The Greatest
Speech, Ever

Albumen photograph of Abraham Lincoln is known as the "Gettysburg Lincoln," because it was made only eleven days before giving his immortal speech. Taken by Alexander Gardner in his Washington D.C. studio.

The Greatest Speech, Ever

The Remarkable Story of Abraham Lincoln
and His Gettysburg Address

by James L. Cotton Jr.

Foreword by former
Senator Howard Baker Jr. of Tennessee

History Publishing Company
Palisades, New York

Copyright@2013 by James L. Cotton, Jr.
Cotton, James L.
LCCN: 2013947674
ISBN: 9781933909929 (QP)
        1933909927
ISBN: 9781933909912 (eBook)
        1933909919
SAN: 850-5942

Cotton, James L. Jr.

The greatest speech ever : the remarkable story of
Abraham Lincoln and his Gettysburg Address / by
Judge James H. Cotton ; foreword by Senator Howard
H. Baker Jr. -- 1st ed. -- Palisades, NY : History
Publishing Co., c2013.

p. ; cm.

ISBN: 978-1-933909-92-9 ; 978-1-933909-91-2
(ebook)
Includes bibliographical references and index.
Summary: Not only a scholarly assessment of the
Gettysburg Address and its impact on America, but
also an absorbing look into Abraham Lincoln's
life.--Publisher.

1. Lincoln, Abraham, 1809-1865. Gettysburg
address. 2. Lincoln, Abraham, 1809-1865--
Political and social views. 3. United States--
History--Civil War, 1861-1865. 4. United States--
History--19th century. 5. Soldiers National
Cemetery (Gettysburg, Pa.) 6. Consecration of
cemeteries--Pennsylvania--Gettysburg. I. Title.

E475.55 .C68 2013   2013947676
973.7/092--dc23   1311

Published in the United States of America by
History Publishing Company, LLC
Palisades, New York

Printed in the United States on acid-free paper
First Edition

A CONFESSION FROM THE AUTHOR

SOMETIMES IN THIS BOOK, INSTEAD OF REDUPLICATING THE "PECULIAR" spelling or capitalization of words originally used by Abraham Lincoln and contemporary observers of his life, as they appear verbatim in primary sources, I substituted a modern counterpart. And sometimes I chose otherwise, electing to use the "peculiar" version, often without inserting the clumsy word "sic." I took this erratic literary approach, because at times, such peculiar wordings can be a distraction to the reader; or conversely, they can provide an extra layer of insight into the speaker or writer of those words. Thus, I have invoked my right of poetic license to do what I believe best connects with the reader. However, I never allow such editing to distort the writer's or speaker's intended meaning. Note that I do not brand those "peculiar" spellings used by Lincoln and his contemporaries as misspelled words. To do so, feels condescending. Folks here in our Appalachian Mountains have some of their own special spellings, too. As President Andrew Jackson put in, "It is a d_ _n poor mind, indeed, that can't think of at least two ways to spell any word." Perhaps Old Hickory had a point.

To Lisa, Caroline and Luke . . .

For all the reasons that matter.

TABLE OF CONTENTS

Foreword By

HOWARD H. BAKER, JR.

You are about to undertake a journey into the life of our sixteenth president; a journey that will yield not only a greater understanding of what are, arguably, America's most admired words, but also a deeper understanding of their author, Abraham Lincoln. Judge Cotton's book is not only an fascinating and scholarly assessment of the Gettysburg Address and its impact on America, but also an absorbing look into Abraham Lincoln's life. Indeed, as the subtitle of the book states, it was a "remarkable" life.

It is also remarkable that nearly one hundred and fifty years after his tragic death, we still yearn to know more about Abraham Lincoln, to better understand him. Each passing decade it seems we gain more insight into the man. Yet he remains mysterious, elusive and complex. Maybe we can never fully know Lincoln.

Like many Americans, Lincoln was introduced to me at a young age. I was taught by my beloved Grandmother Ladd, that as fiercely independent and self-reliant East Tennesseans (my grandmother slept with a nickel-plated 32 pistol under her pillow), we were unique in our politics, our attitudes, and in our place in history, when it came to our relationship with Abraham Lincoln. Along my educational and political path, I was encouraged by my father, Howard H. Baker, Sr., an attorney who served in both the Tennessee Legislature and U.S. House of Representatives, to embrace the initiatives of Lincoln's Republican Party. Later, I found myself even closer to the Lincoln legacy when I married a Dirksen from Illinois.

My home, the mountains of eastern Tennessee, also bound me to Lincoln. President Lincoln carried a great concern and fondness for the people of eastern Tennessee. Likewise, we have always carried a great respect and affection for Lincoln. The distinguished university and repository of Lincolniana, Lincoln Memorial University in Harrogate, Tennessee, is a manifestation and living legacy of that mutual respect and admiration East Tennesseans and President Lincoln held for each other.

However, it is what Lincoln has meant to all Americans, not only those in his time and in ours—but to those Americans yet to come – that is his greatest legacy. When I have visited the battlefields and Soldiers' National Cemetery at Gettysburg, first and foremost, I am deeply impacted by the magnitude of the sacrifice made by those brave Americans. And when I have read the timeless words of the Gettysburg Address that are enshrined there, or see them on the wall of the Lincoln Memorial or the page of a book, I am reminded that all Americans, each and every one of us, are *legatees* of the contributions of Abraham Lincoln.

One encounter with the Lincoln legacy, in particular, made a life-time impression upon me. When I was first elected to the U.S. Senate in 1966, I was soon invited by my father-in-law, Senator Everett Dirksen, to speak at a Lincoln Day luncheon in Springfield, Illinois. After the event concluded, Senator Dirksen gathered me up from the crowd, so we could go —as he put it—"to meet my Mr. Lincoln." It was a cold, snowy day that February, as we set out for the Oak Ridge Cemetery, a few miles away.

When we arrived, the entrance gate was locked, which did not, of course, deter the irrepressibly resolute Senator from Illinois. Dirksen promptly summoned the cemetery supervisor, who kindly opened the gate and joined us.

Eventually, we arrived at the site of Lincoln's tomb, and entered the somber place, just the three of us.

As we stood in the chilled air of the small, but impressive rotunda that shelters Lincoln's final resting place, Senator Dirksen, in his booming, baritone voice, began to expound, eloquently, upon the greatness of our sixteenth president. As Senator Dirksen's warm and affectionate words bounced from the stone walls that surrounded us . . . I could not help but wonder . . . if Lincoln, himself, might come up to join us.

During the many years that I had the privilege to be a public servant in Congress or the White House, at times, I was a front-row witness to some of America's most glorious moments, and some of her darkest hours. Whether our nation was wrestling with the dangers of the Cold War, the constitutional crisis of Watergate, the deep political division of Vietnam or the trauma of September 11, 2001, the words of the Gettysburg Address have always been there like a shining beacon in the night to guide us, giving our people and its leaders a sense of direction that honors the creed of American democracy handed down to us by the Founding Fathers.

Lincoln, after all, taught us the importance as Americans, of knowing our own history. Lincoln longed for Americans of his time to be mindful of how their nation came to be. By using the looking glass of the past, Lincoln better understood the grim and challenging reality in which he served as President. As President Lincoln struggled with the Civil War and slavery, he found guidance and sustenance from the Declaration of Independence and other writings of the Founding Fathers, whose vision of America inspired his thoughts and words. Now, through the living legacy of his Gettysburg Address, we—as today's Americans—are made ever mindful of how America came to be. Lincoln's words from that speech have not only extended the vision of the Founding Fathers to every generation of Americans that have followed him, but helped to sculpture the democracy that touches the lives of every American, still today.

The words of the Gettysburg Address have become so indispensable to us, so essential to the framework of our modern democratic republic, that it is natural to ask the intriguing question . . . if Lincoln had failed at Gettysburg, would America have survived?

Thankfully, we will never know. A better historical fate awaited us. President Lincoln would not fail. The Gettysburg Address, over time, would become a speech for the ages. And America, against all odds, would survive what Lincoln called "the fiery trial." But most importantly, America would endure, although imperfect, as one nation—a nation, in Lincoln's immortal words, built upon a government ". . . *of the people, by the people, for the people.*"

Howard H. Baker, Jr.
Huntsville, Tennessee

PREFACE

THIS IS, OUTWARDLY, A BOOK ABOUT A SPEECH THAT FOREVER CHANGED America, and the remarkable man who wrote and spoke it. This is, inwardly, a book about love of country.

Like most Americans, the September 11th, 2001 attack on our nation, turned my thoughts inward about the future of our country and my family. America, after all—despite its historical failings with race and gender—has always been the symbol and promise of freedom and equality in the world—a place of new beginnings.

Among the myriad of emotions I felt, I found myself rattled by the white-hot intensity of hate against America and Americans that motivated the attack, and the unfathomable depth of the cultural divide which allowed other humankind to celebrate that death and destruction.

I wondered . . . what has happened to us? And why? Can America no longer remember itself? And if America is still the predominant guardian of the sacred promises of freedom and equality in the world—and notwithstanding, continues to be hated and reviled by so many across the earth—what will become of America? What, then, will become of the world? Is America at risk because it has cast away its core values, and surrendered to the tenacious social forces of materialism and meism? These questions continued to burn.

A year later . . . on September 11th, 2002, I was mesmerized as I listened to the Gettysburg Address read in New York City, at Ground Zero. Lincoln's words were read without introduction, without stridency, without promotion of the reader, allowing the power and dignity of the words to exalt themselves.

Suddenly, I knew where the answers to my questions lay. They were written within a document that contained the meaning of America. It was *The Gettysburg Address*. In those timeless, rarified words, Lincoln was stretching out from 1863 to speak to today's Americans—to all humanity.

It was then . . . September 11th, 2002 . . . that the journey of this book began.

Most of my life, I have been infatuated with the words of Gettysburg Address, because they are unlike any other in history. They are iconic words, not only because they were exactly what America needed at that time and place at Gettysburg—not just for their wisdom and poetic beauty—but also because they are made out of the raw, sinewy materials that were uniquely Abraham Lincoln's life. Out of the sweat, the toil, the suffering and the hope of his human spirit. Words, eventually, sombered by Lincoln's martyrdom. They are words that have pierced the heart and soul of every American, and forever engraved in the American consciousness the creed of freedom and equality. Words . . . that are "American scripture."

By design, I strived to make this book more than a specialized monograph about the Gettysburg Address. Accordingly, I have digressed along the way in telling the story about the great speech, taking side excursions and backroads into Abraham Lincoln's remarkable life—exploring his father-son relationship and hardscrabble childhood, his formative years as a young man in New Salem, the vexing issues of slavery and colonization, and his courageous but controversial Emancipation Proclamation. After all, to fully understand how the Gettysburg Address came to be, one must understand how Abraham Lincoln came to be. Part of the greatness of the Gettysburg Address is that the DNA of Lincoln's life, is found in every word.

Through the course of his life, Lincoln would develop a relaxed style of politicking that was frank, easygoing and light-hearted. "My politics is short and sweet," Lincoln liked to say with a smile—"like the old woman's dance." And so were his words. When Lincoln wrote and spoke, he used words that were simple, precise and pithy—not the showy, elevated language that was so popular among politicians of his day. He recognized that the sound, the rhythm, and the origin of the words he chose, meant everything.

Abraham Lincoln came up as a boy busting rails and sod on dirt farms in Kentucky and Indiana, wrestling on the bluffs of the Sangamon River, surveying ground with a compass and chain, flatboating down the Ohio and Mississippi, leading a rowdy company of hungry soldiers up the murky, mosquito-infested Rock River, running a mill, working as a postmaster, managing a general store, arguing law before rural juries and judges, campaigning in big and little towns, debating his political opponents and giving speeches on the hottest, most controversial topics of the day—all of it, a life woven inextricably from the conversations, customs and heartbeat of the common, everyday people.

This, the poverty, the endless sorrows, the mind-numbing work, the harsh father, the hunger to read and learn, the storytelling, the intellectual prowess, the ambition, the rivers, the pressures of the presidency during our Nation's only Civil War—all of this—was Lincoln's life. This—all of this—was Lincoln's education, the primordium of his word skills and his great speeches, like the Gettysburg Address. Lincoln, after all, knew little of polite society or universities. And he had only a thimble's worth of formal education. Instead, Abraham Lincoln often labored, laughed and raconteured with the mudsills and tinkers of the uneducated, working class. Lincoln's words were, in their purest form, a people's language—language that was eloquent in its own simplicity, rough-hewned from the rigors of life. As one Springfield lawyer once put it, Lincoln never spoke "beyond the people."

Lincoln's life not only shaped the words of the Gettysburg Address, but those words—just 272 of them—breathed new life into the Declaration of Independence and have helped to shape the self-governing republic that baptizes all of us as Americans. They are words known and admired all over the world, and are, perhaps, the most familiar work of all American writings.

The pages of this book are teeming with quotations from "eyewitnesses"; that is, people who actually saw and heard Lincoln, first hand.

I have done so, because the fascinating observations of those who were the opportune witnesses to Lincoln's life, folks who were the eyes and ears of rarified history, bring Lincoln alive in a more three dimensional way for our generation, and those yet to come.

I carry a hope that this work will be a "first Lincoln book" for many readers, and that its pages will not only reveal how words can make and sculpt history, but that it will also breathe life into our sixteenth president for them, the same way the melodic prose of Carl Sandburg first brought Lincoln alive for me as a young boy.

For those who have already read a book about Lincoln, I am hopeful this one will be another in their repertoire; and that this book will be a lasting reminder, from Lincoln's captivating and uniquely American life, that the word "impossible"—when it comes to the perseverance of the human spirit—ought to be spoken with the greatest reluctance.

James L. Cotton, Jr.
760 Grape Rough Rd.
Oneida, Tennessee

**"There's a divinity that shapes our ends,
Rough-hew them how we will."**

From Hamlet, often quoted by Abraham Lincoln to his
law partner and old friend, William H. Herndon.

CHAPTER ONE

PROLOGUE: A HOUSE DIVIDED

"Nobody believes in him anymore."
—George Templeton Strong
Diarist & Prominent NYC Lawyer
Writing About President Lincoln
During The Early White House Years

ON THE AFTERNOON OF THURSDAY, NOVEMBER 19, 1863, THE lanky, angular, six-feet-four frame of President Abraham Lincoln rose from the wooden platform nailed together on a knob of dirt called Cemetery Hill. Before him stood thousands of people, waiting anxiously, on his words.

The place was Gettysburg, Pennsylvania.

As the applause gently swelled, Lincoln awkwardly approached the front of the platform, where he would speak. In his hand he clutched two pieces of paper, containing the words to a short speech. It was a place where as many as twenty thousand people had gathered on a beautiful autumn day to stand amid the sea of graves and honor the thousands of soldiers who had fought and fallen there.

It has been said that America was born in Philadelphia, and saved at Gettysburg. Perhaps so. Only four and a half months earlier, on the first three days of July 1863, this small, crossroads town of Gettysburg was the eye of the Civil War's hurricane. Soldiers from the North and South, more than 160,000 of them, had gathered for mortal combat there. It was General Robert E. Lee and his Army of Northern Virginia's going-for-broke invasion of Northern territory. Most Civil War battles were fought on Southern soil. This bold attack by the Confederacy took place, for the second (and last) time, in a northern state located entirely outside of the claimed boundaries of the Confederate States of America.

Lee was a brilliant and brave general. But the decisions he made at the Battle of Gettysburg were more akin to the strategy of a riverboat gambler, than a seasoned military commander. By July 4th—the end of the three day battle at Gettysburg—more than fifty-one thousand human beings were dead, wounded, or missing. The Confederacy would suffer twenty-eight thousand of those casualties; the Union's Army of the Potomac twenty-three thousand.

It was a blizzard of blood. During the ghastly fusillade, a bullet hit a human being, on average, about every four seconds.

The Battle of Gettysburg had become the zenith of pain and suffering that had poured out of a war where Americans killed Americans. A bitter war fought between states, that pitted father against son, brother against brother, family against family. It was a superhuman struggle where both sides were willing to give all they had—possessions, limb and life—for what they believed. And they did.

Looking back in time, the fact that President Lincoln was present on the speaker's platform that day at a soldiers' cemetery in Gettysburg, is remarkable—if not providential. A cloud of uncertainty hung over Lincoln's trip to Gettysburg. He was very uneasy about it all. The President did not like to travel away from Washington to make a speech, and he rarely did so. He was especially reluctant to leave the Nation's capital, with a war going on. *The* War. A war that would eventually claim more than 750,000 lives—more than all other American wars, combined.

The Civil War was the most frightening crisis in the history of the young nation called the United States of America, at that time, made up of thirty-four states—the "Union" as they often called it in those days. Like the biblical ninth plague that fell upon Pharaoh's Egypt, the black darkness of this internecine war would cover the Nation for four years. The very existence of the United States, still an infant nation, was hanging, precariously, by a thread. And the thread was frayed.

It was a war that produced constant crisis during Abraham Lincoln's presidency, demanding his sisyphean attention. In fact, Lincoln would be the only U.S. President, ever, whose entire presidency was mired in war. During major battles, Lincoln would spend as much as eighteen hours a day at the telegraph office in the War Department building, often into the small hours of the night—and sometimes until the stars disappeared into the candescence of dawn—his long legs canted against a table next to the telegraph machine, where he received dispatches from his generals and heart-wrenching battle reports. As communications entrepreneur and author Tom Wheeler has pointed out, Lincoln's telegraph office was the Nation's first "situation room."

It was a war, from beginning to end, that also produced severe stress and exhaustion on the President. His public poise belied the private anxieties that often robbed him of quality rest. Many nights during the course of the War, Lincoln would go with virtually no sleep. Lincoln's friend, Noah Brooks, encouraged the President to get some much needed rest. "I suppose it is good for the body," Lincoln replied. "But the tired part of me is *inside*, out of reach." Dogged by this constant fatigue throughout the War, Mary Lincoln said her husband sometimes just "keeled over" with fainting spells. The Civil War, for President Lincoln, was death on the installment plan.

Shortly after Abraham Lincoln was elected to the presidency, but before he took the oath of office, things were already looking bleak for the country—and for Lincoln. So bleak, in fact, that out-going President James Buchanan, with his conical spike of top hair—the paragon of all lame-duck presidents—was already telling folks visiting the White House that he was going to be "the last President of the United States." He was, however, the last and only bachelor president. One day, a band of reporters huddled around president-elect Lincoln in Springfield, anxious to hear from the new President. "Well, boys," Lincoln would remark in a jovial tone, "your troubles are over, now . . . mine have just begun." It was the understatement of his life.

Even before Confederate gun-fire rained down on Union-held Fort Sumter to light the fuse of a yet unenvisaged Civil War, Lincoln's new-born presidency was hit with pre-shock tremors of the terrible conflict yet to come. Lincoln had inherited a Union Army of merely sixteen thousand men, who were sorely unprepared and strewn about, mostly, in outposts along the Indian frontier. He was also the unfortunate beneficiary of a dismembered federal government that already had seven states in the deep South seceded from the Union by the time Lincoln took office on March 4, 1861. These seceded states were borne of a new government, called the Confederate States of America, with its capital first established in Montgomery, Alabama, and later transferred to Richmond, Virginia.   Four more states that were on the precipice, would pull out from the Union shortly thereafter. More border states (that is, Union states with slavery that "bordered" both the Union and the Confederacy) were teetering on the razor's edge.

Lincoln had become the President of the United States completely unaware, if not inexcusably naïve, of the grave and perilous condition of the country. A man who had never managed an operation more manifold than a small-town, rural law office, was now chief executive over the highest office in the land and managing a national civil war. In fact, during the first few days of his presidency, Lincoln was still leaning on the hope that the South was a rebellious child that would see the error of its ways and eventually return home. "The last hope of peace," Lincoln said, "may not have passed away."

But hope is not a strategy. On the horizon, just beyond Lincoln's myopic line of sight, was the reality of an inevitable collision between an immovable object, the Union's right to self-preservation—and an unstoppable force, the South's right to self-determination. Lincoln had convinced himself that there must be a way for the Nation to avoid a civil war. Surely, he thought, there was a way to bring the Northern and Southern states back together, peaceably.

There wasn't.

When the anvil of reality finally dropped on Lincoln, and he came to grips with how dangerous and irreversible the situation really was, he was stunned. And dumbfounded. One of Lincoln's earliest miscalculations as President—and a big one— was that he terribly underestimated the heat and intensity of secessionist feelings in the Southern states. Lincoln refused to see the Confederacy as a separate country. And he refused to refer to Jefferson Davis as "President Davis." In Lincoln's early assessment of discontent in the deep South, "secession" amounted to no more than a rebellion of radical, rabble-rousing individuals. In fact, people in the North would call the Civil War the "War of Rebellion."

In the same way it was incomprehensible to Americans before

September 11, 2001 that enemies of our country, in a suicide mission, might hijack commercial airliners and crash them into city skyscrapers—in early 1861, it was unimaginable that the country, in an act of national suicide, would turn upon itself in a civil war.

In his heart, Lincoln thought the political leadership of the South would never go so far as declare war on the national government. In the first few days of his administration, Lincoln was allowing caution to trump confrontation. "The people of the South have too much sense to attempt the ruin of the government," Lincoln said shortly after his election. He believed that a pro-Union majority existed among ordinary people in the South, who had been seduced into secession by the slave-owning aristocrats. Most Southerners did not own slaves; only about one-third of white people in the South were members of slave-owning families. The majority of slaveowners were not the rich operators of the large-scale plantations, but were small-farm operators and work crew supervisors. However, many more white non-slaveowners were cuffed to the economic machinery of slavery, through their buying and selling of goods, jobs, and their leaseholds with slaveowners.

Many Southerners, particularly in the Upper South, did not believe that secession would lead to war, either; some even joked, in what would become a cruelly ironic quip, that any blood spilled because of secession could be mopped up with only a "handkerchief." That first few months of secession, many in the North thought the "rebellion" would be over by Christmas. But when it came to understanding the Jacobinic war sentiments of Southern powercrats, who had frocked the President as "King Abraham I" (in sarcastic reference to King George III), Lincoln was wrong. Dead wrong.

But Lincoln wasn't alone in his underreckoning of the potency of the secession movement. In the genesis of Lincoln's presidency, his Secretary of State, William H. Seward—at that time, viewed by many as the stealthy "brains" behind Lincoln's administration and the *e'minence grise* who was calling all the important shots, Seward cultivated this view and, also came to a blundered conclusion about the Confederacy's true intentions.

Seward, generally a warm and friendly person, who by nature was inclined to be an appeaser, had even gone so far as to indirectly communicate with agents from the South, in what would now be called "back-channel" diplomatic discussions, trying to reach an agreement for a "peaceful" solution with the Confederacy that would prevent the country from splitting in two and lapsing into a bloody civil war. Seward had taken it upon himself, early on, to become the Lincoln administration's sole diplomatic voice. In this self-appointed, lone wolf role, Seward likely overreached the jurisdictional authority of his office in some of these undercover negotiations with the South.

In a cautious, conciliatory diplomatic approach, Seward conducted these "negotiations" under the gullible, mistaken belief that if the Federal government backed-off the burgeoning Confederacy and quietly relinquished Fort Sumter, and avoided any words or actions that could be interpreted as military aggression towards the Confederacy— the desire of patriotic unionists in the Upper and Middle South not to fracture the country would eventually prevail over radical pro-secessionist sentiments in the Deep South, allowing the intensity of the conflict to wane, and thus, avoiding war and preserving the Union. That is, if the Southern states were left alone to wander in the wilderness of secessionist isolation for a while, they would, like the prodigal son, eventually return to the arms of their Union father.

But any belief on Seward's part that peace without slavery was possible, was naïveté on steroids. Slavery was the cornerstone of socioeconomic order in the Deep South. The reality was, that the immensely powerful planter autocrats behind the Confederacy wanted to have their cake and eat it, too. They wanted both national autonomy and slavery, including the expansion of slavery into the new western states, which would provide the South with broader economic opportunities. And they wanted them, forever.

Seward found himself in the coy game of moving around the chess pieces of clandestine government to create what he believed to be advantageous diplomatic delays. These delays, he calculated, would allow secessionist fever to eventually fade, especially if the South was not provoked. But the Confederacy knew something Seward (and Lincoln) didn't. There was no way pro-Union sentiments would percolate up and spread across the South to a level that would save the country. Lincoln's administartion had terribly underestimated secessionist passions, and overestimated Southern unionism. The prodigal son wasn't coming home; he was gearing up for war on dear ol' dad.

President Lincoln bucked, hard, when he finally learned of the true, deep-dyed intentions of the Confederacy. A cool and highly educated John Forsyth, Jr., who was appointed by Confederacy President Jefferson Davis to be one of three commissioners for the national government of the Confederacy and "negotiate" with the Union, later revealed that the true strategy of the South was "to play with Seward," in order to "delay and gain time until the South was ready." The Grandmaster Seward, had been checkmated.

With tact and aplomb, Lincoln would put Secretary Seward back in his proper authoritative place, and reclaim his presidential role as the preeminent leader and voice for the Federal government. Lincoln would have no part of any "peace compromise" with the Southern states that sawed the Nation in half and turned a blind eye to slavery. For Lincoln, who would be branded by critics as an inveterate "compromiser," there was no room for any compromise on this issue. Any deal that allowed the Southern states to go their own way to form a separate government, and gave them a free ticket to transplant slavery into the Western states, was an unholy alliance—a deal, in Lincoln's own words, that "acknowledges that slavery has equal rights with liberty, and surrenders all we have contended for." This time, the word "compromise," in Lincoln's mind, was no more than a sugar-coated sop, in which America would be acquiescing to its own destruction.

All of this made for an unstable and unnerving start for a harried president-elect. During the first month of Lincoln's presidency, William Seward characterized the administration in a private memo as one "without a policy, either foreign or domestic." In late 1861, Lincoln's Attorney General, the long-whiskered, Poseidon-faced, work-weary, Edward Bates, who had respect for the President but had no confidence in what he saw as Lincoln's lax management style, would write in his diary, "he [Lincoln] lacks *will* and *purpose*, and, I fear he has not the *power to command*." George Templeton Strong, an influential lawyer from New York City, part-time Lincoln supporter and full time worry-wart, would chide the President: "Nobody believes in him anymore." Lincoln's old buddy, Republican Thurlow Weed would predict:

"Lincoln is gone." In the eyes of many, Abraham Lincoln was sitting astraddle of a gimcracked administration. President Lincoln would later sum up those early years of his first term as being "under great and peculiar difficulty."

Certainly, once he took the reigns of the presidency, Lincoln was a gradualist in his approach to curing problems. Ever the slow-moving pragmatist, Lincoln would often shift political positions to adjust to changing events and newly-emerging developments. It was Lincoln's nature, as a peacemaker, to mollify and mediate to avoid conflict. But as President of the United States, he would never compromise on one issue: *his indefatigable commitment to save the Union.* Because of that commitment, President Lincoln never allowed himself to become a passive, disengaged commander-in-chief who was afraid to soil his hands in military affairs of the country. President Lincoln would grab hold of the levers of War like he did the handles of a plow in his youth, becoming a hands-on manager of the Civil War.

After all, it was Lincoln's war. Fate can be a harsh handmaiden. Justified or not, Abraham Lincoln had to carry much of the personal responsibility for the Civil War. Lincoln was elected President in 1860, wedded to the Republican Party. It was a new, untested party—a party built upon the political platform of eliminating slavery from the country. Lincoln's election, in which he did not get a solitary electoral vote from any of the fifteen slave states, was the straw that broke the camel's back. The frenzied, rapid bail-out of Southern states from the Union was a direct and proximate consequence of the election of Abraham Lincoln, the "Black Republican" they called him, and the rise of his anti-slavery party to the presidency.

Lincoln's ascension to the highest office in the land instantly deepened the intransigence of the slaveowner class of the cotton states, who viewed Lincoln's election as an intolerable act of provocation. The Deep South saw permanent separation from the Union, and then war, as its only remedies.

One newspaper in Georgia wrote: "Let the consequences be what they may . . . the South will never submit to such humiliation and degradation as the inauguration of Abraham Lincoln." To the Confederate states of the South, Lincoln had become the great white political Devil.

The 1861 election of Abraham Lincoln as President of the United States would transform the political and socioeconomic landscape of America with a force of suddenness, weight, and velocity that would not be seen, again, until the ascension of Franklin Delano Roosevelt to presidential power in 1933.

Secession would break loose on Lincoln with terrifying speed. The bleeding out of the Union first began with South Carolina. Then Mississippi left the Union. Next came Florida, then Alabama and Georgia. Louisiana followed, then Texas. Virginia next, then Arkansas, North Carolina, and finally Tennessee. These Southern states wanted to break loose from Lincoln and his Republican party's vision and brand of government, and form their own. They called it the Confederate States of America—and its mission was to keep a tight grip on its institution of slavery. Unimaginable as it was, the country had, in fact, turned upon itself.

Yes . . . it was Lincoln's war.

With this burden of responsibility hanging over him like Damocle's sword, Lincoln would become rapt not only in the weighty matters of generals who directed the war battles, but also in the minutiae of the infantryman who fought in the war battles. For instance, Lincoln, an amateur inventor and holder of a patent himself (U.S. Patent No. 6469, a device to lift boats over shoals and obstructions in shallow water; Lincoln whittled out the model for this patent, which is on display at the Smithsonian's National Museum of Natural History), was keenly interested in the mechanical design of war armaments and weapons. Lincoln was a science and technology geek, even before the advent of pocket inserts.

For instance, the President enjoyed test-firing the latest rifles, like the Spencer breech-loading carbine rifle, at a shooting range set up for him near the White House. An incurable tinkerer, Lincoln tried out new gunpowders in his fireplace, tested signal lights from the top of a Washington building, and personally funded the design of a "primitive" machine gun (that didn't work). Inventor Edward D. Tippett sent a letter to Lincoln, asking for only forty minutes of the President's time to demonstrate (by mathematical equation) a "self-moving machine" powered only by gravity, that came to him in a vision and would end the

War. Lincoln would file this letter away, under a handwritten label that pretty much summed up the crackpot idea: *"Tippett: Crazy-Man."* If an inventor showed up at the White House, hawking a new gadget with military application, he was usually given an quick audience with the President. (Tippett's idea, however, didn't make it.)

During that same time, the President could be found at the War Department hunched over battle maps that were sprinkled with colored pushpins marking the locations of the armies, and discussing battle strategies with his commanders. He was always trolling for a new strategy or weapon to give the Union Army a military advantage. Science and war, in Lincoln's view, were a perfect match. President Lincoln pushed the use of a cutting-edge concepts in naval warfare, such as the "ironclad ship" and mortar-firing boats for river battles. When a hot air balloon flew over Washington, D.C., likely the first aeronautical motion he had ever seen, Lincoln realized its valuable military application and convinced its owner, Thaddeus S.C. Lowe, to partner with the Federal Army so the balloon (Lowe called it his "aeronautic machinery") could be used to spy on Southern troops. There is also the uncorroborated but irresistible story about bullet-proof vests. The concept of steel-reinforced body armor got hot early in the War (for obvious reasons). Lincoln, as it goes, insulated himself from an endless cavalcade of would-be body armor inventors wanting a personal audience with him, with one qualifying proviso that could only be a creature of his crafty wit: before meeting with the President, the bullet-proof vest had to first pass a military test-fire *with the inventor wearing it.*

Lincoln, an admitted neophyte in military operations, would give himself a crash-course in military stratagems, by checking out Halleck's *Elements of Military Art and Science* from the Library of Congress. Just six months after Lincoln checked out this book, he would hire the irritable author himself, Henry Halleck (nicknamed "Old Brains") to assist as a military adviser during the War. Just as he had been all of his life, he was a fast learner. In this war-room environment, Lincoln's keen intelligence would begin to reveal itself.

Within weeks after the outbreak of the Civil War, President Lincoln would begin to formulate the critical strategic components he believed were necessary to keep the Nation intact, over and above winning head-to-head military battles: he would have to gin-up widespread feelings of patriotism across the Union (patriotism is needed most, it seems, during a time of war); dramatically increase the size of the Union army; implement a widespread military draft for the first time in American history; make near-dictatorial use of his executive war powers, suspending habeus corpus to lock up Confederate sympathizers without charges or a trial, and suppressing publication of pro-secessionist newspapers; play every political card to prevent secession among the Union slave "border" states; engage in international negotiations to keep foreign countries from assisting or diplomatically recognizing the Confederacy; blockade the South from essential goods and war resources; and protect the Nation's capital, Washington, D.C., from Confederate take-over. Assistant Secretary John Hay, who affectionately referred to his revered boss President Lincoln in his diary as "the Tycoon," colorfully described Lincoln's multi-task skills like this: "The old man sits here and wields like a backwoods Jupiter the bolts of war and the machinery of government with a hand equally steady and equally firm."

As the War moiled on, galvanizing Union generals to move and fight became a grueling and frustrating daily ordeal for President Lincoln. Until late in the War when the President finally placed William Sherman Grant in command of the Union Army, Lincoln himself, was arguably the best general he had. In modern jargon, Lincoln micro-managed the Civil War, fully immersing himself in the grim, day-to-day details and military strategies.

There were times, however, when Lincoln got more picayune details shoveled onto his presidential plate than even he had an appetite for. Sometimes he about choked on them. Folks were constantly smuggling their requests for jobs and favors into the White House. Petty irritations seemed to have easy access to the President. Once a buck private in the Union Army somehow gained access to President Lincoln (which was not very difficult), whining to the President about his petty grievances and begging for an executive office transfer to the Quartermaster Corp.

Despite being extremely tired and busy, President Lincoln patiently listened, eventually telling the private, "Well, my man, that may all be true—but you must go to your officer about it." But that wasn't good enough. Like fingernails repeatedly dragged across a blackboard, the soldier continued to repeat his gripes, over and over, grating Lincoln's patience. Some visitors can stay longer in one hour, than others can in one day. This was such an occasion. Finally, the President wearied of the man planted in his office, and could take no more.

Looking out of the south window of his Executive Office towards the Potomac River, Lincoln raised his scepter-like finger and sternly scolded the soldier: "Now, my man, go away! I cannot attend to all of these details," he fumed. "I could just as easily bail out the Potomac with a spoon."   Lincoln's sarcastic analogy, spoken to defuse his own frustration, was rooted more in reality than exaggeration. Had Lincoln really been dipping a spoon into the Potomac for every decision and detail he dealt with during the Civil War, the water table of that great river surely would have been lowered.

So, it seemed, that when it came to the War, what Lincoln called the country's "fiery trial," no matter was too insignificant for the President's attention or his compassion. A good example of this occurred about five weeks before the President's November 1863 trip to Gettysburg. Lincoln sent a letter to General George Meade (who, back in July, was the victorious Union commander at the Battle of Gettysburg), notifying Meade that the father of a fifteen-year-old Union soldier had come to him, asking the President to intervene and stop his son's execution by firing squad.   The teenage soldier, Private August Blittersdorf, was scheduled to be shot the next day at Mitchell's Station, Virginia for the crime of desertion.

At a time when President Lincoln's attention was mired-up in war strategies, wrangling with quirky and recalcitrant Union generals, preparing his vitally important Annual Address to a newly-elected Congress, living under the veil of constant death threats, dealing with political turmoil in his Cabinet, managing foreign relations, and facing his most important speech of the War in Gettysburg, Pennsylvania in little more than a month—he still took the precious time to meet face-to-face with the young soldier's desperate, panic-stricken father.

Lincoln, justifiably, could have refused to meet with the condemned soldier's father—or given him the bum's rush with a few token words and a clap on the back, quickly sending the father, empty-handed, on his distraught way.   But such a cold and indifferent response was just not in the man. That same day after meeting with the young soldier's father, Lincoln wrote an urgent letter that was immediately delivered to Gen. Meade, saying: "I am unwilling for any boy under eighteen to be shot."

Although no formal reply from Meade about Blittersdorf has ever been found in the historical record, certainly, because of the President's immediate intervention, the life of the boy soldier was spared. In an age when the most impressive credentials on the résumé of a big time, national level politician were traditionally considered to be grandilo-quent speech-making, a celebrated war record, blue-blood pedigree or a classical education (Lincoln had none of these). Lincoln, in contrast, would be the first president in American history to bring moral qualities into the realm of powerful political skills, qualities such as compassion, honesty and humbleness.   It was those qualities that saved Private Blittersdorf. And in those qualities, lies the greatness and lasting legacy of his presidency. They are virtues that separate Abraham Lincoln from all other U. S. Presidents.

* * *

As the Gettysburg event drew near in the fall of 1863, the pace of the War had calmed a bit. However, the previous spring and winter months had been some of the most dismal for the Union. The President was still grappling with the insuperable distractions of running a war-torn country. The U. S. Treasury was about wiped out. Angry mobs engaged in violence and vandalism. There was widespread Lincoln-bashing. No shame or limits existed when it came to humiliating the President.   Lincoln was depicted as a gorilla, baboon and a monkey. One group of Democrats who hated Lincoln and his politics, the Copperheads, printed a pamphlet entitled "Abraham Africanus I," which told the story of the President making a deal with the Devil, and selling his soul, so he could become the dictatorial ruler of the United States of America.

President Lincoln was on shaky political ground even with Northern voters. Hard-core abolitionists who wanted immediate black emancipation, felt Lincoln hadn't fought fast or hard enough against slavery. Democrats felt he had fought too hard against it. Others, just wanted rid of him. Northerners from both parties were still burning mad from the military draft Lincoln had implemented that summer of 1863; they didn't like being forced by government edict to fight, let alone fight over the issue of slavery. Many were becoming restless and cynical about the purposes behind the War—and even violent.

Riots in Northern cities protesting Lincoln's military draft became white hot, with much of the violence directed at African-Americans, even their homes and inner-city orphanages. Hundreds of people died in the mob violence. Blue collar workers in Northern industrial cities, particularly Irish-Americans, were hostile and embittered by the draft; in their view, why should they be jerked away from their families, and put in harm's way far from home, to free slaves who would then migrate North and take-over their jobs? Adding to the intensity of the public anger, these draft rules contained loopholes which favored the rich, and discriminated against the poor and the working class. If you were drafted and wealthy, you could hire a man for the exorbitant sum of $300.00 to take your place; or you could pay a fee to the War Department and be released from your military obligation. It reminds us of the old adage that politics is often used to get money from the wealthy, and votes from the poor, all under the façade of protecting one social class from the other; except that this time, the poor and the working class weren't buying it.

People in the 1860's were asking the same question, made popular a century later in a 1960's song performed by the band "Country Joe and the Fish" during the turmoil of the Vietnam War. That anti-war anthem asked Presidents Johnson and Nixon the simple but piercing question, framed in a catchy melody: **"And its one, two, three . . . what are we fighting for?"** The people of the Civil War era were demanding an answer to that same question, from President Lincoln. Are we fighting to save the Union?—or fighting to put an end to slavery? Which is it? **What are we fighting for?** This was the question President Lincoln had not answered, and would not answer, until his speech at Gettysburg.

Despite key Federal victories at Vicksburg and Gettysburg back in July 1863, the military efforts of the Union Army that fall season of the Gettysburg event, under Lincoln's leadership as commander-in-chief, seemed to be squandering the spoils of those victories by failing to follow up and deliver the killer blow to the Confederacy, allowing the horrible war to drag on. This meant more blood. More suffering. More human slaughter. All of it, on Lincoln's executive watch.

Nevertheless, despite the augury of discord and distractions surrounding him, on November 10, 1863, Lincoln would formally announce his plans to attend the dedication of a soldiers' cemetery in Gettysburg, Pennsylvania. He had privately made the decision to go a few days earlier, leaving himself about two weeks or so to synthesize his thoughts and pull together the words of his speech for that occasion. But in this chaotic administrative environment, it would be only two days before the ceremonial event, as Lincoln's top Cabinet secretary John G. Nicolay would later recall, that a fiendishly over-worked President Lincoln would know, with absolute certainty, whether he could even make the trip to Gettysburg.

The president's staff had first arranged for Gettysburg to be a one day excursion, leaving very early in the morning on Thursday, November 19, 1863 and getting back in Washington on the same day, around midnight. They knew the President was very busy and uncomfortable being physically separated by time and distance from Washington, D.C., the heartbeat of war strategy and communications. They endeavored that he lose only one day from his already overloaded schedule. But Lincoln was very uneasy about such a crammed-up, one-day travel itinerary. The mission was too important to fail. "I do not like this arrangement," the President told his Secretary of War Edwin Stanton on Tuesday November 17th, as he sized up the original travel schedule. Lincoln worried that if his train broke down—an all-too-common occurrence in those days—he could miss the whole event. "I do not wish to so go," Lincoln replied about the idea of compressing the entire trip into a solitary day, "that by the slightest accident we fail entirely."

Lincoln, somehow, sensed the portentous importance of his appearance at Gettysburg. There was too much at stake. An extra travel day was needed. Thus, under Lincoln's order, Secretary Stanton would arrange a schedule that was "of abundant margin and . . . less fatiguing." The presidential train would leave for Gettysburg a day early, on

Wednesday the 18th, which was the day before the cemetery dedication event.

Only three of Lincoln's Cabinet—namely, his friend and confidant Secretary of State William Henry Seward; the loyal, hatchet-faced Postmaster General Montgomery Blair, from a powerful political family, who was extraordinarily well read and carried himself with the self-righteousness of a man with strong and fixed beliefs; and his new Secretary of the Interior by lucky default, the pliant and pleasantly ursine John P. Usher—would accompany the President to Gettysburg. Seward and Blair were tightly aligned with the President; Usher, more restrained and remote in his relationship. But the entire Cabinet was invited by the President. In fact, Lincoln pressed upon his Cabinet to go. He wanted them all there, as a demonstration of political unity. The problem was—there wasn't much.

The members of the President's Cabinet were not only busy with their upcoming reports to Congress, but the Cabinet itself was in a state of political upheaval. Behind-the-scenes political maneuvering and back-stabbing were the top priority of some Cabinet members. At various stages of Lincoln's first term in office, at least three men in his own Cabinet had carried strong cravings for the presidency. Sometimes, they turned on each other. It was a Cabinet, for most part, made up of the ingredients of intellect, conflict, indecision and ambition, with a pinch of loyalty to the President sprinkled in.

One thing was for sure—the cast of characters that filled Lincoln's Cabinet at the time of the Gettysburg trip, was not the steadfast, unified phalanx of support the President of the United States wanted and needed to effectively govern during the ongoing national crisis.

The truth was, there was little public sympathy for the President and his Cabinet troubles. Many savored the thought that Lincoln had cooked himself in his own pot of political soup. That's because Lincoln had committed what appeared to be political suicide. The President had appointed some of his most outspoken political adversaries to his own Cabinet. Every single member of Lincoln's Cabinet had more experience, more schooling, and more public prestige than he. And all of them, initially, considered their judgment superior to that of the President. As one friend close to the President cautioned him: "They will eat you up!" Lincoln didn't much care if his Cabinet liked him (although he would have preferred it); but he did want smart, Republican, anti-slavery men who could do their job and render him valuable advice. When Lincoln was questioned about his Cabinet choices, he would reply, simply, they were the "strongest men" for the job. He called them his "compound Cabinet."

It was a gutsy, high-risk decision on Lincoln's part, putting political opponents in his own Cabinet—one that in the long run, would turn out to be an act of ingenuity. But in the early days of his compound Cabinet, President Lincoln was a blossoming political virtuoso, stuck in an ensemble of dissention. Over time, however, Lincoln's character as a man—his honesty and compassion; his willingness to take ultimate responsibility for the mistakes of underlings; his sharing of compliments and credit; his ability to gently handle the strong egos that girded his presidency; his capacity to forgive and overcome petty grievances, and forge friendships with those who had opposed or insulted him in the past; his steady, even-tempered emotional strength during grim crisis, all of this, together, would eventually endear these political adversaries to their President. Months later, William Seward would, privately confess to his wife, Frances, "the President is the best of us."

One of the immutable tests of effective presidential leadership is being able to build bridges, especially with political rivals. And Lincoln would stretch across the great divide of differences, to build them. Patiently, painstakingly, purposely, President Lincoln would guide the Union to victory over the next few years, exercising such deliberative and focused willpower, as Carl Sandburg wrote, that "those who had sought cunningly to lead him, slowly found that he was leading them."

As each month, then each year of Lincoln's presidential term passed, and the Union continued to survive, his Cabinet began to gradually understand that Abraham Lincoln was *unforegoable*, the only man alive who, at that grave moment in history, was able to carry the terrible load of the presidency. The lack of confidence and respect for Lincoln that prevailed among his Cabinet and close advisors in those early years of his administration, by the tragic end of his presidency, would fructify into their highest regard and admiration for the man.

But at the particular time of the Gettysburg trip, the most prominent feature of the President's "compound Cabinet" was that it only *compounded* Lincoln's mounting problems.

Some of the more disloyal members of Lincoln's Cabinet ridiculed the President behind his back, and tried to hamstring his policies. Some of them even concocted excuses and maneuvered their way out of the Gettysburg trip, knowing that President Lincoln wanted and needed them to go. Francis E. Spinner, the head of the U. S. Treasury, who looked like the fortune-teller Professor Marvel in the 1939 movie *The Wizard of Oz*, being cocksure in his own prediction, openly joked about Lincoln's trip to Gettysburg to consecrate the soldiers' cemetery, by sarcastically puffing: "There's a d_ _n good scripture for that ... let the dead bury the dead."

Not long before Lincoln would travel to Gettysburg to give his speech, one prominent author and lawyer who visited Washington observed that "the most striking thing is the absence of personal loyalty to the President. It does not exist." Some in Lincoln's own Republican party, a party split into a daisy-chain of factions, even wanted to court-martial Lincoln. This tumultuous political environment at the time of the Gettysburg trip, super-charged by an ongoing fratricidal war threatening to destroy the country, made it a terrible time for Lincoln to leave Washington.

But the President's public trip to Gettysburg was about to have, privately, even a more dubious start.

CHAPTER TWO

A DUBIOUS START

"Abraham—if you go to Gettysburg, I know Tad will die."
—Mary Todd Lincoln
Family Residence, White House
November 18, 1863

JUST AS LINCOLN WAS ABOUT TO GET AN EARLY START ON THE morning of Wednesday, November 18th, 1863—the departure day for the Town of Gettysburg—Mary Lincoln had a "conniption fit," as they would sometimes say in those days. And brother, could Mary Todd Lincoln pitch a fit. On some occasions, she would even fling herself into childish tantrums, rolling around on the carpet, screaming with caterwauling intensity, yanking on her dark hair, until Lincoln capitulated to her demands.

However, this time, Mary had good cause. Her reactions were not out of proportion. Their ten-year-old son, Thomas, was very sick, tossing in bed with fever. "Scarlatina," the newspapers called it. Scarlet fever. "Tad" as the Lincolns lovingly nicknamed Thomas (short for "Tadpole"), apple of the President's eye—with his boundless mischievous energy and childhood speech impediment—was being attended with the best care possible. However, child mortality was extraordinarily high. Children of the mid-nineteenth century were frequently kidnapped from their parents by death.

Medicines for Tad were being fetched from Thompson's Drugstore, just up the street from the White House, and a devoted nurse stood vigil at his side. But Tad's physical deterioration, as he laid on his sickbed,

41

resembled the fatal listlessness into which their son Willie had slipped only a year and a half earlier. Clammy with fear, Mary begged and pleaded with Lincoln not to go, afraid beyond senses that Taddie might follow Willie to the grave. Her passionate cajolery usually prevailed upon her husband. Just the day before, Mary had cancelled her plans to travel to Gettysburg because of Tad's sickness. Now, she wanted Lincoln to do the same.

Mary told her husband, in a fretful, desperate tone, "Abraham, if you go to Gettysburg, I know Tad will die."

Lincoln made every effort to reassure Mary, to soften her fears. Still, it did no good. Sometimes, Lincoln must have thought . . . Mary could be so sad and fatalistic in her outlook towards life. But he knew exactly how Mary felt. He often felt that way, himself. It was the "hypo," as Lincoln called it, a sorrowful feature of his being, a melancholy, that seemed stamped upon the soul of the man. Today, some would call it clinical depression. It was Lincoln's cross, and would shadow him all of his life.

* * *

Lincoln's last and youngest law partner, William H. Herndon, once famously commented of Lincoln that "His melancholy dripped from him as he walked." No one has ever measured, even the poets and authors of the great tragedies, how much sadness the human heart can bear. If such a measurement were done, it is difficult to imagine a heart that was more tested than Abraham Lincoln's.

Although the practice of psychobiography is a tedious and sometimes controversial analysis, it seems abundantly clear from those who were around Lincoln and who knew him best (especially those who knew him long before he set his sights on the presidency), that his personality was tilted towards depression. It was, most likely, a psychological mark upon him since birth. James Lemen, Jr., an Illinois lawyer (his father was greatly admired by Lincoln for leading the anti-slavery movement in Indiana) who knew Lincoln through the Bar, vividly described that Lincoln had a "settled from of melancholy," which was sometimes pronounced and sometimes slight, but was "always sufficient to tinge his countenance with a shade of sadness." When one surveys the constant deaths, disappointments and difficulty that were the fabric of his life, Abraham Lincoln's struggles with depression, his fatalistic ethos, are better understood.

Much of what Lincoln would eventually become as President was made and forged in the fire of suffering. Lincoln was a person who, by his very nature, pulled himself into introspection. Often, depression is the by-product of the deep, self-coerced introspection that comes from suffering. It is from that suffering, from that self-coerced introspection in Lincoln, that emerged a man who was uniquely equipped with the wisdom, compassion and emotional durability to become one of the greatest presidents in American history.

To a large extent, Lincoln's remarkable achievements as President of the United States were manifestations of his self-awareness and his resourceful use of suffering. Although written hundreds of years before Lincoln's birth, the spectral words of the Greek dramatist, Aeschylus, from his play *Agamemnon*, seemed predestined to come wailing down the centuries and fall upon our sixteenth president, when one considers Lincoln's profound transfiguration of suffering into wisdom:

> "He who learns must suffer. And even in our sleep, pain that cannot forget falls drop by drop upon the heart, and in our own despair, against our will, comes wisdom to us by the awful grace of God."

Mary Lincoln was mired in depression, too. Hopelessly mired. Unlike Mary, however, there was something about the anima of Abraham Lincoln that made it possible for the man to suddenly snap out of his doldrums of depression. That was what distinguished his and Mary's individual battles with overwhelming sadness. Grief is as personal as fingerprints. Each person has to cope with grief in their own way. But Mary Lincoln could never break loose from its hydraulic grip. By the time of Gettysburg, her suffering had become who she was. Lincoln, instead, was in touch with his own melancholy temperament, and eventually learned how to pull himself out of it. As his lifelong friend Joshua F. Speed witnessed, the President's moods "could readily brighten," a quality, Speed said, that "was an aspect of his uniqueness."

Lincoln realized that to rise above the tide-waters of his depression, he had to keep moving . . . he had to keep on going. Much like the hip 1970's slogan, Lincoln's approach to suppress the melancholy was to "keep on, keeping on." The history of civilization has taught us that many of the greatest human accomplishments are realized, not by brilliance or strength, but by raw perseverance. And Lincoln had it. He was always looking forward. There is a popular saying attributed to Lincoln, that appears on T-shirts, mugs, in books and on the Internet. Lincoln says, "I am a slow walker, but I never walk back." There is no proof that Lincoln ever said this. As a Lincoln quote it may be a spurious, but it is spot-on in describing how he turned his depression into a lever for growth. *Perseverance.* It is lasting historical testimony to Lincoln's mental toughness during his presidency, that his private battles with depression never shut him down. He was always able to maintain a clear vision, and a calm, steady strength about his presidential duties.

Lincoln's lightening change of moods were possible, in part, through his love of humor and storytelling. Through the years, he had become a marvelous raconteur. Laughter, for Lincoln, was a life force that gave him balance, clarity and resilience, buffering him from the storms of life. And it whetted a natural inner craving he had, for good ol' fun. After telling a good joke, the President would slap his thighs with both hands, laughing effusively at his own joke until it became contagious to everyone in the room. "This reminds me of a story," Lincoln would invariably say, as he began to spin the yarn of a good tale.

One contemporary remembered that when Lincoln told a story, his "eyes would sparkle with fun." Lincoln got the same pleasure from a good joke or a funny story as others got from a shot of whiskey or a leg of lamb. A favorite Lincoln story around the White House was about a young and anxious soldier, who was telling his family good-bye as he was departing for the Civil War. His proud, loving sisters, as Lincoln told it, had made their brave brother a going-away gift—a belt, which they suggested be smartly embroidered with the inspirational slogan, *Victory or Death.* "No, no...don't put it quite that strong," their brother replied. "How about one say'in, *Victory . . . or Get Hurt Pretty Bad.*"

As he told a perfectly paced story, Lincoln's features increasingly arranged themselves, almost dutifully, into a glow-in-the-dark grin, as he closed in on the funny punch line. Whether telling the story of the short-legged Frenchman in the snow whose britches erased his tracks as he walked, or the preacher who really got religion after getting a lizard in his pants—for Abraham Lincoln, humor was an anti-depressant drug with no side effects.

By the time of the Gettysburg event, the White House had become the blotting paper for many worries and sorrows, so a generous dose of collegial male laughter at White House meetings, whether Abraham Lincoln dispensed or partook in it, kept him emotionally grounded. President Lincoln got a kick out of entertaining aristocratic, upper-crust visitors to the White House by telling them backwoods stories in a strong Hoosier twang. Most folks have privately entertained the thought that it would be nice to have a pin that would puncture arrogance. Lincoln had one. It was a straight pin made of humor. Occasionally, when a politician at the White House got a little too puffed up and full of himself, Lincoln would use a good joke to pierce a hole in the fellow's stuffed shirt, so some of the hot air would leak out. If you didn't have a sense of humor, you were pretty much unarmed, and at Lincoln's mercy.

A man is never completely broke, it seems, who can still laugh. And in that regard, Lincoln never emotionally slipped into the red. His sense of humor, and his innate timing in using it, never abandoned him. He used much of his spare time reading humorous satire and funny stories. Lincoln's humor could be urbane, backwoods, or even a bit crude. Whatever the subject, Lincoln's humor was the centerpiece of his unfailing mental stability and sheer stamina as President, a part of the gestalt of his presidency. A good laugh helped to purge himself of the superhuman pressures that squeezed on his very being. As his lifelong friend Judge David Davis recalled, Lincoln was always telling jokes to "whistle off sadness." On once occasion, Congressman James M. Ashley from Ohio sprung to his feet, all worked up and objecting to Lincoln cutting a joke as a side diversion from the intense discussion taking place, over a pending crisis. Lincoln, in reply, perhaps placing a hand on the uptight Republican's shoulder, said, "Ashley—I have great confidence in you and great respect for you, and I know how sincere you are. But if I couldn't tell these stories, *I would die.* Now you sit down."

Lincoln could laugh at himself, too. Even when he was the butt of a humiliating cartoon, or a cruel comment that ridiculed the clothes he wore or mocked the oddity of his physical features—personal insults that he lived with from childhood to his death—Lincoln could be dog-gone funny about it all. During one of his epic senatorial debates with Stephen A. Douglas, as legend has it, the smooth and accomplished Douglas, before a huge crowd, openly accused Lincoln of being "two-faced" on a political position. Lincoln quickly countered the man proudly known as the "Little Giant" (so called, because Senator Douglas was "little" in stature at five feet four inches and a "giant" in Illinois and national politics). "I leave it to my audience," Lincoln snapped back. "If I had another face, do you think I would wear this one?" A gale of laughter followed.

One humorous story, that got a lot of circulation around Washington during the War, in parlors, over fence rails and in the news-papers, involved two silver-haired, Godly women discussing the war. One of the elderly Quaker ladies remarked, "I think Jefferson Davis will succeed because he is a praying man." To which the other woman countered, "But so is Lincoln." "Yes," said the first lady, "but when Abraham Lincoln prays, the Lord will think he's joking." Lincoln really got a kick out of this one; it was one of his favorites.

Later during his presidency, Lincoln would reflect, pensively, on the thread of demeaning insults that had been woven into the tapestry of his entire life, and write a personal letter to the Shakespearean actor James H. Hacket, expressing with a touch of both hurt and humor, "I have endured a great deal of ridicule without much malice; and received a great deal of kindness, not quite free from ridicule. I am used to it."

In what would become the remarkable drama of his life, Lincoln, indeed, would wear both the masks of tragedy and comedy.

* * *

DESPITE THE PRESIDENT'S talent to instantly shift emotional gears, still, a dank air of lingering, unreachable sadness seemed to always hover over the Lincoln household. That's because death kept mighty close company with the Lincoln family. Few things are as democratic as death. But even in their age of foreshortened lives (the average life expectancy when Lincoln was elected president was about forty-two years), the Lincoln family seemed to suffer a cruel and inordinate deficiency of mortal years. During their lifetimes, both Abraham and Mary Lincoln would learn to endure the unendurable—relentless, gut-wrenching grief—grief, enough, to make the word falter on the lips.

First, death claimed Abraham Lincoln's infant brother, Tom, at the Knob Creek farm in Kentucky. Little Thomas' grave would not be found until 1933, near the Knob Creek homesite. For Abraham—just a young boy—it was his earliest encounter with the pain and emptiness that travels with death.

A few years later, while living in the southern Indiana wilderness called Little Pigeon Creek, his "angel mother" Nancy Hanks Lincoln, a tall and sinewy, dark-haired woman with sharp cheek-bones and sad eyes, summoned nine-year-old Abraham and his older sister Sarah to her bedside after several days of debilitating, horrible suffering. She had the "milk sickness."

If free-roaming cattle got to the tall growing, white-blossomed poisonous plant called "white snakeroot," and ate it, they in turn passed it on to humans through the cow's milk. If you drank the tainted milk, and your tongue turned white, all hope dissolved. It was the mark of death, which was painful and certain. Uncontrollable trembles. Convulsive vomiting and searing intestinal pain, followed by paralysis. Finally, a blessed coma. Then death. It was though months of suffering the likes of terminal bone cancer had been, somehow, hideously compressed into a single week. Dying was worse than death. This was how Nancy Lincoln greeted death on October 5, 1818, bravely, surrounded by loved ones. She was only thirty-four.

Nancy Lincoln was an uneducated but intelligent woman (she could read but not write), whose family was "the joy and care of her life." Her last words spoken to her children Abraham and Sarah pleaded with them "to be good and kind to their father—to one another, and to the world." It was a solemn creed of kindness Abraham would accept—one that would forever instill in her only son a sensitivity towards all living things, profoundly shaping his life—and that someday, would shape the country.

The boy Lincoln would help his father build his mother's coffin, cut out of green pine with a whipsaw, tearfully carving out the pegs that would hold the sad box together. In bitter, unspoken grief, they would carry Nancy Lincoln a quarter-mile through the woods, the fall leaves beginning to turn, to the peaceful site of a beautiful green hill. There was no pastor within thirty miles, so they conducted a humble family funeral and gently laid her in the earth, just like they had done for Nancy's uncle and aunt, the Sparrows, who died from the deadly "milk sick" just a few months previous. In the tradition of the time, they would wait several months for a preacher, to give her the funeral service she deserved. Only after her son's assassination, would a gravestone be placed at the site of Nancy Lincoln's burial. "All that I am, or hope ever to be," Lincoln would say many years later to his old law partner and friend, William Herndon, "I get from my mother, God bless her." The lifelong pain of her loss was so great, Lincoln rarely spoke or wrote of her.

Just ten years later, Abraham's adored sister Sarah, married to Aaron Grigsby, would unexpectedly die just hours after her stillborn baby. It was a painful death for the young woman barely under twenty-one years of age, who lost her life giving birth to her first child. Sarah was only two years older than Abraham. One neighbor remembered the sadness that broke over him that day: "We went out and told Abe [about his sister's death] . . . I will never forget the scene," as the awful incident was recalled. "He sat down in the door of the smokehouse and buried his face in his hands. The tears slowly trickled from between his bony fingers, and his gaunt frame shook with sobs."

Then, as a young man, there was the crushing loss of Lincoln's sweetheart perhaps his fiancée, the pretty, auburn-haired Ann Rutledge—the girl he courted back in New Salem, Illinois. Her life was suddenly taken by the "brain fever," likely typhoid fever. Lincoln once said, after plunging into depression at that time, that he could not even bear the thought of it raining on her grave.

A few years later, after his marriage to Mary Todd, when Lincoln was practicing law in Springfield, he and Mary would suffer the first of what would eventually be the tragic death of three children. It was their second son, Edward Baker Lincoln, whose expression instantly glowed when the word "Father" was spoken in his presence. "Eddie," as his parents called him, died just a few weeks shy of his fourth birthday. Pulmonary tuberculosis likely took the boy, after fifty-two days of terrible suffering.

Soon after Lincoln's election to the presidency, he would suffer another devastating loss. In a cruel twist of fate, the first officer to die in the Civil War would be one of Lincoln's dearest friends, Elmer Ellsworth. Lincoln loved the young soldier from Illinois like a son. A few years earlier in Springfield, he had learned the law as a clerk under Lincoln's tutelage. In what would be the first thunder-clap of personal tragedy for the Lincoln family arising out of the Civil War, Colonel Ellsworth was cut down with a double-barreled shotgun while tearing down a Rebel flag from top of the Marshall House hotel that was located just a few miles from Lincoln's Executive Office. Learning of Ellsworth's shocking, unexpected death, in a rare display of raw emotion during his presidential years, a stunned Lincoln wept, sobbingly, covering his face with his handkerchief. Lincoln struggled to absorb the sudden obliteration of such a fine young man. Two reporters who inadvertently walked in on the chap-fallen President, weeping in the White House library, were shaken and deeply moved to see this occur, as they put it, "in such a man, and in such a place." Sometimes, in the stress of an exceptional emotion, we act without ambient consciousness of people and place. Lincoln had done so. Lincoln would close his letter to Colonel Ellsworth's parents with these unforgettable words: "May God give you that consolation which is beyond all earthly power." The words of French novelist, Marcel Proust, perhaps, best capture Lincoln's emotions that day: "It is often hard to bear the tears that we ourselves have caused."

In the late Fall of 1863, the season of the Gettysburg event, Abraham and Mary Lincoln, as First Family, were still in mourning from the devastating loss of their eleven-year-old son William Wallace Lincoln—they called him "Willie"— who died in his pitiable struggle with typhoid fever the year before. The Lincolns never recovered from the loss of Willie. The boy was smart and sweet, and showed so much promise. Lincoln saw much of himself in Willie. Most around the White House thought he strongly resembled his father. Willie gave his parents so much joy and hope. After he died, joy never fully returned to the White House. In the first days following Willie's death, Lincoln would go alone, secretly, to the place of entombment, and gently lift the coffin lid. He wanted to be near the boy, and look upon his face one last time, even in death. His love for Willie was inexhaustible—as was the pain.

Then there was the endless tide of fraternal blood and death pouring out of the Civil War, all on Lincoln's presidential tenure. Lincoln's administration supported the Nation's first draft law passed by Congress, pulling these young men, many of them against their will, into harm's way. His signature on this conscription act had summoned legions of men and boys, fathers, sons and brothers, to their violent deaths. "The cry of the widow and orphan," John Hay once remarked, "was always in [Lincoln's] ears." Because of this, some anti-war media had transformed Lincoln from a public servant into a public serpent. One bone-chilling political cartoon even depicted President Lincoln as a vampire, literally sucking the lifeblood out of Columbia (a beautiful goddess often used by artists in the nineteenth century as a patriotic symbol of America), with Columbia desperately crying out, "You have swollen the earth with the blood of my children."

Mary Todd Lincoln would have three half-brothers and a brother-in-law killed in the Civil War, all of them dying for the cause of the Confederacy. In one dark six month period, the Lincoln's buried their son Eddie, Mary's father, and her grandfather. Most of Mary's family were Southerners and eventually became estranged and deeply embittered at the Lincoln family over the War. Even worse, Mary had to hide her grief over the death of loved ones from the South, to politically protect her husband and avoid stoking-up the growing accusations that she had Southern sympathies.

It is no wonder that Mary could never gain her emotional footing in the White House, as she lost family to both death and disaffection. The endless tears she shed would literally damage her eyes. In an era before the transformative world of psychotropic medications, there was little that could be done for Mary. The Todds would become a singular apologue of what the War had done to families and the Nation. The President once remarked, during those difficult years in Washington, that "even the Heavens are hung in black."

Surely, it seemed so.

During his fifty months in the White House, hanging on to a moment of joy for President Lincoln was like trying to hold quicksilver; when he clutched his hand around it, just as instantly it was gone, chased away by another tragedy. And so it always was for Abraham Lincoln. When life began to sweeten a little—death intervened. It was a life that both haunted and sculpted the heart of the man.

* * *

That morning of November 18th, 1863, Lincoln must have wondered, after hearing Mary's emotional plea that he not go to Gettysburg, whether she would ever be able to cope with Willie's death. Down deep, he knew the awful answer—there was just no getting over the loss of Willie—for either of them, ever.

Lincoln tried to calm Mary before leaving for the train station that morning—"Now there, Mother," he would say in a tender, soothing tone. Cupping her face with her hands, she covered eyes which had reached a sadness of incurable depth. Mary required more emotional support than her husband, or anyone, could ever hope to give.

There she was the morning of the Gettysburg trip, still wearing her black, bombazine mourning clothes, a year and a half after Willie's death. Indeed, the White House itself seemed dressed in Hamlet's black. The place had become a caldron of misery for the Lincoln family. Mary herself once described, in a disturbingly real metaphor, the sadness she suffered as "the fiery furnace of affliction," writing that she feared she was in "deep waters" that were going to "overwhelm" her. And, eventually, they would. While Lincoln seemed to convert suffering into the brilliance of mature leadership, Mary was shut down physically and mentally by it. She had just about foundered on grief. It had demented her. Two sweet boys, gone. And their oldest son, Robert Todd Lincoln, detached and away for good, at school. Unfathomable grief. Unquenchable sorrow.

Mary was right—Lincoln privately deliberated that morning, as he listened to her heartfelt and frightened appeal for him not to go to Gettysburg. They could not lose Tad. They could not bear to lose another. The President and Mary surely wondered, in their frightened, private-most thoughts, whether death had already wrapped itself around their family like wraiths of damp fog that would not lift.

As Abraham and Mary belabored his decision to go to Gettysburg, the President, undoubtedly, asked himself the agonizing question: "Do I dare leave my sick boy, to make a few remarks over soldiers' graves in Gettysburg?"

After all, what was it that was urging Lincoln to Gettysburg? No one around the President knew, with certainty, why he was going. But they were well aware that the trip involved both political benefits and risks for the President. And physical risks, too. Every mile of railroad track exposed Lincoln to danger. Still, no one really knew what was on Lincoln's mind, or what he hoped to accomplish at Gettysburg. All that really mattered is that Lincoln knew.

Like the eternal cadence of ocean tides returning to the shore, the Preamble to the Declaration of Independence kept returning to the President's thoughts, over and over, as it had for many years. As President Lincoln reflected on the words in that revered manuscript of 1776 that defined American democracy—and the desperate need of the people to understand the reason for the War—he began to realize that he had an inescapable rendezvous with a soldiers' cemetery in Gettysburg, Pennsylvania.

He had to go.

And his heart longed to go. President Lincoln wanted to see and walk upon the battlefields at Gettysburg. As a surveyor, he had learned long ago that if one is observant enough, during moments of quietude and contemplation—the land will speak to you. The original Americans—Native Americans—had known this for centuries. Lincoln wanted to hear what the battlefields of Gettysburg had to say.

There was also some political expedience in the President going to Gettysburg. Lincoln was facing a reelection bid, and shrewd enough to keep a windsock in the political breezes that were blowing about. He knew that the governors of several key Northern states, whose support he desperately needed to recruit more soldiers from their states—would be at Gettysburg. And so would reporters from all over the country. Even dignitaries from foreign countries. Lincoln was also well aware that the telegraph could report to just about every city and settlement in America what he said and what he did, within minutes of it happening. The newborn Associated Press, which was rapidly maturing into a powerful communications machine, would be there. Lincoln's second Attorney General, James Speed, later said that the President told him "he was anxious to go [to Gettysburg] . . . and desired to be prepared to say some appropriate thing."

The fact that President Lincoln was willing to do two things he ordinarily avoided like the plague—that is, make a public speech and travel a great distance from Washington—suggests that Lincoln believed he had something of great importance to tell the people, and that Gettysburg was the right place to say it.

For several months, the President had felt an aching need to speak directly and forthrightly to the people about the War. Trusted advisors who had the ear of President Lincoln, strongly encouraged the same. Maybe, Lincoln pondered, Gettysburg was, at last, just the backdrop he needed to make an important speech to all Americans—a special place and time to give meaning to the War—and to give the people a message of hope for the future.

The bottom line was that Lincoln wanted—and needed—to make a speech at Gettysburg. Only the President of the United States could explain why the War was necessary, and why the War had to go on. Yes, the Gettysburg Address would be a war-speech. But it had to be much more. Somehow, he had to make sense, out of the senseless. Lincoln knew he had to speak to all Americans, in words they could all understand. It had to be a message about the future of their country—and what America must do, to survive.

Still, there were some who thought it was bad politics for President Lincoln to make a speech at Gettysburg, figuring he would hurt his reelection chances with a clumsy or embarrassing speech. But by the time Abraham Lincoln had climbed aboard the presidential train to Gettysburg, any thoughts of the political backwash that might surge over him from speaking at the cemetery dedication had become a subordinated concern, deeply buried in the recesses of his mind.

Going to Gettysburg transcended politics. The urgent, compelling reason to go to Gettysburg was that the President hungered for the people to understand the War. And the people hungered for understanding. And hope.

In his heart and mind, Lincoln had no choice. He had to go to Gettysburg. It was time to deliver a special message to the people. Not time in the ordinary meaning of passing time, like the time shown on a clock—but "Kairos" time—time as it was meant in ancient Greece. Kairos, for the Greeks, was a specific and urgent moment, that when fully realized, cries out within the person to make a decision.

Gettysburg was Kairos.

Mary remained adamant that her husband should not go to Gettysburg. And it was gut-wrenching for Lincoln to think about leaving, especially with Taddie so sick and wanting his father by his side. But somehow, it seemed the right thing to do. Something inside was pulling him to Gettysburg, like a team of plow horses.

It was Wednesday, November 18th, 1863, the day before the Gettysburg cemetery dedication. The time had come for President Lincoln to depart for the train depot at Union Station. His worryworn visage reflected a man who was both burdened and conflicted by his decision, leaving behind him at the White House an overwrought Mary Lincoln and very sick little boy.

For Abraham Lincoln, it was not only a dubious start—but a departure wrapped heavily in trepidation and melancholy.

CHAPTER THREE

BOARDING PASSES INTO HISTORY

"William goes with me."
—President Abraham Lincoln
Memo to Treasury Department
November 18, 1863

FINALLY, AFTER THE EMOTIONAL TURMOIL THAT HAD TAKEN PLACE inside the Executive Mansion that morning, the tall, discomfited figure of President Lincoln slowly emerged from the White House. His shoulders and head were slumped with worry about what he was leaving behind; his lips pursed with apprehension about what lay before him. James B. Fry, Lincoln's provost-marshal-general and personal escort, already had the Chief Executive's horse-drawn carriage ready to go to Union Station. It was approaching the noon hour, and Lincoln was running late.

Officer Fry gently urged the President to hurry, reminding him that there was no time to spare in getting him to the train on time, to assure his timely arrival in Gettysburg. Lincoln gave Fry a smile, telling him that the situation reminded him of a story of a fellow back in Illinois, a convict, who was being escorted by the Sheriff's men down the road to a set of gallows, where he would be hung in public. As Lincoln told it, crowds of excited, curious people eagerly raced towards the execution site, pushing and shoving, scrambling their way past the condemned man to secure a good view of the event, until he suddenly hollered out: "Boys, you needn't be in such a hurry to get ahead . . . for there won't be any fun, till I get there." Underneath the humorous veneer of

Lincoln's story, it seemed that the President, himself—like the condemned man in his story—was not as eager as everyone else to face what
lay ahead of him the next two days.

The President would travel to Gettysburg in a specially-commissioned four-car train. Compared to the train ride that Lincoln traveled
more than two years earlier in route from his home in Springfield,
Illinois to Washington, D.C., on his way to become the sixteenth
President of the United States—a bumpy, swerving endurance trip of
twelve days, two thousand miles and two dozen different railway sys-
tems—this luxuriant, half-day ride was like going from the outhouse to
the penthouse.

Climbing aboard the train that morning must have been especially
painful for President Lincoln. Not only was Tad sick, but he was thinking of his son Willie. Precious and precocious Willie. It had been nineteen unbearable months, since he passed away. Willie had showed so
much promise—he glowed both in academics and in adult company.
The handsome, fun-loving, blue-eyed boy was always absorbed in trains,
taking imaginary trips from one end of the country to the other. Young
Willie could holler out the names of railways and train schedules all over
the eastern part of the country, like nobody's business. How Willie
would have loved to ride on such a fancy train! The President surely
reminisced for one precious but evanescent moment, how he used to
play the part of the locomotive and pull his "dear rascals," Willie and
Tad, up and down the streets in Springfield, Illinois in a tiny wagon.
The boys adored their father.

As Lincoln eased himself down on the soft, opulent seating of the
President's train, he may have been reminded of the comfort of his old
law office sofa he had custom-made for his long frame. The sofa served
the dual role of his nap site and as a wrestling ring for the boys, "which,
after many years of service," according to his old law partner William
Herndon, "had been moved against the wall for support." Sometimes
Willie and Tad would wear themselves out and fall asleep on the sofa at
the end of a long day.

Abraham and Mary Lincoln were loving and kind parents, who were
also long on indulgence and lax on discipline. Willie and Tad were
unconstrainable whirlwinds of energy and mischief. Back in the days of

Lincoln's law practice in Springfield, it wore raw on law partner Billy Herndon's nerves ("I wanted to wring their little necks," he once admitted) when the boys rummaged through the law office like wild hogs in a peach orchard. Herndon was convinced that "had they sh_ t in Lincoln's hat and rubbed it on his boots, he would have laughed and thought it smart." Accordingly, the law office in Springfield was always a mess. Lincoln, himself, added to the gaum. Documents scattered over his desk and the floor like fallen November leaves; reminder notes and unpaid bills crammed inside the band of his stovepipe hat; orange rinds and apple seeds all over the floor, where Lincoln enjoyed his favorite snacks and pondered on his cases. Those were hectic and hard days for Mary, when Lincoln was away for long spells practicing law on the Circuit, leaving her all alone to handle the boys. He was gone from home far too much. But still, they were good years for the family. Before they moved to Washington.

Pulling out from Union Station in Washington, D.C. towards Gettysburg, leaving behind a sick boy and distraught wife, President Lincoln may have been reminded, by sad contrast, of how happy Mary was less than three years ago, smiling and buoyant as she proudly stood behind him, as he gave his first inaugural speech. How, that night at the inaugural ball, unburdened by the first family's image as parvenu Washingtonians, she danced on air and dazzled the crowd of five thousand guests. Mary was resplendent in her beautiful blue silk evening gown, swathed in a gorgeous French lace tunic. Surrounded by her loving and enthralled Todd family of sisters and cousins, Mary was raptured in the joy of the occasion. How her blue eyes sparkled that evening as she felt the part of Parisian grace. Why, she had even taken a dance with Lincoln's old debate and senatorial nemesis, Stephen A. Douglas! Those were sweeter times, indeed. More laughter at home. More joy in life. By the time of Gettysburg, however, things had changed. There was so much heartache. The presidency had taken a heinous toll on the family. And the full price had yet to be exacted.

The Gettysburg trip of roughly eighty miles would take about half of the day, if spared breakdowns. Lincoln would ride in the fourth car, of the four-coach train. It was a plush and well-appointed "director's car," originally built for the personal use of the president of the Baltimore &

Ohio Railroad, the prestigious John W. Garrett, who loaned it to President Lincoln for the trip. The stern section had been partitioned off to create a separate compartment, filled with seats next to the walls. The ride on that director's car, even at a top speed of twenty-five miles an hour, would be a level of grand and sumptuous comfort in railway travel to which Lincoln was unaccustomed, even as President of the United States—but surely enjoyed. Early on, Mary Lincoln had planned on joining the train ride to Gettysburg too, until Tad got sick. The First Lady (Mary was the first presidential wife to wear this title) had a hearty appetite for extravagant furnishings, what President Lincoln sometimes frustratingly referred to as his wife's "flub-dubs." No doubt, such a luxurious trip would have been right down Mary's alley.

Riding the rails along with the President and his three Cabinet members were his young but loyal Cabinet assistants, first secretary John G. Nicolay and second secretary John M. Hay; his Commissioner of Public Buildings, Benjamin B. French, who had written a beautiful hymn especially for the Gettysburg program; diplomatic emissaries from Canada, France and Italy (invited in a tactical effort to annul any Confederate sympathies those countries might harbor); Charlotte Everett Wise, the winsome daughter of the keynote speaker for the Gettysburg event, Edward Everett, as escorted by her husband, Naval Officer Henry Wise; a dozen soldiers from the recently created military division known as the Invalid Corps, dressed in snappy, sky-blue uniforms, who served as ceremonial bodyguards for the President; the talented Marine Band; and other diplomats and headliners in the Republican party. Lincoln had cushioned the atmosphere of this train ride to Gettysburg by surrounding himself with fellow Republicans and a politically-friendly entourage for this trip to Gettysburg.

Even for this short junket to Gettysburg, there were serious concerns for the President's safety. As the Civil War animosities intensified, Lincoln's staff would constantly remind him that he was "in danger of a violent death, every minute of the day." Because of assassination fears— fears, as history would tragically play out, that would become a cruel reality—precautions had to be taken.

* * *

Ward Hill Lamon, a thick-chested, burly fellow, with a black pomaded coiffure and thick goatee-stache, who had the look and swagger of Buffalo Bill Cody and whose customary wearing apparel included a toggery of guns, knives and brassknucks—was a part of the small, tight consortium of people that formed Lincoln's inner circle of advisors. He traveled to Gettysburg a few days ahead of the President, to work on the logistics of the big event. Lamon was one of the President's oldest and closest friends. And he had married the daughter of Lincoln's old law partner, Stephen T. Logan.

Lincoln and Lamon had rode together on the Eighth Judicial Circuit, practicing law across a wide span of the Illinois towns and countryside. Furthermore, Lamon had been a loyal and tireless campaign aide for Lincoln's runs at the Senate and Presidency. Not only was he a raucous joke-teller, but he could also strum a pretty mean banjo. Lincoln really enjoyed hearing Lamon play Stephen Foster tunes. A lawyer by trade, Ward Lamon discovered that he was better suited for another occupation, bodyguard of the President of the United States.

Lamon, a former champion, took his job seriously. Very seriously. A big, bold man who was tough as a $2.00 steak, and former champion wrestler (at six feet two inches, he was one of few people who could nearly stand eyeball-to-eyeball with Lincoln. Lamon was obsessed with the President's safety. With his Southern drawl and tendency to brag and drink too much, Lamon rubbed some of the upper crust in the Washington crowd a little raw. Scottish-born Allen Pinkerton, who was head of the Pinkerton National Protective Agency and the famed father of modern detective agencies, once called Lamon "a brainless egotistical fool." Others who knew Lamon intimately, who knew his courage and dedication to the President, would have disagreed. But there was one thing about Ward Hill Lamon that no one disagreed about. He was incorruptibly loyal and willing to step in front of a bullet or blade to save the life of the President.

Lincoln sometimes thought his friend Lamon was sort of a fussbudget about his personal safety, and a bit overanxious about it all. Lincoln did not want to be like an unseen, untouchable king kept aloof from the people by imperial guard. This mindset caused Lincoln to be terribly slack about his own security. On one occasion, Lamon would scold

President Lincoln in a letter: "I regret that you do not appreciate what I repeatedly said to you in regard to . . . your own personal safety. *You are in danger.*" In frustration over these matters of security, Lincoln would vent to John Nicolay, "I cannot discharge my duties if I withdraw myself entirely from danger." To keep himself perfectly safe, Lincoln sarcastically told Nicolay, he would have to "lock [himself] up in a box."

The truth was, Lamon was rock-solid right. Lincoln was in grave danger, 24-7. There would be an open bounty on his head, throughout his presidency. And down deep, Lincoln knew it too. He began to realize that the safety of the President of the United States and the stability of the Union as central government for the country, were inseparable concerns. So Lincoln made Ward Lamon—"Hill" as the President and close friends often called him—in charge of his security and the U.S. Marshal for Washington, D.C.

And Marshall Lamon was tough-enough for the job. Any twitch of suspicious movement towards the President would get you clobbered. On one occasion, the barrel-chested Lamon was so ferocious in making an arrest, that he nearly killed the poor fellow before he was locked up. "Hereafter, when you have occasion to strike a man," Lincoln afterwards chided Lamon, "don't hit him with your fist; strike him with a club or crowbar, or something that won't kill him." When threats towards the President got fever pitch, the well-armed Lamon would roll himself up in a blanket, like a burrito made of guns and knives, and sleep outside the Lincoln bedroom door.

Shortly after Lincoln's election, a fellow named Joshua Allen visited the president-elect in a campaign office Lincoln still had open in Springfield, Illinois at the state capitol building. Allen wrote on January 26, 1861, a letter to his mother, telling her of his observations in Lincoln's office:

"He [Lincoln] has got stacks of preserved fruit and all sorts of such trash which is daily receiving from various parts of the South, sent him as presents. He had several packages opened and examined by medical men who found them all to be poisoned."

By the time President Lincoln traveled to Gettysburg in November 1863, threats to his life were nothing new. In fact, they started in 1860 right after his nomination in Chicago, and continued to plague his presidency, from its very beginning to its violent end. When Lincoln received letters threatening his life, which he regularly did, he discreetly filed them away in the drawer of his pigeonhole desk . . . eerily enough, labeled "*Assassination.*" When he penciled-in that file label, Lincoln—in the cruelest of all ironies—had assigned a title to the last chapter of his life.

* * *

The first leg of the Gettysburg trip would take the President to Bolton Station in Baltimore, Maryland, where the presidential train was shifted over to the north central tracks next leading to Hanover Junction in Pennsylvania. This stop in Baltimore may have left Lincoln feeling uneasy in his car. For President Lincoln—as the famous line goes — it was probably "déjà vu all over again." The President's thoughts surely flashed back only thirty-two months in time, when Baltimore was a stop on the last stretch of his inaugural train ride to Washington. At the last moment, the itinerary of that trip was suddenly altered. Lamon and Pinkerton feared an attack on Lincoln's life at the same train station in Baltimore. In an abundance of caution, Lincoln was covertly whisked to Washington for his March 4, 1861 inauguration, incognito, in the middle of the night by special train. Even as Lincoln stepped into the special train, Pinkerton's detectives cut telegraph lines, so word could not escape that Lincoln had departed.

Although the details of the "Baltimore Plot" are unclear, it seems a plan to kill Lincoln outside of the Calvert Street Railway Station in Baltimore had been hatched by a secretive political camorra of xenophobic racists called the "National Volunteers." Frederick W. Seward (the thirty-year-old son of Lincoln's Secretary of State, William H. Seward), in collaboration with Allan Pinkerton, brought secret information about the assassination plan to President-elect Lincoln. Today, the National Volunteers would be identified as a fringe, radical, paramilitary organization. They were organized, dangerous and they meant business.

Since Lincoln's shocking election on an anti-slavery plank, the National Volunteers were obsessed with preventing his inauguration. Their anger burned deep against Lincoln. Maryland was a border slave state, and its flagship city of Baltimore was a churning hot kettle of

Southern sentiments and secessionist activities. (Only a small percent-
age of people in Baltimore even voted for Lincoln.) Baltimore's streets
had long been reputed to be violent habitats. The dangers were real.
And the plot had a real chance of success. Certainly, then-Senator
William H. Seward, and also General Winfield Scott, who was fussy and
pompous but one of the most admired military minds in the country,
thought so. If radical Confederates could capture or kill the newly-elected President before he was even sworn into office, the whole political
infrastructure of the Federal government might collapse.

So, at the insistence of Lamon and Pinkerton, and with Lincoln's
reluctant consent, the plan to secretly transport the President-elect by
clandestine train several hours ahead of his public schedule were put
into motion. The testy Pinkerton also preferred that no one else in the
President's tight circle of advisors know of his covert train connection,
but Lincoln demanded that Mary be told.

The stealthy subterfuge worked. Lincoln traveled only with Lamon
(who rode with both hands on his pistols) and made it safely into
Washington at the break of dawn. The President stepped off of the train
in Washington, safe and unseen, until a voice frightenly pierced the veil
of twilight: "Abe, you can't play that on me." A startled Lamon and
Pinkerton instantly surged to subdue the mysterious, perhaps dangerous
man who had eyeballed the next President. Lincoln intervened. In
twenty-first century idiom, Lincoln had been "punked" by his friend,
Congressman E.B. Washburne, who had, somehow, got in on the secret
plan and showed up to welcome his old buddy. (To his lasting credit,
after the Civil War was over, Washburne advocated that large Southern
plantations be carved up and sold, to compensate freed slaves.)

Soon after Lincoln's inauguration, the story of his secret night ride
escaped. Embarrassing scuttlebutt circulated about Lincoln. One version even had the President-elect sneaking into Washington for his first
inaugural, under the dark cover of night dressed like a woman.
Cartoons lampooned the President-elect as a cowardly buffoon, some
depicting him slipping into the Nation's capitol wearing the disguise of
a Scottish tam and kilt, dancing a Highland jig. Lincoln's fair weather
supporter, George Templeton Strong, worried that "this surreptitious
nocturnal dodging," as he artfully bloviated, would sully the President's

"moral" image. Even back then, as it is today, politics was the toughest of all verbal contact sports.

This fabricated story of Lincoln skulking into Washington, at a time of grave crisis when the country needed brave leadership, dressed like a woman or a Scotty—along with the horselaughing that never failed to cap it off—quickly spread all over the capital city, and rippled out even further. Although President Lincoln had a hard bark when it came to ignoring the endless barrage of personal and political slander against him that came with the job, this one really got under his skin. The stories were humiliating. The episode had sullied his reputation as a man of steady courage and strength, an image he had carefully cultivated during his presidential campaign, and on this inaugural tour into Washington.

Actually, what really happened on Lincoln's hegira into Washington that night, was that he had switched his usual stovepipe hat and frock coat for a wide-brimmed farmer's hat which he could bend down over his face (given to him at the New York stop) and an oversized coat that he draped over his shoulders like a serape, to hide his distinctive stature, not an easy chore. It was an effective disguise. But Lincoln was embarrassed to the bone by the swirl of demeaning jokes and bad publicity over the incident that implied he had made a weird, cowardly entrance into the Nation's headquarters. Henceforward, the President forever swore off of such disguises and middle-of-the-night rigmarole, danger or not.

Despite Lincoln's obstinate self-pledge to never again don disguises as a security measure, and even though the President would later downplay the Baltimore risk, the frightening reality of the danger that night in Baltimore was validated by this hair-curling fact: the train originally intended to transport the President-elect and his family—which was the subterfuge train carrying only Mary Lincoln and their children—was actually detained in Baltimore by a terrifying mob of Southern sympathizers and likely some Plug Uglies who were bloated with violent urges. The mob screamed at the new First Family, yelling out vulgarities against Lincoln, calling him, among other epithets, the "black ape." How frozen with fear Mary and the boys must have been. History could have been disturbingly detoured that night, had the president-elect actually been on that train.

A few days before Lincoln was sworn into office, the great American poet, Walt Whitman caught a glimpse of the newly-elected President as he worked his way through an uneasy and packed gauntlet of people in downtown New York City. It was a stop-over on Lincoln's inaugural trip to Washington, D.C. Whitman surveyed the faces and collective body language of the crowded streets, and later speculated that "many an assassin's knife and pistol lurked in hip or breast-pocket" in that mass of people.

The dangers and threats against Abraham Lincoln's life seemed so real, so imminent, that when the president-elect eventually rode in an open carriage down the muddy, dirt road called Pennsylvania Avenue for his first inauguration ceremony, he must have felt like Odysseus traveling the watery maw that flowed between Scylla and Charybdis. The city was plied with anti-Lincoln sentiment and Lincoln haters. Lincoln undoubtedly knew that someone out there in the crowded streets, unseen, wanted to kill him. There was danger at every side. Union sharpshooters perched on the tops of buildings like modern day SWAT teams, and Federal soldiers heavily guarded street intersections. Even so, reminiscent of President John F. Kennedy's open motorcade in Dallas, in hindsight, it is shocking that President Lincoln was not driven to his inauguration in a safer, closed carriage. For the first time in history, protective barriers were erected to physically separate the President and his podium guests from the massive crowd. The horrifying possibility of presidential assassination had, for the first time—and forevermore—entered into the American political psyche.

* * *

As Lincoln traveled another train route—this time, eighty miles of train rails to Gettysburg, Pennsylvania—there was little thought about the danger. The danger was just as real as it had been in Baltimore, thirty-two months earlier. And on Pennsylvania Avenue, at his inauguration. There was plenty of spots along the way to sabotage a train. Or even kill or kidnap the President. The Confederacy had become quite skilled at disabling the North's railway lines. Even so, Lincoln understood that the wind blows hardest atop the flag pole. He had come to accept that being in the path of hate and harm was a cross he must carry as President of the United States. Especially in a country ripped asunder by civil war.

But there was also danger in not going to Gettysburg. A more subtle one. It was the danger of unfavorable public opinion. Bad press, run amok. If the President and commander-in-chief of the Nation's military had appeared frightened or intimidated by Southern threats of violence—backing out of a potentially dangerous rail trip to Gettysburg—it could have triggered a panic wave through the people and politicians of Northern states who were confident (and perhaps overconfident) of their eventual victory in the War—and empowered those in the South who made such threats.

Storms do not move the mountain. Likewise, fear does not move the strong and wise leader. Abraham Lincoln would not be moved. He would not allow himself to become a prisoner of fear. There was no room in Lincoln's thoughts to even hesitate about making the trip.

So it was on to Gettysburg.

Brimming with its political grab bag of people, the President's train rolled towards western Pennsylvania. However, one member of this presidential entourage was not a cabinet member, nor a business tycoon or politician. He wasn't a secretary to the President, an influential reporter, or a high-ranking military officer. He couldn't even call himself a citizen.

He was simply known as William H. Johnson.

Johnson was a young African-American who was President Lincoln's valet, barber and occasional bodyguard. In the custom and language of that day, he was Lincoln's paid "servant." William Johnson was the only servant at the White House brought to Washington from Springfield by the Lincolns.

Johnson, with his very dark skin, stood out and had some early difficulty being accepted on a White House staff of other African-American servants—a group of cooks, maids, stable-hands, seamstresses, gardeners, wagon drivers, and housekeepers—most of them, of lighter mulato color. Johnson struggled to fit in. The other servants saw Johnson as an outsider, and treated him as such, despite their commonality of race. The irrational intolerances that sometimes emerge from human nature and skin color can create a peculiar pot of race relations. And in this case, it did. To ease tensions, Lincoln found a spot for Johnson at the Treasury Department. Soon, Johnson's honesty and reliability, his industrious and tireless work, made him Lincoln's favorite and most trusted servant.

Yet, those close to the President knew very well that William Johnson was much more than a factotum. He was a man of integrity—a loyal and discreet friend to the President—with whom Lincoln often entrusted messages and confidences, and even his personal safety. On that departure morning of November 18th, as the genus of powerful and influential men arranged to ride in a special car with the President of the United States, Lincoln made it abundantly clear that there was one person—a man who had no inherited or elected prestige, no lofty rank, no elevated social standing, or even citizenship—who had better be on the presidential train with him, when it pulled out for Gettysburg.

Firing off a cryptic memo to the Treasury Department that morning, Lincoln brusquely ordered: "William goes with me to Gettysburg."

And so it was. William H. Johnson, the most unlikely passenger of all—likely the only black man aboard—along with the fortunate handful of others chosen to ride in the director's car to Gettysburg, had not only received a prestigious invitation to travel with the President.

They had received boarding passes into history.

CHAPTER FOUR

THE RIDE TO GETTYSBURG

"Father Abraham, come out . . . your children
want to see you!"
—Pastor M.J. Alleman
At Hanover Station, PA.
November 18, 1863

WEDNESDAY, NOVEMBER 18, 1863. IT WOULD TURN OUT TO BE A beautiful, clear travel day.

The presidential train with its payload of impressive people would take a steep route northeastwardly from Washington, D.C. to Baltimore, Maryland; then wheeling north, it traveled to Hanover, Pennsylvania; and finally, turning back west to the small town of Gettysburg, a rural community in south-central Pennsylvania of about 2400 people.

The rails hummed, as miles of track were gobbled up by the presidential train. Despite the burdens clinging to his mind, the President grew upbeat, enjoying conversation with those around him. It was one of his few breathing spells from the burden of presidential demands and duties.

As Lincoln peered out the train window, scenic murals of undulating landscape, sprinkled with homes and barns and bantam communities, sailed by. Throngs of well-wishers, gawkers and the curious would gather at the brief railroad stops along the way, hoping to catch a glimpse of the President of the United States through his car window, or from the train balcony. With a little luck, the train might stop at their station. Why, they might even get to shake his hand.

At the same time the President Lincoln's train was chugging its way to Gettysburg, a separate, specially-commissioned "Governor's train" was making the same trip. It was departing from Harrisburg, Pennsylvania, the state capital. Only thirty miles from Gettysburg, this excursion would not pull out from the Harrisburg station until five o'clock in the afternoon. As the fickle hand of mechanical fate would have it, they should have left earlier. This train carried the Governor of Pennsylvania, the handsome, forty-six-year-old Andrew G. Curtin, and a salon of other political heavyweights, that included eight current and former governors of Northern states, high-level military officers and politicians, along with a garrison of musicians and reporters.

Virtually all of the journalists and newspaper reporters that would make this train ride to Gettysburg with Lincoln were pretty cozy to the President and his politics. For most part, the Republican press would have the upper journalistic hand at Gettysburg. Cocooning himself with such an arrangement was no accident. Lincoln was super-sensitive to the power of the print media. And he knew how to use it.

Very early in his career of partisan politics, Lincoln had been sort of a newspaper man himself. He (with likely help of others) anonymously published a wagonload of letters—hundreds of them—in the *Sangamo Journal* in Springfield, sometimes under the pseudonym of an illiterate but wily farm widow named "Rebecca." In those days, when it came to political newspaper print, the quill and pad were often converted to the quiver and the bow. Lincoln's razor-sharp letters to the *Sangamo Journal* were no different. Both humorous and cutting, these epistolary newspaper battles were a nineteenth century version of present-day political attack ads, often directly aimed at smearing and discrediting one's opponents.

One barrage of Lincoln's anonymous attack letters, written in the late summer of 1842 during his old state politics days, targeted an unpopular fiscal policy of the Illinois Democratic administration, in particular, mocking and piling up insults on its state auditor, James Shields. At the time, Shields—a vain, spunky little Irish fellow—was a bigwig in Democratic politics. In one biting letter to the *Sangamo Journal*, "Aunt Becca" and "Jeff" engage in the following chatty dialogue: "Shields is a fool, as well as a liar. With him, truth is out of the question, and as for getting a good bright passable lie out of him, you might as well try to strike fire from a cake of tallow. . . I tell you, aunt Becca, there's no mistake about him being a Whig . . . if I was deaf and blind I could tell him by the smell." Today's political commentators might say Shields had been "swift boated."

Shields eventually deduced that Abraham Lincoln was the likely author of these letters that blackguarded him and his recent state proclamation. Unfortunately, Shields was born about a century too early to benefit from Yogi Berra's sage advice of "Never answer an anonymous letter." So he did. Shields, who was short on fuse and long on pride, angrily demanded a "full . . . and absolute" retraction from Lincoln.

Some historians believe Mary Todd (whom Lincoln would marry just a few weeks later) may have written some of these caustic letters against Shields and his Democratic party. The witty, brash, headstrong future First Lady, who had a blue-blood education for her day (she spoke fluent French) and a penchant for politics, was very capable of composing such political assaults, both with the tongue and the pen. She spoke and argued with razor-sharp skill. The better weight of evidence suggests, however, that Lincoln was the guilty ink slinger. Nonetheless, when it came to putting a retraction in the local newspaper, a stubborn, young Lincoln, who, perhaps in an act of chivalry was deflecting the political heat away from the true author, Mary, wouldn't budge. Or apologize. From Lincoln's perspective it wasn't personal, just politics. Shields saw it differently. Feeling angry and publicly humiliated, the hot-blooded Shields challenged Lincoln to a duel, a fight to the death.

Under dueling protocols of the day, known as the "code duello," Lincoln got his pick of the deadly weapons to be used. Lincoln chose calvary swords. Each man would stand next to a board placed on the ground, which they could not cross and then fight to the death. Lincoln must have felt the dark irony that his ghost writing might turn him into one. He shrewdly selected swords instead of the customary pistols, to take full advantage of his seven inch height advantage over Shields (not to mention his ax-swinging prowess), and some believe, to call Shield's attention to the absurdity of the dangerous event. And it was no secret that Shields, having military experience, was a fine marksman. Publicly, both men were willing to spill blood in the name of honor. Privately, both wanted to save their lives and save face. Problem was, neither Lincoln nor Shields could invent a manly and dignified exit strategy out of the duel, once the fuse was lit.

Unable to stop the gravitational pull of the deadly-serious affair, eventually, on September 22, 1842, the reluctant adversaries showed up at 4:00 p.m. on the banks of the Mississippi River, broadswords in hand, ready to fight to the death. They had taken their bloody affair to the opposite side of the river—the Missouri side, rather than the Illinois where there was a law against dueling. Lincoln would later sum up the situation like this: "I did not want to kill Shields and I did not want the d_ _ ned fellow to kill me."

Fortunately, during the last few moments before the duel began, friends of both combatants who had scrambled desperately to the scene were able to peacefully mediate the conflict. Swords were never pulled from their scabbards. Both Lincoln and Shields had realized that discretion really was the better part of valor. The duel which could have ruined both men's lives and consigned Lincoln to political obscurity—whether it ended in his survival or death—instead, ended with a handshake. The hatchet (or in this case, the sword), was buried.

This incident evoked uncomfortable, shameful memories for Lincoln, and thereafter, he flat-out refused to talk about it. It offended him if someone even asked about it. But Lincoln did learn from it. It taught him that personal attacks that go too far, even in politics, can backfire. And it was an act of self-betrayal in his personal belief to use cool, calculated, impassioned reason to resolve heated problems. In a fascinating twist of fate, twenty years later, after Abraham Lincoln became President, James Shields, a self-made immigrant, would serve under him as a Union general in the Civil War, and would later distinguish himself in American history by being the only person, ever, to serve in the United States Senate from three different states. It was apparent: the more these men learned about life, the more they were able to forgive.

* * *

By the time of the Gettysburg trip, President Lincoln had learned from his *Sangamo Journal* days and his "scrape with Shields" (as he called it), an immutable rule of politics: if you get in a mud-slinging contest, you'll always get some on you. Lincoln had also become keenly aware of another constant in the political universe: good press helps and bad press hurts. Lincoln shrewdly understood that public opinion was not only pliable, but also the key to political survival. "Public opinion in this country is everything," he once declared in an 1859 speech in Columbus, Ohio. Public opinion was constantly on his mind. When Lincoln was shot at Ford's Theatre, he had several favorable newspaper clippings in his wallet.

The great Shakespearean and film actor Sir John Gielgud once said of young Jean Seberg, who came from the small mid-western community of Marshalltown, Iowa, that "she had learned to be a star before she became an actress." It was much the same for Lincoln. He had learned to be a politician before anything else. Lincoln knew that a successful politician had to till and fertilize journalistic soil, in order to harvest a good relationship and good print with the press. And that's exactly what he did. After all, that is how you get your brand of message out to the people. So when the President's train pulled out for the destination of Gettysburg, Pennsylvania, well-stocked with friendly reporters, Lincoln already had the plow-spade thrust into the ground.

The Governor's train, rolling out of Harrisburg, was scheduled to catch up with the President's train at the Hanover Junction Station in Pennsylvania. But the locomotive had engine trouble. Like our delayed and bumped airline flights of today, delays from the train break-downs were just a fact of life. "Are we there yet?" is not a colloquialism unique to the twenty-first century. Folks in the 1860's often asked the same question when they took a trip by rail. A good dose of patience, mixed with a few ounces of corn derivative taken internally before your train departed the station, for many, was the recommended travel ritual of the day. Good conversation and music helped to shorten the journey for others on the Governor's train. Still, it would be a red-eyed 11:00 p.m. before the Governor's train made it to the Gettysburg Station that evening, nearly six hours late and lagging way behind the earlier arrival of President Lincoln's train.

For the President's train, though, it was smooth sailing. No strung-out delays when they switched tracks. No aggravating engine break-downs. No pesty cattle stops. A mighty fine train ride, indeed.

Despite many stops along the way to Gettysburg, the longest holdover of the whole trip for the President's train would be about eight minutes, at the train depot in Hanover, Pennsylvania. It would also be the junction drawing the largest crowd. Hours before Lincoln's arrival in the tiny rural town, the train station was already jam-packed with hundreds of people who had been arriving for hours, hoping to lay eyes on the President of the United States.

When the presidential train finally pulled into the Hanover station, Lincoln initially remained inside the director's car, probably hoping to stay seated and relax during the brief train stop. Perhaps he was preoccupied with executive duties or collecting his thoughts about tomorrow's speech at the soldiers' cemetery. Whatever it was keeping the huge crowd of onlookers from seeing their beloved President, they would have no part of it. Like the repeated cheers of a inspired theatre audience clamoring for an encore performance, the gathered onlookers began to yell and call out for the President, over and over, trying to cajole Lincoln to step outside and say a few words.

Several rounds of cheers failed to coax the President out of the director's car. Suddenly, the Reverend M. J. Alleman, Pastor of the St. Mark's Lutheran Church there in Hanover, bellowed out like a clap of thunder, *"Father Abraham, come out, your children want to see you!"*

Like a foghorn cutting through a still night, the preacher's thunder-call on behalf of his passionate congregation of spectators, pierced through the noisy crowd and into the director's car like a hot knife through butter—jarring the President's attention. It worked. Moments later, President Abraham Lincoln would emerge from the director's car, onto the train balcony, removing his stovepipe hat as he ducked through the confined threshold of the train-car door.

After making some opening comments to the large crowd, the President, as was his habit, attempted to inject some levity into the gathering. **"Well, you have seen me, and, according to general experience—you have seen less than you expected to see."**

Laughter broke loose from the crowd.

Lincoln continued: **"You had the Rebels here last summer, hadn't you?"** Heads in the crowd nodded in affirmation. Some, no doubt, muttered "Yes."

Pushing ahead with his impromptu, light-hearted banter, the President then asked the crowd, **"Well, did you fight them any?"** Lincoln was making reference to the June 30th invasion of their community by the flashy Calvary commander J.E.B. Stuart and his Confederate troops, which took place the day before fighting broke out at Gettysburg.

But there was a problem. No one laughed. For the people of Hanover, "fighting the Rebels" was no joking matter, since it had brought with it the plundering and destruction of their homes, livestock and farms, and blood on their streets. There was nothing funny about "fighting" for survival, or attending the funerals of soldiers killed in action. Nothing funny, at all.

Lincoln's flippant question tossed out to the Hanover crowd was met with frosty silence—cold as the steel rim of a wagon wheel in winter. Half of making a good speech is knowing when to stop. And Lincoln went a little too far. Some of the crowd was reported to have left the gathering, disappointed in the President's remarks.

What was the President thinking when he made those inappropriate remarks? Like all modern-day presidents do on occasion, he had laid a political egg. A gaffe. At this train stop, Lincoln probably felt he had opened his mouth, just to change shoes.

The force of the crowd's sudden demand for a speech may have caught Lincoln off guard, and rattled him a bit. Perhaps he was groggy from a brief nap. It is possible that Lincoln's thoughts of what to say to the people of Hanover at that particular moment, had tangled up with preoccupied thoughts about what lay before him in Gettysburg. Whatever the reason, the President's unbuttoned remarks there at Hanover station were clumsy and ill-suited for the situation. At best, the moment was awkward for the President; at worst, downright embarrassing. No doubt, the quiet stillness of the crowd, stunned by his insensitive remarks, must have hurt Lincoln, personally. It surely reinforced his public image among some who heard, that he was more jokester than statesman. And it was another sour lesson that reinforced his insecurity about making unrehearsed speeches. Thankfully, the cumbersome interval of silence was mercifully disrupted by a group of ladies who emerged from the crowd to present flowers to the President, and give him a hand-crafted flag.

On a more positive note at the Hanover station, Lincoln was introduced to Daniel Trone, the telegraph operator who had enjoyed the proud moment, last summer, of sending the July 3rd telegram to Secretary of War Gideon Wells, proclaiming the Union victory at the Battle of Gettysburg.

Even better, one proud little fella brought President Lincoln an apple, polished up like a diamond. It had been picked off of a tree from his family's homeplace. Both the President and the boy would always remember that moment with great affection. Their two impish smiles proved it.

There would be other brief stops along the way for the President, where he would make better use of his words. At one memorable pause of the presidential train at another site, a pretty little girl raised a cluster of rose-buds above her head, stretching them up to a window left open on the President's car.

She called out in a childhood lisp, "Flowrth for the Prethident! Flowrth for the Prethident!"

Lincoln heard the little girl. The child's speech impediment surely reminded Lincoln of his son Tad, reviving his deep worry for the boy, lying sick back in Washington. Most folks around the Executive Mansion had trouble understanding young Tad because of his speech defect (likely a cleft lip and palate). But not his father. Lincoln—"Papa-day" (his attempt to say "Papa Dear") as he was affectionately called by Tad, always understood the boy. No matter what Lincoln was doing, no matter how busy he was, conferring with war generals, conducting cabinet meetings, engaging in military strategy sessions, when Taddie burst into the room and made a bee-line for Papa-day's knee, Lincoln stopped everything and gave his son undivided attention. Perhaps Lincoln's many months away from home during campaign and speaking tours, or the loss of Willie, accounted for this.

Here at this train stop, again, the President would stop everything to give attention to a child, this time, to the tiny flower girl. The President stooped over and kissed the little girl on the top of her head, telling her: "You'er a sweet little rosebud yourself. I hope your life will open into perpetual goodness and beauty."

That's why everyday folks loved their President. Many saw him not so much as their President, but as a father, or as a friend. There was an insuppressible stream of kindness—genuine and unaffected kindness—that ran through Abraham Lincoln. Kindness is a thing that needs to be practiced each day, like playing a fiddle. And in daily devotion to his mother's dying words, Lincoln practiced kindness. It was always most poignantly revealed when he was in the presence of the suffering, or the helpless—especially children. He would gently pat the crown of their head with his huge hand. Like sadness, kindness was a primal instinct in Lincoln, a quality borne out of the last words of his dying mother that resided in a place deep within the man, like iron ore in a mountainside. Children, like the little flower girl, always brought a smile out of the President no matter how dark and difficult the day.

At other train stops along the way to Gettysburg, folks would serenade the President with the affectionate, hymn-like song, *We Are Coming Father Abraham*. Lincoln would, in turn, gratefully bow, and appease the audience with a few remarks. They would sing:

"We are coming, Father Abraham,
Three hundred thousand more.
We are coming, coming our union to restore.
We are coming, Father Abraham,
With three hundred thousand more."

The lyrics for this wildly popular song were anonymously written by a New York banker and abolitionist, James Sloan Gibbons. In early July 1862, President Lincoln had pleaded for an additional 300,000 volunteers for the Union cause. Gibbons composed the song while treading behind an assembly of Union soldiers on a New York City street; their rhythmic tempo of marching inspired him to write several verses. After it was quickly set to music, Gibbon's song sold an incredible half-million copies of sheet music. In a strange twist of copyright fate, Gibbons would not get credit for writing the song until twenty-two years after the Civil War was over.

Lincoln couldn't carry a tune in a bucket. But he sure loved to listen. This song, which fueled a new, fatherly public image of President Lincoln, pleased the President very much, although in the humble way that was his grace, he was inclined not to openly admit it. For the people, it was an anthem to pump-up Union morale and honor their beloved President. For the President, it was good politics and a good song, a musical salve that soothed the soul during turbulent times. Songs not only had great impact on President Lincoln, but also the people who endured the Civil War, both North and South.

The ever-increasing popularity of songs like, *Yes, I Would the War Were Over* and *When This Cruel War Is Over*, were telling the President and the politicians how ordinary people really felt about the War, and what they were going through. *Bear This Gently to My Mother* was more than just a sad song; it related the painful, heartbreaking reality of thousands of young soldiers, many of them still boys, who wrote their mother a final letter of good-bye, the evening before they died in battle.

A year or so before Lincoln's trip to Gettysburg, a hauntingly beautiful ballad called *Lorena*, popular on both sides of the Mason-Dixon line, literally became a Siren's song for Southern troops. Confederate soldiers became so homesick after hearing the bewitching song, that many of them deserted. One Confederate general, John Hunt Morgan, was so enraged by the mesmerizing effect of the song on his troops (he called it that "cursed ballad"), that he ordered his officers to kill the songwriter if they encountered him. Apparently, even song writing was a potentially hazardous activity during the Civil War. In the 1950's, the song *Lorena* was used in two movies, *The Searchers* and *The Horse Soldiers*; it seems the director of those movies, John Ford, had become captivated by *Lorena*'s spell, even a century later.

* * *

But for a few brief stops here and there, the President had several hours of rail time in his director's car. It gave Lincoln some unencumbered time to read the newspapers, an indulgence he rarely had time for in Washington. But did the President use some of that time on the train to work on the Gettysburg Address?

Persistent folklore has it that Lincoln, in a flash of inspiration, conceived and scribbled the Gettysburg Address on the back of an envelope or a piece of wrapping paper that was picked up from the railroad car floor. Even Andrew Carnegie, the future railroad and steel tycoon, who was only twenty-seven years old at the time of the Gettysburg trip and supervising military telegraph operations and railroads in the east, like others after Lincoln's death whose imagination was richly fed by a heartfelt yearning to be historically connected to a martyred and beloved president—would later recall a place in the story for himself, which was that quixotic and pivotal moment in history, while riding with Lincoln on the train to Gettysburg. And what moment was that? Why, it was when Carnegie reached paper and pencil to the President, so that Abraham Lincoln, in a moment of spontaneous inspirational combustion, could compose his next day's speech—which, in an astonishing chapter in history, would turn out to be the famous Gettysburg Address. At least, that's the way Carnegie's business associate, Charles M. Schwab, told it. No doubt, Andrew Carnegie had later wished he was there.

He just wasn't.

Such Walter Mitty fantasies popped up like spring clover, after Lincoln's death. For years after Lincoln's assassination, many others, like Carnegie, would cast themselves into an imagined scene of revised history, literally placing themselves in close proximity of Abraham Lincoln at some important or even inconspicuous moment in his life. Sometimes, an artist's brushstrokes—like today's photoshop manipulations—were used to stretch and reshape history. So many imagined people were depicted in paintings as being present all at the same time in the confined 9 by 17 ft. bedroom at Lincoln's deathbed scene in the Petersen House, sometimes stretching the tiny room to hold, as seen in the Alonzo Chappel artistic rendering, *forty-three mourners* that it has been given the name of "The Rubber Room Phenomenon."

Even Governor Curtin, apparently in a memory lapse, would later claim that he was on the president's train, and that he cut apart envelopes to provide Lincoln the paper upon which to write his immortal speech. Problem was, the Chief Executive of Pennsylvania wasn't there. He was on another train—the "Governor's train"—originating from another city. And William Slade (not to be confused with servant William Johnson, who really was in Gettysburg with Lincoln), another African-American servant at the White House, claimed, as told years later by his daughter, that he listened to Abraham Lincoln practice his speech as he composed it, line for line, in the President's boarding room at Gettysburg. According to his daughter Nibbie, William Slade even recalled the President consulting with him about his speech from time to time, saying, "William, now how does that sound?" There was one problem, however. William Slade never made the trip to Gettysburg.

So what was this all about? It seems as though people wanted, somehow, to be close to their tragically-taken president. They wanted their own personal and special moment next to a man who had been elevated in death to a status of near sainthood.

These Lincoln fantasies, for their heartfelt creators, were more fancy than fraud. They were often motivated by raw and sincere emotion. Perhaps it was a form of bereavement. They loved their President, now gone, forever. They wanted to rub shoulders with history. And memory, as someone once said, always seems to smile upon the highest bidder.

All of this was a peculiar phenomenon of human behavior much like the one of recent years where people, from everyday citizens to prominent actors, authors, politicians and celebrities, even a Pulitzer Prize winning historian—people who were otherwise highly credible and immensely successful in their lives—found themselves infatuated by the political martyrdom experienced by combat veterans of the Vietnam War. Allowing fantasy to blur and reshape their own reality, these people inserted themselves into fictional scenes of heroism, tragedy and human drama in Vietnam, even though some of them had never stepped foot on the soil of Southeast Asia. The layers of these types of self-indulged fantasies are almost always peeled back by the hand of time, and thus exposed, often causing painful embarrassment for those who invented the stories and their families.

After Lincoln's death, not only did people want memories of a moment with their President, they also wanted a memento touched by their President. Like true believers on a quest in search of an ancient holy relic, folks feverishly sought out tangible objects that had been in direct contact with Abraham Lincoln, at any point in his life. These things took on a numinous quality. Physicians and others who attended Lincoln after he was shot, even those involved in the post-mortem process, clipped locks of Lincoln's hair. Even President Lincoln's favorite horse, "Old Bob," suffered the indignity, after Lincoln's death, of having the hair from his mane and tail purloined for souvenirs.

Somehow, it is still sad, even when removed a century and a half after the events, to read about these Lincoln confabulations and quests for mementos, knowing how desperately those in pursuit wanted a moment next to Lincoln, or wanted to touch something touched by Lincoln—longing for a physical connection with history and their immolated president.

* * *

Before leaving for Gettysburg, Lincoln had struggled with enough time back in Washington, D.C. to hammer out the words to finish the entire speech. Time was on short supply. Very short supply. The President would have, at most, only two weeks to prepare his Gettysburg Address; perhaps as little as two days. The White House staff was aware that the President's time, even to prepare an important speech like the one he would deliver over the soldiers' graves at Gettysburg, was a scarce commodity. "Duties" of the President, later remarked Lincoln's third-position secretary William O. Stoddard, "prevented elaborate preparation" on his speech. Lincoln's top secretary, John G. Nicholay, would notice about the time of the Gettysburg trip, the President's "want of opportunity" as he put it, "even to think leisurely about what he might desire to say."

That's because the War was soaking up most of the President's time. And on top of everything else, Lincoln had been trying to squeeze in some time to write his upcoming Annual Address to Congress which was, in itself, a very important war-time speech. So Lincoln knew, when he left Washington, that his speech would have to be finished when he got to Gettysburg, and only then, when he could pry loose some private time at the place where he would spend the night.

But not on the train.

The atmosphere on the President's rolling and jerking train that day on November 18, 1863 was fine for "skirmishing" through the newspapers (as Lincoln called it), and the good fellowship of swapping stories and "politick'in"—but did not lend itself to the quiet contemplation Lincoln needed to author the most important speech of the War—a speech worthy of such a serious and somber event.

This seemingly indestructible story, that Lincoln in a eureka-like moment of inspiration, dashed off the Gettysburg Address onto the back of an envelope, while riding the train to Gettysburg—is pure myth. It is also an enchanting, seductive story that has risen to almost parable status. It is impossible to pinpoint the germ of the tale, but no doubt, it has been given extended life by stacks of early Lincoln biographies, and most poignantly and perpetually, through a tiny book written in 1906 by Mary Raymond Shipman Andrews. It is titled *The Perfect Tribute.* And it is perfect, as the propagator of this most famous Lincoln myth of all. The forty-seven page Andrews book—beautifully written but entirely fiction—was required reading in schools all over America for years and has even been made into two movies, breathing even more life into the myth.

Lincoln's oldest son, Robert, still believed the story, even twenty years after his father's death. "My father's Gettysburg Address was jotted down in pencil," Robert Lincoln said, "in part, at least, on his way to the place." Even Harriet Beecher Stowe, the famed author of *Uncle Tom's Cabin* and outspoken admirer of the President's Gettysburg and Second Inaugural speeches, believed (and wrote) that Lincoln authored the Gettysburg Address on a piece of paper "in a few moments, while on the way to the celebration." However, it is no more than a beautifully-written, captivating tall tale woven from cloth of fantasy—not fact. It just never happened that way.

Still, Lincoln probably took time on the train ride to ponder about his speech. He may have even scribbled some thoughts or pneumonic devices on scraps of paper to help him commit parts of his Gettysburg speech to memory. History, often a jealous mistress of such private scrawl, leaves us no hard evidence of such notes. But old habits die hard. And Lincoln had long ago developed the habit, when he read powerful words or heard a well-turned phrase, of jotting down those keepsake words on scraps of paper, and then stashing them away in a desk drawer, or in his stovepipe hat. Lincoln would save these scraps of paper, what were often called "memoranda" in that era, sometimes numbering them. At some point in the future, he would thoughtfully assemble and sew the memoranda together like a patchwork quilt, to construct a good speech.

Years later, one fellow would recall that he was only a young boy when the President's train stopped for a few minutes at the Hanover Junction train station in Pennsylvania, before heading on to Gettysburg. He remembered peering into a window of the President's car, and seeing Lincoln "using the top of his high hat . . .as a makeshift desk," as the President wrote on a piece of paper. This was something the President was known to do. Others claiming to be in the director's car on the way to Gettysburg would vaguely recall the President laboring over some document and writing notes to himself along the train ride.

The complete lack of written evidence and the wildly inconsistent and incredible versions of those who claimed to see Lincoln write out his speech on the train, ultimately, seem to foreclose any possibility that is really happened. Some said the President wrote on an "envelope" drawn from his pocket; others said someone handed him a "piece of cardboard" to write on. Some said Lincoln wrote the speech on his knee, surrounded by "laughing . . . chattering" people; others remembered that he retired to a private place in the rear of his car.

General James B. Fry, who was with Lincoln the entire trip to Gettysburg, was "quite sure" that any claims of the President writing his Gettysburg Address on the train were in "error." Fry, who enjoyed a stellar reputation for honesty, said he had "no recollection seeing him [Lincoln] writing or even reading his speech during the journey." Adding, that "there was hardly any opportunity for him to read or write."

The President's trusted assistant, John G. Nicolay, who was around Lincoln the entire train trip to Gettysburg and a keen, credible observer of the 16th President wrote in 1894, in a February issue of *The Century Illustrated Monthly Magazine*, that "There is neither record, evidence, nor well-found tradition, that Mr. Lincoln did any writing, or made any notes, on the journey between Washington and Gettysburg."

As Lincoln scholar and clergyman Louis A. Warren wrote in 1964, with tongue-in-cheek: "Apparently, after leaving Washington, every time the President held either pen or pencil in his hand along with a piece of paper, onlookers concluded he was writing the [Gettysburg] address." It seems that when human beings yearn to be close to history—memories, which seem too convenient—probably are.

If we know anything about Lincoln's habitudes of speech-preparation, it is this: Lincoln would have never waited until his train ride to Gettysburg to begin writing one of the most important speeches of his political career—a speech he would deliver the next day before thousands of people and a swarm of print and telegraph media. A habit is a coat made of cast iron. And if Lincoln had a habit that he regularly wore, it was that he always sharpened his important speeches on the whetstone of revision. He crafted his speeches in a slow and laborious fashion—for him, a tedious process, in order to lathe and hone down his words so they would fit with precision to the purpose needed. Lincoln needed plenty of time to construct major speeches because he reasoned, methodically, and wrote, methodically.

Although the historicity of an event is best proven (or disproven) by the contemporaneous accounts of reliable, unbiased, first-hand witnesses or tangible scientific evidence, it is often impossible to do so. Sometimes such evidence simply does not exist. If Lincoln wrote any of the Gettysburg Address on scraps of paper that day, on the train, there is no hard historical evidence of it. And contemporary accounts of the goings-on inside Lincoln's train are contradictory and vague, reminding us of the fallibility of human memory. From a forensic perspective, writings made on nineteenth century trains invariably reveal the wobbly penmanship inflicted by a bumpy, swerving, vibrating ride. No such "wobbly" documents have ever emerged, which are claimed to have been written by Lincoln on the train to Gettysburg. All one needs to do is examine the draft of Lincoln's 1861 "Farewell Speech" to the people of Springfield that the president-elect reduced to writing (after he gave the speech) while riding the trains that carried him from Illinois to Washington to be inaugurated. The swerving, bumpy motion of the train is clearly revealed in Lincoln's penmanship of his Farewell Speech, especially when it is compared with Lincoln's elegant and fluid handwriting in the First Draft of his Gettysburg Address.

Maybe Lincoln scribbled out a note or two on the train, in some of his private moments. Maybe the President tucked them in his hat or jacket, and then discarded them, later, when he finished composing his speech in Gettysburg. We probably will never know. But one thing seems immutably certain: *the Gettysburg Address was not written out on the train ride to Gettysburg.*

Whether or not President Lincoln wrote some of his speech on the train that day, the odds are still pretty good that the Gettysburg Address was on his mind when the presidential train pulled out of the Hanover Junction, heading down the last stretch of track to the Town of Gettysburg. It was there, according to some of Lincoln's staff, the President politely excused himself from the camaraderie of good conversation, choosing to retire himself to the solitude of the "study," a more private section at the rear of the director's car. It would be a very long day. He needed a respite of solitude.

And time to think about tomorrow.

CHAPTER FIVE

MISGIVINGS

*"The proposition to ask Mr. Lincoln to speak at the Gettysburg
ceremonies was an afterthought. The President of the United States
had been invited to be present—
but Mr. Lincoln was not invited to speak."*
—Colonel Clark Carr
Illinois Commissioner
Gettysburg Cemetery Commission

As President Lincoln captured a few private moments on the train ride to Gettysburg, his thoughts may have turned to what his critics had been not-so-privately saying. He had surely caught wind of their misgivings about his speaking at the dedication of the soldiers' cemetery. Some on the Gettysburg Cemetery Commission were concerned that a Lincoln speech might not adequately capture the seriousness of the event. They had a point. Sometimes Lincoln's off-the-cuff remarks could be poorly chosen for the occasion.

Others wondered whether or not the President could rise above partisan politics if he made a speech at Gettysburg. They feared Lincoln would make a campaign speech, to kick off his run for reelection. After all, Abraham Lincoln had politics in his blood; and some would say he was a pretty clever, if not a wily politician. Certainly, Lincoln's gangly and forlorn manner helped to conceal the sharper edges of his ambitions, and disguised a man of remarkable political finesse and dexterity.

But there was something critics did not understand about Abraham Lincoln. Although he loved politics, Lincoln had grown and matured during his presidency into a man who came to reject the politics of personal destruction and revenge. It had not always been that way. As a younger man working his way through the spit-and-fight, rough-and-tumble world of state politics in Illinois, and like the rest of his political peers, Lincoln had sometimes behaved as a hack politician. Once, he and his political colleagues jumped out of a window to kill the chances of a voting quorum, and another time, he dropped into the legislative chamber through a trap door in the ceiling. About all politics in those days got personal and was full of backroom wheeling-and-dealing, logrolling, trading political influence for favors, and dirty tricks. Arguably, not much has changed.

It must be remembered that in Lincoln's time, politics was the main entertainment of the day. It was a true spectator sport, in settings that might be best described as political versions of *The Jerry Springer Show*, where hyped-up crowds participated in the act of political theatre. They cheered, whistled, hissed and hollered. They interrupted, laughed at and jeered at the candidates, whether on the stump or stage. Fisticuffs were a regular attraction. Occasionally, there was some gunplay.

In one celebrated incident in Springfield, state representative Lincoln was sharing the stage and exchanging political punches with an influential, blue-blood politician and former circuit judge named Jesse Thomas. Thomas claimed to be a Whig like Lincoln, but often talked and sounded more like a Democrat. All of this had riled Lincoln and his Whig party; they felt the apostate Thomas, expletives deleted, was a tongue-wagging two-face and political traitor. To settle the score, Lincoln and Thomas had squared off, toe to toe, in a public debate.

Thomas would lead off, giving his best stump speech. Then it was Lincoln's turn. In gatlin gun style, he launched an unmerciful and unrelenting attack on Thomas. Lincoln not only put a verbal cleaver to Thomas's politics, but went on to carve up Thomas himself, by mimicking Thomas's voice and facial gestures and even caricaturing his peculiar tics and mannerisms (Lincoln had a natural talent for this)—all while the boisterous crowd roared in laughter at Thomas, humiliating him like Quasimodo in the town square at Notre Dame Cathedral.

In what modern wrestling fans would call a "smackdown," Lincoln had, in public, verbally bludgeoned Thomas into submission. Thomas pitifully broke down in front of everyone, ran from the speaker's platform, crying like a schoolboy who had scuffed his knees on the playground. One eyewitness account said Thomas began to "blubber like a baby."

This became famously known as "the skinning of Thomas." Despite the instant euphoria that came from giving Thomas a public "whoop'in," young Lincoln soon realized that he had gone too far. When Lincoln rang Thomas' bell going for a political knock-out punch, he crossed the line of decency—even by the wild and woolly standards of Illinois state politics. Lincoln may have later reflected on the admonition of kindness his mother gave him on her deathbed, when he was only nine years old. Whatever his thoughts, we know that Lincoln felt bad about the incident, so bad that he looked up Thomas the next day, apologizing for what he had done. But the damage was done. One cannot unring a bell.

Politics does not build character; it only reveals it. And Lincoln did not like what had been revealed in him that day. Lincoln realized that tearing someone down personally in public, is a dishonest way of praising one's self. This ugly incident with Jesse Thomas would burden Lincoln, and consequently, mark the beginning of his growing reluctance throughout the rest of his public career to use personal humiliation as a political weapon in speeches and debates.

After he became President, it must have embarrassed Lincoln a bit to think back upon some of those raucous political stunts in the state legislature. That was the way politics was played back in Illinois. Most politicians of the time (and now, too, for that matter) practiced the old saw that it was easier to "forgive" a political enemy—once you got even with them. But once he became President of the United States, there was nothing vindictive that remained in Abraham Lincoln. "Getting even" wasn't on his agenda. Or his mind. It just wasn't in the man. Lincoln had come to realize that life was both too short, and too long, to carry a grudge.

Maturity is a plant of slow growth. Lincoln had grown and matured along the path to the presidency. The trial and afflictions of the highest office in the land had extracted the last drop of political malevolence from his veins. "I shall do nothing in malice," Lincoln would write in the summer of 1862 to Cuthbert Bullitt, in reference to his war-time presidential duties, "What I deal with is too vast for malicious dealing." And as President, Lincoln walked his talk. There would be no meanness in any of President Lincoln's speeches, ever.

But revenge in politics—especially against an incumbent, war-time President—was as much a reality, as killing was a part of the War. Like it or not, President Lincoln could not elude the politics of the Civil War. As it became painfully obvious that the Civil War was going to be a long and bloody military conflict, the President understood that having the better army, alone, was not enough to assure Union victory. He also needed to win the battle of public opinion.

* * *

The hand of war often fits nicely into the glove of politics. To be reelected, Lincoln needed the people's support both for the War, and the purposes for which it was being fought. And thus far, Lincoln had failed miserably on both counts. So it is understandable that the nerves of many Northern political bigwigs, along with the members of the Gettysburg Cemetery Commission, were taut as bridge cable when they learned Lincoln was invited to speak over soldiers' graves at Gettysburg. They worried that Lincoln—who was facing a tough reelection campaign just over the horizon in 1864—would cave in to his political nature and politicize his speech at the Gettysburg ceremonies.

The President, surely enough, needed a political boost—maybe even a miracle—to get reelected in the 1864 election. Lincoln had the support of most Republicans. But the anti-Lincoln factions came in all stripes. There were, of course, the abolitionists, who wanted immediate emancipation of African-American slaves. They were deeply roiled over what they saw as Lincoln's sluggardly approach to abolishing slavery.

There were the "War" Democrats, who attacked the President's handling of the War, but supported the Union military and aggressive war efforts against the Confederacy. They felt a bungling Lincoln trampled on Constitutional liberties, and antagonized his generals, interfering with their work. Some of their outspoken political leaders and newspaper editors who were harshly critical of Lincoln's administration, were arrested when habeus corpus was suspended, further embittering them against Lincoln.

Then, there were the "Copperheads" who also went by the grossly misleading nickname of "Peace Democrats"; a befitting-named political den of Northerners who were mostly mid-westerners from Illinois, Indiana and Ohio with southern, agrarian roots. They pretended loyalty to the Union but were, at their core, sympathetic to the cause of the Confederacy. They brazenly exploited racism over jobs in the North, especially among white Irish-Catholic immigrants, coining the slogan, "Rich man's war, poor man's fight." The Copperheads, who seemed to never offer public statements without deducting from the sum of human decency, loathed President Lincoln and were obsessed with his removal from office, whether by ballot or bullet. They were anti-New England. Anti-industrialist. They were anti-war and anti-Lincoln. But most of all, they were anti-emancipation. In their view, Lincoln was an exemplar of tyranny, who had provoked the South into war and was bent on destroying the civil liberties of white Americans. They wanted to return to the "old" America . . . "the Constitution as it is—the Union as it was."

Others in the North felt Lincoln's autocratic use of executive war powers had made him into an out-of-control dictator, as they watched the President stretch his constitutional authority to the breaking point by snuffing out the right of habeas corpus, shutting down newspapers that voiced Southern sentiments, and locking up thousands of civilians who revealed Confederate sympathies. One popular political cartoon depicted President Lincoln as a grinning, long-tailed, claw-footed monster, stomping on constitutional rights and dangling an apple of "emancipation" just out of the reach of a grasping African-American soldier. So much of this ugly, violent-toned, anti-war sentiment was being ginned up against Lincoln in the homefront of the North, stoked mostly by Copperheads, that Lincoln referred to this lack of Union solidarity as "the fire in the rear."

And there was a faction of Northerners who were angry at Lincoln over the military draft and his Emancipation Proclamation. Even Lincoln's own Republican party was splintered by sectional bickering. Some groused that the President gave too much weight to the concerns of fickle border states. Others thought he was indecisive, and spent more time telling jokes than tending to the Nation's business.

Some Northerners blamed the President for not ending the war sooner; they wanted to cut a deal with the Confederate States of America that would allow the Southern states keep their slavery and go their own way. Another group of Northerners liked the President and were anti-slavery, but could no longer stomach the North's heavy loss of life. War fatigue was spreading in the North with the fury of the small-pox contagion. On top of that, some of Lincoln's own Cabinet and generals were publicly and privately peeling the paint off of him.

At one point, with all of this undermining the Union's cause and his presidency, and on top of that, his commander over the Army of the Potomac, General McClellan getting typhoid fever, and the Federal Treasury nearly broke, Lincoln told Army Quartermaster Montgomery Meigs , *"the bottom is out of the tub!"*

It surely seemed so. A political feeding frenzy had been unleashed on the President. In politics, when you're right, no one seems to remember; when you're wrong, no one forgets. And the liability side of Lincoln's political ledger—that is, the things people thought he got wrong—was rapidly growing. Looking back, it seems to have defied all odds that President Lincoln wasn't assassinated during his first term in office, having so many haters and so little security.

Lincoln was surely aware that no president had been re-elected in more than thirty years, since Andrew Jackson. He didn't need a crystal ball to see that the chances of his own re-election in 1864 weren't looking so good, either. The politically-sinister Salmon Chase, holding a position in Lincoln's own Cabinet even while Lincoln was in route to Gettysburg was trying to position himself to be the next Republican candidate for president. Lincoln's close friends encouraged him to boot Chase for his promiscuous disloyalty, but the President, in his near-infinite forbearance, wouldn't. He felt Chase ought to have a fair shot at the Republican nomination if the party wanted him. Others in the North were even talking-up his own military leaders, Generals Grant and McClellan, as candidates for president.

Lincoln was on a political high-wire. And there was no safety net. He was even managing his own reelection campaign. Politically bruised and battered, with voter discontent and dissatisfaction festering up across the Northern states, Lincoln was worried he could not be reelected. Deeply worried. And justifiably so. It was worse than even he knew.

Mary Lincoln, who always seemed to be stretching both the family's budget and the social boundaries for women of her time to the breaking point, had become a political liability, too. Some believed she harbored Southern sympathies, or was even a spy. Her occasional haughty demeanor and mercurial temper didn't help much either. Finding comfort in her possessions, especially after Willie's death, and longing for aristocratic acumen and acceptance, she became a compulsive shopper, frequenting posh department stores in Manhattan for clothes and purchasing expensive Haviland china for Executive Mansion dinners. She swapped political influence for private donations and expensive gifts. In shopping spree after shopping spree, the fashionista First Lady spent thousands of dollars purchasing haute couture dresses, accompanied by pricey gloves during one stretch, she bought about four hundred pairs in three months, shawls and jewelry. Her unpaid tab for these extravagances exceeded $25,000, a blooming fortune in those days, and more than President Lincoln's annual salary. She tried to get John Hay fired when he refused to turn over the budgeted White House stationery money to her personal use, and she got rid of the first Commissioner of Public Buildings when he balked on paying for a fancy White House dinner event out of the "manure" fund. An incurable but sympathetic spendthrift, Mary Lincoln had also overran her White House appropriations by nearly $7,000, refurbishing a shabby and run-down White House, all of this, unknown to a war-preoccupied Lincoln, and debts he would have to personally pay if he lost his bid for reelection.

Mary Lincoln had unwittingly turned herself into a campaign issue.

The upcoming 1864 presidential election would be a referendum, by popular vote, on Lincoln's management of the War and his Emancipation Proclamation. Even worse for candidate Lincoln, it would be the only presidential election in American history held during a civil war. Lincoln could have single-handedly postponed the presidential election by use of his war-time powers. But in a remarkable act of political restraint and selflessness—an act kindred to George Washington turning down the opportunity to be "king" of America— Lincoln chose not to. Not having a free and open election, in Lincoln's view, was inconceivable. To do so, he warned, would appear as though the Confederacy had "already conquered and ruined us." By refusing to postpone the election at the risk of personal defeat, Lincoln took an important step in forever shaping the American presidency and authenticating the American form of democratic self-government.

But losing the election was a real possibility. Perhaps, even a probability. "Mr. Lincoln is already beaten," newspaperman Horace Greely would write. "He cannot be re-elected." In fact, in a secret memo that sounded like a political death rattle, Lincoln predicted his own defeat. "You think I don't know I am going to be beaten," the beleaguered President confided in a friend about his chances for a second term, "but I do." Then Lincoln bluntly added, "and unless some great change takes place *badly beaten.*"

It seemed Abraham Lincoln, at the time of his Gettysburg trip, was destined to be a one term President. . . unless the bottom could be put back in the tub.

* * *

The official invitation sent from David Wills on behalf of the Gettysburg Cemetery Commission to President Lincoln did not go out until November 2nd (1863). A week later, on November 9th, there was an announcement in the Boston Daily Journal that "President Lincoln has determined to be present at the [November 19th] consecration . . . and participate in the ceremonies." On the very same day, Lincoln sent a letter to his former law partner, Stephen T. Logan, inviting Logan to Gettysburg and telling him, "It will be an interesting ceremony." Clearly, by November 9th, President Lincoln had made up his mind to go to Gettysburg.

And he had less than two weeks to compose the Gettysburg Address.

This was mighty short notice to the President of the United States, even by nineteenth century customs. Was the President's belated invitation to Gettysburg no more than an afterthought? At first impression, it would seem so. Sending the President an invitation to speak little more than two weeks before the event itself, certainly smacks with the insult of Lincoln being a last minute choice. After all, Edward Everett, who would be the featured speaker at Gettysburg, had received his invitation back in September.

However, the "late" invitation sent to Lincoln was, in all likelihood, a formal invitation to follow-up on verbal invitations that had been earlier related to the President. Lincoln's staff (probably Lamon) and David Wills, most surely, had informally communicated with each other about the Gettysburg event on a date well before the November 2nd formal invitation was sent to the President. In fact, on October 11th, Wills advised a journalist with the Philadelphia Inquirer that Lincoln was "expected to perform the consecration service" at the cemetery dedication event, suggesting the President already knew, by that date, he had been invited to Gettysburg. The impeccably polite and professional Wills would not have leaked this information to a newspaper reporter unless he was sure the President, beforehand, had been personally invited). Furthermore, Governor Curtin, a staunch Republican, surely mentioned the plans for the Gettysburg ceremony when he personally visited President Lincoln in Washington, in late October—political courtesy would have dictated no less. All of this means that President Lincoln may have had more time to think about his Gettysburg remarks—perhaps five to six weeks—than historians once believed.

Undoubtedly, it was a great honor to have the President of the United States speak at the Gettysburg ceremonies. But on the other hand, some members of the Gettysburg Cemetery Commission apparently questioned the fitness of Lincoln to speak at such a "grave and solemn occasion." They worried that Lincoln's remarks might be coarse and insensitive, or that the President might launch into a campaign speech from the speaker's platform.

The member on the Gettysburg Cemetery Commission from Lincoln's home state of Illinois, Clark E. Carr, certainly thought there were serious doubts among the members of the Commission about inviting the President to speak at Gettysburg. Carr was Lincoln's friend. Whether or not Carr's sentiments reflected those of the entire Commission, is debatable. But years later he would explain, with piercing candor, that "The proposition to ask Mr. Lincoln to speak at the Gettysburg ceremonies was an afterthought." Colonel Carr went on to describe the unflattering sentiments of the Commission about Lincoln's invitation to speak at the cemetery dedication, when he added that "it did not seem to occur to anyone [on the Commission] that he could speak on such an occasion." In fact, Carr strongly insisted that when it was suggested that the President speak, "there was immediate and vigorous objection."

Many contemporary historians have questioned Colonel Carr's take on this whole affair of Lincoln's belated invitation. Like the man who caught a big fish, which continued to grow each time he would tell the story, Carr seemed to stretch and recast his story as the years went by, ever modulating it towards the more dramatic "Lincoln was an afterthought and unfit speaker" version. The colonel had a tendency, it seems, to get a bit carried away with big events. For example, Carr "stretched" the size of the crowd in Gettysburg during the ceremonies to be an incredible 100,000, and described Lincoln's horsemanship in the cemetery procession as being something akin to the featured equestrian performer in a rodeo show. In balanced historical hindsight, it seems that the Commission unquestionably wanted President Lincoln to attend the Gettysburg ceremonies; but it may have had reservations about having him speak there.

Part of the Commission's concerns about having Lincoln speak at Gettysburg, if they had any, would have been the President's shaky reputation as a public speaker. For many in high political places, Lincoln's speaking skills for such an important and serious national event were, at best, an unknown quantity. Others, simply put, felt Lincoln could spin a good yarn but was a third-rate speaker. The reason for the President's wobbly reputation as a public speaker was twofold: image and historical timing.

First, there was a strong imprint on the public consciousness—especially among many Northern bluebloods and Eastern elites—that Lincoln was an awkward, uncouth, bedraggled backwoodsman with an insatiable habit of telling cornpone stories. To see President Lincoln at ceremonial affairs in formal attire, uncomfortably squirming in his fancy duds and fidgeting with his bow tie, his huge, kid-gloved hands hanging like curtains over the front edge of an opera box, telling a corny joke at the first sidebar opportunity, would have probably reinforced such an impression. Secondly, Lincoln's writing and speaking style, comprised of simple, straightforward and succinct diction, was not what the general public wanted or expected from their statesmen or headliner orators.

In Lincoln's era, the gold standard for popular orators was long speeches that entertained. Steeped in patriotic and religious platitudes, and garnished with operatic voice inflections and bombastic, high-flying rhetoric, these speeches could last two hours or more. (Aside from a few of the premier speakers, most antebellum oratory was long on words and short on substance; that is, speeches that we would think of today as having more sizzle than steak.)

In defense of the Commission's possible trepidation in asking President Lincoln to speak at the Gettysburg ceremonies, it is fair to point out, as Carr himself would later emphasize, that most members of the Commission had never actually heard Lincoln give a speech. In an age without radio, television, Internet or even voice-recording devices, relatively few Americans—especially members of the Commission and Congressmen from states far removed from Washington—had ever heard the President's voice. In fact, about the only live words folks had heard from Abraham Lincoln, had been entirely political in nature—not a national memorial service for soldiers killed in action.

Aside from a couple of eulogies in his past, Lincoln had no track record, no oratorical résumé, to reassure the Commission he could effectively deliver a speech in this nationally- important setting. His public ken, among some, was that of a political wag who told jokes and slapstick stories, not a serious orator who could give a somber speech over the graves of fallen soldiers. This was a man, after all, who did not sound like Washington aristocrats or speak in the idiom of the educated gentry elite. Lincoln was a mid-westerner, the first President born west of the Appalachians, who greeted folks with a "Howdy." He often responded to a speech introduction, in a lingering drawl, with "Thank you for those kind words, Mr. Cheerman," and said "git" rather than "get", and "thar" instead of "there." On his inaugural trip to Washington as president-elect, the New York media unmercifully ridiculed Lincoln on the twangy, syncopated, hick-toned way he pronounced "inauguration" (something like, "in—agger-rayshun").

Something else may have worried the Gettysburg Cemetery Commission. It was an ugly rumor that had dogged Lincoln, ever since the President had returned from the battlefields of Antietam (near Sharpsburg, Maryland), a year earlier. Lincoln had visited Antietam shortly after the violent battle was over. Antietam, with its twenty-three thousand casualties, was the bloodiest one-day battle in American history.

As the slanderous story went, President Lincoln, General McClellan and U.S. Marshall Ward Lamon, along with some others, rode together in an ambulance wagon across the butchered landscape of Antietam to survey the battleground and discuss war strategy. When Lincoln and his entourage arrived at the site known as the old stone bridge, a place where the wounded still lay suffering and the dead bodies of soldiers were stacked up the highest, it was told that "Mr. Lincoln suddenly slapped Marshal Lamon on the knee, and called on Lamon to sing a comic song."

At the nub of the awful story was a twisted, exaggerated version of what really happened. Lamon did respectfully sing some songs along the route for the President. One sad song that was a Lincoln favorite, *Twenty Years Ago*, especially moved the President. And then, to leaven the accrued sadness, Lamon performed a light-hearted song or two, in particular one called *Picayune Butler*. That's all that happened. But the sickening lie that Lincoln and his group had lampooned a sacred battlefield and engaged in some macaab humor by singing bar-room type songs over the dismembered bodies of the fallen soldiers spread like wildfire by newspaper and word-of-mouth. Rumors without a leg to stand on, it seems, always find another way to get around. *The New York World*, a newspaper which swallowed the political prevarication whole, would print this mean, acid-etched little ditty:

> "Abe may crack his jolly jokes
> O'er bloody fields of stricken battles,
> While yet the ebbing life-tide smokes
> From men that die like butchered cattle."

All of this, of course, was a terrible lie. The author, Joseph Scovill, disclaimed that it was "only a joke." But it was too late. In 19th Century parlance, "the horse was already out of the barn." The truth was that no one in the President's group—including McClellan—was offended by the songs; they were not sung on the battlefield; the incident occurred sixteen days after the battle; and no bodies were seen.

Still, it is no wonder the members of the Commission were skittish about Lincoln speaking at the consecration of a soldiers' cemetery. Political lies, because they are somehow inherently believable to the masses, are probably the most devious product created by the alchemy of intellect. A good many people probably believed this one on Lincoln, including some of those who would hear Lincoln deliver his speech at Gettysburg. Although General McClellan was there at Antietam with the President, and knew perfectly well that this story was not true, he would never publicly rebuke the story. This allowed the savage story to fester. Scandal mongering is as old as politics itself. McClellan, who was soft on slavery and hated Lincoln's backwoods stories, probably hoped to get some political mileage out of it, when he ran for President against Lincoln in 1864. He probably did, at least from the Copperheads. And Lincoln was as powerless as a palsied hand to stop it. It is very possible that one of the thoughts Lincoln carried with him to Gettysburg, was that he would have the opportunity, by speaking there, to excise the political demons of this lingering story.

Colonel Carr, in his personal account of this whole affair of Lincoln's invitation, seemed to gently insinuate that the Commission was squeezed a bit, to make sure that President Lincoln got invited to say a few words at the dedication ceremonies. If so, Governor Andrew Curtin, who liked the President and whose state was the home soil of the soldiers' cemetery and host of the dedication ceremonies may have done the squeezing. Carr too, claimed to pressure the Commission on Lincoln's behalf, telling the *Chicago Journal* in an interview that despite the opposition to the idea of Lincoln speaking, the Commission "finally yielded to my demands."

However, Abraham Lincoln, a pretty savvy reader of political tea leaves in his own right, would have been tuned in to the Commission's anxieties. Even in his days back in the Illinois State legislature, Lincoln was revered by his political peers for his x-ray vision into the strategies of political opponents. Although there seems to be no proof of it in the historical record, President Lincoln may have sent word through his White House staff, to assuage the Commission's concerns about the subject-matter and tone of his speech. After all, Lincoln wanted to go to Gettysburg. He was pleased to get the invitation to speak. And the Commission wanted the President of the United States to be there, at Gettysburg. They just didn't want him to say too much. How could they control what Lincoln would say? For many of the Northern political intelligentsia and wealthy business tycoons of the "cod-fish aristocracy," and some of the Gettysburg Commission itself, Lincoln was the bull and the cemetery dedication ceremony was the china shop.

In the official invitation sent to the President on November 2nd, 1863, David Wills was mustering all of the politeness and tact that his wordsmithing abilities as an attorney would allow, when he requested that President Lincoln, "set apart these grounds to their sacred use," by limiting the length of his speech, as Wills delicately put it, to only "a few appropriate remarks."

David Wills also wanted to hammer home the point in his letter to Lincoln, as diplomatically as possible, the type of "remarks" he felt the people wanted to hear from their President—words, as Wills described it, that would inspire "a confidence that they who sleep in death on the Battle Field are not forgotten by those highest in Authority." Wills had the insight to realize that the greatest laurel of honor that could be bestowed upon the fallen soldiers at Gettysburg and the most meaningful source of comfort to their families was that they never, ever, be forgotten. Will's advice is still relevant and true, today. To be remembered, is the only repayment America's fallen soldiers have ever wanted, since the Nation's 1776 beginnings, for making the ultimate sacrifice in defense of liberty.

In retrospect, the words David Wills used in the Commission's invitation to President Lincoln to speak at Gettysburg, seem to be subliminally voicing the whispered misgivings about Lincoln that were held by the Commission and many prominent politicians of the day. But the message in Will's letter was crystal clear. *Mr. President, please keep your speech short and serious.*

Not in his wildest imagination could David Wills have realized that when he sent Lincoln an invitation to speak at Gettysburg—an invitation which delicately asked the President to both constrain the boundaries of his remarks and make sure the soldiers killed in battle were never forgotten. He had given to Abraham Lincoln, who always designed and built his own speeches, the architectural footprint for the greatest speech ever delivered on American soil.

The die was cast.

CHAPTER SIX

THE BIRTH OF A SPEECH; A DECLARATION, REBORN

"I have never had a feeling, politically, that did not spring from the sentiment embodied in the Declaration of Independence."
—Abraham Lincoln
Independence Hall
Philadelphia, PA
February 22, 1861

WHEN PRESIDENT ABRAHAM LINCOLN CLIMBED ABOARD THE train AT Washington's Union Station—his destination, Gettysburg, Pennsylvania—in all likelihood, he had about half of his first draft of the Gettysburg Address already written, as he would later tell his Attorney General, James Speed.

Before putting pen to paper, Lincoln had already forged some ideas in his head about the short speech he would give at the dedication of the soldiers' cemetery. Lincoln's inspiration would be the Declaration of Independence. In fact, that great document, particularly the words contained in its iconic Preamble, had long been a beacon light to guide Lincoln's thoughts about the future of America, especially during the Civil War. The President had devoted much private thought to the words and meaning of the Declaration of Independence during the last decade of his life—a document he once referred to as the foundation of America's "ancient faith."

Lincoln believed the Declaration of Independence made a promise, inviolate, to all Americans. And through the years leading up to his presidency, and as President, he would often speak of that promise.

When Lincoln stopped in Philadelphia on his inaugural trip to Washington, D.C. to become the sixteenth President, he got the chance to visit and speak at Independence Hall, the venerated place where the Declaration of Independence was given birth.   Lincoln, after alluding to the deep political divide looming over the country, would say that he "would rather be assassinated on this spot than surrender" the liberty America had gained in the Declaration of Independence. Ironically, this same hall was the site where Lincoln's body would later lay in state after his assassination, one of numerous stops the President's funeral train would make before he was buried in Springfield, Illinois.

Gathered at that hallowed hall of liberty on February 22, 1861, the birthday of George Washington, Lincoln could not suppress his great affection for the Nation's founding document, and he had its sacred promise on his mind when he told the huge crowd, "It was that which gave promise that in due time, the weights would be lifted from the shoulders of all men, and that all should have an equal chance." He went on, saying that "This is a sentiment embodied in that Declaration of Independence."

In Lincoln's view, the Declaration of Independence contained America's promise of freedom and equality that gave every human being—without regard to the color of their skin—the opportunity, as he put it, to have "an unfettered start, and a fair chance, in the race of life."

Only four months before the Gettysburg trip—the electric night of July 7, 1863—an inspired and overjoyed President Lincoln gave what was likely the longest unrehearsed speech of his presidency on the White House lawn. The Marine Band had just livened up the jubilant crowd. "I do most sincerely thank Almighty God for the occasion on which you have called," he would proclaim.

The huge crowd, flush with excitement, was celebrating the Union's two great victories that had occurred that same week at Gettysburg and Vicksburg. What a week it was for the Union! Led by General Grant, Vicksburg was a key military and psychological victory for the North, which resulted in the Confederate armies being cut off from all of the central part of the Mississippi River. And Gettysburg brought a crushing end to Lee's penetration into Northern territory.

In these off-the-cuff but passionate remarks made by the President at this July 7, 1863 serenade, it was clear that the democratic ideals of freedom and equality, which were core principles around which the words of the Gettysburg Address would be built, were already bouncing around in Lincoln's head. Unsure in that impromptu moment of the specific number of years since the passage of the Declaration of Independence, Lincoln, referring back to that glorious phrase from Thomas Jefferson's Preamble, told the exuberant throng of people:

> "How long ago is it—eighty odd years—since on the Fourth of July, for the first time in the history of the world a nation by its representatives, assembled and declared as a self-evident truth that 'all men are created equal.'"

There it was. Lincoln had detonated into the presidential political arena a bombshell of American thought: *no person should have dominion over another.*

The President went on to say that the true motive behind the Confederacy's war against the Union was "an effort to overthrow the principle that all men [are] created equal." Lincoln was telling his lively audience that Independence Day is meant for all people who seek out America in pursuit of liberty. Some people talked of "freedom" for slaves. A few spoke of "equality." But Lincoln had come to realize, after much reflection on the words of the Declaration, that you cannot have either of them—until you have both. And then it happened. The words and thoughts on both freedom and equality that had been incubating in Lincoln's mind during the previous decade, were—for the first time in his presidency— launched into the public domain.

But Abraham Lincoln's bond of admiration for the Declaration of Independence, as evidenced in his July 7th speech, was no whim or passing fancy. Nor was it political rhetoric. Lincoln's expanded thoughts on human equality, as inspired by the words of the Declaration of Independence, had laid springloaded in his mind for many years.

Even further back, before assuming the presidency, in a speech he made on July 10, 1858 in Chicago. Lincoln would eloquently explain that even immigrants who came to America, people with no blood or political lineage connecting them with the Founders of America, were entitled to the same assurances of liberty and equality promised in the Declaration of Independence, as were birth-right Americans.

Lincoln wanted all people, including *immigrants*, to be able to look to the core ideals of the American Revolution. This was radical political thought. And politically dangerous. With those sort of words, Lincoln ran the risk of turning the revered Declaration into another divisive issue, another bone of bitter contention between the North and South, between Republicans and Democrats, just like the ongoing turmoil over the question of whether slavery was permitted under the Constitution. Nevertheless, in his Chicago speech, Lincoln would audaciously proclaim that immigrants . . .

". . . cannot carry themselves back into that glorious epoch and make themselves feel that they are part of us, but when they look through that old Declaration of Independence, they find those old men say that 'We hold these truths to be self-evident, that all men are created equal,' . . . that it is the father of all moral principle in them, and that they have a right to claim it as though they were blood of the blood, and flesh of the flesh of the men who wrote that Declaration, and so they are. That is the electric cord in the Declaration that links the hearts of patriotic and liberty–loving men together, that will link those patriotic hearts as long as the love of freedom exists in the minds of men throughout the world."

But still, even further back—in a speech Lincoln made on October 16, 1854 in Peoria, Illinois, perhaps the longest he ever gave—it was evident that Lincoln's search for historical authority to support the elimination of slavery, the operative words needed from the Declaration of Independence were already crystallizing in his mind. When Lincoln made his 1854 Peoria speech to kick-off a tour of anti-slavery lectures, he would become a potent and high-profile voice in opposition to slavery. For the first time in his political career, Lincoln was thrusting into the public spotlight those simple but striking words of human equality recited in the Declaration. Lincoln was also throwing a sharp elbow of sarcasm into the proponents of slavery who argued that it was "a self evident lie" to interpret the Declaration of Independence in a way that made black people equal with whites, when, in his Peoria speech, he told the audience:

> "Near eighty years ago we began by declaring that all men are created equal; but now from that beginning, we have run down to the other declaration, that for SOME men to enslave OTHERS is a 'sacred right of self-government.' These principles can not stand together . . . whoever holds to the one, must despise the other.
>
> Let us re-adopt the Declaration of Independence, and with it, the practices, and policy, which harmonize with it. Let north and south—let all Americans—let all lovers of liberty everywhere—join in the great and good work. If we do this, we shall not only have saved the Union; but we shall have so saved it, as to make, and to keep it, forever worthy of the saving. We shall have so saved it, that the succeeding millions of free happy people, the world over, shall rise up, and call us blessed, to the latest generations."

Lincoln's White House speech in 1863, his Chicago speech in 1858, and his 1854 speech in Peoria, make it clear that the core principles upon which the Gettysburg Address was built were not suddenly born in Lincoln's head on the train ride to Gettysburg—or even during his presidency. The gestation of those thoughts was much longer. By the time Abraham Lincoln boarded the train to Gettysburg to make a speech over a soldiers' cemetery, the Declaration of Independence had been whispering into his ear its sacred covenant . . . *all men are created equal . . . all men are created equal* . . . over and over, for many years.

When the Declaration of Independence spoke to Lincoln, it did so clearly and unambiguously about what a democracy in America should be, especially at a time when political forces in the South argued their hallowed belief in "state's rights" and used tortured interpretations of a silent Constitution to justify slavery and dividing the Nation into two separate governments. "I have never had a feeling, politically," president-elect Lincoln said at Independence Hall, "that did not spring from the sentiment embodied in the Declaration of Independence."

The Constitution may have provided the essential framework for creating a democratic republic form of government, but in Lincoln's view, the Declaration of Independence was the moral foundation blocks underpinning that governmental framework. The Declaration of Independence had vested in America a set of inalienable, God-given moral principles. They were principles that could not be usurped by government, by king or by man. Principles that Lincoln was counting on to put the Nation back together. And free a people. Lincoln's sentiment was this: what the Bible meant to Christians, morally, the Declaration of Independence meant to Americans, politically.

Slavery, Lincoln believed, was a "monstrous injustice" and a living contradiction of the expressed promise made in the Declaration of Independence that states "all men are created equal," whether or not Thomas Jefferson consciously intended his words to extend that promise beyond white males to slaves, immigrants and people of color. Lincoln most powerfully and succinctly defined his view of American democracy as early as August 1858, when he wrote:

"As I would not be a slave, so I would not be a master. This expresses my idea of democracy. Whatever differs from this, to the extent of the difference, is no democracy."

* * *

However, abraham lincoln did not enter the presidency as a warrior-king championing the fight against slavery. When he became President of the United States, he was not the "Great Emancipator." He was not even an abolitionist. Far from it.

In the ascending course of his career in state and national politics, Lincoln, sometimes spoke inconsistently about racial equality, and he took a cautious, sometimes ambivalent, position among those abolitionists in the North that argued for the immediate destruction of the institution of slavery.

Privately, Lincoln despised slavery. He always did. Lincoln often characterized himself as "naturally anti-slavery." Publicly, however, in his early political career, Lincoln was more cautious than courageous. He believed the immoral, socioeconomic system of slavery was on borrowed time. Lincoln theorized that if the expansion of slavery into the western states was stopped (which he zealously fought to do; it was this issue that fired him up to enter national politics), and slavery in the South was isolated and contained there, it would, over time, suffocate to death under its own oppressive weight. It would be an end to slavery, he reckoned, without a civil war or ripping the Nation in two. In the beginning of his presidency, Lincoln was unwilling to become an deep-dye abolitionist—at the time, an extremely radical, outside-the-main-stream, career-ending political stance—if, as he surmised, slavery in the South was already on the "course of ultimate extinction."

Lincoln's full and unconditional commitment to emancipation for African-Americans would evolve over time, steadily and gradually. Lincoln never said a nice thing about slavery during his entire life, but neither was he a lifelong abolitionist. In his first presidential term, he focused primarily on stopping the spread of slavery, rather than elimi-nating it where it already was entrenched. Lincoln would enter the presidency an eventual abolitionist, but not an immediate one. Like most white, anti-slavery people outside of the South (but not all), Lincoln believed there were inherent differences between the races, and he carried with him some of the racial stereotypes towards black people that prevailed in his era. Some of these racial stereotypes became visi-ble during Lincoln's famous senatorial debates with Stephen Douglas.

During those 1858 debates and speeches, often held before white, racist-oriented crowds who were already antagonistic to Lincoln's poli-tics, Douglas unrelentingly played the race card against Lincoln, by claiming Lincoln believed in full "equality of the races." These were, for most part, code words of that era for support of interracial marriage and black suffrage, a taboo position on black civil rights that had no chance of becoming a reality at that time and which was tantamount to political suicide. Many whites of that era carried a deep-rooted, almost psycho-neurotic fear of intermingling the black and white races, which was called "miscegenation."

Lincoln dodged these political grenades that Douglas tossed at him by saying, "I . . . am in favor of the race to which I belong, having the superior position." Lincoln also told his debate audience: "I have no purpose to introduce political and social equality between the white and black races." These statements, when isolated and read alone, are probably the most racist things Lincoln ever said in public, and are often quoted out of context of the debate and political circumstances, unfortunately by Lincoln critics. They are, on their face, plain and simple, an endorsement of white supremacy.

However, in that same debate Lincoln went on to say which is rarely quoted along with the first statement that "the Negro" should be "entitled to all of the natural rights enumerated in the Declaration of Independence, the right to life, liberty and the pursuit of happiness . . . as much entitled to these as the white man." Lincoln was willing to concede a belief in the white-dominated society that then prevailed and he was a part of, to prevent his debate audience from turning him completely off before he could get to his most important message, which was that black people had "natural rights" that were violated by the institution of slavery. Douglas argued that only white people of direct European descent had "natural rights."

Lincoln understood from growing up on a farm, the old saying that went: "pigs get fat—hogs get slaughtered." If Lincoln took the "hog" approach in his debate against Douglas, and argued that black people should have both "natural rights" (the right to "freedom"; that is, no human being should be a slave) and "civil rights" (the right to full social equality; that is, the right to citizenship, vote, own property, marry freely), he would get politically slaughtered and his anti-slavery voice lost in the rubble. If he went for all—all would be lost. However, if Lincoln took the "pig" approach, advocating only for "natural rights" for black people—not the larger, more explosive, demagogic-vulnerable package of "civil rights"—in his view, it gave him his best chance of political survival so he could vigorously fight what he saw as the most-pivotal and pressing issue, which was the expansion of slavery into the Western territories. Essentially, Lincoln was telling his white audiences that they didn't have to give up their white-dominated society, and they didn't have to agree to black civil rights, in order to oppose the expansion of slavery.

Today, some of Lincoln's debate exchanges sound racist and they are, particularly when examined in a contemporary vacuum, in and of themselves. By context, time, place and circumstances, are crucial to understanding what motives were behind those words. Lincoln hated slavery. He believed it would eventually destroy America. And he was willing to do anything, politically, to stop its spread across the country.

Lincoln could no more escape from the fallout of his generation's political and social construct of race, than we can ours. It is painfully uncomfortable for those who deeply admire Lincoln to discover that during his early life, particularly the pre-presidential years, that he attended blackface minstrel shows, occasionally told "darkie" jokes, and that he sometimes used the word "cuffy" (an old slang term for a black person) and the "N" word. Yet, in his own time, Lincoln was considered a progressive when it came to issues of race. That's because these inherently racist activities and conversation were cultural staples of his time and place. Most churches, even in the North, condoned white superiority. Republicans who fought hard to end slavery were called "Black Republicans." Racial slurs were even directed personally at Lincoln, himself, because of his dark complexion and strong anti-slavery beliefs. When Lincoln entered his suite at the Willard Hotel on his inaugural trip to Washington, he was greeted by a note threatening his life and saying he was "nothing but a goddern Black ni _ _ er." It reveals how deeply ingrained and ubiquitous racial prejudice was in nineteenth century America.

Skin color has always sculpted America. And race has always been the rawest of all political nerves. It still is. This was the reality of the times in which Abraham Lincoln lived, and served as President. He was a white man, in a white man's world. Even white women, like First Lady Mary Lincoln, were second class citizens when it came to social and civil rights. They could not even vote, and wouldn't, until 1920.

Strangely, the ill-gotten privileges that came with skin color seemed to connect some white people together, most glaringly in the plantation aristocracy of the Deep South, with a sense of community. Their "whiteness" was a sort of cultural bond. America was not the multilingual, multicultural, multiracial nation we know today. It is difficult and brackish to understand, but in the same way that Native Americans, Asians, African-Americans and Hispanic communities in this country, today, often feel a strong, overarching sense of ethnic pride and cultural commonality, there were white people in Lincoln's era who felt a social and sometimes aristocratic connection about their Caucasian ethnicity. The severe difference was, of course, that the nineteenth century culture of whiteness was, in reality, a belief in white supremacy (not cultural pride), a belief that fertilized the soil of bigotry, hate and slavery. The social complexities undergirding this social phenomenon are, of course, beyond the boundaries of this book and admittedly difficult to historically quantify, but should be recognized because they undoubtedly deepened the intransigent roots of slavery, and encumbered the cause of black emancipation.

Although it is historically misleading to appraise Lincoln only through the lens of our contemporary standards of race relations, neither does Lincoln's era of racism exonerate him from his own prejudices. Historians cannot give him a pass on this. There are no excuses. But understanding cultural climate of his time does mitigate, and gives us perspective on the formidable political and social obstacles President Lincoln faced in advancing the cause of black emancipation in a white-dominated society and the middle of a civil war. And it reflects upon his remarkable growth on this cause during his presidency.

The truth was, very few white people of the 1850's and 1860's, even among the "radical" abolitionists, believed in full black citizenship, and that all races should be socially, economically and politically equal, in every way possible. And early in his presidency—neither did Abraham Lincoln.

In fact, Lincoln had no firm plan to abolish slavery when he assumed the presidency. When Lincoln took office in 1861, slavery had never been more deeply woven into the fabric of American life, thriving under the protective guard of the U.S. Supreme Court and constitutional law. As the distinguished professor and Smithsonian historian James Oliver Horton has pointed out, between the seventy-two years that George Washington and Abraham Lincoln were elected president, fifty of those interim years had slaveowner presidents; and all presidents during that era who got second terms in office, were slaveowners.

Initially, Lincoln wanted to preserve the Union as it had existed in its antebellum form, before the Civil War broke loose. Using the measured and restrained approach of leaving slavery alone to die a natural death in the South and stopping its expansion in the western states,

Lincoln hoped to avoid the full-blown outbreak of secession and civil war. Accordingly, he would attempt to placate the South and head off the war, by promising in his First Inaugural Address that he would not "interfere with the institution of slavery in the states where it exists," adding that "I have no right to do so, nor do I have the inclination to do so." And Lincoln attempted to calm the political leaders of the slavery-splintered border states and angry Northern "Peace" Democrats, who were engaging in constant race-baiting tactics against him, by telling them that the purpose of the War was not to eliminate slavery, but rather to "put the flag back" for the Nation.

In the late summer of 1862, President Lincoln would write an open letter to abolitionist-journalist Horace Greeley, replying to Greeley's earlier editorial letter in his *New York Tribune*, famously known as "The Prayer of Twenty Millions." Greeley had argued in his "Prayer" for immediate black emancipation, calling out the President and criticizing him for his more gradual, cautious approach to abolishing slavery. Lincoln knew Greeley had his thumb on the scales of public opinion, and could not be ignored. He publicly answered Greeley:

> "I would save the Union. If there be those who would not save the Union, unless they could at the same time save slavery, I do not agree with them. If there be those who would not save the Union unless they could at the same time destroy slavery, I do not agree with them. My paramount object in this struggle is to save the Union, and is not either to save or destroy slavery. If I could save the Union without freeing any slave I would do it, and if [I] could save it by freeing all the slaves I would do it; and if I could save it by freeing some and leaving others alone I would also do that."

In these frequently quoted and misunderstood words of Abraham Lincoln, a key point is often lost, however, and it is this: President Lincoln was employing a polemic technique which he had adroitly used both as a lawyer in the courtroom and as a senatorial candidate in his debates with Stephen Douglas. Through this technique, which was in technical jargon a contrapunctual approach to debate, Lincoln would concede a minor point that was of little or no ultimate consequence, in order to give more force and weight to the major, most important point of his argument.

More simply, Lincoln would give in on an argument that didn't mean as much, to shift momentum to the one that did. This was a tactical method of selective conciliation—this time being presented by President Lincoln in the court of public opinion—that he used to inject the power of persuasion into his most crucial argument. Leonard Swett, Lincoln's close friend in the Bar and politics, and himself, one of the most highly-demanded lawyers in Illinois, explained Lincoln's method this way: "By giving away six points and carrying the seventh, he carried his case . . . the whole thing hanging on the seventh," as Swett put it. Lincoln would "trade away everything," Swett insisted, "which would give him the least aid in carrying [his case]." Making it clear that Lincoln's conciliatory approach was based in strength of strategy not intellectual weakness, Swett added: "Any man who took Lincoln for a simple-minded man [because of this approach] would very soon wake up with his back in a ditch."

In his response to Greeley's open letter, Lincoln bluntly said, that if necessary, he would not free the slaves if that was the only way to save the Union. When Lincoln wrote this controversial line, freeing the slaves without winning the War had become impossible. There was no real possibility of it. And Lincoln knew it. By saving the Union, Lincoln could at least keep alive the possibility of ending slavery; a possibility that would have surely died if secession prevailed. So Lincoln was willing to concede an improbable point in his argument (i.e., "If I could save the Union without freeing any slave I would do it . . ."), in order to give more force and weight to his most important one—which was, above all else, *save the Union.*

Contemporary critics have used these words in Lincoln's open letter to Greeley to paint him as a President who cared more about preserving white America than he did freeing the slaves. It is a fair and appropriate inquiry, but it's just not the case. This is, unfortunately, often an ideological-driven criticism, a distortion of historical fact asserted to fit a modern political agenda. In fact, at the same time Lincoln was responding to Greeley's newspaper editorial, he had already privately written the first draft of his Emancipation Proclamation, and revealed it to his Cabinet. Lincoln, clearly, was already on the move to eliminate slavery, and was beginning to see the saving of the Union not as the ultimate goal, in and of itself but rather, the means to achieve an even higher moral cause which was the Nation's realization of a democracy that celebrated the freedom and equality of all races.

Furthermore, if Lincoln's sole and exclusive motive was to preserve the Union, and nothing else—that is, he didn't really care about ending slavery—he could have instantly increased his political popularity by dumping his anti-slavery position as soon as he was elected president (Lincoln got only 39.8% of the popular vote in 1860), and thus, gained a lasting peace and a permanent Union by avoiding a civil war; all of this bought, however, in return for the Mephistophelean bargain of allowing slavery to leapfrog into the Western territories and take even deeper, institutional root in the South. But President Lincoln chose otherwise. He would not forsake his commitment to eliminate slavery. When the time and opportunity became politically ripe, Lincoln would eventually combine together the goals of saving the Union and black emancipation, so that America, if it survived, could realize the promises made in the Declaration of Independence.

In the crucible of his mind—and as reflected in his Greeley letter— Lincoln had boiled the factious issue down to its raw, brutal reality: *if the War was lost, then the cause of black emancipation was lost.*

But lincoln was also a political pragmatist. He was President of the United States, struggling to keep a fractured nation from flying completely apart in a civil war, not Don Quixote confronting the windmills. Had Abraham Lincoln pursued the presidency on a pure abolitionist, equality-for-all-races agenda, seen then as a wildly radical, fringe position, he would have never been nominated for President of the United States, let alone elected. And had Lincoln never been elected, who knows how long, perhaps decades, the cause of black emancipation would have been stalled.

For this reason, during his first months in office, President Lincoln was cautious not to define the Civil War in terms of eliminating slavery, but instead, by advocating that the main purpose of the War was to preserve the Union. By using this approach, Lincoln hoped to have his cake and eat it too. That is, he wanted to both rouse the support of most Northerners (especially those who were willing to fight to save the Union but not fight over the issue of slavery), and not alienate the Southerners with unionist leanings who were not planter class and did not own slaves. Lincoln, himself a Southerner who was born in Kentucky and worked the land, had an abiding respect for those common, self-reliant, working-to-make-ends-meet, Southern people.

During his presidency, Lincoln found himself straddling the massive contradiction between law and morality. He believed slavery was a moral abomination. But he was also well aware with his legally trained mind, that he did not have the constitutional authority, acting alone as President of the United States, to abolish slavery. Lincoln, through the years, had developed a deep-dyed respect for the rule of law and the Constitution. He wanted to eventually impose a lawful and permanent death on slavery. Only a constitutional amendment could do that. Such an amendment required approval by both the U.S. House of Representatives and Senate by a two-thirds vote, and then ratification by three-fourths of the states—a supermajority, constitutional equation that involved the Southern states. Obviously, a constitutional amendment in the middle of the Civil War was impossible.

This issue of slavery was not only fueling the fires of bloody conflict with the South, it was also complicating Lincoln's efforts to lead and unify the North in fighting the War. Many Northerners felt betrayed over the military draft President Lincoln had initiated shortly before his trip to Gettysburg, in the mid-summer of 1863. They bitterly accused Lincoln of shifting the main purpose of the War from the battle cry of preserving the Union, over to the cause of abolishing slavery, what they railed as the "abolitionist war." This was a cause they deemed unconstitutional, since the Constitution (as it existed then, before the passage of the Thirteenth Amendment) did not expressly prohibit slavery. As the President's critics angrily put it, they did not want to be forced to fight Lincoln's "unconstitutional" war.

And they were right. At least about the Constitution providing a legal sanctuary for slavery. One out of every seven people in America was a slave. In South Carolina, more than half of all people in that state were slaves. By the time Lincoln was elected President, there was four million people languishing in human bondage in the South. And the U.S. Constitution was of no use in helping them. Why? Because the Constitution was coldly silent on the guarantee of "equal rights" for people of color. The tragic fact was that the Constitution legally permitted slavery to exist in the states that already had it. As it was written, the Constitution was assuring the perpetual existence of slavery. The proponents of slavery were using this insidious but powerful legal tool of constitutional reasoning to trump moral arguments for human equality.

Lincoln found himself impaled on the horns of this political and moral dilemma.

Politically, when Abraham Lincoln placed his hand on the Bible and took the oath of office as President of the United States, he gave his solemn oath before the Nation "to preserve, protect and defend" the Constitution. After all, Lincoln himself had promised in many public speeches to always obey the U.S. Constitution, and had long preached about the solemn obligation to uphold it, saying the document was "unalterable." Lincoln also looked to the Constitution, ideologically, in support of his argument that states were not lawfully allowed to secede from the Union. Even as far back as 1838, when Lincoln gave a speech in Springfield to the Young Men's Lyceum, he pounded on the importance of having "a reverence for the Constitution and laws," like the highest political law of the land, the U.S. Constitution.

Morally, Lincoln believed with every fiber of his being that slavery was wrong; and he realized that "the rule of law," that is, blind obedience to the Constitution on the issue of slavery, violated what he considered to be the highest moral law of the land, the Declaration of Independence. The legal right to own slaves, did not make it morally right. And, Lincoln believed, a democracy without morality could not survive.

Law and morality were in a head-on collision.

The trouble was that many people on both sides of the Mason-Dixon line, who were blinded by a racial prejudice that had been carved deeply into their minds and culture by a social matrix of tradition, ignorance and economic forces, believed that people of color were not entitled or worthy of civil rights. Among slaveowners in the South, black people were considered to be mere chattel property, like livestock. Even in the "free territory" of the North, black Americans labored under a system of economic servitude. New York City, as the Nation's financial center, supplied a large portion of the capital (textile factories, technology, international shipping ports) that allowed the plantation economy in the South to thrive. And the white populace of the North enjoyed the fine clothes and linens, and the wages and jobs at factories that cotton brought, along with a cornucopia of agricultural products, all of it produced in the South on the back of slave labor.

Nations are not punished for their sins, it seems, but by them. Slavery had chopped up America with an ideological meat cleaver, leaving behind a bleeding, fragmented country that was ripe for rebellion and violence.

Even people in the Northern states were terribly divided over slavery.

The "abolitionists," with their religious fervor for abolishing slavery, wanted the evil institution of slavery immediately eliminated, no matter the costs or consequences. They had the moral courage to call slavery what it really was: human barbarity on a massive scale. And they needed courage. Many whites in the North hated the abolitionists, blaming them for stirring up racial tensions. There were mobs that hunted down abolitionists, terrorizing them into silence, or sometimes even killing them. If you were an abolitionist, you were probably in danger.

One of the most fiery, impenitent, and confrontational of the white abolitionists was William Lloyd Garrison, influential owner of an anti-slavery newspaper in Boston called the *Liberator*. Garrison's anti-slavery sentiments had calcified into dogma. The bald, bespeckled Garrison, who looked the part of a stern schoolmaster, pulled no punches about how he felt about Lincoln's milder anti-slavery position. As titular leader of the white abolitionists, Garrison believed Lincoln's gradualist approach to eliminating slavery, glaringly apparent at the emergence of his first term as President, was unprincipled and weak-kneed. He carped that Lincoln was "nothing better than a wet rag." And Garrison felt the same about the Constitution. "I WILL BE HEARD," he bellowed in his speeches and articles, guaranteeing he would fight to the last breath to end slavery.

Garrison meant it. He excoriated anyone and everything—churches, preachers, political parties, politicians, even his own country—if they were soft on slavery. Garrison viewed the Constitution itself as a septic document, not a sacred one, because it had been composed by slaveowners. In a public display of radical discontent against his own government, much like the opponents of the military draft in the 1960's who publicly burned their draft cards, Garrison did the unthinkable by burning a copy of the U.S. Constitution which he called "a covenant with death, [and] agreement with hell" in public protest of what he viewed as a failed compact with the people.

Then, there was the more moderate coalition of anti-slavery people in Lincoln's own Republican Party who did not support the abolitionists. They vigorously opposed the extension of existing slavery, but viewed the abolitionists as a fringe group of extremists who were willing to sacrifice the Nation in their fight against slavery. They believed slavery would eventually die its own death in the South, and favored a more cautious, gradual plan towards black emancipation. Most of his presidency, Lincoln tried to hold the tottery center between these two political factions—a razor's edge—as he desperately tried to prevent the disintegration of the country.

The North even had its own proponents of slavery, mostly in the "border" slave states of Delaware, Kentucky, Maryland and Missouri. Although these border states—the "Upper South"—were still clinging to Union membership, they always kept their sails tipped into secessionist winds. Lincoln knew that losing even one border state would be a fatal wound to the Union. Maryland was especially critical; if it fell to the Confederacy, the Nation's capital would be sealed off from all contiguous Union territory and soon, itself, collapse. As the President told his friend Orville H. Browning, "I think to lose Kentucky is . . . to lose the whole game." The constant machinations required of the President in keeping these border states from flipping over to the cause of the Confederacy, an event which would have literally divided the country into equal halves and doomed the survival of the United States of America, turned Lincoln into a political contortionist.

Of course, the slave-owning, plantation class of the Deep South felt the abolitionists and anti-slavery coalitions in the North were not only lighting the fuse for slave uprisings, but even worse, trampling on their "constitutional" rights to own property (slaves) and to self-determinism ("state's rights"). Even Southerners who did not own slaves still bartered with, leased land from, sold goods to, brought crops from or were employed by slaveowners, putting the lives and livelihood of many ordinary people in the South in direct contact with, and often dependent upon, a slave-driven economy. In the collective mind of the Southern people, Lincoln and his Yankee states had declared genocide on the Southern way of life.

But many in the slave-free states of the North harbored bitter feelings of bigotry too; they feared freed slaves from the South would come to live in their state, taking low-pay white jobs, clashing with white immigrants who had already moved there to work, and overrunning their neighborhoods. Other Northerners just wanted the bloodshed to stop, whatever it took; they were willing to make a deal with the South to end the awful War, by letting them have their God-forsaken slavery.

The *New York Times* would report that at the time of the Gettysburg ceremonies, a distinguished traveler from Great Britain witnessed, in disgust and disappointment, that in Northern cities the black people at hotels and railway stations were not seen as "men and brothers," but looked upon as "dogs."

Even when African-Americans eventually served as soldiers in the Union army, unlike their white counterparts, they got less pay and no enlistment bonuses, and were routinely ridiculed and assigned to the most menial, back-breaking chores. They often received discriminatory medical care, and unusually harsh and demeaning military punishment for mistakes and insubordination, including lashes and whippings, that mirrored the barbarity inflicted upon Southern slaves. For every black soldier that died on the battlefield, nine more died of disease, mostly a result of discriminatory medical treatment.

Slavery was a harsh lesson for the Nation in mass social ethics, reminiscent of (but, of course, not comparable in the genocidal scope of human death) the collective apathy of the majority of ordinary German people to the Nazi's deportation of Jewish families into the concentration camps. It was not the minority of villainous slaveowners and slave-trading monsters in America that sustained the evil of slavery, but rather, the vast majority of church-going, hard-working, everyday people, both

North and South, who knew in their heart of hearts, the moral wrong of slavery—but chose to say or do nothing. "There may be times when we are powerless to prevent injustice," holocaust survivor and Nobel Laureate Elie Wiesel once wrote, "but there must never be a time when we fail to protest."

Slavery was an American sin . . . not just a Confederate one.

If, somehow, Lincoln had been able to immediately free the slaves, as abolitionists were pressuring him to do, he feared that such an act would cause the fragile border states, that were geographically sandwiched between the Union and the Confederate states, to jettison into the waiting arms of the Confederacy, an event, Lincoln concluded, that would have assured defeat for the North, and foreclosed all hope to save the Union and free the slaves.

Furthermore, Lincoln worried that he would lose support for the War in the North, if the predominant, national theme of the Civil War turned into a fight to end slavery, not saving the Union. Many Northern soldiers were ready to fight and die to save the Union, but not for the cause of freeing the slaves. Before Gettysburg, the Nation's collective conscious had not yet come that far.

And there was another problem, rooted in mid-nineteenth century racial prejudice. If Lincoln freed African-American soldiers to fight in the Union army, the President was, ultimately, ordering black men to kill whites, a morally repugnant and abominable act in the eyes of many Northerners and Northern soldiers. In fact, General McClellan, head of the Union Army, a small but powerfully charismatic man with an akimbo stance and messianic impulses, who throbbed with disdain for Lincoln. McClellan sometimes brazenly referred to his Commander-in-Chief as "a well-meaning baboon" and the "Gorilla." He had intimated to political friends and military underlings, in what could have been a frightening scenario, that if the President freed the slaves, it would encourage thousands of Union soldiers to lay down their weapons and go home. In one stroke, it would have been an instant, cataclysmic collapse of the Nation's military infrastructure.

On the other hand, President Lincoln believed that if slaves in the

South were freed, it could help the Union's cause by disrupting the enormous economic engine of human labor that produced the lifeblood of food, clothing and money for the Confederacy. But the law of unintended consequences lies in wait around such strategies; dismantling the infrastructure of the Confederacy's economy would inevitably hurt the entire country, both nationally and internationally. Confederate states made up nearly half of the Nation's land mass, and possessed the manpower of four million slaves. The Southern region of plantation states had become a turbo-engine for the national economy, producing seven-eights of the world's cotton and the largest concentration of millionaires on earth. The advent of the high-tech cotton gin in the antebellum South, like the emergence of the microchip in today's Santa Clara region of northern California, had fused together technology, money and manpower (slavery) to turn the plantation economy into a global financial juggernaut. The Deep South had become the Silicon Valley of its time.

Slavery had become the ultimate moral, political and socioeconomic Gordian Knot. Right and wrong had never been so complicated for a young America.

* * *

In fact, Lincoln himself, was struggling with right and wrong over an issue connected with slavery. It was called "colonization." During a good portion of his presidency, and the years leading up to it, Lincoln harbored a belief in the colonization of African-Americans. It was a concept launched to prominence in 1827 by Lincoln's political mentor, Henry Clay, and Lincoln had probably fallen under the influence of Clay on this subject.

Colonization was a plan to assist freed slaves in relocating their homes to what is present-day Panama, an island near Haiti, or to the African country of Liberia. It was capitulation to the popular social theory that there was a regrettable but "unconquerable prejudice" in the country, and that it was impossible for the black race, whether slaves or free, to "amalgamate with free whites." It seems incomprehensible today, but in Lincoln's time there was a widespread fear among whites that they could never, under any circumstances, live together in harmony and social equality with African-Americans.

It is important to recognize, as a footnote to this darker side of Abraham Lincoln's historical ledger, that he supported voluntary colonization. Despite being an intrinsically dreadful and racist concept, colonization, for Lincoln, was not a deportation plan. Lincoln never advocated nor believed in the forced removal of African-Americans from the country, although some on the radical fringes of the colonization movement, no doubt, did. At the apex of the colonization movement to Africa, in 1832, less than one thousand blacks left the country for Liberia; most of them were in bondage and promised freedom if they emigrated.

These advocates of colonization were convinced they were taking the moral high-ground on slavery. Even the rabid abolitionist William Lloyd Garrison once supported colonization, later rejecting it outright. Even the iconic antislavery book that turned the world's attention to America's institution of human bondage—*Uncle Tom's Cabin*—concludes with "a black's dream of freedom in Africa." Most of the pro-colonization crowd were anti-slavery, at least to some extent, but they were also wedded to the notion that the successful social integration of a dark-skinned race into a white-dominated America was virtually impossible. In further perpetuation of this ill-conceived social concept, when colonizationists looked at the world around them for working models of racial integration, they could find no existing post-slavery, multiracial communities with significant black populations that lived in peaceful, equal and civil accord. There were no such places.

Colonization, its advocates believed, gave black people a fresh start in another place, far away from the white people who detested them. They argued, with a sort of moral self-flatulence, that colonization would rid the Nation of the dangerous and de-stabilizing presence of slavery, and reinstate the civil rights of African-Americans in their "long lost fatherland." Lincoln once quoted Henry Clay at his eulogy, seeming to act as a surety for his words, by saying "there is a moral fitness in the idea of returning to Africa her children," because those returned "will carry back to their native soil the rich fruits of religion, civilizations, law and liberty." In fact, before he became president, Lincoln had taken an active role in the Illinois State Colonization Society. As late as December 1862, in a message to Congress, President Lincoln would say: ". . . I strongly favor colonization."

In the paternalistic view of its supporters, colonization seemed to be a peaceful, non-confrontational way to bring an end to slavery, and do it without the eruption of barbarity otherwise expected. Initially, it was a plan for relocating slaves escaped from the South, but it eventually expanded into a more aggressive project of eliminating slavery in the Union's border states a shameful sore-spot for anti-slavery Republican leadership. The rationalization of colonization by most of its proponents, though profoundly wrong and misguided, appeared to be founded with some measure of good intent and compassion; but those benevolent motivations, most likely, were as much a soothing salve for white concerns as those of African-Americans.

Propitiously, President Lincoln would soon learn from Frederick Douglass and other African-American leaders he invited to the White House (he was the first President in American history to do this), that black people were fully vested in America's future, just like white people—most of them born in America, living here for generations, and having no knowledge of their ethic or tribal origins. This delegation of black Americans respectfully told the President they wanted no part of colonization. Douglass, with his intense, blazing eye contact and fierce intelligence, eloquently but firmly reminded Lincoln of how slaves and the black race had helped to build America. And indeed they had. Africans were brought to Jamestown, Virginia as early as 1619, working a system of indentured servitude or slavery to shape America's first colonies. When Lincoln pondered on the large-scale enlistment of black soldiers, and their bravery and dedication in fighting for the Union—he realized the idea was immoral and unjust. Lincoln searched his heart. And finally came to understand. America was their home. People of color were Americans, too. The same as himself. This misguided, poorly-conceived, impractical concept of colonization, a praxis borne of ignorance and desperation, was eventually discarded by President Lincoln.

Lincoln now realized that the advocates of colonization were picking Dead Sea fruit. He would never consider it again. Shortly thereafter, Lincoln's young secretary John Hay would write with obvious relief, "I am glad the President has sloughed off the idea of colonization."

Lincoln and his administration even explored the idea of the federal government purchasing the freedom of slaves living in the four border states. The government would pay slaveowners the fair market value of their slaves, and then free them. It was "compensated emancipation." At first blush, this seemed to be a simple and straightforward solution that might tilt the War in the Union's favor, saving the Nation blood and treasure. After all, how could the continuation of a bloody civil war with no end in sight cost less than purchasing the freedom of a finite number of slaves?   Lincoln was counting on support from Southern unionists. But there was a problem. Many in the Upper South were as doggedly rigid in their social views of race as they were in the Deep South. Slavery had become inculcated even into the culture of the border states, too. It was a way of life. There was no way the border states would give up slavery in a "cash for slaves" government program. As a cover for their true motives (to keep slavery), the majority of representatives from the border states rejected the compensated emancipation proposal, alleging (falsely) that the U.S. Government could not afford to fund the program. Ultimately, Lincoln could not risk losing the border states to the Confederacy, over this unorthodox and unworkable idea.

Lincoln and his administration were stuck at Morton's Fork on the issue of slavery, and were groping for answers. All possible solutions that might save the country noxious, or not, were placed on the discussion table. As Lincoln explained in his Annual Message to Congress on December 1, 1862, his administration would have to "think anew, and act anew" to find workable answers. Today, we would say "think outside the box."

Throughout this fumbling, groping process of searching for solutions to the War and slavery, Lincoln, to his credit, kept an open mind. He told powerful newspaperman and founding editor of the *New York Tribune*, Horace Greeley, that "I shall try to correct errors when [they are] shown to be errors; and I shall adopt new views [so] fast as they appear to be true views."

What no one knew was that by mid-1862, in Lincoln's mind, what were previously (by political necessity) the separate and disassociated issues of preserving the Union and black emancipation—were suddenly fusing together—and becoming unpartible pursuits in what Lincoln envisioned as a new birth of freedom for the country. At the very time President Lincoln was discussing colonization and compensated emancipation with African-American leaders like Frederick Douglass, he was already privately drafting the Emancipation Proclamation and beginning the process of irrevocably committing all of the resources of the presidency and the Federal government to the destruction of slavery.

Fortunately, there was no permanent marketplace for these toxic ideas of colonization and compensated emancipation. In both situations, the "cure" was as bad as the malady. But the failure to find a peaceful solution to eliminating slavery made a negotiated end to the war impossible. It was too late. The cancer of slavery had already spread into the bone marrow of America.

* * *

Ultimately, President Lincoln would look to the words in the Preamble of the Declaration of Independence for the moral authority he needed to solve the Nation's crisis. And as inspiration for his Gettysburg Address. The Founding Fathers had been breast-fed on the writings of the English philosopher, John Locke. Lincoln, too, deeply believed in John Locke's ideal of liberty and equality as a natural right— a God-given right—perhaps, understanding it better than Thomas Jefferson himself. In Lincoln's judgment, where the Constitution failed in protecting the American ideal of freedom and equality for all people, in contrast, the Declaration of Independence provided the Nation its only hope for redemption from the sin of slavery. And the Declaration of Independence could not be amended by Congress to accommodate slavery, a vulnerability of the Constitution.

Not until the Thirteenth Amendment to the Constitution was finally adopted as law of the land on December 18, 1865 abolishing slavery, eight months after Lincoln's assassination, would the U.S. Constitution be finally given a blood transfusion with the egalitarian principles flowing from the heart of the Declaration of Independence.

But before the passage of the Thirteenth Amendment, President Lincoln would bet the house, and his speech to dedicate a soldiers' cemetery in Gettysburg, Pennsylvania, on the words of the Declaration of Independence. Lincoln believed those words made it clear that freedom and slavery could not cohabitate in the same country. Only the promises made in the Preamble of the Declaration of Independence, what Lincoln had referred to in his 1858 speech in Chicago as "the father of all moral principle," could give the Constitution the precious gift of a moral conscience.

From its 1776 beginnings, a profound lie had begirded America's touted image as "land of the free." The truth was, many were free; but many were not. After all, the fortunes of thousands of white men from the original colonies, many of whom were brave, selfless patriots and devoutly religious, were also tied to the economic machinery of slavery. George Washington, the Father of America owned slaves. Thomas Jefferson, author of the Declaration of Independence, owned slaves. Benjamin Franklin, America's great polymath owned slaves. Patrick Henry, who famously screamed "Give me liberty or give me death!," and helped ramrod the passage of the Bill of Rights . . . owned slaves.

In fact, many in Lincoln's time, and some scholars today, believe that those words of Thomas Jefferson in the Preamble, the iconic words, "all men are created equal, "were, in Jefferson's mind, intended only for "new" Americans, being those of British lineage who came to or were born on American soil. That is, was Jefferson speaking of a narrower "legal equality" for British descendants only? Or did he mean a broader "social equality" for everyone? We cannot be sure, for we are not privy to Jefferson's inner-most ideological thoughts as he put quill to parchment. Even the Chief Justice of the U.S. Supreme Court, the corpse-like Roger B. Taney, an old Jacksonian Democrat who was a former slaveowner and lead architect of the infamous *Dred Scott* decision (considered by most historians to be the worst U.S. Supreme Court decision in history), insisted in his tortured reasoning that when Jefferson composed the phrase, "all men are created equal," he only meant that white British subjects born in America were equal to white British subjects born in Great Britain.

Justice Taney, by his 1857 ruling in the *Dred Scott* case, had clipped the Declaration's wings and used the Constitution's flaw by omission—that is, its silence on the legality of slavery—to support the Supreme Court's ruling. The Taney Court decreed that free slaves were not citizens with inalienable rights, but items of property. Going even further, the Taney-led justices opined in their 7-2 decision that Congress had no right or power to ban slavery in any of the American territories, because U.S. citizens were guaranteed the rights of life, liberty and property (that is, slaves). The U.S. Supreme Court was telling Congress it could not stop the spread of slavery in the newly-emerging western states, and telling all black people, whether free or not, that they were not "a part of the people" included in the Declaration of Independence, and thus, they, nor their descendants would ever become American citizens. As the pallid Chief Justice wrote in his own grim and odious words: "Negroes had no rights the white man was bound to respect."

Slave power had captured the highest court in the land.

Looking back, a strong case can be made that Taney's racist decision in *Dred Scott*, as much as any single factor, accelerated the Union and Confederacy down the collision course to war. And it provided legal sanctuary for the most rich and powerful slave-owning class in the world. It reminds us of the venerable adage that men make history; but that they seldom know the history they are making.

The U.S. Supreme Court, from President Lincoln's standpoint, had twisted America's sacred, founding words, "all men are created equal," into a hypocritical, meaningless, patriotic mantra. Taney, born in the year following America's birth, had neutered the Declaration of Independence.

Even before his 1861 election to the presidency, Lincoln had no tolerance for Roger Taney. Lincoln publicly criticized Chief Justice Taney and the *Dred Scott* decision, arguing that it violated the terms of the Nation's founding document, the Declaration of Independence, which Lincoln believed was a moral compact with the people. In what must have been an incredibly uncomfortable situation for both men, Chief Justice Taney, whose appearance that day was the mastery of the embalmer's profession, would administer the presidential oath of office to Lincoln at his first inaugural. Justice Taney's narrow and tortured interpretation of the Declaration's words not only excluded "Negroes," but also excluded from its promises and protections, as Lincoln pointed out, "all white people outside of Britain."

Once he assumed the highest office in the land, in a rare exercise of presidential gall and muscle, Lincoln would eventually use his war powers and Emancipation Proclamation to ignore an edict of U.S. Supreme Court. He would refuse to comply with Dred Scott.

This time, at least for the duration of the War, Lincoln had neutered the Taney decision.

Thomas Jefferson's words—no matter what his "original intent" may have been, no matter what the Taney court decreed—in Lincoln's eyes, were plain and unambiguous. They said . . . **all men are created equal**. Lincoln found no nationality qualifiers—nor did he find any words of racial or ethnic exclusion in the Declaration of Independence.

It was during this maelstrom of political, socioeconomic and military conflicts that Lincoln became convinced that the Civil War would either make or break America. The ideals of the Declaration of Independence were facing the ultimate test. The very survival of the only democratic republic in the world was at stake. America would weather the storm of the War, emerging stronger, or be destroyed. For Lincoln, true democracy, made of both freedom and equality that extended beyond white males of British lineage to people of all races and colors, as plainly written in the Declaration of Independence, was America's only hope.

During the course of his presidency, Lincoln would abandon his bridled and hedgy approach towards the abolition of slavery, and ideologically mature into a man devoted to the elimination of human bondage in America, root and branch. Ever thinking, listening, learning, straining, Lincoln would emerge from out of his prejudices. President Lincoln's issuance of the Emancipation Proclamation on January 1, 1863 validated his fulfillment of that maturation process and his unconditional commitment to freedom for all African-Americans. And he would never turn back. In an April 4, 1864 letter to Albert Hodges, a year before his death, Lincoln would powerfully and succinctly write: "If slavery is not wrong, nothing is wrong. I cannot remember when I did not so think, and feel." Nearly a year later, in his Second Inaugural Address, Lincoln would proclaim slavery as the cause of the War. And a few weeks later on April 11, 1865, before an excited crowd on the White House lawn, in what would be the penultimate public event of his life, only three days before he was fatally shot at Ford's Theatre,

Abraham Lincoln would be the first President in American history to publicly broach the idea of black suffrage, at a time which was generations before his wife Mary or other women would have such a right to vote. A handsome young actor in the audience that evening, who preferred to be called "Wilkes," angrily commented to those around him: "That is the last speech he will make."

And it was.

By the time the final pages of his presidency and life were being turned, the metaphysical transformation of Abraham Lincoln into a man wholly committed to the elimination of slavery—body, mind and spirit—would become complete. He came to realize that the bloodguilt of the Civil War could be absolved by one thing, and one thing only: the death of all slavery.

Thus, for President Abraham Lincoln, the War would become a fight to both save the Nation and destroy slavery. These dual purposes for fighting the War, finally, would be melded into one.

* * *

By mid-november 1863, Lincoln's thoughts about what he would say on November 19th to the people at Gettysburg—about slavery, the War and the blood sacrificed—were beginning to congeal into words. The Declaration of Independence, heavy on his mind for the last decade, would be his inspiration, the taproot for his speech at the soldiers' cemetery.

Still, the President was feeling the pressure of preparing his speech under severe time constraints, as he was in the difficult throes of converting vapory thoughts to actual words. Lincoln needed words at Gettysburg that would anchor the Nation on the rock of democracy, as it was perfectly described in the Declaration of Independence. And he would pull from the cleft of that rock both freedom and equality.

Americans had long sung the hymn of freedom. But the song of equality had been silent. Lincoln had come to realize that freedom and equality were mutually indispensable. And soon, in his speech at Gettysburg, he would tell all Americans:

There could not be one, without the other.

CHAPTER SEVEN

WHY, GETTYSBURG?

"God pity us! God pity us!"
—Nurse Ellen Harris
Letter to her Husband
From Gettysburg, PA
July 9, 1863

To UNDERSTAND THE GETTYSBURG ADDRESS, ONE MUST UNDERSTAND what happened at Gettysburg, Pennsylvania the first week of July 1863. And its aftermath.

The Battle of Gettysburg was a bitterly-fought three-day battle that took place during July 1st, 2nd and 3rd of 1863. Wednesday, Thursday, Friday. It was a Union victory, arguably, that was the tipping point in the Civil War. And it was one of the bloodiest battles ever fought in American history.

Although the Union Army, under the command of Major General George G. Meade, would ultimately prevail at the Battle of Gettysburg, it would be a Cadmean victory. The devastating human toll and psychological reckoning of this battle on both armies are revealed by the fact that it would be Confederate General Robert E. Lee's last offensive battle of the War; and neither side, afterwards, would engage in a major battle for nearly a year.

Strangely, it was the shortfall of gravediggers that triggered the chain of events leading to the Gettysburg Address.

The problem was both simple—and simply overwhelming. After the Battle of Gettysburg was over, as though there had been a hail storm of soldier corpses, as many as ten thousand dead bodies, lying where they fell in battle, were scattered about in ghastly fashion over the Gettysburg streets, farms, mountain sides and fields. Some were left prostrate, uncovered; others were thinly buried just a few inches under the soil or a pile of stones.

When most troops were gone and heads had cleared from the fog of war, a terrible and overwhelming reality fell on the people of Gettysburg. The countless dead needed burial. Who, and how, would they do it?

The project would require the unthinkable. The loading of uncovered corpses for burial, by the thousands. Then there would be the shoveling and scraping away of shallow graves—hundreds upon hundreds of them—and the process of identifying the soldiers found in those opened pits. Lifting and loading the exposed remains. Putting the bodies into boxes, and then moving them for more dignified interment or shipment home. Thousands of new graves to be dug. Thousands of coffins to be built. Thousands of coffins to be loaded and transported to the train depot, for shipment to loved ones for burial in other states. Moreover, hundreds more were dying each day from their mortal wounds; they too, would need proper burial.

Out of sheer desperation, the Town of Gettysburg ran a public notice, pleading for help:

> "To all Citizens,
>   Men, Horses and Wagons wanted immediately, to bury the dead and to cleanse our streets, in such a thorough way as to guard against a pestilence. Every good citizen can be of use by reporting himself, at once, to Capt. W. W. Smith, acting Provost Marshal, Office, N.E. corner Centre Square."

There were few takers. Folks in Gettysburg were not rushing to volunteer. In fact, hardly any showed up at all. Who could blame them? In a time before science had unlocked the secrets of microbes and viruses, people were frozen with fear of disease from the human and animal carrion. In their eyes, the rotting carnage was the propagator of death. Anyway, as a practical matter, how many burial crews could be produced from a town of 2400 men, women and children, with many men already gone to War?

On July 7, 1863, one of the local newspapers, the *Gettysburg Compiler*, would capture in words the dreadful moment of gut-wrenching pain and loss felt by families when they were notified that their loved ones had been identified as casualties of the War—a timeless, chilling description that has lost none of its poignancy, still today:

> "Every name . . . is a lightening stroke to some heart, and breaks like thunder over some home, and falls a long black shadow upon some hearthstone."

It was a harsh and horrible reality: there were just not enough townspeople and resources in tiny Gettysburg to handle the monstrous situation that had fallen on them like a biblical plague.

Some of the Union dead were identifiable only because their names were written on scraps of paper and nailed to planks of wood pulled from fences or ammunition boxes, then thrust upright into their shallow graves like the stone-wedged sword of Excaliber. Others were identifiable . . . only by God.

Then there were the Confederate dead, the corpses in gray, thousands of them. Confederate carnage seem to lay upon the ground, everywhere. Hundreds of the Southern casualties had been placed into mass, anonymous graves, buried in long trenches. Dozens of Confederate bodies were laid side by side in the same furrows, like piano keys buried under a lid of dirt. Union Sergeant Charles Blanchard witnessed 108 Confederate soldiers being placed into a single trench.

After the battle was lost, General Lee's desperate retreat left hundreds of Confederate soldiers quickly interred under thin blankets of dirt and stones. John B. Linn, a young attorney and amateur historian who walked the rainsoaked battlefields just three days after the battle, commented in his journal on July 7, 1863 about some scantily-buried soldiers from a South Carolina regiment, writing that "you could feel the body by pressing the earth with your foot." A decade would pass after the Battle of Gettysburg, before Confederate dead would all be removed from field burials and re-interred with dignity in their own honored soil.

Some Confederates, lying naked and starving on remote battlesites, simply bled out and died before help would come. Others were left wedged between mammoth crevasses of rock, their bodies swelling in the shimmering waves of heat that filled the ragged contours of the fissure. Many got no burial at all. Eyewitness Daniel A. Skelly, just a boy at the time, reported that the Confederate dead were "lying on their backs, their faces towards the heavens, and burned black as coal from exposure to the hot sun." The sky began to slowly fill with returning buzzards previously scared away by battlefield gunfire, steadily, cautiously, lowering their gliding pattern towards the earthly carnage. A few weeks after the battle, a Union soldier described some of the battlefields where Confederates were shot and fell, without burial, as looking like "a vast bone yard."

Lee had lost one third of his army.

When townspeople climbed from under their homes, and out from their potato cellars and larders on the rainy daybreak of Independence Day, 1863, they would not be in the instant spirit of celebrating a national holiday. Instead, they were witness to an apocalyptic scene out of time and place, frightenly similar to the one described in H.G. Well's fictional novel *War of the Worlds*, where people emerged from their hiding places and peered out in stunned disbelief at the decimated landscape following the earth's alien invasion.

There were thousands of decaying horse and mule carcasses strewn about the roads and countryside in the twenty-five square mile battlefield, their gas-bloated stomachs splitting open in the steamy heat. Farm animals, too. Just about everywhere you went, there was an unbearable stench. Sarah Broadhead, who lived on Chambersburg Street with her husband Joseph and daughter Mary, expressed the foreboding felt by all Gettysburgers when on July 11th, she wrote in her diary: "I fear we shall be visited by pestilence, for every breath we draw is made ugly by the stench."

Thousands of dead horses ramified the landscape. William T. Livermore, a Union soldier in the 20th Maine Infantry, wrote to his brother Charles that he, alone, had nineteen horses "in the bigness" of his [Charles'] barnyard. Something had to be done about these dead animals, they said, before they poison the air. "Pile kindlin' and pour kerosene over'm, and set fire," somebody hollered out. Thousands of dead horses, mules and other livestock were burned. It seemed to help, at least the pitch black smoke kept the flies at bay. And burning flesh, it seemed, was more tolerable than rotting flesh. Folks soon learned that it was best not to burn the carcasses next to a house or barn, though. Too risky. They had to be dragged off with ropes and a mule, and then set fire.

A putrid, fecal stench percolated in the air, rising from the commingling of the body waste and dung of more than 200,000 men, horses and mules that had descended on tiny Gettysburg for three days, and the smell of human and animal decay. Bad air would bring bad disease, the people thought. Chloride of lime was sifted about, everywhere; before it dissolved in the rutted, mud-bogged roads and fields, the white disinfectant powder had the look of a new-fallen snow in summer. Twelve-year-old Mary Elizabeth Montfort, who lived in Gettysburg at the time, described it quite plainly in her diary when she wrote, "The terrible smell all through the town is worse than the time we found a dead rat behind the loose boards in the cellar." Stacks of arms and legs—ghastly byproducts of the amputation tables—were piled up in trenches like firewood, still oozing blood, rotting in the heat. Even in the fetid-hot temperatures of July, windows had to be kept tightly shut both day and night.

Gettysburg was filled with a netherworld odor, a noxious cocktail of rotting flesh and excrement, that permeated lungs and minds.

The ground heaved with twisted corpses, many of them, mouth and eyes wide open. John Howard Wert, who visited the site only three days after the battle, would write that there were "festering corpses at every step. . . in some cases nothing but a few mutilated fragments and pieces of flesh were left . . . it was one vast, hideous charnel house." Some injured soldiers, writhing in pain in creekbeds and unable to crawl to safety, drowned in the flash floods that poured down shortly after the battle. Heavy rains would raise the creeks as much as seven feet, dissolving the thin blankets of dirt covering the quickly-buried corpses, exposing hands and arms of soldiers who, even in the stillness of death, seemed to beckon for dignified burial. Liberty Augusta Hollinger, a local teenager, somehow had the composure as she walked across town on family errands, to gather up army coats, and drape them over the hands and feet protruding from the washed-out soil. Maybe the Lord was washing away the bloodstained earth with the rain, some surely conjectured.

The people of Gettysburg were in collective shock. Walking about, dazed, with a stick of camphor or a bottle of peppermint oil held under their noses, they surveyed what was left of their village. There is an old African proverb that says when elephants fight, it is the grass that suffers. The town of Gettysburg had been plowed over and plundered by two elephantine military forces. Livestock was stolen or shot. Gardens, trampled flat. Cellars, looted. Corn and wheat fields grinded down under the feet of troops. Apple trees plucked bare. Many roads were furrowed and beaten down to an impassable, rain-drenched muck by brigades of trampling boots and wagon wheels. Some streets had to be "corduroyed" with wood planks, to regain their use. Hundreds of thousands of bullets were scattered over roads and fields like acorns on the floor of a vast oak forest.

Splintered dead trees stood on the horizon, like giant gnawed bones. Some of the larger trees in the fierce battle zones were literally sawed off, six to ten feet above the ground, by the rip-saw of bullet fire exchanged between the armies. Homes were left ransacked, pilfered and destroyed. Windows were shot out, everywhere. Bullets were riveted into houses, barns, fences and even bedstands. Stores were stripped of their merchandise. Headstones in the town cemetery, broken to pieces.

Choking heat. Corpses and animals, cooking in the sun. Blue-bottle flies and roaming hogs, having their way. Worms and maggots, fastened hideously, to both the wounded and the dead. The awful smells. The eerie quietude of ubiquitous death. Like a scene out of the old *Twilight Zone* television series where the protagonist awakens in a deserted rural town with no sounds or signs of life in it—Mary Horner, a local who lived on Chambersburg Street, would recall the strange and unearthly phenomenon that no song birds could be heard "for weeks after the battle."

The Town of Gettysburg, a place that three days earlier, had been a serene, pleasant little venue, had become a slaughterhouse, a mountainous heap of sorrow, suffering and blood. A place where the extent of suffering was off of the human Richter Scale.

For the people of Gettysburg, their town was their entire world. Their pastoral community, over three days of unbridled violence against people and property, had metastasized into a place blighted by death and destruction. As Nurse Ellen Harris wrote from Gettysburg to her husband on July 9th: "God pity us! God pity us!"

During the first week of July 1863, the Town of Gettysburg had become what distinguished Civil War historian Gabor Boritt would describe as "the site of the greatest man-made disaster in American history."

* * *

Just before the Battle of Gettysburg broke out, both militaries were operating, strategically, pretty much stone-blind. They had no idea about the location of each other's armies. In fact, neither General Lee nor General Meade planned or wanted to engage in battle at Gettysburg. Lee was hoping to lure the Northern Army into a battle close to Cashtown, Pennsylvania. Meade, who had taken over command only a few days earlier, had cherry-picked the site of Pipe Creek where he planned a major battle with the Confederacy. As fate would have it, both generals were wrong. And caught off guard. So surprised were Lee and Meade by the outbreak of fighting at Gettysburg, that neither one of them made it to the battlefield until the second day of combat. Both generals were shocked that the fuse of their next major battle had been lit in the inauspicious village of Gettysburg.

And how was that ominous fuse lit? Although the series of events leading up to this unlikely and unforeseeable battle on Gettysburg soil are a denouement that defy a single, cause-and-effect explanation, Gettysburg lore has it that the triggering event for the epic battle was this: on July 1st, a group of Confederate soldiers were scouting and per-haps interested in going into Gettysburg to privateer some supplies. Southern troops were in desperate need of shoes, food and medicine. Word may have reached the Confederacy, from troops earlier passing through, that there were tanneries in town, where Gettysburgers regu-larly crafted shoes and boots. For the invading militia, their pilfering expedition into this quaint little Pennsylvania town, at first impression, must have seemed like snatching a few cookies out of momma's cookie jar in the middle of the night, since they did not know Union soldiers were there. However, unexpectedly, a calvary screen of Union soldiers encountered these Confederates at a road crossing near the edge of town. The vanguards of two armies had inadvertently stumbled into one another. In military terms, these accidental encounters are known as "meeting engagements." The first shot fired was by a Union officer from the Illinois calvary, who had bummed a carbine rifle from his sergeant. Men and bullets had mixed.

The bloodletting had begun.

* * *

For the thousands of wounded soldiers who would somehow survive the three-day battle, worse horrors were yet to come.

There was a cruel shortage of trained, military medical help left behind. Both armies were guilty of this. The injured and near-dead were hauled to medical help in "avalanches," those wretched, horse-drawn, springless ambulance carts of both two and four wheel variety, that jerked and convulsed so violently, they often worsened the injuries or finished the poor soldier off. Soldiers (sometimes musicians) from the Union army, along with the help of Confederate prisoners (who, under such dire circumstances, had been granted "parole"), operated the avalanches, driving the wheelbarrows of suffering through the rough and rocky terrain.

The armies also left a pitiful shortage of medical supplies for the wounded. Often, armies did not carry much medical supplies with them, anyway, and had little to spare. The dirty-little secret of some field commanders was that they did not want to be bogged-down with the weight and bulk of medical supplies and ambulance wagons. Less medicine, more room for ammunition. Less weight, troops are quickened. Battles were won with guns and bullets, not gauze and morphine. The ability to move thousands of soldiers faster, quieter and further than the enemy, could be the difference in victory or defeat. Quickness enhanced survival. Kill the enemy, before he killed you. It was the brutal reality of winner-take-all combat. And it was why people in both the North and South sang songs like *When This Cruel War Is Over*, and began to call the Civil War the "cruel war." *Because it was.*

However, much chatter and debate persisted among folks in Gettysburg about how the injured "Rebels" should be treated, and sermons were preached from the pulpits that pleaded for "Christian compassion." In fact, there was growing sentiment to set aside a plot of land for the Confederate dead, "for the sake of common humanity," one local newspaper editorialized. But this was not to be. Some citizens were angry about the idea of ministering to the Confederates or providing them any comfort. Others called the injured Confederates "white trash," a pejorative term that had recently emerged into the American lexicon and would, unfortunately, stay. Perhaps the bitterness was understandable. After all, these same Rebels had gashed open their community to the bone and left thousands of wounded and dead Union soldiers—some of them family and friends—lying on their own soil. It was a cruel, but necessary law of war, they said. First, you take care of your own.

Still, for most part, there was little intentional cruelty or neglect from the people of Gettysburg, towards the wounded soldiers from the South. There was some isolated accounts of barbarity, no doubt. And there was some profiteering of fresh food and supplies, driven by the diabolical duo of scarcity and greed. The darkest side of humanity always reveals itself in war. But in many barns, homes and churches, soldiers from the North and South lay side by side—made equal by the parity of their inhuman suffering. Some Gettysburgers even became emotionally bonded to Confederate soldiers who were being nursed back to health in their homes.

When Reverend Henry Bellows, who was in charge of the U.S. Sanitary Commission, walked about Gettysburg in the early hours following the battle, he discovered a barn packed full of wounded Confederate soldiers, their woeful configurations covering both the floor and loft. It was obvious; Lee had left behind his most hopelessly mangled men. Blood from these dying soldiers "filtered through the cracks and knot-holes" of the hayloft, dripping on the poor souls lying below. In a vivid metaphor of a scene in the afterlife, Reverend Bellows would later describe the sorrowful scene he found in that barn: "Those above in the barn might almost be said to be in heaven, as compared to those below in the stable, who might with equal truth be said to be in hell. For upon heaps of dung, reeking with rain and tormented with vermin, the wounds still undressed . . . lay fair and noble youth." Reverend Bellows would lament that "furnishing attention to 20,995" wounded human beings could not be fixed "by anything short of arch-angels."

And then it happened. Angels did appear, those made of flesh and blood. They were divinely inspired women, white and black. One wid-owed African-American woman from Gettysburg, Lydia Hamilton Smith, repeatedly drove a borrowed horse and wagon across Adams County to collect food and clothing, and spent her entire life savings on supplies to minister to the wounded, soldiers from both the North and South. It seemed black Americans, even in their era of bondage and deprivation, had a special, seraphic capacity for forgiveness, and com-passion.

With many of the menfolk in Gettysburg gone away to the war, women—previously relegated by society to cleaning, child raising and cooking—suddenly, were breaking out of the ideology of Victorian domesticity, doing anything and everything they could, mind and mus-cle, to help. Many Gettysburg grandmothers, mothers, wives and daughters worked day and night to the point of mental and physical col-lapse, caring for and comforting the mangled men and boys, otherwise left to die naked and hungry in the rain. These brave and strong women became indispensable to the recovery of Gettysburg.

Frantic searches were commenced by commanders for Union MIA's. Major C.H. Weygant of the 124th New York, like hundreds of others, was wandering about in the eerie, death-scented dark of night, trying to find wounded soldiers missing from his regiment. Suddenly, out of the blackness, he would hear human sounds of suffering—tortured, forsak-en sounds—that would haunt him all of his life. In a real-life scene out of Dante's *Inferno*, Major Weygant would find close to three thousand men among a thicket of trees, moaning and thrashing about in pain, the wild glare of trauma in their eyes, crumpled together in their torn, blood-caked uniforms, lying in pools of commingled blood. It was what would become the Civil War's own unique chamber of horrors, an amputation site. He later described the dreadful episode in his own words:

"The thick foliage caused dark shadows to fall upon these acres of mangled bleeding human forms. Away down through the trees flickering lights could be seen, the reflections of which fell with ghastly effect upon the corps of surgeons who, with coats off and sleeves rolled up, were gathered at, or moving rapidly to and from about the amputating tables. After a moment's hesitation at the edge of the woods I resolved to attempt to pick my way through towards where I hoped to find the objects of my search . . . several in a state of delirium were shouting as if upon the battlefield, and others, believing I was a surgeon, besought me to stop just a moment and bind up the wounds from which their life-blood was ebbing.

Presently a man I was about stepping over, sprang to his feet, shook in front of me a bloody bandage he had just torn from a dreadful, gaping wound in his breast, and uttered a hideous, laughing shriek. This sent the hot blood spurting from his wound into my very face. Then he threw up his arms as if a bullet had just entered his heart, and fell heavily forward across a poor mangled fellow, whose piercing wails of anguish were heart-rending beyond description. I could endure no more, and wheeling about, hurried over the wounded and dying to the open field again, and returned to the regiment, glad that I had informed no one of my intended errand of mercy, for I was heartily ashamed of the weakness which had caused me to turn back."

The care of these wounded masses of Union soldiers had been left to an overwhelmed group of one hundred or so medical officers assigned to stay after the battle by General Meade (only three dozen of them were actually army surgeons), and a group of stout-hearted volunteers— many of them women—who worked, day after day, night after night, without sleep. Some surgeons collapsed with fatigue; other became "butchers" in the eyes of their patients and onlookers, as the horror and exhaustion of it all seemed to strip them of their humanity. Covered in blood, these caregivers looked into gaping wounds, and into the eyes of the dying. Thousands of them. Without rest. One nurse who worked the long, blood-stained tables set in the woods for amputations, would describe that first week after battle, writing that "for seven days, it literally ran blood."

Nurse Emily Souder could not bear to look at the place where limbs were sawed off with the cold operation of an assembly-line factory: "The amputation-table is plainly in view . . . I never trust myself to look toward it." Nurse Souder would recollect burying her head in a pillow, to shut out "the cries" and "shrieks" coming from a nearby church being used as an amputation site. Another nurse would have burned into her memory forever, the heartbreaking scene of a father and his son lying side by side, bonded by unbearable pain and hopelessness, each of them having a leg gone. Three of every four surgeries performed was an amputation. It was necessary butchery. If a ball hit your arm or leg, the best chance of survival was a straight, fast, bonesaw cut removing the whole mangled limb. Chloroform was administered to the soldier amputees in a cattle-horn or rag, clamped like a vise over their mouths. The right dosage of the sweet-smelling anesthesia got the poor soldier through the gruesome sawing process; too much paralyzed the lungs and killed him, outright.

"Too horrible to describe," is how Fannie Buehler, a Gettysburg local, described the sounds wreaking from the amputation tables in the Adams County Courthouse. She remembered covering her ears, so she would "not hear the groans of those poor unfortunate men." Fannie also recalled that "the Regimental Bands . . . came every afternoon and played patriotic airs in front of hospital," to drown out the blood-chilling screams and wails of the amputees.

Making a horrible situation even worse, the public was beginning to descend on Gettysburg, by the thousands. As Daniel Skelly, a young clerk at Fahnestock Brothers Store would observe, the town "was filled up every day by people coming from all over the country—fathers, mothers, brothers, sisters hunting their wounded or dead [at] the scenes." Some were even digging up corpses, searching on their own for loved ones. And then came the morbidly-curious gawkers and the souvenir scavengers, rummaging through burial sites . A journalist with the *Public*

Ledger out of Philadelphia, in an article published about twelve days after the battle ended, offered this sobering advice to people who might be thinking of coming to Gettysburg to see what was going on:

> "A word of well meant advice. Let no one come to this place for the simple purpose of *seeing*. To come here, merely to *look* at the wounded and dying, exhibits a most vitiated and disgusting taste. Besides, every such visitor is a *consumer*, and adds to the misery of the sick, but subtracting from the means that should be given exclusively to them. Let all that come, come with stores for the sick, and ready to work for them, but let all mere sightseers *stay at home*."

The entire Town of Gettysburg had been converted into a community complex of hospitals for the wounded. The suffering was profligate. Every house, pole shed, church, school, tavern, stable, grain bin and barn was needed. And like a congregation of Good Samaritans, the people of Gettysburg gave them up, willingly. The wooden floors of many Gettysburg homes, for years to come, would remain black from blood stains, like the "damned spot" on Lady MacBeth's hands, that could not be scrubbed out.

Rows of white medical tents sprang up, hundreds of them, everywhere. Eliza Farnham, one of many who volunteered to nurse the wounded and dying, described Gettysburg to a newspaper correspondent as "one vast hospital." Nurse Sophronia Bucklin wrote that these long strands of hospital tents, stretching out over the landscape, were like "great fluttering pairs of white wings, boarding peacefully over those wounded men, as though to shelter them from further evil." The exterior walls of these white, embracing, angelic-winged tents, however, belied the hell on earth, inside.

But what would be done with the thousand-fold dead?

The first-hand testimony of a young Connecticut soldier, assigned to search a designated area of a battlefield for bodies, provides a glimpse into the stark scene:

> "The dead lay all about, some with a smile upon their faces,

and others horribly contorted as if the death agony had there been photographed or modeled in clay. As [our] burial party was going over the rebel field, suddenly someone shouted to a comrade, 'Look out! There's a Johnny aiming at you!' And, sure enough, there he was, with his musket in position across a large stone and his face down on the breech. He had been struck in the forehead in the act of firing, and was instantly killed. There was not the slightest thing in appearance to indicate that the soldier's alarm was not well founded."

Shortly after the battle, Union officer Robert Stiles would attempt to convert the unspeakable to written word, when he recorded this grisly but commonplace scene he and his men encountered in a Gettysburg field:

"The sights and smells that assailed us were simply indescribable—corpses swollen to twice their original size, some of them actually burst asunder with the pressure of foul gasses and vapors. I recall one feature never before noted, the shocking distension and protrusion of the eyeballs of dead men and dead horses. Several human or unhuman corpses sat upright against a fence, with arms extended in the air and faces hideous with something very like a fixed leer, as if taking a fiendish pleasure in showing us what we essentially were and might at any moment become. The odors were nauseating, and so deadly that in a short time we all sickened and were lying with our mouths close to the ground, most of us vomiting profusely. . .".

Three days after the battle, Lt. Colonel Alfred B. McCalmont of the 142nd Pennsylvania Volunteers, a lawyer by profession before the War, was leading his brigade across the fields touching the war-worn Emmitsburg Road. McCalmont would relate his dreadful observations in a letter sent to his family on July 9, 1863:

"The ground was still marked with newly made graves, with

the bloated and disgusting bodies of horses with their mouths open and eye-balls protruding. Many human bodies were still unburied and the faces were black and the teeth grinning horribly. The trees were shattered by shot and shell. Wheat fields were trodden down. War had done its work . . . "

Indeed, war had done its work. And Gettysburg had become inhumanity, incarnate.

* * *

In the same way that a modern-day governor or FEMA director would tour a natural disaster at ground level, to get an up-close-and-personal view of the crisis, Governor Andrew G. Curtin of Pennsylvania responded quickly by traveling to Gettysburg on July 10th, only one week after the fighting armies had left the battlefield. Governor Curtin would come to Gettysburg intending to help the tiny town by any means he could. But the paramount concern on his mind, before his arrival, was that it be made possible for the bodies of Pennsylvania soldiers to be shipped back to their homes and families so they could be given an honored and dignified burial.

However, the Governor was not prepared for what he would see once he stood on Gettysburg soil. Who could be? Governor Curtin said his "heart sickened" at what he observed. The death and destruction was worse—unimaginably worse—that he could have concocted in his most dark and wanton dreams.

Governor Curtin soon realized that there was far more to do than just transport bodies back home to their loved ones. Gettysburg had been violated, body and soul. Somehow, the once vibrant little community would have to be restored to health. But how? The dead and wounded were everywhere. Most roads were impassable; others still blocked by military barricades left behind. Food and supplies were gone. Telegraph communications chopped off. Railroads severed.

Fear of disease from exposed corpses and carcasses, which were strewn out on all points of the compass, was rapidly mutating into public panic. And rightly so. Typhoid fever, diarrhea and diphtheria, in that era, were as deadly as grape-shot and minie' balls. Flash floods had drowned the land. The west branch of the marshy "Plum Run" stream was completely clogged up, not with the usual beaver dams, but from the swollen bodies of Confederate soldiers.

Even hogs, starved and running at large, became feared monsters in the insane aftermath of the battle, which as one Union soldier described, "magnified the surrounding horrors." When a kind-hearted father and son from Gettysburg discovered the corpse of a Northern soldier in the vicinity of the train depot, they carried the soldier's body and put it in an outbuilding, terrified the hogs would rip him apart during the night. One Union soldier experienced the unspeakable x-rated horror of watching a hog eat his amputated leg. He was tormented by the ghoulish memory for years, telling how he somehow felt the intense pain on the stub of his severed leg, as he watched the hog, before his very eyes, pull the flesh from his dismembered limb.

The town itself seemed to weep, inconsolably, in despair.

What was Gettysburg to do?

Governor Curtin would turn to a bright, young, energetic attorney and banker from Gettysburg to come up with a plan to handle the dead and save the town. His name was David Wills.

Despite achieving wealth and prominence in his community and in Adams County, the patriotic Wills also carried a deep love for his state and country, and was committed to public service. Wills accepted the formidable assignment, becoming the Governor's proxy in both responsibility and authority to get the job done. The bearded Wills, only thirty-two years old, but loaded with talent and ambition, was just the right person for the job.

Wills would throw himself wholeheartedly into the woe-smitten project, working day and night, assisting bereaved Pennsylvania families retrieve the bodies of their mourned husbands and sons. Bringing back home the remains of loved ones meant everything, in a way that can only be understood by those who had suffered the infinite emptiness of the loss.

But the numbers were overwhelming.

Thousands of Union soldiers from states all over the Union, their bodies scattered throughout the length and breadth of the battlefields, still rested in shallow, undignified graves at the place where they fell. Many of those graves were washing out, leaving the corpses promiscuously exposed among the rocks, roots and meadows. Wild animals plundered the others. And the digging up, handling and shipping of these decomposed bodies in the scorching, humid heat of summer had the people of Gettysburg on the fringes of panic, fearing the outbreak of terrible disease.

At first, the Northern states outside of Pennsylvania wanted to transport their dead back to their beloved homeplaces, where they could be put to rest in family cemeteries and churchyards of their own state and their own faith. Tradition and religious sensibilities encouraged it. But this situation was different. Governor Curtin and state officials had a deep-seated fear that when these thousands of decomposed bodies were carried home, a plague would surely follow them.

One thing was becoming clear—the massive exhumation, identification and then transportation of thousands upon thousands of corpses to seventeen states outside of Pennsylvania was not the answer to the loathsome predicament. No town had ever faced this before. This was *terra igcognita*.

The monstrous crisis, however, would not overwhelm a smart and determined David Wills. Acting with valuable assistance from others, Wills would catalyze a plan that would rally and pool the resources of the eighteen Union states which had suffered the loss of soldiers in the three day battle. The plan would make it possible to bury the thousands of bodies of Union soldiers, whose homes were scattered all over the Northern states, in the town of Gettysburg, Pennsylvania. They would be put to rest with honor and dignity at the place where they fought and died. It would be, uniquely and exclusively, a solders' cemetery.

On July 24, 1863, just three weeks after the Battle of Gettysburg had ended, David Wills penned his first report, since being placed in charge of the project by Governor Curtin. It was a lengthy letter to Governor Curtin, laying out his ideas for a innovative burial plan and reasons for creating a national military cemetery.

Wills was a compassionate man. But his main concerns were not about the wounded soldiers; they would be cared for. His deepest and most oppressive worries were about the dead.

Wills realized that the most daunting challenge facing Gettysburg was figuring out a way to dispose of thousands of rotting corpses, in a way that would both bring dignity to the dead, and prevent the spread of disease. Three years after the battle had ceased, with raw and unrestrained candor, Wills would remind the Governor of the horrors that had befallen Gettysburg:

> "In many instances arms and legs and sometimes heads protrude, and my attention has been directed to several places where the hogs were actually rooting out the bodies and devouring them . . . humanity calls on us to take measure to remedy."

Persuaded and impressed with Will's plan, which was that all of the states having soldiers killed in combat would politically and financially join together to create a new military cemetery, Governor Curtin gave it his full endorsement and support. This idea of moving soldiers' bodies from their original graves and relocating them to one massive burial place was a radical break with tradition, because in America's past history soldiers were often buried, quite literally, where they fell in battle, unless returned to their families. This time, tradition would be subjugated to dire necessity. A centralized soldiers' cemetery was an idea whose time had come.

Wasting no time in launching his recovery plan, the first step Wills would take was to form a multi-state commission made up of the eighteen Union states that lost soldiers at Gettysburg. They would be formally called the "Gettysburg Cemetery Commission." Each participating state would contribute a ratable share of the costs in design and construction of the national cemetery, along with the costs of the exhumation and reburial process. Wills, a Republican himself, would chair the Commission. The governors of each of the eighteen states would designate a special commissioner to sit on the Commission, giving each of the ally states a voice and influence in the project. Officially, Wills would be acting as "agent" for the Governor of Pennsylvania and all of the participating states.

This was, in its entirety, a project put together by and for the participating states. Not until David Wills would invite the President of the United States to speak at the dedication ceremonies, would the Federal Government be brought into the picture. Eventually, though, with the clout of the Commission behind him, Wills would press upon the Federal government for some extra assistance; as a result, the War Department shipped thousands of wooden coffins to Gettysburg, free of charge. And Wills would begin organizing a grand but solemn ceremony to dedicate the cemetery. This ceremony would be attended by a retinue of distinguished guests and featuring the most famous orator in the Nation as its principal speaker. The Gettysburg attorney believed such a momentous ceremony featuring renown speakers was necessary, because, as historian Garry Wills put it, David Wills "felt the need for artful words to sweeten the poisoned air of Gettysburg."

Decisive and determined, David Wills was ramroding the Herculean project into a reality, and by the first week of November (1863), he would convert what had originally been a multi-state burial project into a national event.

The young lawyer's concept to save Gettysburg was a Daedalian plan. It was the only way to restore public health, and sanity. And it gave hope to the people of Gettysburg that they could recover from the tidal wave of death and destruction that had submerged their town. It was a project that would give CPR to a community that was struggling to breathe after the blunt-force trauma of two fighting armies dropping on them, full weight and velocity.

On October 15th, 1863, just one month before the Gettysburg cemetery dedication event, David Wills would next invite public bids on two multi-service contracts, one contract for the grim task of recovering the buried and unburied bodies of Union soldiers, trying to identify the decomposed corpses, and moving them to the new soldiers' cemetery. The second contract was for digging graves in the new cemetery and burial.

Identification of soldiers' remains was very important, obviously, for the sake of their families; but also because Union corpses had to be separated from the Confederate ones. No Confederate soldiers would be allowed to be buried in this cemetery honoring the sacrifices of the Union Army. Just the mention of such commingling of graves would have been vulgar and repulsive to Northerners. Out of the thirty-four bids received by Wills, the highest would be $8.00 per body. The low bid, $1.59. So at $1.59 per body, F.W. Biesecker, a local citizen, won the dreadful contract.

Wills and Biesecker quickly employed Samuel Weaver, a white man, as superintendent in charge of removing the corpses of soldiers from their obscure and lonely graves that were scattered throughout the Gettysburg countryside. Weaver would then pick his own assistant, a fellow named Basil Biggs, who was a self-taught farm veterinarian and coffin-maker (a timely skill), and only one of a handful of African-Americans in the Gettysburg area who had the right to call themselves a "citizen." With work crews made up mostly of black men and boys, Biggs dug the corpses out of the ground and placed each body in its own white pine coffin.

Weaver, who possessed the diverse and practical skills of operating a dray-wagon and a camera, was the ramrod of the exhumation project. The grisly work would being on October 27th.   As he would later report in writing to David Wills, "There was not a grave permitted to be opened or a body searched unless I was present. I was inflexible in enforcing this rule." But Weaver was more than a drayman and photographer. In a real life 1860's episode of *CSI: Gettysburg*, Samuel Weaver was pioneering the skill of modern forensic investigations, as he analyzed clothing fragments, necrotic skin color, pocket contents, notes and letters, mementos, dental bridges, military gear and grave location to assemble a collection of forensic clues that might lead to the accurate identification of a soldier.   Weaver confidently described his forensic process to David Wills, like this:

> "... I saw every body taken out of its temporary resting place, and all the pockets carefully searched; and where the grave was not marked, I examined all the clothing and everything about the body to find the name. I then saw the body, with all the hair and all the particles of bone, carefully placed in the coffin, and if there was a head-board, I required it to be at once nailed to the coffin. At the same time I wrote the

name, company, and regiment, of the soldier on the coffin, and numbered the coffin, and entered in my book the same endorsement. This book was returned to your office every evening, to copy and compare with the daily return made by the Superintendent of the interments in the Cemetery. In these scrutinizing searches, the names of a number of lost soldiers were found. They were discovered in various ways. Sometimes by the pocket diaries, by letters, by names in Bible, or Testament, by photographs, names in pocket-books, descriptive list, express receipts, medals, names on some part of the clothing, or on belt, or cartridge-box, [etc]."

Superintendent Weaver went on to explain to Wills his clever and reasoned identification process:

"It may be asked how we could distinguish the bodies of our own men from those of the rebels. This was generally very easily done. In the first place, as a general rule, the rebels never went into battle with the United States coat on. They sometimes stole the pantaloons from our dead and wore them, but not the coat. The rebel clothing is made of cotton, and is of gray or brown color. Occasionally I found one with a blue cotton jean roundabout on. The clothing of our men is of wool, and blue; so that the body having the coat of our uniform on was a pretty sure indication that he was a Union soldier. But if the body were without a coat, then there were other infallible marks. The shoes of the rebels were differently made from those of our soldiers. If these failed, then the underclothing was the next part examined. The rebel cotton undershirt gave proof of the army to which he belonged. In no instance was a body allowed to be removed which had any portion of the rebel clothing on it. Taking all these things together, we never had much trouble in deciding, with infallible accuracy, whether the body was that of a Union soldier or a rebel. And I here most conscientiously assert, that I firmly believe that there has not been a single mistake made in the removal of the soldiers to the Cemetery by taking the body of a rebel for a Union soldier."

In less than two weeks after bids were advertised, crews were already on the job, working daylight to dark, carrying out their grisly assignments. At best, about 50-60 bodies a day was all the hard-working men could get done on a "good day" (that is, when bodies were easily removed and identified, weather cooperated, and they didn't have to be hauled very far). The State of Massachusetts insisted upon taking care of its own, so it joined the project, eventually burying 158 of its dead in the soldiers' cemetery.

The remains of Union soldiers, after being probed with a steel hook for identification and then removed from the clutches of their shallow graves, would be swathed in military blankets and placed in coffins, a cushion of wood-shavings added to rest behind their heads. Then the coffins were hauled by horse-drawn wagons to a site called Cemetery Hill, where they were lowered with ropes or rolled down rails into the rectangular pits that were their final resting place. All of this was done in strict accordance with the plan developed by the cemetery architect. A more sad and gruesome job is hard to conceive. At night, David Wills would religiously tally and record the data on the day's burials.

Slowly, but surely, Gettysburg was coming back to life.

In addition to enduring the unthinkable sights and smells encountered by burial crews, the identification of bodies was made even more difficult because hundreds of Confederate soldiers were buried wearing parts of Union uniforms taken off of captured or killed Union soldiers. When the remains of a Confederate soldier were identified, most often, under a pile of rocks or in a washed out, shallow grave located at the very site where the soldier fell, the body was put back in the ground by Biggs and his crew at the same place where it was found. There was no pay for an "enemy grave." Even though no grave was dug, fresh dirt would be quickly piled upon the Confederate corpse as a "deed of decent respect." Some around town whispered that Sam Weaver had sympathies for the Confederate dead. How could he not? It was known, even if unspoken, that many of these Confederate casualties were poor farm boys, often hungry and homesick, who had fought out of a sense of honor and dignity, dying a long distance from home and family. They also knew, instinctively, had they been born on Southern soil, they too, might be lying in that shallow, unmarked grave; after all, honor dictates that you stay and fight with your people.

Weaver firmly believed that not a "single mistake" was made in the identification and interment project. However, this difficult exhumation process undoubtedly resulted in a few Confederate soldiers being mistakenly buried with full honors beside Union soldiers. Still, Weaver and his crews did amazingly good work for their time. And their few burial mistakes would not have troubled President Lincoln. (It is sometimes lost, from a historical perspective, that Lincoln was born in Kentucky, descended from Virginia ancestors, and married into a family with strong Southern moorings, giving him a Southern-steeped understanding of honor.)

* * *

Before the burial project began, under Will's guidance, a plot of about seventeen acres of land, L-shaped like the slanted foot of a hockey stick, was purchased with state money at a price of $2,475.87. The deed would be titled to the State of Pennsylvania although nine years later, the cemetery would be transferred over to the U.S. Government. But it could not be just any piece of ground. The place chosen for the soldiers' cemetery meant everything. This land for the soldiers' cemetery had to be at a site irreproachably worthy of the noble and sacred purpose for which it was destined.

There was such a place. A perfect place. A piece of ground called Cemetery Hill. It would be nestled next to the existing "Evergreen" civilian cemetery. Wills described the selected site for the soldiers' cemetery, best, in his own words: "It is the ground which formed the apex of our triangular line of battle, and the key to our line of defenses. It embraces the highest point on Cemetery Hill, and overlooks the whole battlefield. It is the spot which should be specially consecrated to this sacred purpose."

David Wills would hire the most famous landscape architect in the country, Scottish-born William Saunders, to design the cemetery, and to create a special monument site within the cemetery that would over-look the entire battlefield and serve as the centerpiece of this sacred ground. Saunders was a passionate botanist. During his distinguished career, he would develop hundreds of trees, shrubs and plants that are thriving throughout America, still today. Saunders was also the preem-inent spokesman for an avant-garde movement of the time known as the "world cemetery" association. This movement became a cultural phe-nomenon, and promoted what was then the fashionable architectural concept of "rural cemeteries."

These rural cemeteries—a concept inspired by the Greeks—were pastoral settings designed to allow the living and the deceased to jointly commune. The goal of the architect was to make the rural cemetery a quiet and beautiful place where the borders of both life and afterlife became contiguous. A place that blended with the beauty of nature, and inspired spiritual contemplation.

Although it seems odd today, the nineteenth century was a time of Victorian influence when American society was deeply intrigued by death and its appurtenances, such as séances, mourning clothes and jew-elry, hair keepsakes from the departed, elaborate grieving rituals, post-mortem photographs and cemeteries—especially cemeteries. This cul-tural fascination with death and cemeteries was not as macabre as it might seem, at first impression. It is often said today that every family has been touched by cancer. During the Civil War, the same was said about untimely death. Virtually every family was touched by the prema-ture death of a loved one, by bullet or disease. Moreover, the death of a child or children was a heart-breaking but almost inevitable part of nineteenth century family life. So inevitable, that books of etiquette and advice on how to handle the loss of a child, became literary staples. Lydia Marie Child, in her popular 1831 work titled *The Mother's Book*, encouraged mothers to discuss, with sweet but chilling frankness, the possibility of death with their children, and to make sure "the idea of death [was] not only familiar but pleasant to [the child's] imagination," so that the child's death and journey to Heaven with the angels, as she put it, would be "like going to a happy home." Sadly, *The Mother's Book* was consulted with unconscionable frequency, nearly one out of every two people that died in this era was a child under the age of five.

Interest in the afterlife and spiritualism became the rage because it spooned with the deepest needs of mid-nineteenth century Americans. This was a generation who prepared themselves to look death squarely in the face. Millions of Americans were engulfed with spiritualist fervor. The business of "mediums" was booming. And the idea that the living could talk to their deceased friends and kinfolk, or become closer to them in the sanctuary of a beautiful and happier cemetery setting, had a comforting and popular appeal. These scenic, uplifting, flora-filled cemetery settings were becoming much preferred to the gray, dreary burial lawns that were so commonplace.

William Saunder's cemetery design for the soldiers' cemetery at Gettysburg would reflect these rural cemetery influences.

But Saunder's work would be more than just latching to a fad; it would be creative and dexterous. This was no surprise. Saunders brought impressive credentials to the project. He had designed the first "rural cemetery" in America back in 1831, known as the Mount Auburn cemetery, in Cambridge, Massachusetts. It rivaled the great burial grounds of ancient Athens, and gracefully melted into the natural landscape. Mount Auburn Cemetery is historically rich and exquisitely maintained, still today. Interestingly, the principal speaker for the cemetery dedication at Gettysburg, Edward Everett, had previously played a key role in the earlier creation of the Mount Auburn cemetery, and was an avid supporter of Saunder's rural cemetery model. In less than two years after giving his keynote speech at Gettysburg, Everett, himself, would be buried at Mount Auburn. Furthermore, President Lincoln, whose words would eternally consecrate the rural cemetery at Gettysburg that had been designed by William Saunders, in less than two years, would be laid to rest at Oak Ridge Cemetery, in Springfield, Illinois, a burial place, ironically, landscaped by William Saunders.

In his own words, William Saunders would eloquently describe his architectural vision of the rural cemetery to be built on the battlefields of Gettysburg:

"The prevailing expression of the Cemetery should be that of *simple grandeur*. Simplicity is that element of beauty in a scene that leads gradually from one object to another, in easy harmony, avoiding abrupt contrasts and unexpected features. Grandeur, in this application, is closely allied to solemnity. Solemnity is an attribute of the sublime. The sublime in scenery may be defined as continuity of extent, the repetition of objects in themselves simple and common place. We do not apply this epithet to the scanty tricklings of the brook, but rather to the collected waters of the ocean. To produce an expression of grandeur, we must avoid intricacy and great variety of parts, more particularly must we refrain from introducing any intermixture or meretricious display of ornament."

When William Saunders first immersed himself into the Gettysburg project, he was a bit perplexed by the peculiar shape of the tract of land the Commission had proposed for the soldiers' cemetery. However, the Commission's purchase of some extra land gave Saunders the architectural boost he needed. Saunders was then able to skillfully design an interment plan for the cemetery where every soldier's grave would receive a physical placement on the ground that reflected equal dignity, prominence and honor for the soldier, his state and his country. No simple task, indeed, considering the highly-sensitive social and political sentiments of the time.

Early in the project, Wills accidentally struck a raw nerve with Massachusetts and the Cemetery Commission. His first impression was that it would be a logistical nightmare to sort out the thousands of corpses, state by state. So his original plan was to bury Union soldiers in the newly-formed cemetery, grouped together, in random fashion. That is, an Ohio soldier might be buried next to a Michigan soldier. An Indiana soldier next to a Vermont. Certainly, it would have simplified and hastened the interment process.

However, this plan of "promiscuous" burials, as it was distainly called, was vehemently opposed. No doubt, these soldiers from Maine, Wisconsin, New York and from all of the eighteen Northern states— had fought passionately to preserve the Union. But people from these eighteen states also felt equally passionate about preserving their state identities. In the world of mid-nineteenth century politics, loyalty to one's state, the recognition of an individual's state heritage, and even state's rights, themselves, was an emotion and creed that ran as deeply and passionately as Americans feel, today, about issues like civil rights and freedom of speech. At Will's request, Saunders went to work on solving this problem. A "balanced" approach to honor these burial sensitivities was the answer.

To accomplish a balanced goal of both "distinguished" and "equal" burial, Saunders laid out the individual burial spaces by dividing them into separate, curved sections, with each section being designated for one of the participating eighteen states. Thus, Delaware soldiers were buried together in their own state section, as were Michigan soldiers, and so on. Accordingly, Saunders had honored the sacred state affiliations of the individual soldiers. These state sections were then arranged in a series of semi-circles around the centerpiece monument. This left each state section an equal distance from the main, central monument that stood in the soldiers' cemetery. The two ends of the cemetery would be reserved for the unidentified. As Saunders described his own work: "The position . . . of each interment, is relatively of equal importance."

Eventually, under this plan, 3,512 Union soldiers would take their final resting place on Cemetery Hill. Of those, 979 would be "unknown." And they remain so, today.

William Saunders' work was nothing short of brilliant. Through equal spacing of individual burial plots from the location of the centerpiece monument in the cemetery, without regard to a soldier's rank, Saunders had brought the democratic, egalitarian ideals of both honor and equality to recognize the accomplishments of each and every one of the individual martyred soldiers, and their home states. After all, these men—whatever their rank or status in life—had all given their lives in equal sacrifice, so they should be laid to rest among brothers of the same state, equally. And, at the same time, Saunders had maintained visual, architectural focus on the single majestic monument standing at the highest point, the epicenter of the cemetery—like the Great Tree of Moreh—to *forever* recognize the Union victory and valor of the entire group of fallen soldiers.

The needed balance had been struck. In the language of a modern metaphor, both the individual and the team had been equally distinguished, and honored. Saunder's work was an architectural masterstroke painted on a canvas of raw land. It would be the first national cemetery in America.

Fate, again, had pulled Abraham Lincoln into its wake.

CHAPTER EIGHT

LINCOLN ARRIVES IN GETTYSBURG

*"Never in my life will I have the same opportunity of seeing
so many of the great men of the nation again."*
—Josephine Fortney Roedel
Written in her Diary
From Gettysburg, PA
November 18, 1863

THAT EVENING OF WEDNESDAY, NOVEMBER 18TH ABOUT 5:00 P.M., President Lincoln's train, embroidered with red, white and blue buntings, and dressed up with evergreen and jasmine wreaths, finally reached the Gettysburg station on Carlisle Street. A large, enthusiastic crowd waited there in the setting sun to welcome the President. In that crowd stood the President's host for the next twenty-four hours, local attorney David Wills.

Also there to greet Lincoln, among a coterie of other dignitaries, was the grand old man of Massachusetts himself, Edward Everett, the featured orator for the Gettysburg dedication. Everett was anxious to see the President, and especially pleased to reunite with his adored daughter, Charlotte, and his son-in-law, who had rode on the train with the President.

Celebrities were rolling into tiny Gettysburg like Hollywood movie stars on *Academy Awards* night. During the next twenty-four hours of strolling about Gettysburg, one might see a congressman or senator chatting with folks on a street corner; a foreign ambassador milling about; a governor browsing in a store, or conversing with a crowd next to a church; a famous military general or presidential cabinet member rocking on a porch; a world-renowned orator riding a carriage in the middle of town; or even the President of the United States, striding across the public square. As Josephine Roedel, enamored by the famous people and goings-on all around her wrote in her diary, "Never in my life will I have the same opportunity of seeing so many of the great men of the nation again." Gawking, abounded.

Ward Lamon, and Lincoln's Commissioner of Public Buildings, Benjamin B. French, who was assisting Lamon, had caught an early morning train out of Baltimore earlier in the week and arrived in Gettysburg on Friday, November 13th. The purpose of this earlier trip to Gettysburg was to meet with David Wills, so they could iron out the final details for the November 19th program. David Wills had been working feverishly for two months to organize this huge, once-in-a-life-time event—what Wills in his own words predicted to be "a very imposing and solemnly impressive" ceremony.

Lamon and French, by taking a early train to Gettysburg, had worked together with Wills to firm-up arrangements for the President's travel, lodging, security and personal appearance schedule before Lincoln arrived. But their train ride was no pleasure trip, even for the gregarious Lamon, usually full of ribald humor, funny stories and banjo tunes. Lamon and French may have second-guessed themselves on their decision to catch a train to Gettysburg on the perfidious date of Friday the 13th. They found themselves riding on a train to Gettysburg that was pulling cars packed with hundreds of secessionist prisoners from the South. In all likelihood, hungry, hostile prisoners. Fitting into the environment of that train ride like two skunks at a Sunday School picnic, even in separate train cars, Lamon and French probably could not wait to get to Gettysburg Station, and get off that train.

Upon arriving in Gettysburg earlier the previous week, Lamon and French booked hotel rooms at the Eagle Hotel and immediately got with David Wills at his home. They wasted no time in getting to work. The trio collaborated intensely during three days of planning sessions to tighten-up the logistics for the array of ceremonial events set for November 19th.

History, it seems, has not paid worthy attention to the genuine spirit of cooperation between these three men, Wills, Lamon and French, which over three days ripened into a synergy, resulting in their completion of a remarkable amount of important planning. It was an amazing feat, under oppressive time constraints. Among other things, they added a grand parade to the ceremonies, that would be made up of thousands of distinguished guests, military personnel, bands and civilians who would walk together from the public square in Gettysburg to the soldiers' cemetery. They believed this processional, led by the President of the United States, would lend great inspiration and dignity to the program. And they were right.

David Wills recruited Ward Lamon to take on the job of chief marshal over the ceremonial parade, and superintend the event. He also asked Lamon to serve as master of ceremonies for the dedication program at the soldiers' cemetery. Lamon proudly accepted. They agreed that Benjamin French who was a good friend of Lamon would assist Lamon in these responsibilities. After spending three days in Gettysburg doing advance work, Lamon returned back to Washington on Monday, November 16th, and that very evening, he would organize and brief the support staff that would accompany the President. Like the suitcase life of modern-day Secret Service, U.S. Marshall Lamon would turn around and leave Washington the very next day, returning back to Gettysburg on Tuesday the 17th, to prepare the way for the President's trip that would take place on the 18th. There was no actual Secret Service at this time. Ironically, the agency would be created by President Lincoln on April 14, 1865, the day he was shot by Booth. The signed legislative papers were on Lincoln's desk, when he died.

* * *

With the organizational work done, Ward Lamon—who Lincoln fondly referred to as "my particular friend," was relieved to be at the train station and see President Lincoln arriving safely on November 18th in Gettysburg. He always worried for the President when he was not there by his side. History would tragically validate Lamon's concern; when President Lincoln was fatally shot less than two years later at Ford's Theatre, Lamon was not there. He had been dispatched to the defeated and occupied capital of the Confederacy, in Richmond Virginia, thus pulling him away from Lincoln's security detail.

As the President's train pulled into the depot on Carlisle Street in

Gettysburg, Lincoln had parted the venetian blinds and peered out the window of his car. He could not avoid seeing the empty coffins. Boxes of death immodestly stacked up on the platform at the train depot, and elsewhere, lying in wait to be filled by the casualties of war, a war crushing down on Lincoln's mind and body like a cold granite millstone. "How many more coffins must be filled," Lincoln surely pondered, "before it is over?"

Those stacked coffins at the Gettysburg train depot would become a site that eternally haunted the President, as haunting, perhaps, when in his youth he flatboated down the Ohio River and saw African-American slaves in transit, ripped from their families. They were beaten, starved, and shackled to boats, as Lincoln remembered it, "like so many fish upon a trot-line," being hauled to their destinations of cruel bondage. Lincoln would later share with his close friend Joshua Speed that the recollection of those slave boats was "a continual torment to me." Likewise, the memory of those coffins at the Gettysburg train station would linger in the President's mind, coffins awaiting the bodies of men who died shackled to a ship of war from which they could not escape, and ripped apart from their families to fight it, this time, with Lincoln at the helm.

When Lincoln alighted from the train into the thick, lively crowd, cheers and applause broke out. "The next President," they enthusiastically yelled. "Father Abraham. . . Father Abraham." The Marine Band played as the President began his crowded, escorted walk of two blocks to the home of David Wills, a residence located in the public square of Gettysburg. Wills, Everett and General Darius Couch, along with a single guard from the Invalid Corps, would escort the President to his destination. A fine dinner and friendly people awaited him there. And it was the place where President Lincoln would spend the night.

The President, as always, gave thanks to the excited crowd, nodding his head in appreciation, smiling, shaking hands. But for the moment, these polite reactions by President Lincoln were purely perfunctory. He barely noticed the music and applause. The stacks of coffins were still on his mind. So was the bloodshed. There was tomorrow's speech, still unfinished, to think about, too. Before leaving Washington, the President had shared with Ward Lamon his private concerns about the speech he would give at Gettysburg, telling his trusted friend that he was worried he would not be able to "fill the measure of public expectation" that had been thrust upon him. Lincoln felt the awful weight of uncertainty—the War, the upcoming election, tomorrow's speech. The uncertainty of it all.

Dusk waned. Moonlight was beginning to shimmer off of the train cars.

The President's thoughts must have wandered away from the pomp and ceremonies greeting his arrival, from the warm reception he had received, and turned back to the question that nagged him like a toothache, deep inside:

"Will I choose the right words, tomorrow?"

CHAPTER NINE

THE PRESIDENT BECOMES A HOUSE GUEST

"There was so many people that
there was no comfort."
—Susan Holabaugh White
Letter to her Husband
November 20, 1863

PRESIDENT LINCOLN WOULD BE AN HONORED GUEST IN THE THREE-story Gettysburg home of David Wills and his wife, Jennie Smyser Wills. Joining him there would be Edward Everett, the featured speaker for the dedication ceremony, and the popular Governor of Pennsylvania, Andrew Curtin, that is, once Governor Curtin eventually arrived on the very late Governor's train. The Wills home was the largest on the public square in Gettysburg, located at York and Baltimore streets. Attorney David Wills, who would later become Judge Wills, had moved his law office into this house. It was, in its day, a grand and impressive mansion, reflecting the wealth and prestige David Wills had achieved in his community.

As soon as Lincoln arrived at the Wills residence, he climbed the stairs to his upstairs quarters on the second floor, for some private time. During this brief hiatus from travel and people, Lincoln could get a little rest from the long ride, and take some time to continue work on the first draft of tomorrow's speech.

The Wills family was very proud to have President Lincoln, along with the famous Edward Everett and the Governor of Pennsylvania as guests in their home. What an exciting evening it must have been for

David and Jennie Wills. Someday, their home would be filled with the sounds of seven children. But on that special evening, it was filled with the conversation of celebrities!

Following a brief time alone in his room that evening, Lincoln came downstairs to join David and Jennie Wills, Edward Everett, those of the President's cabinet that made the trip, and other dignitaries for dinner. More than twenty guests would enjoy Jennie Will's sumptuous meal. The only disappointment was the absence of a number of other interesting and high-powered guests, like Governor Curtin and other chief-executives of Northern states. They were still stuck on the rails en route to Gettysburg, riding the mechanically-plagued Governor's train. Most likely, the delicious leftovers were saved as a midnight snack for those delay-weary travelers. Fine hospitality would have allowed no less. This dinner at the home of David and Jennie Wills would be a culinary fusion of local, state and federal politics.

For the Wills family, the gathering must have seemed surreal and almost kafkaesque. That night, their home was filled with the sweet aroma of good food, friends and celebrities, and the pleasant, hopeful voices of good conversation. Yet, just four months earlier, the wine had been turned to blood. This same house had been identified by a red flag as a make-shift hospital, filled with the rancid odor of open wounds and blood-soaked bandages, and the desperate, forsaken moans of wounded and dying men. This surreal experience of David and Jennie Wills was surely a gripping topic of conversation that evening.

During dinner at the Wills house, rambunctious and restless groups of people—thousands of them—who clustered and traipsed about in the public square outside of the Wills home—singing, cheering and yelling out for "Old Abe" and "Father Abraham" to make a speech—constantly interrupted the occasion.

After the fine meal that evening, this group of well-heeled guests mingled briefly for an impromptu reception in the Will's parlor room. The mood was light and upbeat. David Wills, acting like a modern day press secretary for President Lincoln, made sure the roaming and story-hungry horde of journalists were sealed off from the social event being held inside of his home. Even in those days, the news media was always on the prowl for a politician's foot-in-mouth moment or a nuance in a speech that could be twisted into a hot controversy. As frustrated *Philadelphia Press* reporter John Russell Young complained, Lincoln "became invisible" to the press early that evening, and "could not be enticed" to come out—still a valuable skill in the repertoire of modern presidents. This reporter-free zone, no doubt, liberated the conversation.

President Lincoln talked with Edward Everett that evening, along with many others. Everett, impressed with the decorum of the President, would note in his diary that Lincoln, among the many dignitaries, was "in gentlemanly appearance, manners and conversation . . . the peer of any man at the table."

Although there is no detailed historical record that reveals "with whom" and "about what" Lincoln spoke that evening at the dinner and reception that followed, odds are, the President shook hands and spoke to everybody. He was extraordinarily patient in that way, and in these situations he always listened more than he talked. Lincoln's friend and political adviser, attorney Leonard Swett, said Lincoln "would listen to everybody; he would hear from everybody; but he never asked for opinions." Certainly the War was discussed. And, perchance, the President's bid for reelection. This was an era when the topics of religion and politics were not only the main topics of conversational pastime, but through the medium of sermons, speeches and debates, were often the favored entertainment of the day. These nineteenth century social settings, along with townhalls, barber shops, general stores and street corners, were the blogospheres of their day, where people exchanged opinions and political banter. This reception in the Will's parlor would have been no different.

About ten o'clock that evening, despite the pleasant atmosphere of the reception, Lincoln politely excused himself from the gathering, and returned to his upstairs room. It was a good time to work on the ending of tomorrow's speech. He hoped to get the first draft of his speech done, that night.

But working on tomorrow's speech would not be so easy. Lincoln's window faced the public square. Even inside the house with windows closed, Lincoln could still hear the thousands of people gathered out in the public square, whooping it up next to the Wills home, hoping to steal a glimpse of the President. "Hurrah for Old Abe," they yelled.

"God save our President," and "Father Abraham, the next President," some of them shouted, tossing their hats high above their heads. Unfortunate for the President, their cheers and serenades pierced the walls where he was trying to think and write.

Those close to Lincoln said he had a knack for blocking out distractions while he worked—a skill born out of necessity from his days as a lawyer, trying to work at the office with folks dropping in without appointments to chat a while, and surrounded by the pranks and plundering of two energetic boys. It was a skill he surely needed that evening. Suddenly, another chorus rings through the crisp night air: "We are coming Father Abraham, three hundred thousand more. . . ."

Eventually, the loud but laudatory beckoning of the crowd, and the unrelenting serenades of the 5th New York Artillery band and a singing group, persuaded the President to come to the window of his second floor room. He smiled and waved to the enthused crowd, signaling his appreciation. But it wasn't enough. They wanted a speech from their President. Henry Holloway, stuck in the thick crowd that evening, remembered that "Nothing would do— the President [had to] come forth." After all, it was the expected custom of the day for a statesman or dignitary to respond in-kind to such serenading with a few words of gratitude. To ignore a serenade was high-handed and impolite. Custom aside, Lincoln wanted to thank them. He was tired, but appreciative of their support.

Overriding his fatigue, President Lincoln left his room, came down the stairs and emerged through the York Street door of the Wills house, and positioned himself on the steps.

Applause and loud cheers erupted. "Never did a mortal have a more enthusiastic greeting," later wrote J. Howard Wert, a local Gettysburger. The boisterous group began to call out, "Speech, Father Abraham . . . speech!"

Tired and keenly self-aware of his clumsiness with off-the-cuff remarks, Lincoln artfully dodged their cries for a stump speech. **"Thank you for this compliment,"** he opened, telling the excited gathering that **"The inference is a very fair one that you would hear me for a little while, at least . . . were I to commence to make a speech."**

Enthused replies of "yes . . . oh, yes," no doubt, came from the whipped-up crowd.

The President wanted to give them something—if only a dollop of remarks—that would show his gratitude.

Lincoln then told the frisky crowd that he was not appearing before them for the purpose of making a speech, **"for several substantial reasons . . . the most substantial of these,"** he quipped, **". . . is that I have no speech to make."**

A wave of laughter rolled over the adoring crowd. They thoroughly enjoyed the President's humorous banter, soaking up in every word. They sensed some more was coming.

And they were right. The President wasn't finished.

"In my position, it is somewhat important," Lincoln said, **"that I should not say any foolish things."**

To which a smart-aleck buried in the crowd instantly wisecracked, *"If you can help it."*

Belly laughter, most surely, broke loose, again.

Still quick on his feet from his days of trying cases as an Illinois circuit rider, and publicly debating the formidable "Little Giant" Stephen A. Douglas, the President verbally counter-punched the smart-aleck (no doubt, to the delight of everyone there), by cleverly replying, **"It very often happens that the only way to help it is to say nothing at all."**

Again, laughter filled the audience. Then, tactfully lowering the final curtain on his remarks for the night, Lincoln announces: **"Believing that is my present condition this evening, I must beg of you . . . to excuse me from addressing your further."**

Applause surged. The crowd loved it. And the smart-aleck—in the popular parlance of the day—had been "catawamptiously chawed up."

Almost instantly, a smiling President Lincoln would step back into the Wills house. As one reporter wryly characterized Lincoln's remarks: "He had said nothing—but he said it well."

Meanwhile, the congregated audience began to lumber en masse to the house next door, gathering in front of the Harper place, where they serenaded and played music for Secretary of State, William H. Seward. Exhibiting his distinguished profile, that showcased his huge ears and a nose shaped like a jig sail and nearly as big, with his erudite vocabulary, the small, wiry, slightly stooped Seward stepped outside the home and treated the hungry crowd to a long and serious anti-slavery speech. Seward, already mellowed out from an early nightcap or two, passionately railed against the evils of slavery and the Southern cause, calling the later "treason that is without justification and without parallel." And he emphasized the critical importance of safeguarding America's democratic form of government, what he described as "the purest, the best, the wisest, and the happiest [government] in the world," from the divisive and destructive forces of the "misguided" Confederacy.

Seward finished his speech by giving prayerful words of gratitude to God, "for the hope that this is the last fratricidal war which will fall upon this country," a nation which Seward rhapsodized as "the richest, the broadest, the most beautiful, and capable of a great destiny, that has ever been given to any part of the human race."

Steward's lush oration, bristling with patriotism and vilification of the Confederacy, was the "speechification" fix the crowd wanted that night. And they got it. Seward was probably stalking an opportunity to make a speech at the Gettysburg occasion, since he had been slated to take Lincoln's place as a back-up speaker at the next day's cemetery dedication ceremonies, if the President could not make the trip. Seward had some prefabricated remarks, ready for delivery. This was his shot, and by golly, he took it.

After Seward's speech was concluded, the distinguished group of guests staying at the Harper house that night went back inside and huddled around the fireplace to listen to the voluble Secretary of State, who, in stream-of-consciousness fashion, riffed on a variety of topics for several hours. The scholarly and debonair Seward, a muser of political thought and philosophy, would become the cynosure of the gathering. And bask in the moment. Benjamin French, who was also a guest at the Harper's, was mesmerized by Seward's discursive conversation about their world. French would later write that he "seldom, if ever, met with a man whose mind is under such perfect discipline, and is so full of original and striking matter."

Much like Seward, Benjamin French was a likeable and gentlemanly man of even keel, who enjoyed people and delighted in both light-hearted and enlightened conversation. He seemed to enjoy rubbing shoulders with those in the circles of political and social power. Perhaps French, despite being about the same age as Seward, as he listened to the wise, savoir-faire Secretary of State, saw a mentor in the man. Captivated by Seward's renaissance-man aura that evening, French would glow that Seward's "conversation, no matter on what subject, is worthy of being written down and preserved [into] one of the most interesting and useful books of the age. . . he is one of the greatest men of this generation."

Like a bus-load of starving people stopping at every drive-thru restaurant window in town, this huge, wandering group that first congregated in front of the Wills house to serenade Lincoln, and then swarmed the Harper house to beckon a speech out of Seward, would continue their nocturnal foraging for more speeches. "Bewildering the night" with serenades, as reporter John Russell Long recalled, they even convinced the starchy, stiff-backed Postmaster General, Montgomery Blair, and the Governor of New York, Horatio Seymour, a Democrat who was openly critical of President Lincoln, and even toying with the idea of running against him, to climb aboard the speech wagon. And much more speech-making would reverberate throughout the night. Some of it flowing from the fountainhead of sobriety; some of it, otherwise.

Eventually, the lively social atmosphere of the Wills home would begin to wind down, and guests sought to retire for the night. They hoped for some sleep before tomorrow's big day of ceremonies. David Wills must have felt some pride, and rightly so, in organizing this national event and providing "room-and-board" for its distinguished line-up of famous people. However, Mrs. Wills—a *pregnant* Mrs. Wills—may have privately entertained the notion of a "bed-and-board" divorce. *Not really.* Mrs. Wills was a wonderfully supportive wife and gracious hostess. But the uncomfortable reality was that her husband had generously overextended his invitations of lodging in their home. At last count (as noted in Edward Everett's diary), at least three dozen people were chock-ablocked, miserably, into the Wills house. There was probably more. And one of them was the President of the United States!

Only President Lincoln and Edward Everett had the incomparable luxury of their own bed. Every other bed had at least two or more tenants, jawbone to jowl, a common sleeping arrangement in the nineteenth century. Still, regardless of the century, comfort lies not in custom, but in elbow room. Even Governor Curtin, who was a late arrival at the Wills house that evening, getting there about eleven o'clock, due to the breakdown of the Governor's train, came up a mattress short. The Governor quickly discovered the uncomfortable reality that he had no bed to sleep in, unless he shared a bunk with Edward Everett. When the Governor from the land of Pennsylvania was most in need of his executive veto powers, they were, in the land of Nod, rendered quite useless. With heart and kidney troubles, combined with a heightened sense of self-dignity, Everett cringed at the idea of a bunkmate, and would have no part of it. "The fear of having the Executive of Penn. tumble in upon me," Everett fretted in his diary, "kept me awake until one." This left that same Governor of Pennsylvania, who, ironically, had cloaked David Wills with the position and prestige he wore for this national event , roaming about in the dark of night to find another place to sleep, if he found one at all.

Charlotte Wise, Everett's charming and doted-upon daughter, whom he affectionately called "Charlie," fared even worse. Assigned to a bed shared by two other women, Mrs. Wise and dainty company were unceremoniously awakened in the middle of the night, when their bed frame suddenly snapped under the load. In that time of genteel Victorian etiquette, the collapse of the bed, no doubt, was blamed on faulty craftsmanship, rather than the overabundance of human weight.

The acclaimed architect of the Soldier's National Cemetery, William Saunders—despite the honored position he would fill on the platform of distinguished guests the next day—never found a bed to rest in that night. Saunders was relegated to catching a few hours (or minutes) of sleep, sitting upright, in a jam-packed parlor room. Even the Baltimore Glee Club, the talented singers who would be featured in tomorrow's prestigious program, had no place to sleep. The entire cast of twelve singers and their director Wilson Horner would show up at the home of Smith McCreary and his daughters, who had a house near the public square. The good-hearted McCreary family made space on the floor for the chorale group, in a kind gesture repeated by many other Gettysburg citizens that night.

As Susan H. White, a visitor in Gettysburg who was submerged somewhere below the high tides of the Gettysburg masses, fumed in a letter to her husband back in Ohio, "There was so many people that there was no comfort." Comfort, indeed, had become a rare commodity. It was a harsh lesson in the principle of supply and demand. When it came to capturing a comfortable place to rest that night in Gettysburg, it was the law of the jungle. It was every man, woman, child. . . and even governor . . . for "himself."

* * *

Back up the street at the Wills house, the crowd had finally thinned, and the President had settled in his room. Lincoln hoped the little teaser of a speech he gave in front of the Wills house would be his last public remarks for the night. The President was tired, and he needed a cease-fire on interruptions so he could wrap-up tomorrow's speech. And before going to bed, he wanted to walk over to the Harper house—hopefully, taking a draft of tomorrow's speech with him—and have a private visit with his trusted friend and adviser, William Seward.

Later, Lincoln's assistant secretary, John Hay, wrote in his diary his own uninspired description of Lincoln's after-dinner dialogue with the massive crowd (and smart-aleck) that had earlier occurred in front of the Wills house: "The President appeared at the door, said his half-dozen words meaning nothing and went in."

The implacably loyal and usually apercu Hay, this time, just didn't get it. What Lincoln said, and how he said it, had sailed completely over young Hay's head. Lincoln's handful of words to the expectant crowd in front of the Wills home that evening meant far more than "nothing." The President's words meant everything to those who heard them. Lincoln had chosen to speak to the people, rather than ignore them. It was the President's way of demonstrating, with his unique blend of humble and humorous words, that he was no better than they were—that they were all cut from the same cloth.

With his trademark humor and wisdom, he had pulled off some oral legerdemain by both avoiding the physical taxation of making a full-blown speech, and still quenching the thirst of the friendly but high-strung crowd who wanted to hear something from their president.

It was quintessential Lincoln.

CHAPTER TEN

THE NIGHT BEFORE

"The tranquility of the little town [was]
completely broken up."
—Nurse Emily Souder
Letter to her Cousin
From Gettysburg, PA
November 18, 1863

To MOST OUTSIDERS, THE TOWN OF GETTYSBURG MAY HAVE APPEARED to be just an inconspicuous, wide-spot-in-the-road on most maps, but at this particular crossroads in time—the third week in November 1863—the little Pennsylvania community was bursting at the seams with visitors. Thousands and thousands of them. They came by foot, horseback, buggy, covered wagon and train.

Just the previous July, Gettysburg had been turned inside-out, completely upheaved by three days of fierce battles. By the following November, it was happening all over again. But this time, the night before the great event, it was fierce battles for a place to stay.

The *New York Times* wrote, "People from all parts of the country seem to have taken this opportunity to pay a visit to the battle-fields." It must have seemed that way. Almost every home in tiny Gettysburg was crammed full of guests, with thousands of people roaming around, looking for a place to sleep, throwing down their coats and blankets on the dirt floors of stables and barns, bedding down in wagons, train cars and corn cribs, and stretching out on the slat boards of porches and hotel floors. A comfortable place to lie down, as the locals would say, was "as scarce as hen's teeth."

It was an evening of brilliant moonlight. If you were fortunate enough when night fell, you might get permission to use a front porch chair or barn loft to rest in, at least until daybreak. Many of the doughtier visitors, not so fortunate, spent a long, cold night sleeping in open fields. Some drifted aimlessly, until dawn. The earnest hope was to get off of one's feet for the night.

Marching bands playing all over town. There was unbridled urge for merriment. Music, songs and celebrations went on in the streets, wildly, and loudly, all night. Whiskey and speeches flowed, and stoked some occasional rowdiness. Some folks who partook too much, in the slang of the day, got "corned." Sorties of the *Star Spangled Banner* fired out from the darkness throughout the night, repeatedly, eventually serving as a revelry call for those unfortunates within earshot at sunrise.

People caroused, cavorted and meandered about. They hooped and hollered, sang, back-slapped, and played fiddles and banjos. Vocal refrains of *We Are Coming, Father Abraham* echoed through the cool autumn night. Some argued. Some fought. Some passed out, cold.

These were palmy days for peddlers who hawked pieces of battlefield gear and spent war ammunition all over town, their portable souvenir shops sprinkled about like lemonade stands. Back in July, marauding packs of visitors had foraged through the battlefields for guns and trinkets of war, and no doubt, some of their plunder had shamelessly emerged for public sale. Customers converged upon these vending shacks like farm trout rising to corn, anxious to purchase a token for their pocket like a pressed penny from today's theme parks; they wanted something, a keepsake, to memorialize the big occasion. Bullets—especially parts of a tree with a bullet embedded in it—were the most popular. Newspapers of this era all too often reported of deaths and serious injuries occurring to people who handled live shells they found on the battlefields.

Words like "God save the Union" and angry references to the "Rebels," the "arch traitor Jeff Davis," and the "treasonous outlaws" of the Confederacy, seemed to be on everyone's lips. Noise, tramping-about, and politickin' filled the night air. It was pickpocket heaven.

Even Lincoln's top secretaries, Nicolay and Hay, hit the town for some food and fun. They moved about the popular watering holes to slake their thirst, enjoying a shot or two of whiskey, taking on the role of conversational scouts, getting a pulse on the bristling tempo of political talk. Much of the jaw-boning and bull sessions around town were election talk, and about the War: Would "Honest Abe" make it back to the White House? What would come of the Emancipation Proclamation? When would the Rebels finally be crushed, and the War end? Should Jeff Davis hang? Somewhere, tangled up in the arguments and altercations, squeezed between the speeches and serenading, and wedged among the pontificating and punching, opinions varied.

Sleep was scarce, whether you wanted some, or not. Surely, deeply religious families who had traveled to pay their respects, or those still grieving a loved-one killed in battle on the fields or rocky outcroppings of Gettysburg, were deeply offended by the hucksters peddling their war trinkets at every turn and shocked by the wild revelry. Although cultures and customs change over the centuries, human nature it seems, does not. At the 150th anniversary of the Battle of Gettysburg, when thousands of visitors again descended on the most famous little town in America, some were offended by the omnipresence of vendors selling hats, T-shirts and cheesy trinkets next to revered battlefields.

Like the movie title from an old spaghetti western, the evening was a strange amalgamation of the good, the bad, and the ugly. For those rightly appalled, they simply had to clinch teeth and bear it, no matter how many times drunks hollered out "God save the Union" and old Union chestnuts like the *The Star-Spangled Banner* and *Battle Hymn of the Republic* rang out, over and over again, throughout the night.

Nothing could have been done about it anyway. The peaceful little town, for one night, had taken on the rollicking atmosphere of a circus. There was no way to put the lid back on. Still, it did not matter. Somehow, it was all under control. Tomorrow would be a serious, somber day. But for this one night, folks would unwind—and rightly so—from the months of war fatigue that had so cruelly and relentlessly pressed down upon their lives.

Lincoln's right-hand men, Nicolay and Hay, would spend the evening with John W. Forney, who was Secretary of the Senate. They swapped stories, sang songs, had a few more shots of tanglefoot, "belted out a few choruses of *John Brown's Body* led by the youthful John Hay, and then, as a grand finale, listened to a loosened up, long-faced, wrinkled-browed John Nicolay recite his inspired rendition of the classic, *The Three Thieves*. The whisky consumed, under the circumstances of these painful performances, surely qualified for "medicinal purposes."

Nurse Emily Souder penned a letter to her cousin on that evening, writing that "The tranquility of the little town [was] completely broken up." And was it ever.

This event had rocked Gettysburg's world.

* * *

Later that night, between nine and ten o'clock, after having dinner and saying a few words to the crowd of serenading supporters outside the Wills house, President Lincoln returned to his second floor room, to work on tomorrow's speech. Outside Lincoln's bedroom door was Sergeant Hugh Paxton Bigham, a Federal Calvary soldier. Sergeant Bigham would maintain a constant vigil at the threshold of Lincoln's room that evening, not only as security, but also to relate messages to and from the President.

At one point, President Lincoln sent his servant William H. Johnson downstairs for some writing paper, and to request that David Wills visit him in his room. Wills promptly went up to Lincoln's quarters, where he found the President "with paper, prepared to write." Wills recalled President Lincoln as saying that he had "just seated himself to put upon paper a few thoughts for tomorrow's exercises." Lincoln asked David Wills to bring him up to speed on tomorrow's panoply of events, so he would know exactly "what was expected of him." Wills would later write that it was at that time, he had a "full talk" with President Lincoln on the agenda for the next day's ceremonies, and then left Lincoln's room.

After David Wills had briefed the President on tomorrow's itinerary, Lincoln likely continued to work on his speech, especially the ending, which was not yet the way he wanted it.

At about eleven o'clock that night, Governor Curtin finally arrived at the Wills house, excruciatingly delayed by the mechanical troubles of the Governor's train. Governor Curtin dropped by Lincoln's room to greet the President. As the Governor later recalled it, the President was positioned at his writing table, where he was scribbling on a "very large yellow envelope," that apparently contained other pieces of Lincoln's writings. Moments later, President Lincoln left his room under the guard of Sergeant Bigham, eased down the steep flight of stairs from the second floor, and strolled out of the Wills house into the street.

The President stepped around the corner and entered the home of Robert and Harriet Ann Harper, where Secretary of State Seward and other dignitaries were staying. The man of the house, Robert G. Harper, was the editor of the local Gettysburg newspaper, the *Adams Sentinel*, and a devoted Republican (just like his newspaper).   Like the Wills house, the Harper house had been converted to a hospital back in the first week of July, its rooms filled with grievously wounded soldiers.

Notwithstanding the late hour, the President was heading over to the Harper's residence to see William Seward. In his hand, Lincoln was carrying some sheets of paper. Most likely, it was a draft of tomorrow's speech.   Both Governor Curtin and David Wills would specifically remember President Lincoln carrying with him these pieces of paper upon which he had been writing. Lincoln and Seward spent about the next hour together, in private, at the Harper's home.

That night, did Lincoln and Seward talk about the speech the President would give the next day? No one knows for sure. But we do know that Seward was well read and a polished wordsmith himself. And that Lincoln valued Seward's feedback. Frederick W. Seward (who was serving as Asst. Secretary of State under his father), once observed about Lincoln and his father that, "As they sat together by the fireside, or in the carriage, the conversation between them, however it began, always drifted back into the same channel, the progress of the great national struggle."

Maybe the two friends discussed the content of the speech Seward gave earlier in the evening, and the demeanor of the large crowd outside the Harper house that he delivered it to, the same crowd that first serenaded Lincoln in front of the Wills house, after dinner.   Maybe they smiled, and their spirits lifted, as they heard out in the street the Baltimore Glee Club's harmonious renditions of "We are coming Father Abraham, three hundred thousand more!" They may have talked about who and what they had seen in town that evening, or about the War.

Or the situation with little Tad, sick back in Washington. Or, perhaps, all of these things.

Surely, Lincoln and Seward would have discussed the speech the President had brought with him. Lincoln, by now a journeyman public speaker, was astutely aware that the way a speech reads on paper can be dramatically different from how a speech sounds when it is actually spoken. He knew that the only way to get a feel for the rhythms, pauses and inflections of a speech, was to actually speak it. It was a regular part of Lincoln's speech preparation to practice saying his speech, out loud, to see how it sounded. Then, he would give his speech a test run on discreet friends who would offer him some feedback. In this regard, William H. Seward, "Henry" as Lincoln referred to his valued friend, was the perfect partner for appraising the President's speeches. After all, why else would the President have brought his speech with him?

Seward's home back in Washington was on Lafayette Square, the closest one in proximity to the Lincoln family's residence in the west wing. Henry Seward carried a pair of learned and experienced shoulders upon which Lincoln often leaned. The gregarious and inveterately pragmatic Seward had become a valuable asset as presidential adviser, and also Lincoln's closest friend. Seward's son, Fred, would remember that the friendship between Lincoln and his father "had grown very close and unreserved."

This candid and trusted relationship between Lincoln and Seward was not only of great value to the two men, but to the Nation, as well. They had co-opted each other's knowledge and experiences in life. Lincoln and the elder Seward would routinely meet and stroll the White House grounds, the President often chomping on an apple, Seward with a cigar pinched between his fingers. They were a peculiar sight, the President at six-feet-four, his Secretary of State coming in a foot shorter. Sometimes they discussed gravely serious matters. Sometimes they politicked. At other times they engaged in unrestrained laughter at the crack of a good joke or a good story told. Both of them had a great affection for humor. Both were naturally kind men. Both possessed sagacity. And both had loving but melancholy wives whom they sometimes found hard to understand and appease. There was much common ground between them.

These two friends, Lincoln and Seward, would almost die together seventeen months later. At the same time John Wilkes Booth was stepping into the presidential box at Ford's Theater on April 14, 1865, pointing a derringer to the left side of Abraham Lincoln's head—muscular co-assassin Lewis Powell (a/k/a "Lewis Paine") was forcing his way into William Seward's bedroom where he was recuperating from a carriage accident, putting a razor-sharp bowie knife to Seward's neck. It would come to be known as the "night of horrors." Only Seward—not Lincoln—would survive. (Although Seward's face and neck were horribly slashed by Powell, a metal cervical collar would deflect the blade from Seward's jugular vein and miraculously save his life. Despite his grave injuries, he would later hold his Cabinet position with the succeeding Andrew Johnson administration, purchasing Alaska from Russia two years later. Seward's purchase of Alaska for the U.S. Government, despite being laughed at and harshly ridiculed in its time, is arguably one of the greatest, negotiated government land purchases in modern history.

In the past, William H. Seward had assisted the President in crafting other important speeches, including Lincoln's 1861 Inaugural Address. Did Seward assist Lincoln in writing the Gettysburg Address? A day or two after President Lincoln delivered his speech at Gettysburg, Seward was asked this very question. Seward instantly set the record straight by replying: "No one but Abraham Lincoln could have made that address." Seward left no room for historical conjecture. There was no ghost writer for the Gettysburg Address. It was pure Lincoln.

When looking back on Lincoln's and Seward's meeting at the Harper house that night of November 18, 1863, odds are, Henry Seward was the first and only person to read or hear the Gettysburg Address, in its entirety, before it was spoken by Lincoln the next day at Cemetery Hill.

* * *

As Lincoln prepared to leave the meeting with Seward around midnight, the host of the house, Robert Harper, suddenly called out towards the street, "The President of the United States." In a gesture unthinkable for today's Presidents, Lincoln stepped off of the Harper's porch into the town square—and straight into a dense, mosh pit of people. The President's one-man security detail, Sergeant Bigham, would lead the way.

But for the six-feet-four Lincoln, at one time in his salad days a stout and sinewy, 180-200 lb. man renowned for his talents in wrestling—there would be no physical intimidation. Once, during his Whig party days, at a state campaign rally back in Illinois, a youthful Lincoln spotted one of his friends being whipped and flailed in the crowded building. Lincoln cut his way through the thick mass of rowdy people. Strong as garlic in a mustache, Lincoln grabbed the attacker by the nape of the neck and the back of his britches, and tossed the fellow several feet through the air, head first, out of the building.

Lincoln, of course, was now older and worn down, but he still knew how to handle himself in a crowd. Indeed, navigating himself through a lush thicket of clamoring folks, some of them, in the colloquial of the day, having "a brick on their head" (they were drunk), was nothing new to the President, even inside the White House. That's because Lincoln operated a wide-open White House. He was one of the most approachable and accessible Presidents in American history.

Lincoln made himself available to both the most humble and high-flutin of folks who strayed in for a peek or were wanting something from him. When going over to his Executive Office on the east end, for a good portion of his presidency Lincoln had to get there by walking from the family's living quarters in the west wing through a corridor known as the "central hall"—a cattle-shoot filled with the body odor, tobacco spit, cigar smoke, muddy boots and chin-wagging of dozens of visitors, politicians and kinfolk (most from Mary's family), many of them beseeching Lincoln for jobs, favors and political appointments. With free admission, the White House was probably the top tourist attraction in a marshy, begrimed, foul-smelling capital city otherwise full of unfinished buildings, overpriced boarding rooms and half-built monuments.

The patronage job system in Washington made Lincoln flat-out miserable. It drained his time and energy, when he could least afford it with a war going on. Scores of people, all of them wheedling on the President for something, would descend daily on the White House, as John Hay colorfully described it, "like Egyptian locusts." Lincoln felt as if each visitor plucked out a hunk of his life essence, piece by piece, "with thumb and finger" he once said, leaving him emotionally and physically emaciated. In fact, Lincoln was so hounded by favor-seekers during the early part of his presidency, followed by the Union's crushing defeat at the Second Battle of Bull Run, he once facetiously remarked that he felt like going out on the White House lawn and "hanging himself."

Once, as persistent Lincoln mythology has it, an opportunistic office-seeker anxiously awakened President Lincoln, late into the night, to tell him that one of his political appointees had suddenly died. "Mr. President," asked the hopeful officeholder, "could I take his place?" "Well," recoiled Lincoln, "if it's all right with the undertaker, it's all right with me." On another occasion, Lincoln would exclaim in frustration, "There are too many pigs for the teats!", as dozens of pushy, contentious people horded at the White House for a handful of political offices. Some of Mary's family—who had more gall than gumption, had voted against Lincoln and still expected a political appointment.

But Lincoln added to his own misery, when it came to dealing with the incessant aggravations of patronage demands. Despite his complaints about it, Lincoln chewed more that he bit off. Lincoln embraced the process of plugging friends and political supporters into federal jobs with more attention than any president since Andrew Jackson.

And Lincoln turned up the knob on his self-inflicted misery index another notch, when, on a regular basis, he would open up the White House for afternoon receptions to the general public. The President would meet with just about anyone who wanted to talk with him. He called these melee sessions his "public-opinion baths." Aptly described, since Lincoln often found himself submerged to the shoulders in a brimming cauldron of people—all of them wanting something. Even when he wanted to leave his office just to grab a bite to eat or take a nap at the family's residence, Lincoln had to pass through that horror chamber called the central hall, where a duke's mixture of folks laid in wait just to buttonhole him. And, unmercifully, they did. Eventually, an extra door was installed, so Lincoln would have the simple, quiet pleasure of having direct access to his family's private quarters in the White House, without having to circumnavigate his way through the crowded hallway.

By the time of his trip to Gettysburg, President Lincoln had plenty of practice being at the center of friendly mobs and occasionally, not-so-friendly ones.

So on this midnight in the Gettysburg town square, President Lincoln would handle himself in this stoked-up crowd , just fine.

"Speech, Give us a speech Father Abraham," the gathering in the public square continued to yell out. But not at this late hour. It had been a long and exhausting day. President Lincoln was upbeat in mood, but weary. He gracefully declined. "I can't speak tonight, gentlemen," he politely said, telling the extant crowd that he would see them, "tomorrow" and then, he bidded them, "Good night."

Sergeant Bigham would lead President Lincoln back to the Wills house, plowing a row through the crowd to make the short but smothering walk across the street possible. "The way was very dark," Bigham would recollect, with the President telling the young Calvary soldier, "You clear the way and I will hold on to your coat." During the crossing, David Wills joined Lincoln and Sergeant Bigham, to aid the President's return to his quarters. Wills observed that President Lincoln held in his hand "the paper on which he had written his speech." A vigorous round of cheers and applause followed the President all the way back to the Wills home.

It was after midnight. Another chorus of "We are coming, Father Abraham, three hundred thousand more," rang through his windows. But maybe there was a few more quiet moments left in the day to fire up a gaslight and put a few more brushstrokes on tomorrow's speech that he started back in Washington. Then, he could retire for a much-needed, short night's sleep. There would be enough time early tomorrow morning, perhaps, for the President to give it a practice run or even write out a second draft of his speech—a "clean" copy to read by—when he delivered his remarks from the speaker's platform.

* * *

When Lincoln finally retired for the day and pulled back the bed covers, he must have thought, again, about Taddie. He already missed the tenderhearted boy, terribly.

He and Tad had grown especially close since Willie's death. Both devastated by the loss, they needed and comforted each other. Lincoln often called the puckish Tad his "little sprite." They played checkers and read books together. Tad and his father raised a menagerie of animals at the White House, like rabbits, horses and dogs, including a mutt named "Jip" who unashamedly reclined in Lincoln's lap at the dinner table. There was even a pet turkey (perhaps, Lincoln's private penance for the wild turkey he shot as a boy, that so grieved the tender-hearted Abe that he never again intentionally killed another large animal). And they raised two goats, "Nanny" and "Nanko," that napped or "chewed their cud" in Tad's bed.

Although Tad did not have his father's natural ability for school or books, he was a clever and creative little thinker in his own way. Even when he was knee-high to a milk stool, Tad had a quick take on folks visiting the White House. He could sort the good guys from the others. Tad was very proud of his father, and even tuned-in to his father's political image, once remarking, "Everybody in the world knows Pa used to split rails." (Interestingly, Tad was the only member of the Lincoln family who would ever have his photograph formally taken with Abraham Lincoln, not even Mary. Any other family photos we see in books are art work or cut-and-paste composites, versions of today's photo-shopping.)

Tad liked to shake down some of the visitors who were waiting to see his father, requiring them to pay him a nickel before they could enjoy the company of the President. "Do you want to see old Abe?," Tad would ask. When they flipped him a coin for the favor, sometimes the grinning boy would point to someone else standing around the White House.

Once, Tad came to his father, asking him to grant his Zouave-dressed doll "Jack" a presidential pardon. According to Tad, Jack was facing certain execution for falling asleep at his military post. In reality, this was frequent grounds for court martial during the Civil War. President Lincoln would dutifully issue an order of clemency for the derelict doll, proclaiming in writing that "The Doll Jack is hereby pardoned by order of the President." This whimsical pardon of Jack may have been the most judicious use of that presidential power that Americans have seen, since.

Tad would often hang close to the President in his Executive Office all day, often wrapping his arms and legs around Lincoln's timber-like leg like a honeysuckle vine, playing games—and pranks (like eating all of the strawberries allocated for a State dinner)—until finally, late in the evening, the curly-haired boy would wear out and fall sound asleep under a table, or next to the warm fireplace. Lincoln would cradle Tad in both arms, toting him to his big bed, where he spent many nights sleeping beside his beloved Papa-day.

During the course of the evening in Gettysburg, the President had been brought a telegram from Mary that answered his prayers— Taddie was "slightly better," it said. His fever must have broken. It had been a withering day.

Now, Lincoln could sleep.

CHAPTER ELEVEN

A GLORIOUS MORNING USHERS IN THE SPEECH

"It was a clear autumn day . . ."
—Nurse Emily Souder
Letter to her Cousin
From Gettysburg, PA
November 20, 1863

THE GREAT DAY had arrived.

It was Thursday morning, November 19th. The ominous, dark clouds that first appeared at a warm and humid dawn, would eventually evanesce into a gloriously beautiful, sunny morning in Gettysburg. Folks were stirring early. Calvary bugles echoed through the air at the first blush of dawn. Artillery fire rumbled mightily across the quiet, dew-covered battlefield. "It was one of those very few November days in our climate," recalled Henry Jacobs, a nineteen-year-old seminary student, "that are adapted for open-air audiences and open-air speakers . . . almost balmy." It was Indian summer.

A perfect day.

Rising early, President Lincoln would take a few minutes to chat and exchange pleasantries with Edward Everett, the ceremonial speaker around whom the day's program was organized. These two national figures may have discussed the general theme of their upcoming speeches, so not to trample upon each other's words. Or, they may have carried over the topics of their conversation from the previous evening, which they had at the Will's home.

Lincoln admired Everett. Everett, in every way, was a gentleman who always conducted himself with impeccable manners and aplomb. Even better, Everett was a tenacious supporter of the Union and hated slavery. On those two issues, Lincoln and Everett were of one mind. The year before, the President had recruited this eloquent, patriotic man—despite Everett's early criticisms of Lincoln and his outspoken reservations about the Emancipation Proclamation—to serve as an ambassador to Europe. Everett had declined the President's offer back then. Now, Gettysburg had finally brought them together.

Afterwards, President Lincoln and Secretary of State William Seward rode by carriage to the battlefield. No one else went along.

Such carriage excursions were not new to the President and the man who had become his closest advisor. Back in Washington, Lincoln and Seward often took buckboard rides over to military posts in the northern part of Virginia, where they would chat around campfires and eat a supper of beans with Union troops. Lincoln always enjoyed talking with common soldiers, often those of lower rank, perhaps the influence of his experiences as a foot soldier in the Black Hawk War. Some of the President's finest speeches were made to soldiers in the field, as they departed or returned from military engagements. When made with a dear friend like Henry Seward, these journeys to visit troops, for President Lincoln, were never long. These men had formed a fusion of fellowship and truly enjoyed each other's company.

How strange fate can sometimes unfold. Especially, the capricious force of political fate. Lincoln and Seward, just three years earlier, had been not-so-friendly political opponents for the Republican nomination for President. The shaggy-eyebrowed, cigar-smoking Seward had been the consummate Washington insider, the establishment favorite. Seward was so convinced that he would get the Republican nomination for President, that he kept a loaded cannon in front of his home, to be fired in celebration of his party's selection. Then there was the backwoods lawyer, Abraham Lincoln, a long-shot, dark horse outsider. Shockingly, on what some would see as a political fluke, Lincoln would win his party and the Nation. How ironic that the man who, as President, would often be harshly criticized for too much compromise, rose to the power of that presidency in 1861 as a compromise candidate. (Lincoln once referred to his improbable election as being "accidentally selected.")

William Seward handled his shocking defeat to Lincoln with dignity, harboring no grudges. Impressed with Seward's intelligence, experience and political skills as a former governor and senator from New York, Lincoln invited Seward to join his Cabinet. Seward graciously accepted. Even after Lincoln brought Seward into his Cabinet, they had to iron out a few wrinkles in their working relationship. Less than a month after Lincoln's inauguration, Seward had composed an audacious letter to the new President, recommending, essentially, that he be put in charge of things, only to be tactfully but firmly put back in his place by his boss. Building bridges with former political rivals like Seward was one of the President's gifts.

This visit to the battlefields had been a top priority of the President ever since the Gettysburg event was first mentioned to him, several weeks earlier. To understand it all, to choose the right words for his speech that afternoon, Lincoln knew he had to enter upon such hallowed ground.

The President had never been to the Gettysburg battlefields, in body. Yet, he was no stranger. He had been there before, in mind. After Lincoln was invited to speak at Gettysburg, he quickly summoned William Saunders, the landscape architect who had designed the Soldiers' National Cemetery at Gettysburg, to his Executive Office in Washington. They met together on Tuesday, November 17th (the day before Lincoln departed for Gettysburg) to go over the cemetery layout. Saunders later recollected that President Lincoln "took much interest in it . . . and seemed familiar with the landscape of the place, although he had never been there." Saunders would also recall that the President was "much pleased" about the cemetery design.

Before arriving in Gettysburg, Lincoln wanted to become familiar with the lay of the sacred land. The President, a former surveyor, had learned much about the topography of the battlefields from telegraph reports he received from commanding officers during the epic three day battle in July. And just three days before leaving for Gettysburg, on Sunday, November 15th, Lincoln dropped by the Washington, D.C.

studio of the famed Civil War era photographer, Alexander Gardner, to have his picture taken.

Lincoln regularly stopped by "Gardner's Gallery" to pose for photo shots. He had no compunction about getting his picture made. During his presidency, Lincoln had his photo taken at least eighty times. Lincoln would sometimes work his way through the tedium of these long photo sittings by reciting soliloquies from Shakespeare's plays. Still, he enjoyed the experience.

For the awkward-faced Lincoln, these photo sessions were not, obviously, a matter of vanity. Lincoln was intrigued by the gadgetry of photography and the idea of freezing a moment in time. And he was heady enough to recognize that photographs, suddenly becoming widely available to the masses, were a powerful political tool to connect with the American people. In fact, Lincoln, accompanied by his secretaries Nicolay and Hay, had visited Alexander Gardner's new studio at the corner of 7th and D Streets in Washington, just the previous Sunday, November 8th. On that day, the Scottish-born, heavily bearded Gardner would take a front-profile, headshot of Lincoln, which would become one of the most reproduced and familiar photographs ever made of the President. This photo would get the name, "the Gettysburg Lincoln," because of its proximity to the Gettysburg event. Lincoln returned to Gardner's studio on the following Sunday, November 15th, likely knowing that Gardner and his brother James had previously captured on film a collection of extraordinary and horrific scenes of the aftermath of the Battle of Gettysburg. The Gardner brothers were working non-stop on a compilation of Civil War photographs which would be published in two volumes (1866) as *Gardner's Photographic Sketchbook of the Civil War*.

The Civil War was the first war captured with photographs. Of course, there was no moving film, only still shots. But newly-developed portable camera equipment took photojournalism to a new place. In the same way that the battlefield scenes shown on the evening television news would expose Americans to the horror of war and irreversibly tilt public opinion against the Vietnam War, the graphic and shocking battlefield daguerreotypes of death and destruction taken by the Nation's first photo-journalists like Alexander Gardner, Mathew Brady, George S. Cook, the Tyson and Weaver brothers, and Timothy O'Sullivan, would eventually intensify the public's growing hunger for an end to the Civil War, both North and South.

Although we do not know with historical certainty, it is incomprehensible that President Lincoln, with his insatiable craving to be informed about every aspect of the War, and his knowing that in only four days he would be walking on those very battlefields at Gettysburg, would miss the opportunity to examine Gardner's battleground photographs while he was there on Sunday, November 15th . Furthermore, Gardner would have been anxious and honored to show them to the President. Those disturbing scenes of human carnage would have had a profound impact upon President Lincoln. And they are breathtakingly powerful and disturbing, still today.

* * *

By the time Lincoln and Seward reached the battlefields that early morning of November 19th, clouds were still overcasting the sky. They would pause first at Seminary Ridge. Death still lingered in the air. So much suffering and sacrifice had taken place here. So much blood had spilled, among the forests and farms of Emmitsburg Road. Then, they would ride to other battle-sites. It was a conflicted panorama. On one hand, there was the breathtakingly beautiful autumn landscape at the foothills of the Southern Mountains, the majestic Alleghenies rising from the background; on the other, even months after the fighting was over, there were the morbid remnants of the human costs of the War.

Shreds of gray and blue coats. Lingering wisps of butternut-dyed Confederate uniforms. Horse and mule bones. Tattered bits of kepis and havelocks. Buttons, weathered to an oyster-shell patina. Frayed pieces of blankets. Muddy fragments of socks, knapsacks, and empty holsters. Cartridge boxes and canteens. All of it, gossamery flecks of former lives, scattered sparsely across miles of battlefields.

The landscape was still pitted with the fresh pockmarks of shallow graves, both taken and empty. Burials had paused only to allow for the cemetery dedication program. The gruesome job would be re-started as soon as the Gettysburg ceremonies were over, but with the winter delay, would not be finished until the following March. Flat boards, half-buried in vertical position, emerged from the killing fields like bony fingers, pointing to corpses still in the ground. The faint but fowl smell of death still leaked from the Confederate dead "buried" at Devil's Den, where graves had been hastily covered, after battle, only with stones; there was no dirt on that rocky ridge for decent burial.

But far more remained upon these battlegrounds than decaying, temporal things—more than cloth, metal and bones. The imperishable was there too. Duty, honor and love; immortal and incorporeal things left behind, that also filled the place, *in saecula saeculorum*. Evermore.

We don't know what was said by Lincoln and Seward that morning on the battlefields. But what they saw, touched them deeply. Lincoln wanted to be there, because he believed the hallowed ground would speak to him. Surely it did.

Looking out at the land where so many had fought, and bled, and died— Lincoln may have recalled the words of George Washington that he read as a young man, who once said, in reflection of being the first President of the United States, that he "walked on untrodden ground." If so, Abraham Lincoln perhaps thought of himself, the sixteenth President, as having "walked on blood-soaked ground."

Lincoln and Seward would have noticed in the distance that people were already wandering about the battlefields. As one newspaper reporter wrote on November 19th, "[There is] not a foot of the grounds that has not been trodden over and over again by reverential feet." Many of them were paying their respects to a member of their family, who died there. Some, looking about the farm pastures, woodland ridges and boulder-choked protrusions of ground, were hoping to find the burial place where their husband, brother or son fell in combat; after all, many soldiers had not yet been re-interred to the new national cemetery. Others, were searching for a sign from a loved one lost, hoping to find a shard of life left behind. Searching their hearts, trying to understand it all.

The President must have searched his own mind and heart. What can I say that will make sure these men did not die in vain? What words will be fitting and proper, he must have thought, to properly consecrate these sacred grounds?

After an hour or so of touring the battlefields that morning, Lincoln and Seward would return to town. Lincoln was hoping to cabbage a little more private time in his room at the Wills house, to polish up his speech, before the start of the parade to the soldiers' cemetery.

First, Lincoln would have breakfast about eight o'clock or so that morning, and then return to his second floor room no later than nine. This one hour hiatus before the assembly of the parade at ten o'clock, perhaps, gave President Lincoln the extra time he desperately needed to quickly write out a second draft of his Gettysburg Address, to use as a reading copy when he delivered the speech. And time, hopefully, to take a few practice runs over it.

John Nicolay would come to see Lincoln that morning of November 19th after breakfast, because he had not seen the President since the presidential entourage arrived the previous evening and, in Hay's words, separated "like a drop of quicksilver spilt." Nicolay would write twenty-two years later, that Lincoln brought half of the Gettysburg Address, written in ink, with him from Washington "in his pocket;" and that the President wrote the other half in pencil "in Mr. Wills house." The serious and trustworthy Nicolay would then forcefully state . . . "I was with him [Lincoln] at the time," which had to be the morning of the 19th.

This account dovetails, perfectly, with what President Lincoln later told his Attorney General James Speed. Lincoln confided in Speed that "he took what he had written with him to Gettysburg, there he was put in an upper room in a house, and he asked to be left alone for a time. He prepared a speech, but concluded it so shortly before it was to be delivered, he had not time to memorize it." Lincoln's own words ("shortly before it was to be delivered") would seem to conspicuously describe the morning of the 19th.

This strongly suggests that during Lincoln's last precious hour available for preparation—the morning of the 19th—he most likely continued to refine his speech, and possibly worked on a few other presidential affairs. A Federal soldier, Sergeant James A. Rebert, who was assigned the proud duty that morning to guard and run orders for the President, arrived at Lincoln's door about nine o'clock, right after breakfast. Rebert later reported that President Lincoln asked him "to wait a few minutes [outside the door] until he finished his writing, which

I found him engaged in on entering the room." The soldier observed that Lincoln "had several sheets of note paper in front of him written in pencil, and several that he was just finishing."

After the President completed his writing, according to Sergeant Rebert, "he folded them all together and placed them in his pocket." That morning, was Lincoln working only on his Gettysburg Address? Or could the President have been completing the paperwork for other official duties that morning? Or both? Did the President fuse together the final draft of his speech from the bits and pieces he brought with him in the large yellow envelope, noticed the night before by Governor Curtin? Was Lincoln quickly re-writing the first draft of his speech, that is, writing out a second draft, to make a "cleaner," more improved delivery copy? We will likely never know, with certainty.

What we do know, however, with reasonable certainty, is that at some point between the early evening of November 18th and ten o'clock the next morning of November 19th, Lincoln completed his Gettysburg Address. And we know that the accounts of Nicolay, James Speed and Sergeant Rebert are a tight fit, in this regard.

Those last few hours of Lincoln's speech preparation, and the question of which draft he used as his delivery copy at the soldiers' cemetery, will always be cloaked in mystery. We can only be sure that Lincoln wrote at least one draft of the speech before he gave it. He may have wrote another. This is where so many distinguished historians part company. However, a credible (but by no means conclusive) case, in the author's view (although it may be the minority view among contemporary Lincoln scholars), can be made for this scenario: Lincoln completed two separate and complete drafts of the Gettysburg Address *before* he delivered the speech at Cemetery Hill. The "first draft" would be started with an ink quill in Washington, D.C. on Executive Mansion letterhead, and then finished at David Will's home in pencil on lined stationary. This "first draft" would reflect Lincoln's handsome and unrushed penmanship, and arguably, the type of flaws that are natural to the composition process.

The President's "second draft" was written, possibly, on November 19th, the morning of the Gettysburg ceremonies. This "second draft" has handwriting that appears to be more about hurried copying than about hurried composition, suggesting Lincoln was rushed in reproducing it. Lincoln, undoubtedly, would have been pressed for time as he wrote out an extra "reading copy" for delivery of his speech at the soldiers' cemetery, which he desperately needed. And what is known as the "second draft" of his speech—which, arguably, is closer (than the "first draft") to the words Lincoln actually spoke at the cemetery—could be it. After all, Lincoln's "first draft" of his speech was a pretty choppy and incomplete version to read from, at such an important occasion and before an audience approaching 20,000 people. It was known by those around the President that Lincoln—a compulsive revisionist—would patiently and dutifully scotch-up important speeches, constantly drafting and re-drafting them, in earnest search of just the right words for the right occasion—even making changes up to the moment the speech was given. The Gettysburg Address, most likely, was no different.

Or, perhaps, Lincoln read from his "first draft," smoothing it out with skillful extemporaneous phrasing; thus writing out his "second draft" after he returned to Washington, improving on it for publication.

It is also possible that Lincoln did not read from the "first draft" of his speech, nor the "second draft"; instead, choosing to speak from another version of the Gettysburg Address that is unknown to us and lost forever.

These are the horns of the great debate about the first two drafts of the Gettysburg Address. The provenance of the first two drafts of the speech, and the historical debate that perpetually begirds them, are addressed more extensively in the post-epilogue section of this book.

Regardless of these historical mysteries, the Gettysburg Address would be the first speech, since giving his inaugural address more than two years earlier, that President Lincoln would prepare and write out, ahead of time. Lincoln had only two weeks, perhaps a few days more, to compose and pin down with exactness the words he would use in his speech. So he had to make earnest and focused use of every quiet moment he could capture to work on his speech before leaving Washington, and then, squeeze in extra preparation time during the Gettysburg trip.

This was no stump speech. Lincoln knew he had to get this one right.

Lincoln's extemporizing could be wittingly good, even brilliant. Or it could sometimes be lousy, little more than a bad joke at a bad time. His impromptu, foot-in-mouth incident on the previous day at the Hanover train station ("Did you fight the Rebels?"), reminded the President that there was no room to shoot-from-the-hip in his Gettysburg speech. His speech at the soldiers' cemetery had to be made of thought and preparation—and of truth. Only truth could speak to the hopelessness and futility that the people felt about the Civil War. Somehow, Lincoln must do with words, what had not yet been done with battles. He must bind the country together.

Nurse Emily Souder would write in a letter to her cousin, that November 19, 1863 "was a clear autumn day."

And more than that, it would be an amazing, unforgettable day.

Chapter Twelve

CORTEGE TO THE SOLDIERS' CEMETERY

"Such homage I never saw or imagined could be shown
to any one person as the people bestow on Lincoln.
The very mention of his name brings forth shouts of applause
. . . even his enemies acknowledge him to be an honest man."
—Josephine Roedel
Written in her Diary
From Gettysburg, PA
November 19, 1863

IT WAS THE SHANK OF THE MORNING, NOVEMBER 19TH.

The parade was assembling in the Gettysburg town square at a brisk and excited pace, in preparation for the ceremonial march to Cemetery Hill. As J. Howard Wert remembered, "The hum of life was everywhere."

Liberty Augusta Hollinger and some of her friends had gathered in the home of the McCreary family, which was located on the public square, just across the street from the Wills house, where President Lincoln was staying. Liberty may have been only sixteen, but she had grown "years" since the horrors of last July, when she volunteered, each day, to clean and dress the wound of a Union soldier who had his arm amputated at the shoulder. Four months later, things were better. Hope was in the air. Liberty was excited about the great activities taking place in her hometown. The McCreary place was an excellent vantage point for the girls to soak-up all of the activities going on in the Town of Gettysburg that morning.

Like so many presidential watchers that day, this group of kids eagerly focused with laser-beam intensity on the home of David and Jennie Wills, hoping to see the President of the United States as he emerged to the street. Governor Curtin and other dignitaries were standing on the front steps of the Wills home, jovially greeting people as they walked by. Suddenly, and unexpectedly, Liberty and her friends got a paparazzi-like glimpse of President Lincoln through the window of the second floor, "pacing back and forth."

"A hush stole over the girls," Liberty would later recall. In a matter of moments, they would see President Lincoln himself, on two occasions, come to the window from his upper room, "where he looked out on the street." The teenager was able to see a yellow piece of paper, about the size of an envelope, clutched in Lincoln's left hand. The President, young Liberty noticed, was "apparently engaged in deep thought," as he glanced down upon the convening masses of people. Liberty especially remembered the "inexpressible sadness of his face," a somber countenance over Lincoln that was, in the eyes of the perceptive teenager, in dark contrast to the upbeat, excited mood of the gathering crowd below him. It was a countenance that would carry over and merge into the speech Abraham Lincoln would give that day, at the south edge of town, at the gathering place called Cemetery Hill.

When Lincoln came downstairs to join the parade ceremonies at about ten o'clock that morning, he discovered that a swarm of newspaper reporters had already invaded the Wills house. A few precious hours of sleep and the excitement surrounding the day's event seemed to ramp up the President's energy level. He was ready to engage in some banter with the press.

Still stairborne, Lincoln told the gathering of reporters that the best thing newspapers could do for the Nation, as he put it, "was to stand by the officers of the army." This was, by implication, a president's earnest request for the press not to criticize him or the country's ongoing military operations when it came to the Civil War. Lincoln wanted (but wasn't naïve enough to believe he could get) the newspapers to print only favorable and supportive stories about the Union's military campaigns—interestingly, a patriotic plea for good press that has been made by all war-time presidents that have followed Lincoln.

As Lincoln tactfully untangled himself from the restless covey of reporters, and worked his way down the steps towards the street on the public square, he was welcomed by a throng of admiring supporters. They cheered, applauded and hurrahed for "Honest Old Abe" enthusiastically shouting, "The next President of the United States. . . The next President of the United States."

Eight-year-old W.C. Storrick, who had walked with his father about two and a half miles from the eastern outskirts of town, got a glimpse of the President at the Wills house "as he was about to start down the steps to the sidewalk." Young Storrick (destined, one day, to become a historian) said he was "awed" by the President's "great height," saying with boyish wonder that "he was the tallest man I had ever seen." With his arsenal of shifty, squirming moves that are natural in eight-year-old lads, Storrick spelunked his way through the cavernous crowd to the landing at the foot of the steps at the Wills house, where Lincoln was descending. Reaching out his hand to the President of the United States from a pack of spectators, the boy would always remember that "I had the honor . . . of shaking his hand."

For the next long while, Lincoln pressed the flesh. Shaking hand after hand. After hand. "Pumping the ol' well" as it was called in those days. Lincoln put on no airs. There was nothing pompous or egotistical about the man. In fact, Lincoln despised arrogance. That's why these people adored their President. These prolonged handshaking sessions often caused Lincoln's hand to swell and knot-up, and painfully so. Today we can still see the actual size of Lincoln's swollen right hand as it looked right after a prolonged handshaking session following his Republican nomination for President, based upon the hand cast of famous sculptor Leonard Wells Volk. Once, when visiting the Union field hospital at City Point, Virginia with General Grant, President Lincoln shook the hand of every single wounded soldier. He then turned and picked up a seven pound ax with the same hand, held it parallel to the ground by the end of the handle for a bit, and then commenced to bust wood for a campfire. Soldiers loved the demonstration. Somehow, in his mid-fifties, he still had the muscular hands and arms of the "ol' railsplitter." For President Lincoln, the handshake was a universal gesture of commonality and fellowship that connected him with the people and the people with him.

Josephine Forney Roedel had traveled in late October from Wytheville, Virginia, to visit and bring some "cheer" to her elderly parents in Gettysburg, her childhood home. She was quite reluctant and melancholy in leaving her husband for the trip, especially during a war, but felt it was her Christian duty to go. She noted in her diary that "the Lord would lead me safely through all the trials if it was His will." Upon arriving in Gettysburg, she soon became "engrossed" with the preparations for the big event. On November 18, 1863 she made these entries in her diary about President Lincoln: "Such homage I never saw or imagined could be shown to any one person as the people bestow upon Lincoln. The very mention of his name brings forth shouts of applause. Even his enemies acknowledge him to be an honest man."

Like the sea of spectators pouring into a super bowl stadium, thousands of visitors were coming into Gettysburg, filling the public square and its connecting streets, to watch or participate in the ceremonial parade to the soldiers' cemetery. A local newspaper, the *Adams Sentinel*, wrote that "Every available spot on the principal streets was occupied." A military band from New York further energized the swelling assembly of people with a one hour concert of patriotic music.

Since nine o'clock that morning, Ward Lamon and Benjamin French, along with six dozen volunteer parade marshals mounted on horseback, had wrestled with crowd control and the logistical nightmare of organizing the hundreds of parade participants. Lamon, who was an excellent horseman, had organized these parade marshals the night before. For the parade marshals, dealing with this massive, unwieldy concentration of people flooding into the town's public square, must have seemed like they were straightening out a barrel of fishhooks.

The crowds were so dense, U.S. Marshall Lamon (no doubt, packing pistols, knucks and knives) had to escort Lincoln between a two-line gauntlet of soldiers, so the President could reach the beautiful chestnut horse he would be riding in the parade. H.B. Crawford noticed the fine saddle on the horse, and the ornate saddle blanket under it, which he said was "a work of art." After climbing on the horse, Lincoln must have wondered if he had climbed upon a Shetland pony, rather than a Calvary steed. Rev. J. B. Remensynder, who attended Gettysburg College, called it "a diminutive pony." With his long legs, the

President's feet were almost touching the ground. One observer hollered out: "Say, Father Abraham—if she goes to run away with'ye—you just stand up and let her go."

It was a comical sight, no doubt. There were lots of smiles and gentle chuckles. The President, with his self-deprecating sense of humor, surely got a laugh out of it himself. In fact, folks noticed that a smile crept upon Lincoln's face, as he nestled into the saddle. "If there had been an accident," in the droll observation of eyewitness Henry Jacobs, "he certainly would not have had far to fall." During those moments, Lincoln probably wished he could have somehow squeezed in Old Bob, his faithful horse back in Washington, on the train he rode to Gettysburg.

Forming a plan that would get local, state and federal government officials, international diplomats, generals and military divisions, choirs, clergymen, college and seminary students and faculty, four military bands, hoards of press, and hundreds of other roaming, fidgety parade participants into place, with the President of the United States sitting on a horse in the eye of the human storm, in an egregious understatement, was no easy task.

The parade participants were organized into three separate groups: the "dignitaries" division, the "civil" division and the "military" division. Ward Lamon was in charge of the dignitaries division made up of President Lincoln and the other distinguished guests, all of whom were gathering in the public square. Because carriages for all dignitaries would have log-jammed the cemetery route, one hundred and thirty horses were brought into the public square for them to ride, an impressive equestrian display, in any century. The civil division of the parade would assemble on York Street; the military division on Carlisle Street.

Lamon knew that for the plan to work, they, in turn, had to work the plan. And work it, they did. During the next hour, President Lincoln stayed patiently on his horse, while Lamon, French and their cordon of black-suited, white-sashed parade marshals scrambled around like drovers, to herd the crowds and get the procession organized. The President, stuck on public display for nearly an hour on his horse, like a lofty statue in the town square, never complained.

At one point, a huge wave of humanity, in what was surely a disturbing breach of security in the eyes of bodyguard Lamon , surged forward, shoving themselves up against the President, who was still on horseback. The scene was ripe with chaos, an assassin's sweet spot to strike. Even then, the ever-congenial Lincoln continued to shake hands, reaching down from his horse to all who approached. Finally, the parade marshals, acting on Lamon's order, pushed the people back away from the President, in order to restore security and give Lincoln some breathing room. These ongoing, unwieldy undulations of the unsettled crowd delayed the start of the parade about an hour.

During this organized mayhem, a telegram was delivered to Lincoln, sent from Washington by Edwin M. Stanton, his Secretary of War, which gave the President some good news about the War and let him know that Tad was continuing to feel better. This telegram noticeably lifted the spirits of the President, and gave him an emotional boost for the taxing day ahead.

Finally, by 11:00 o'clock that morning, the multitude of parade participants had finally been shepherded into position. The grand and solemn cortege to the soldiers' cemetery would mercifully begin.

The Marine Band kicked off the parade by playing an inspirational march, which spooked the President's horse—again, bringing a smile to Lincoln's otherwise somber face, as young Liberty Hollinger remembered it. Liberty was amused that the excited horse under the President "pranced about in time to the music."

The *military division* of the parade, with its sharply-dressed color guard, its squadron of calvary, and its regiment of infantry and two batteries of artillery, would lead off. Joining with the troops of the U.S. Calvary, came two of the finest military bands in the country, the Fifth New York Artillery Band and the Second United Artillery Band. This military assembly was the same official chaperon that regularly accompanied funeral services of the highest-ranking officers in the U.S. military. It was a striking sight.

Next, the President and *dignitaries division* would fall into the procession. President Lincoln rode in a group with his three attending cabinet members, William H. Seward, John P. Usher and Montgomery Blair, and of course, the President's shadow, Ward Hill Lamon. All of the members of the Gettysburg Cemetery Commission from the various states were in this group. So were French and Italian diplomats. John Nicolay and John Hay rode steeds behind the President, with many other distinguished guests following them.

President Lincoln wore a new black suit, dramatically contrasted with a pair of white riding gloves (gauntlets) that covered his wrists. He carried his black stovepipe hat in his hand. Daniel Skelly, thought the President's face looked "lined and sad, [and] bore traces of tremendous worry the ordeal of the war had brought to him." One lady, recognizing that the President was deeply absorbed in the somberness of the occasion, wrote that "He seemed like the chief mourner."

And at other times, Lincoln would offer a smile and a nod, responding in-kind to the crowd's heartfelt and enthusiastic reception. Young eyewitness J. Howard Wertz (who would grow up to become a history professor), later wrote about that day, saying that on occasion, the "waves of warm, loud cheers from the crowd" caused the President's face to be "illuminated with smiles," and that it seemed "his heart was touched."

Annie Skelly could not get a clear view of the President from her crowded place on Baltimore Street, where she stood with her mother across from the Adams County Courthouse. Annie would remember that the crowds were so packed in the street, President Lincoln could barely pass through on his horse. A nice man next to her mother lifted her up, above the heads of the crowd, so she could see the President of the United States. With the unvarnished honesty of a seven-year-old, young Annie's first and most-lasting impression of the President in the setting of this historic occasion was that "He looked rather odd on such a small horse." Lincoln and little Annie, with her innocent candor and keen eye for spotting a humorous moment in an otherwise serious affair, would have likely made quick friends of each other, had they met. It was true. President Lincoln, mounted on his horse, stood out from the procession's skyline, like a lighthouse on the seashore.

But to most onlookers that gathered along the parade route that day, the President, often caricatured as a lumbering, physical oddity, with wild and unkempt hair, and a reputation for always fidgeting with the askewed appointments of his formal clothes, now seemed gallant and poised, more than was expected. Even Lincoln's equestrian skills were apparent. A reporter with the *Boston Journal* confessed: "I must do the President justice to say, his awkwardness, which is so often remarked, does not extend to his horsemanship."

All eyes were glued on the President, wherever he went in Gettysburg. The people watched him, intently. They seemed to notice every little thing he said, and every little thing he did. Most of all, they noticed that President Lincoln was carrying himself in a manner that was reassuring to them, a way that brought dignity to himself and the occasion.

At Lincoln's immediate right on horseback, rode his old friend William Seward. Although a man of noble and refined deportment, even in his rumpled, out-dated suits, Seward—like the "Emperor who had no clothes on"—was blissfully unaware that his pants were unceremoniously creeping up his shins like a flag being raised up a pole, displaying, as a young Marine lieutenant would recollect, a weave of "homemade gray socks" unbecoming of the stately event. This, may have been Seward's first "folly"—not the purchase of Alaska.

Last to join the parade would be the large *civic division*. This section of the parade was filled with fraternal groups and service organizations of all types. They were joined by students and faculty members from Pennsylvania College (now Gettysburg College) and its divinity school, along with delegations of important people from at least eighteen Northern states. Then, in a stirring display of spiritual and patriotic solidarity, hundreds of "unofficial" participants, men, women and children, many of them dressed in their boiled shirts and Sunday-go-to-meeting clothes, fastened themselves to the sternward end of the parade to make the pilgrimage to the cemetery. Many of them hoisted banners and proudly waved flags.

The crowds that had coagulated along the parade route were slenderized by those who rushed to lay claim to a favorable spot of ground at the soldiers' cemetery, less than a mile away. Josephine Roedel spotted "the mass of people who passed through the town in procession," and wisely skipped the parade, hurrying on ahead to the cemetery to stake out a place near the speaker's platform. Seminary student Michael Colver remembered, "long before the hour for the ceremonies arrived, the cemetery grounds were filled with eager spectators."

Of course, there would be some who chose not to ford the might river of people flowing into streets and roads leading to the cemetery. A Gettysburg schoolteacher, Sallie Myers, sized up her view of the situation with a curt entry in her diary, that read: "Saw the President and a great many distinguished men—but had little time to look at them. . . and then came home to work." Teenager Liberty Hollinger, who had, unknowingly, already immortalized herself in history by catching a glimpse of the President inside his room at the Wills house as he prepared for his Gettysburg Address, likewise decided to opt out of the ceremony at the soldiers' cemetery, as she put it, "because of the great crowd."

This melting pot of parade participants surged down Baltimore Street at a snail's pace. There was wailing of funeral music. Dirges played. Songs were sung. Flags, then, often referred to affectionately as "Old Glory," were fastened to most every house and business along the parade route. Flags that were hung on poles were flown at half-mast until noon, by order of Governor Curtin.

Along the congested edges of the parade, many folks, hats removed, would bow to the President. Some, wearing military caps, would touch two fingers to the brim in a salute of heartfelt connection to the President as he rode by, and Lincoln, in grateful return, would smile and give his patented salute consisting of a shy bow of the head and a touch of his hat. Others cheered and waved at President Lincoln. But even the cheers and jubilation the crowds bestowed upon their beloved President that day, were tempered by the solemnity of the occasion. Josephine Roedel, a former Gettysburger who had taken in all of the events, summed up the atmosphere of the day quite well: "Everything passed off very pleasantly, and scarcely one drunken man was to be seen."

It was, remarkably, an atmosphere in 180 degree contrast to the all-night party that had prevailed the evening before. No more of the yelling, better suited for a public wrestling match. No more of the revelry, more fit for a tavern. No more of the celebration, best befitting Independence Day. The people understood the occasion. This was not a political rally or triumphal march of celebrities. At its marrow, this event was a funeral.

The people at Gettysburg that day were proud of their brave soldiers; but still grieving for the dead. Inspired by a visit from their President; yet fearful about their own future. Joyful that the horrid first week of July was over; sad the War was not. This conflicted blend of sentiments and reactions of the people that day—thousands of them—that hedged every street and road, that crowded every corner and cornfield along the route to Cemetery Hill, that quietly wandered about the battlefields—was an amorphous display of the tortured range of emotions left over from the awful war that had washed over them.

Washed over them, like the Red Sea.

CHAPTER THIRTEEN

THE DEDICATION
CEREMONY BEGINS

*"Standing beneath this serene sky, overlooking these broad fields now
reposing from the labors of the waning year, the mighty Alleghenies
dimly towering before us, the graves of our brethren beneath our feet,
it is with hesitation that I raise my poor voice to break the eloquent
silence of God and Nature."*
—Edward Everett
Speaker's Platform
Cemetery Hill, Gettysburg
November 19, 1863

As FUNERAL MUSIC WAILED, THE GREAT PARADE MOVED NEARLY THREE-
quarters of a mile, laboriously up Baltimore Street, then along the
Emmitsburg Road, and finally down Taneytown Road that led to
Cemetery Hill. The short distance to the cemetery took the crowd
about a half hour. John Hay later wrote in his diary that the parade
moved in "an orphanly sort of way."

Artillery guns continuously clapped like thunder in the distance, as
though battles between Lee and Meade were still being fought just
down the road. This parade was a exposition of the people's reverently
restrained, yet patriotic pride in their Union, and how they felt about
their fathers, sons and brothers who gave all to save it.

Shortly after the eleven o'clock hour, the long procession from town
began to pour like cold molasses into the soldiers' cemetery, where
warm ovations and cheers welcomed the President and other dignitaries

that accompanied him. Federal soldiers briskly formed ceremonial lines and silently snapped a salute to the President of the United States as he rode by. The white-gloved return salute from Lincoln's lofty figure, perched atop his chestnut horse, could be seen, impressively, by most of the great crowd.

A cannon fired, in the mournfully slow rhythm of one shot each minute, as the President approached the speaker's platform on horseback. After the Commander-in-Chief was properly honored, the military closed formation around the platform, standing shoulder-to-shoulder as a wall of security for the assembled dignitaries.

Ward Lamon escorted the President towards the three-foot-high speaker's platform. As Lincoln climbed the steps of the platform, the vast audience grew quiet. No applause. No cheers. All hats were removed. There was "perfect silence," the *Washington Morning Chronicle* wrote. J. Howard Wert, standing near the stage that day, said that Lincoln's reception as he mounted the speaker's platform "was one of respect and profound silence." The people were mindful that this was the most sacred and solemn of all human events—the consecration of a burial place.

As the silence broke, David Wills and Ward Lamon, who earlier in the week had carefully planned the seating arrangements for the three-foot-high wooden stage, began ushering the platform dignitaries to their pre-assigned seats. Thirty chairs, in three rows of ten, were positioned on the crowded platform. When Lincoln saw the many dignitaries expecting a seat on the platform, and the modest number of chairs, he may have mentally drawn upon his favorite line about patronage jobs— "they're too many pigs for the teats!"

President Lincoln would be guided to a seat in the front center of the platform. Was the President placed in a distinguished chair? Hardly. A reporter from the *Cincinnati Daily Gazette* wrote that Lincoln was seated in "an old, dingy, uncushioned settee."

Sitting close around the President were Seward, Nicolay and Hay, David Wills, and eventually, the keynote speaker Edward Everett, who had arrived earlier at the cemetery by carriage but not yet taken his place on stage. Seward would sit on the President's left, Everett on his right.

Military units would peel off the procession and assemble to the left of the audience, with ladies from the processional moving towards what was intended to be a reserved section for them on the right. However, at least one cramped, female eyewitness would complain that no such arrangements were available for the ladies; the overwhelming crowd likely disable the plan. This special seating near the rostrum for women, at least by design, was surely a demonstration of the high admiration for the female folk of Gettysburg who had sacrificed and done so much in the crisis.

Every plank nailed on the 12-by-20-foot speaker's platform would be loaded to the rim with a cornucopia of notables and luminaries. They included Lincoln's other two Cabinet members, Usher and Blair; Lamon and French; Henry Wise and his wife, Charlotte Everett Wise; William Saunders, the land architect who designed the soldiers' cemetery; Governor Andrew Curtin and governors of many other Northern states, along with military generals, congressmen, members of the Gettysburg Cemetery Commission, and foreign diplomats. A table was placed behind the speaker's platform for newspaper correspondents and journalists. The bands invited to perform in the ceremony, four of them, were arranged forefront of the stage.

Thousands of people, "an immense crowd" as the *New York Times* would describe it, scrambled and jockeyed for a spot, filling the space in front and sides of the ceremonial platform like a sea of seurat dots. "Oh, what a jam it was," later wrote Philip Bikle, a student at the local college. "I have never been so wedged in a crowd in my life," he would recall. Many of those on the distant, outer fringes of this ponderous gathering of people who could not see or hear, simply gave up and wandered through the battlefields.

While the colossal crowd settled into place, Ward Lamon had to temporarily leave the platform, perhaps to check on the keynote speaker, Edward Everett, who still had not arrived on stage. The program would not start without his presence. During the lull, Benjamin French signaled for Birgfield's Band to begin playing the opening dirge, *Homage d'un Heroes*. This talented band from Philadelphia, which had entertained the cadre of dignitaries that rode to Gettysburg on the Governor's train, set the tone for the ceremonies with this somber, beautifully-played introductory music.

After the dignitaries and distinguished guests assigned to the speaker's platform had filled their seats, and Edward Everett arrived a few minutes later, the Grand Marshal of the event, U.S. Marshal Ward Lamon, approached the front of the speaker's platform. The somber music subsided. The anticipation was over.

At last. The "Great Occasion," as people would come to call it, had begun.

First, Lamon would read aloud the letters of regret sent from some of the big names who had been invited but were unable to attend (for either real or invented reasons): First, there was Lieutenant General Winfield Scott, the brilliant military strategist and war hero, who months before, helped to guard Washington, D.C. after the fall of Fort Sumter, and conceived the famous "Anaconda Plan" to slowly strangle off the Confederacy. The octogenarian commander, whose steely will to fight had long ago outlasted his aching, ponderously large, 6 ft. 5 inch body, would explain in a short telegram sent to David Wills and read aloud, that "on account of infirmities," he could not attend. General Scott's old age, obesity and crippling case of gout, no doubt, made the trip too difficult.

Then there was the long and laborious repine of Major General George G. Meade, the victorious commander at the Battle of Gettysburg. Meade, with deep-cut carpetbags hanging under his eyes, was known by soldiers (behind his back, of course) as "Old Snapping Turtle," for his less-than-handsome features and explosive temper. (Still, Meade was widely respected by his military peers.) In his public letter, General Meade expressed a more-pressing need to remain combat-ready in the field with his military forces: "This army has duties to perform which will not admit of its being represented on [this] occasion." He then expressed gratitude to the people "for your tender care of the heroic dead, and for your patriotic zeal."

Whether or not Meade could have carved out only a few days away from his troops to participate in the ceremony, is debatable. But his decision not to attend was probably for the best. It certainly avoided an uncomfortable rendezvous on the speaker's platform between Meade and Lincoln. As General Meade's regrets were read to the crowd, Lincoln's own "regrets" were likely rekindled, as he reflected on last summer, right after the Battle of Gettysburg, when Meade squandered what Lincoln referred to as a "golden opportunity" to finish off the defeated General Robert E. Lee and possibly end the War. Meade chose not to pursue Lee's badly depleted and crippled army, that after its defeat, was strung out for miles and became trapped beside the swollen waters of the Potomac. Meade's military lassitude had left Lincoln burning-hot back in July, and perhaps, a few smoldering coals still remained.

And there were the regrets sent for the absence of Secretary of the U.S. Treasury, Salmon P. Chase, who wrote: "It disappoints me greatly to find that imperative public duties make it impossible for me to present." Really? "Impossible" to be there? "Impossible," even though his boss, the President of the United States, had found time to attend, and personally asked him to come? When Lincoln heard Chase's "impossible" letter read, it is easy to imagine one word, popular at the time, popping into Lincoln's head . . . *"hornswoggle"* . . . the twenty-first century translation: a cock-and-bull story.

Actually, Secretary Chase was busy back in Washington stacking up dry kindling underneath the President, which he planned to set fire about election time. He despised Secretary Seward, and perhaps was absent because he did not want to ride in Seward's company to Gettysburg. Chase, who was smart, intensively devoted to his career, his religion and his family, did a brilliant job of keeping the Federal Treasury afloat despite the colossus costs of the War. But he was also a vain, pompous man who had a streak of hubris as long and wide as the Potomac (Chase had his portrait put on the one dollar bill for a while). Chase hoped to incinerate Lincoln's chances at being reelected in 1864, because he had convinced himself that he was imminently more qualified than Lincoln to be President. Despite his excuse of "imperative public duties" back in Washington, Chase was somehow finding the spare time to brazenly release "scandalous reports" from the Treasury Department to slander and embarrass Mary Lincoln, as though she didn't already have enough pressing down on her.

The piercing-eyed, impeccably dressed Chase was appropriately named, it seems, for he spent a good portion of his political life "chasing" after the office of the presidency. He suffered an unquenchable thirst to become the President of the United States, and hoped to be elected in the next year's election. In a story that is likely apocryphal but accurately captures Chase's obsessive presidential ambitions, Carl Sandburg relates the story of Chase preening and bowing in front of a mirror, mumbling over and over to himself, "President Chase . . . President Chase."

Interestingly, Lincoln's trusted friend and tenaciously-driven Secretary of War, the surly, stubborn, workaholic Edwin M. Stanton, sporting a beard that resembled a clump of wisteria vine, did not make the Gettysburg trip, either. He elected to stay in Washington, conspicuously, to catch up on administrative chores, and inconspicuously, perhaps, to keep a sharp eye on the disloyal Chase.

After these customary announcements, music was again played to regain quiet attention among the bristling audience. Suddenly, the famed Methodist preacher and Chaplain of the House of Representatives, Thomas A. Stockton, along with the ceremonial speaker for the event, Edward Everett, who rode together by carriage to the cemetery, were ushered across the speaker's platform.

A tidal wave of quietude rolled over the audience. All sound melted away. Heads, again, bowed. Hats were removed. There was reverential silence.

Reverend Stockton, described by one correspondent as having the austere and righteous appearance of someone who had "just risen from the tomb to invoke the God of nations and liberty," moved to the front of the speaker's platform and began to read an elegant and moving invocation prayer held in his hand. This was the era that embraced grand and opulent oratory And the ancient Chaplain would not disappoint:

"O God our Father, for the sake of Thy Son our Savior, inspire us with Thy spirit, and sanctify us to the right fulfillment of the duties of this occasion.

. . . In behalf of all humanity, whose ideal is divine, whose first memory is Thine image lost, and whose last hope is Thine image restored; and especially of our own such nation, whose history has been so favored, whose position is so peerless, whose mission is so sublime, and whose future is so attractive; we thank Thee for the unspeakable patience of Thy compassion and the exceeding greatness of Thy loving kindness. . .

As the trees are not dead, though their foliage is gone, so our heroes are not dead, though their forms have fallen. In their proper personality, they are all with Thee. And the spirit of their example is here. It fills the air, it fills our hearts.

And, long as time shall last, it will hover in these skies, and rest upon this landscape; and the pilgrims of our own land, and from all lands, will thrill with its inspiration and increase and confirm their devotion to liberty, religion and God."

These words would press tears from the eyes of almost all who heard. Including Everett. The President would wipe tears from his eyes, too. As the Reverend concluded with *The Lord's Prayer* . . . **"Our Father, who art in Heaven"** . . . the people instantly, intuitively, joined in together, every word. And then . . .

Twenty thousand Amens.

Most in the audience who heard Reverend Stockton's lengthy invocation were deeply affected by it. A reporter with the *New York Times* called it "touching and beautiful." The *Philadelphia Press* would report: "There was scarcely a dry eye in all that vast assemblage." Lincoln's assistant secretary John Hay, however, thought the good chaplain's prayer went on a little too long. Hay, with his wry and sometimes irreverent sense of humor, wrote in his diary: "Mr. Stockton made a prayer which thought it was an oration."

But the mood of Gettysburg had changed. Religious people who had been appalled by the wild party atmosphere of the night before, were appeased. Reverence had replaced revelry. All was as it needed to be. This . . . was the reason for their pilgrimage to Gettysburg.

Bowed heads raised. Hats returned from hand to head. Now the Marine Band would play the favorite hymn of the day, *Old Hundred*, as the crowd joined in singing the beloved Doxology put to words by

Thomas Ken in the seventeenth century, and still sang in churches all across America, today:

> "Praise God from whom all blessings flow;
> Praise Him all creatures here below;
> Praise Him above ye heav'nly host;
> Praise Father, Son, and Holy Ghost.
> A-men."

The great old hymn helped the people regain their collective composure, that had been lost in the tears of Reverend Stockton's moving invocation.

As the noon hour approached, and after the Marine Band played, it was time for Benjamin French to introduce the featured speaker of the day—the headliner everyone had came to hear. He was, as folks commonly put it back then, the "biggest toad in the puddle." This speaker had an oratory vitae unmatched, anywhere. He was the heir-apparent to the legendary Daniel Webster as the great American speechmaker. This vaunted man on the speaker's platform at Gettysburg had certainly earned his accolades. He was a former governor, congressman, senator, secretary of state, Harvard president, minister to Great Britain, and professor of Greek studies. He had been gushingly referred to as the "master of eloquence" by Ralph Waldo Emerson and "the golden-mouthed orator" by the great Daniel Webster, himself. Hands down, he was the most famous orator in the country.

He was the incomparable Edward Everett.

The silver-haired Everett, even at age sixty-nine, was still a rock star of his day. He commanded speaking fees that made him a lot of money. Although modern dollar equivalencies are very difficult, if not impossible, to calculate with precision, a scholarly estimation (based upon Consumer Price Index [CPI] comparisons of 1860 and modern figures) would put a value on Everett's earnings from public speeches, during his peak, at more than $400,000.00 a year in today's money.

Despite his fame, education and wealth, as a person, Everett was a good and decent man. And a generous patriot for his country. In the previous decade, Everett had raised over $69,000.00 in speaker's royalties (a value approaching two million dollars in modern-day currency), by making 129 speeches all over the north-eastern part of the country on "The Character of George Washington."

Everett would donate all of these speech profits, every cent, even refusing to deduct his travel expenses from the speech earnings, for restoration of George Washington's home and burial place at Mount Vernon that had fallen into a shameful state of disrepair and ruin. This tour-de-force of Everett speeches, alone, would generate one-half of the money needed to fix Mount Vernon.

And at Gettysburg, Everett made the usual rock star "back-stage" demands. For one thing, Everett, who suffered in equal and abundant measure from a healthy ego and bad bladder, required that a two room "convenience shed" be specially built and installed for him, which was essentially a tent fastened to the rear of the speaker's platform.

One side of the partitioned tent would allow Everett the much-needed opportunity to relieve himself, and the other side the privacy for a final vocal warm-up, before embarking on the no-return journey of his taxing, two hour oration. (Unfortunately, Everett's shed was not divided into two sections as he requested, making it essentially a one-room outhouse, from which he had to evict at least a dozen nosey, star-struck platform guests so he could have a few moments of solitude to do his business and get his game face on.) It was from this canvas vestibule that Everett, at the beginning of the program, would emerge and stride across the platform, about thirty minutes late, like Caesar crossing the Rubicon, escorted by no less than a convoy of governors, led by Marshall Lamon and David Wills. Everett was seated on the front row of distinguished guests, along with President Lincoln.

As Everett belatedly approached his seat on the stage that day, about half past the noon hour, all of the distinguished guests on the platform, including the President of the United States, rose to their feet. All hats were instantly removed. Make no mistake about it. Edward Everett had clout. David Wills had originally wanted the Gettysburg cemetery dedication to be held on October 23, 1863, preferring a milder, more pleasant month for this huge outdoor event. Fierce Pennsylvania winters can arrive in November. But Everett needed more time to prepare. "It is . . . wholly out of my power," Everett wrote to David Wills on

September 26th, "to make the requisite preparation by the 23rd of October." As Everett described it, he wanted time to prepare a speech that would present a "full . . . narrative" of the three-day Battle of Gettysburg, and expound upon the Battle's importance to the survival of the country.

Everett also preferred the inspirational ambiance of speaking over the graves of the fallen soldiers, commenting that he felt his speech would be "more effective" if spoken over the soldiers' "remains." And Everett was right; to truly dedicate a cemetery, the sacred words must be spoken over the honored dead. Postponing the dedication ceremony until November would allow time to begin moving at least some of the soldiers' remains from the battlefields for reinterment in the soldiers' cemetery—the honored place that would be consecrated by Everett's oration. The bottom line was this: Edward Everett, the celebrity speaker and linchpin of the entire program, needed more time. So he got it. To accommodate Everett, Wills pushed the date forward almost a month, to November 19th.

Edward Everett, who sometimes referred to himself as "EE," took speech preparation serious. John Quincy Adams would privately exalt in his diary that Everett's speeches were "among the best ever delivered in the Country." His orations were his claim to fame. Even for an old pro like Everett, this speech he would deliver at Gettysburg was a high-profile, big-time speech. The Super Bowl of oration. Like the Golden Age of the ancient Athenians, Everett believed there was no higher calling than to give an oration over the graves of soldiers who had bravely died in battle. The historical significance of the Greek statesman Pericles giving his famous funeral oration over the Athenian soldiers who had died in battle, was not lost on Everett. This occasion demanded a master speech be given by a master speaker.

Weeks earlier, Everett, like a franchise athlete at the professional level, began an intense regimen of speech preparation by consulting with Professor Michael Jacobs who taught at Pennsylvania College, the staff of General George Meade, who was the victorious Union commander at the Battle of Gettysburg, and also Colonel John B. Buchalder, the noted Gettysburg historian, to learn details of the great battle. He canvassed the country for articles, maps and reports that would nourish the content of his speech. And as late as November 16th, just three days before he would deliver his speech, Everett even made an extended visit to the battlefields at Gettysburg, to bring a three-dimensional quality to his speech.

Highly revered speakers like Edward Everett, the oratory pros of their day, wanted full command of their subject matter. They dedicated much research and preparation time to their speeches, time often comparable to the preparation of a college-level thesis.

After composing his speech, Everett even had a Boston newspaper, the *Boston Daily Advertiser*, set it to type, which he received in proof form on November 14th (five days before he would give his speech), and then disseminated copies of his speech to the press and others in advance of the Gettysburg ceremonies. Everett wanted his speech, as soon as he delivered it at Gettysburg, to be ready-made for good newspaper copy—and, as Everett bluntly put it, he did not want his speech to be "mutilated and travestied by the reporters."

That day, November 19th, 1863, superstar Edward Everett would precede Lincoln by unfurling a two hour oratorical fireworks show. It would be a cinemascopic speech exploding with dramatic voice inflections, and sparkling with rehearsed gestures, vivid imagery and elegant words.

But Everett's speech was not just a showy exposition of public speaking skills. And he was no blowhard, pleonastic speaker as some would later paint him, in an effort to portray Everett's two hour speech as an overinflated, windy foil to the greatness of Lincoln's short two minute speech. All one has to do is to read Everett's oration, to know differently. Everett's speech at Gettysburg was a lucid, serious and well-organized dissertation on the ebb and flow of one of the most epic battles to ever take place on the North American continent.

Everett's opening words to his oration, unscripted and extemporaneous, would be splendidly rich and awe-inspiring:

> "Standing beneath this serene sky, overlooking these broad fields now reposing from the labors of the waning year, the mighty Alleghenies dimly towering before us, the graves of

our brethren beneath our feet, it is with hesitation that I raise my poor voice to break the eloquent silence of God and Nature."

These palatial words, bringing together the living and the martyred soldiers together in the spiritual temple of the beautiful natural surroundings, must have especially pleased the architectural prophet of the rural cemetery cause, William Saunders, as he listened from his honored seat on the speaker's platform.

In a "sweet, clear voice" that rifled through the huge audience before him, as eyewitness Henry Jacobs described Everett's vocal talent, and with passionate imagery, the great orator ushered the audience through each day of the Gettysburg battles, each site of human combat and courage: Seminary Ridge and Peach Orchard; Culp and Wolf Hill; Round Top and Little Round Top—"humble" places, as Everett called them, "henceforward dear and famous." Then, with an august resonance of voice that ran chills up the spines of the multitude, Edward Everett promised that ". . . no lapse of time, no distance of space, shall cause [these battle-sites] to be forgotten."

Conjuring up visions of Ancient Greece out of the Battle of Gettysburg, Everett, with his piercing black eyes and snow-white hair, spoke of the fallen heroes of the legendary Battle of Marathon, the epic battle which forced the Persians out of Greece, clearing the way for the birth of Western Civilization. At one point, Everett quoted the Duke of Wellington, telling the great crowd that "next to a defeat, the saddest thing was a victory." Heads nodded in affirmation. Tears, so many of them that day, were living proof of Everett's words.

As Everett waxed eloquent about the battle-sites of the "Titanic drama," he would, with grand strokes of his arms, point towards the breathtaking theatre of landscape that encircled the speaker's platform. Everett looked and spoke like a President. Maybe more "presidential" than the President of the United States, himself. Some even referred to him as "President Everett," from his former position at Harvard University. A man of "apostolic fame," one enamored reporter described him.

At times, Everett would gaze broadly at the audience, and at other chosen moments, look back towards the President, as he spoke. Lincoln would, during such eye encounters, nod his head in affirmation of Everett's words. One person in the audience recalled that Lincoln listened pensively to Everett, keeping "his eyes full upon the speaker," with the President sometimes propping his chin in the palm of his hand, like Rodin's sculpture of *The Thinker*, as he focused on the silver-haired orator. At one point, Everett inadvertently referred to General Meade as General Lee, upon which President Lincoln could be heard to quickly say "Meade," respectfully correcting the speaker.

BUT AS THE conclusion of Everett's speech grew near, the President's thoughts turned to his own. People in close proximity of the speaker's platform noticed that towards the end of Everett's speech, Lincoln put on his glasses, and then removed a paper from his vest pocket, which he read, intently—and moments later, returned it to his coat. "The President became nervous as Everett was drawing to a close," recalled eyewitness Henry Jacobs. "His mind was not on what Mr. Everett was saying," Jacobs added, "but on his own speech."

Incredibly, all of Everett's speech came from memory. Although Everett had a reading copy of his speech on the table that sat next to the speaker, he rarely, if ever, relied upon it. Very few speakers, even today, could commit so much information to memory, and deliver it so eloquently, so beautifully, as did Edward Everett that day.

Everett's speech, as he delivered it to the live audience, was not a verbatim match of the advanced-copy speech he had distributed to the press several days earlier. Everett later admitted in his diary (being a little hard on himself, it seems) that he forgot some parts. Everett had also found it necessary to condense his speech that day, because, as "happens generally" he later wrote, he decided on the platform to elaborate on "several thoughts" that had popped into his head, thereby lengthening his oration. But no one in the audience knew the difference. Although a few folks standing at the hard-to-hear, outer-most perimeters of the great crowd had drifted away by the end of Everett's oration, most thought it was sublime speech-making. And it was.

Bringing his grand oration to a *fortissimo* conclusion, Everett proclaims in his final words to the audience:

". . . as we bid farewell to the dust of these martyr heroes, that wheresoever throughout the civilized world the accounts of this great warfare are read, and down to the latest period of recorded time, in the glorious annals of our common country, there will be no higher page than that which relates . . . *the Battles of Gettysburg.*"

Edward Everett was at the top of his game. Everett received a steady breeze of enthused but reverent applause from the audience and returned to his seat on the speaker's platform.

Immediately, the President rose to his feet to compliment him, warmly pumping Everett's hand. "I am more than gratified," Lincoln said . . . "I am grateful to you." Lincoln was, in fact, very pleased, and equally relieved, with the content of Everett's speech. Although the President had likely read the printed version of Everett's speech, which was released a few days earlier, he may have privately worried about what Everett would say from the speaker's stand. Lincoln's concern would have been that Everett might stray from his text or add something to his speech that was in conflict with the message Lincoln had crafted into his Gettysburg Address.

As Everett concluded his speech, Lincoln surely felt a wave of relief, being discharged of these worries. Now the President knew that he and Everett were both singing out of the same hymnal—the preservation of the Union, above all else. And, on a personal level, they both agreed that the survival or destruction of America hinged on the outcome of the Civil War—and with it, the ideal of republican self-government. At Gettysburg that day, Lincoln's and Everett's beliefs were melded as one. Now, the President had only his own speech to worry about.

Everett had put the Civil War into world context. With his dazzling eloquence and mesmerizing voice, he had made the Battle of Gettysburg as epochal as the ancient Greek battles that were fought at the dawn of civilization. "Magnificent oration," proclaimed the *Washington Daily Chronicle.*

Twenty thousand people, transfixed.

The President's own cabinet secretaries, John G. Nicolay and John Hay, who adored the President and were like sons to Lincoln, thought

Everett's speech had been nothing short of magnificent. Maybe his finest speech-making, ever. Young John Hay, a man with a sarcastic streak in him and not easily bedazzled by grand speech-making, was quite impressed with Everett's two hour oration. Hay glowingly wrote in his diary that "Mr. Everett spoke as he always does, perfectly." Benjamin B. French, whose poem, put to music, would be performed next on the program, later wrote that Everett left "his audience in tears many times during his masterly effort." French further extolled that Everett's speech "could not be surpassed by mortal man."

Everett was totally exhausted. A blanket was placed across his quivering shoulders. A two hour speech in the open November air, bareheaded, left some in concern. He had nothing left. What no one knew, is that he had suffered a stroke the previous year. His health was steeply waning. No wonder he needed a privacy tent to gather himself, physically and mentally. His loving daughter "Charlie," had insisted she sit on the platform of men, close to her ailing father. Lincoln would see that it was done, for which Everett was deeply grateful. In little more than a year, Everett would be gone, buried at Mount Auburn. He, too, had passed through the portal of Gettysburg immortality.

Edward Everett had done exactly what he was invited to do, and he had done it, superbly. He had transformed the Battle of Gettysburg into a colossal inspirational event. It was more than an oration, it was an aria. Everett at Gettysburg, was Pavarotti at Turin, performing "Nessun dorma."

But one more presentation remained on the program, before the President would speak. It was the hymn proudly composed by Benjamin French.

Early in the planning stages of the Gettysburg ceremonies, David Wills diligently tried to secure the appearance of one of the most prominent poets of the day to compose a poem "to be sung or read" for this very moment in the ceremony. Such occasions can be extraordinarily moving, with as when Robert Frost, rather than read, "said" his poem *The Gift Outright* at John F. Kennedy's presidential inauguration.

Wills had invited the distinguished likes of poets John Greenleaf Whittier and William Cullen Bryant and even the renowned Henry Wadsworth Longfellow, who was already a literary legend in his own day. Longfellow was author of the famed long poems, *Song of Hiawatha* and *Paul Revere's Ride*. Longfellow, who was a professor of languages at Harvard (Everett's old academic haunt) and had a son serving in the military, flirted with the idea of coming. Some newspapers even prematurely reported of Longfellow's plans to be at Gettysburg. Longfellow was, however, too busy, apparently composing his famous anthology, *Tales of a Wayside Inn*. Ultimately, all of these poets declined their invitations.

Wills was quite disappointed. He wanted a famous New England poet, a poet laureate, to read at the ceremony. Wills wanted the program, as the *Philadelphia Inquirer* would raise the bar of expectations in describing it, to be "one of the most imposing and interesting occasions ever witnessed in the United States." The cemetery dedication program was, indeed, an ambitious undertaking. History has proved that the event more than lived up to its aspired billing. But, alas, no distinguished poets would lend their talents to the Gettysburg ceremony. Wills had learned that the great bards are sometimes temperamental and idiosyncratic folk, often unamused and even annoyed at what they see as the public patterings of politicians.

To fill this void in the program, Wills desperately turned for help to Lincoln's cabinet. There were no famous poets in Lincoln's cabinet, but there was the versatile and self-assured Benjamin B. French, the Commissioner of Public Buildings. French, who looked like a Victorian-era novelist with his bulging waves of side hair, and his thick, gray, bristle-like sideburns that swooped forward like bicycle handles towards his chin, was, by his very nature, a man of alacrity, who was always eager to please.

French, had already experienced some fair-to-middling success as a published poet. In fact, to ingratiate himself with the First Family and sweeten his chances at landing the job over Federal buildings, a few months back, French had composed a long, silken poem for the pleasure of Mrs. Lincoln. To his lasting credit, French accepted the intimidating, time-crunched assignment of crafting a poem for the dedication of the soldiers' cemetery. And he would come through. While in Gettysburg with Ward Lamon the week before the ceremony, doing advance work for the President's trip, French had stayed up all night on

November 12th, composing a hymn-like poem of five stanzas, which he titled the *Consecration Hymn*.

Put to the music of Wilson G. Horner, and beautifully chanted by the twelve voices of the Baltimore Glee Club just before the President of the United States would speak, the patriotic and spiritual words of the *Consecration Hymn* would bless the hallowed cemetery and pierce the hearts of all who heard:

> "Tis holy ground—
> This spot where in their graves
> We place our country's braves,
> Who fell in freedom's holy cause
> Fighting for liberties and laws.
> Let tears abound.
>
> Here let them rest—
> And summer's heat and winter's cold
> Shall glow and freeze above this mold,
> A thousand years shall pass away
> A nation still shall mourn this clay,
> Which now is blest."

In the early stages of the ceremony, the somber crowd had suppressed its cheers and applause for the day's speakers and program participants. Quietude prevailed. Deep reverence for the purpose of the occasion inspired it so. In fact, when Edward Everett was first introduced, one either overzealous or under-civilized fellow (that one journalist referred to in his newspaper article as "Mr. Idiot."), belted out a cat-call to give the famous Everett the traditional "three cheers"—and was met with icy cold and indignant silence by the audience. But at this point in the program, the performance of French's *Consecration Hymn* had lifted up the funeral-like ambiance of the entire occasion, instantly inspiring a more joyful and uplifted mood among the crowd for the remainder of the program.

Emotions pent up since the mournful walk to the cemetery could, finally, be released. A gale of applause crescendoed from the audience. Tears did abound.

It was, truly, holy ground.

Afterward, there was the conversational rumble of twenty thousand people, moving about and stretching their legs between program events. Tears were wiped from eyes; women, unashamedly with their handkerchiefs, the men, more covertly, with the back of their hands. They were settling in for what they expected to be the next long speech.

It was approaching the two o'clock hour in the afternoon sun.

Suddenly, Cemetery Hill turned quiet as a church service. All eyes were now on the speaker's platform. It was time to hear from their President. Ward Hill Lamon, the grand marshal for the dedication ceremony, shouts out in a piercing, trumpet-like voice . . .

"Ladies and Gentlemen . . . the President of the United States."

A warm and enthusiastic applause follows. . .

The doorway to historical immortality had just been opened for President Abraham Lincoln, who just fifty-four years earlier, was born on a cold, stormy Sunday morning into poverty and obscurity, lying on a pallet of corn shucks and bear skins, in a dirt-floored log cabin built on land of questionable title in Hardin County, Kentucky.

Like the convergence of the Anderson and Ohio waters that had, forever, shaped the course of Abraham Lincoln's early life, now, at Gettysburg, the man and the moment were at confluence, to shape history.

CHAPTER FOURTEEN

A TWO-MINUTE SPEECH; THE BIRTH OF APOTHEOSIS

*". . . that this nation, under God, shall
have a new birth of freedom . . ."*
—President Abraham Lincoln
Speaker's Platform
Cemetery Hill, Gettysburg
November 19, 1863

ABRAHAM LINCOLN HAD ALREADY REMOVED HIS STOVEPIPE HAT FROM his lap, placing it on the planks beneath his seat; fastened around it, a black mourning band in remembrance of his son, Willie.

The tall, lanky frame of the President arises, steps forward a stride or two, and stands at the front of the speaker's platform. A restless twenty thousand people, who had been on their feet nearly three hours, are utterly silent. "The stillness was very noticeable," eyewitness Philip Bikle recalled. For those who had only seen the President in a earlier speech or picture, he looked more aged, more gaunt. His dark, sun-browned face, weary and angular. His blue-gray eyes, sunken.

The pinched contours of Lincoln's tired and inconsolable face carried the marks of his origin, and his journey. Standing in place, the carriage of the President was mildly hunched at the shoulders, leaning forward ever so slightly. He was only fifty-four. Yet, the daily groping for solutions to the War, the bloodletting, the splitting asunder of families and the country, the death of his boys Eddie and Willie, Mary's inescapable struggles with money and melancholy, the endless demands of people and the presidency had left the man worn thin, and hollowed out.

220

This was someone whose face and figure had been chiseled out by life.

Before rising to speak, Lincoln had sat on the front row of the speaker's platform for nearly three hours, wedged between Everett and Seward, where he had listened intently to hymns and prayers, the repertoires of the Marine Band and Baltimore Glee Club singers, and eventually the two-hour oration of Edward Everett.

Abraham Lincoln felt a knot of anxiety in his stomach about the moment that has just arrived. Surely, he was strung tight as a bone corset. There was so much at stake. And it was finally his turn to speak.

What Lincoln felt that day, standing before the mass of humanity at Cemetery Hill, was more than sympathy. His feelings came from the quintessence of empathy. Above all else . . . if nothing else . . . Lincoln understood. He understood how they felt. Why they were there. After all, grief and sadness had been his lifelong companions.

That day, there would come no platitudes from the President of "I feel your pain," a hackneyed phrase in contemporary politics. There was no need. He lived their pain. Abraham Lincoln knew, on an intimate, personal level, the searing pain of inconsolable human loss. His own heart had been swallowed by grief. For months, Lincoln had been haunted by the tears of mothers, widows and orphans, many who now stood before him, who had lost loved ones in what seemed to be an endless war.

Even Pulitzer Prize historian Richard Hofstader, who was by no stretch of the imagination a fan of political icons and often a harsh critic of Lincoln, saw this unique quality in the sixteenth President, writing that "Lincoln was moved by the wounded and dying men . . . as no one in a place of power can afford to be." As Hofstader poignantly put it, "For him [Lincoln], it was impossible to drift into the habitual callousness of the sort of officialdom that sees men only as pawns to be shifted here and there and 'expended' at the will of others."

And the President's face would divulge the realness of his understanding. Charles Young, a twelve-year-old in the audience that day at Gettysburg, later said of President Lincoln, "I remember distinctly his grave and solemn appearance as he . . . faced the audience."

Everett had concluded his magnificent speech. The great orator had no peers, Lincoln must have thought. And deservedly so. After hearing the grandeur of Edward Everett's speech, Lincoln may have even wondered, if only for a fleeting moment, whether he should make a speech at all, at Gettysburg. After all, folded inside his vest pocket was a speech made up of less than 300 words.

Lincoln slowly rose from his chair, "like a telescope drawing," someone was overheard to say. He had already put on his reading glasses. As the President approached front stage from where he would speak, platform boards creaked and popped, overheard by some in the sudden crowd silence. Two pieces of paper, folded, are pulled from his vest pocket. The pages are unwrapped. Lincoln looks up at the vast ocean of faces before him. From the platform where he stood, the President could see the breathtaking vista of the Gettysburg landscape—a perfect and poignant place, a natural lyceum, to deliver his words.

It was also a sad and tragic place. The cemetery was still a work in progress. On that day of the November 19th ceremony, the bodies of 1,188 soldiers had been re-buried there. Another two-thirds of them still awaited their turn at a final resting place; their interments would have to wait until spring, after the hard winter ground thawed.

Fifteen-year-old George Gitt, who got a jump on the crowd and shoehorned himself underneath the speaker's platform, recalled that the "flutter and motion of the crowd ceased the moment the President was on his feet."

From the speaker's platform, Lincoln could see fresh, newly-dug graves in the cemetery, laid out in perfect symmetry; some occupied, others still vacant. The pallid warmth of the late November sun made the faint smells of that fresh dirt, evanescent. Coffins were there too, patiently waiting on their grim delivery. That hill of dirt spread out before Lincoln's eyes was not the exquisitely manicured landscape of green flora that the Soldiers' National Cemetery at Gettysburg is today. That day, Cemetery Hill was a brown, grassless, trampled-down excavation site.

Near the front of the speaker's platform stood about fifty veterans who survived the Battle of Gettysburg, all of them wounded, limbs missing, some propped up on crutches. Lincoln had, on several occasions during the program, glanced over at this group of veterans. The

President looked into their eyes, many of them filled with tears. Eyes are the windows of the soul. What President Lincoln saw there, and what he saw all around him that day on Cemetery Hill, would inspire awe and reverence within. And change him forever.

President Lincoln first took a deep, absorbing look at the words on the papers in his hand, and then began to speak, trying to loosen his vocal chords and suppress the insecurities he felt about the speech he finished only a few hours earlier and made of so few words.

This was Lincoln's opportune moment; one that would likely never pass his way again. Before these thousands who would hear his voice, and the thousands more who would hear his voice converted to the written word in newspaper and telegraph, Lincoln knows he must give purpose and meaning to the blood and brutality of the War. Yes, he must honor the bravery and sacrifices of the dead. But somehow, he must also redefine the purpose of the War in the public's mind. He must make sense, out of the senseless.

He must bind the country together.

This time, Lincoln would not lock his eyes on the copy of the speech in his hand, but looked up, straight into the eyes of the people—thousands of them—who were looking for solace and hope in a time of great uncertainty. Unknowingly, he was about to step into the breach of history.

In a treble, stentorian voice, echoing the biblical sounds and rhythms of Verse Ten of the 90th Psalm which describes the life span of man, President Abraham Lincoln would begin by returning the people to 1776 . . . to the BIRTH of America . . .

"Four score and seven years ago . . .

By the time he spoke at Gettysburg on November 19, 1863, Abraham Lincoln had carried the weight of political history on his shoulders for many years. When he needed them most, Lincoln was reaching back to the words of his serenaded speech at the White House lawn on the hot night of July 7, 1863; and further back to the words he spoke in Chicago on July 10, 1858; and even further back to the words he spoke in Peoria on October 16, 1854. Once again, he was reaching back to the Declaration of Independence.

On this very day, Lincoln had honed to precision his long-held thoughts about the meaning of the Declaration of Independence, and the human experiment that spawned the American Revolution. The birth of America was not the inauguration of George Washington; nor was it the signing of the Constitution. America was born out of the frozen mud, blood and fire of the Revolutionary War—the war of "four score and seven years ago." The defining moment in America's history. Now, another war—the Civil War—had become the next revolution. And the next defining moment, in American history.

Lincoln's universalist interpretation of the Declaration of Independence, and his infusion of its core principles into the Gettysburg Address, was an ambitious attempt to expand freedom and equality to all humankind, not a right to be enjoyed only by white males. The words of the Declaration of Independence, in Lincoln's view, washed over people of all skin colors and creeds, like baptismal waters.

Thomas Jefferson's canonized words in the Declaration's Preamble had once seemed almost supernatural in their power and scope. By 1863, however, they had depreciated down to mostly sentimental value, a residual value held only because the revered manuscript was a piece of national antiquity that had been signed by the Founders. In a time when America condoned the cruelties of human bondage, the words of the Declaration had become weakened, diluted. The great task for Lincoln at Gettysburg was to breathe new life into the Declaration of Independence, to transform it into an instrument of profound moral authority, in order to address the Nation's crisis at hand.

Lincoln, in his Gettysburg Address, was about to stretch the four corners of the Declaration of Independence, and use the federal government for purposes of doing it, in a way likely never envisioned, or intended, by Jefferson. In the eyes of his critics, it was an act of brash, out-of-control "federalism." In this speech he was making at Gettysburg, President Lincoln was undertaking the bold move to bring equality into the equation of American ideals, and trying to carry it out through the strong arm of the national government—a stroke of federalism that, ironically, would have likely troubled the Declaration's author, Thomas Jefferson. Knowing that the US. Supreme Court and many of the individual states had legally justified slavery by leaning on a silent Constitution, Lincoln saw the centralized power of the federal government, even if by bloody civil war, the last, best hope of freedom and equality for people of color.

Lincoln firmly believed that unless the Declaration of Independence was interpreted as an all-inclusive document, that is, a promise made to all human beings, then the great sacrifices of the American Revolution had been lost.

Lincoln saw a *proposition* in the Declaration of Independence—that is, an undertaking yet to be proven and fulfilled. And that "proposition" was simply this: **all people are created equal**. It was a proposition undertaken by America at its conception, but in Lincoln's time, not yet fulfilled. For America to continue to reject this proposition by denying freedom and equality to people of all color and creed, in Lincoln's judgment, rejected the Nation's founding ideals and endangered the liberty of all Americans.

Lincoln had used the word "proposition" hundreds of times in the past. He was very fond of the word. It came from *Euclid's Theorems*, exercises in the power of deductive reasoning, which he often carried in his pocket and read. Lincoln thought the word "proposition" perfectly described America's promise first made in 1776, which was to guarantee the God-given right of equality for all of its people, without regard to color or creed. That is why he insisted on using the word in his speech at Gettysburg, even though it was later reported that William Seward, perhaps after seeing it that previous night at the Harper house, had privately advised against it.

In historical support of this "proposition," the President, in his speech at Gettysburg, was turning back the clock to the time when the pursuit of liberty brought the Nation's Founding Fathers together—a time when a "new nation" was being formed, one dedicated to the principles first expressly promised in the Declaration of Independence, and then reaffirmed through the human sacrifices of the Revolutionary War.

President Lincoln was endeavoring, with his words at Gettysburg, to pull the historical past of America into a contemplative connection with the present.

And with the next twenty-four words of his speech—opening with reference to "**our fathers**," the heroic Founders of America so revered by Lincoln since his first boyhood reading of Weems' *Life of Washington*—the President would boldly launch into the public domain a new and unprecedented interpretation of America's founding principles as they are recited in the Declaration of Independence. Principles, **"brought forth"** with the same epochal human importance as when the Israelites were brought forth out of bondage from Egypt. And further, Lincoln would defend the core tenets brought forth in his Emancipation Proclamation, when he proclaimed:

> **. . . our fathers brought forth on this continent, a new nation, conceived in Liberty, and dedicated to the proposition that all men are created equal.**

Guided by his most sacred beliefs, and his hope for America, he had reaffirmed the reason for America.

Next, President Lincoln would speak to why they had gathered at the soldiers' cemetery:

> **Now we are engaged in a great civil war, testing whether that nation, or any nation so conceived and so dedicated, can long endure. We are met on a great battle-field of that war. We have come to dedicate a portion of that field, as a final resting place for those who here gave their lives that that nation might live. It is altogether fitting and proper that we should do this.**

Then, the President spoke of sacrificial and meaningful death in America. Lincoln would choose words that would consecrate the sacrifices of the fallen soldiers with a sacred mantle of immortality, so that those sacrifices would be forever linked to the principles of democracy contained in the Declaration of Independence. They would be humble and hallowed words, honoring the brave soldiers of the Battle of Gettysburg and the Civil War, who, like their forefathers in the Revolutionary War, fought for the principles of freedom set forth in the Declaration of Independence—many of whom gave their lives and limbs for the cause of liberty:

But, in a larger sense, we can not dedicate—we can not consecrate—we can not hallow - this ground. The brave men, living and dead, who struggled here, have consecrated it, far above our poor power to add or detract. The world will little note, nor long remember what we say here, but it can never forget what they did here.

Lincoln would then tell every American—Americans then and those who would come later—that they have a DUTY to pick up the flag of freedom and equality from the hands of the brave soldiers who had fallen, and carry it into the future. The President was not only consecrating the burial of the brave dead; he was asking the living to honor their sacrifice, by joining together to finish the great struggle looming before them:

It is for us the living, rather, to be dedicated here to the unfinished work which they who fought here have thus far so nobly advanced. It is rather for us to be here dedicated to the great task remaining before us—

Then, with perhaps the only prominent gesture Lincoln made during his speech (according to eyewitness W.H. Tipton)—a sweep of his open hand across the breadth of the soldiers' graves—the President asked the American people for a COMMITMENT . . . a commitment to the cause of freedom and equality for which those supreme sacrifices were made:

—that from these honored dead we take increased devotion to that cause for which they gave the last full measure of devotion—

Lincoln recalled the stirring words of George Washington from that book he first read in his youth, when General Washington walked among the graves of his fallen soldiers, proclaiming, "Their fall was not in vain." Lincoln, inspired by those words, was about to challenge all Americans, those living and those in the future, to NOT FORGET the supreme sacrifices of those courageous soldiers—men who had flooded the altar of democracy with their blood:

—that we here highly resolve that these dead shall not have died in vain—that this nation . . .

Suddenly, President Abraham Lincoln, breathing deeply of the venerated atmosphere all about him, was spiritually moved to add two more words to his speech—two words that were not written on the sheets of paper clutched in his hand. After all, the first breath drawn by the Pilgrims was spent in kneeled prayer at Plymouth Rock.

Perhaps, as Lincoln looked upon the majestic Southern Mountains that embraced the soldiers' cemetery, and the great Alleghenies in the further distance, the words he would add to his speech may have been inspired by a verse in the *121st Psalm*, a book in the *King James Bible* he so loved to read: □*I will lift up mine eyes unto the hills, from whence cometh my help. My help cometh from the Lord, which made heaven and earth.*□

Two profound words are then spoken by the President:

. . . under God . . .

After triangulating history—that is, by reaching to the past for the democratic principles promised in the Declaration of Independence, and pulling them forward to his present time, and then using those principles like a polestar in the night sky to point to the future—the President would speak to the hope for a rebirth of America. By calling for a new birth of freedom, Lincoln was stating a new and higher purpose of the War. Under such rebirth, Lincoln believed, the Nation could move into the future, no longer morally encumbered by what he called the "monstrous injustice" of slavery. A reborn America could then fulfill the "proposition" handed down by the Founding Fathers—the promise of freedom and equality—for all people.

In this speech, Lincoln was providing America with a blueprint for the future. He was stretching democracy further than it had ever been before; further, than even Jefferson and the Founders intended to go. It would be a perfect blueprint for a lasting, democratic self-government, amazingly, made only of three little, but powerfully-placed prepositions—**of**, **by**, and **for**—prefixing the words, "**the people.**" Words, perhaps, inspired by the abolitionist pastor, Rev. Theodore Parker, who thirteen years earlier had passionately written in a sermon that "This [American] idea, demands . . . a democracy, that is, a government of all the people, by all the people, for all the people." And moved by the words of *Proverbs 29:18*, from one of Lincoln's favorite books in the Bible, which says—□ *Where there is no vision, the people perish*□— Lincoln offers hope for the rebirth of America, and in doing so brings his speech to an immortal coda, laying a claim of eternal remembrance upon the final cadenza of words that would follow:

> **. . . shall have a new birth of freedom - and that government of the people, by the people, for the people . . . shall not perish from the earth.**"

The speech was over. Lincoln folded the manuscript in his hand and inserted it back into his breast pocket, then turned from the audience to return to his seat. As he did, Edward Everett sprung from his seat to congratulate the President on his remarks.

For the next palpable moments in time, several excruciating seconds that seemed to last forever, there was blunt silence. Quiet as an empty church. And then, finally, just as abruptly, the gates of applause opened with long, reverential applause.

It was a short speech. A very short speech. It would take Lincoln less than three minutes to deliver the whole thing. It was a speech so short that the photographer assigned to capture the event. . .missed it. The poor man, after shifting around his equipment a time or two for a better angle of Lincoln, ducking in and out from under his black drop cloth—while those around him snickered at his meticulous acts of futility—never got a single photograph of the President of the United States giving one of the most famous speeches in American history. In fact, one of the few surviving photographs of Lincoln at the Gettysburg cemetery dedication is one taken that day by photographer David Bachrach, who took a distant, wide photograph of the massive crowd and unknowingly captured in it a shot of the President sitting on the speaker's platform, his face buried in anonymity for years among an ocean of other faces and figures.

It would be almost a century after Lincoln spoke at Gettysburg, in 1952, that the keen and discerning eye of the legendary Ms. Josephine Cobb, who was then the Chief of the Still Pictures Branch at the Library of Congress, would pick out a frontal shot of a bare-headed President Lincoln, head slightly titled down, surrounded by a blurred circle of friends and dignitaries, from the old negative of this Gettysburg photograph. It was an exciting and important photographic discovery, forensically placing Lincoln on the speaker's platform at the cemetery dedication.

And what moved the President—who as a young man, struggled with religious doubt—to suddenly extemporize the words "under God?"

It seems that over time, the oppressive weight and wear of life had steadily brought about spiritual growth in Abraham Lincoln—a religious sensibility not previously there in his early years. Through it all, as he engaged in mature theological thought about God and immersed himself in the ancient tradition of the inner search, Abraham Lincoln had acquiesced to a Higher Power. Ironically, this was a man who, in his youthful days, was a scornful, religious skeptic, rejecting the strict Calvinism he was raised on and practiced by his parents. Just one year before his Gettysburg speech, Lincoln would write in personal meditation: *"The will of God prevails."* For President Lincoln, the addition of these two words to his speech at Gettysburg was no perfunctory reference to God; they were words of sincere reverence and faith. Words inspired by place and time.

As President, Lincoln was often seen reading his Bible at sunrise when he sought quiet retreat at the Soldiers Home, and during lunch in his Executive Office. Lincoln, the early agnostic, had come to believe in God—a God, he had reconciled, who shaped lives and history. A God that created all people equal. Even in the last public address of his life, a policy speech about Reconstruction—made only two days after Lee's surrender—Lincoln would pause, at its beginning, to remind the American people: "He, from Whom all blessings flow, must not be forgotten." Years after Lincoln's death, Mary Lincoln communicated with her husband's last law partner, William H. Herndon (despite the fact that they did not like each other), about President Lincoln's spiritual experience at Gettysburg. She wrote in her own words that her husband had "felt religious More than Ever, about the time he went to Gettysburg." For Abraham Lincoln, in spiritual terms, Gettysburg was a mountain-top experience.

President Lincoln paced the delivery of his speech that day, speaking in a slow and steady cadence. He spoke plainly, without making self-conscious pronunciations, allowing the dignity of the words to exalt themselves. It is a little difficult to imagine, but Lincoln had a high-pitched, somewhat scrill, monotone speech voice. *But it had exceptional carrying power.* Lincoln's speech voice, after it warmed up, began to mellow out a bit, and had steel in its tone, such that it could be heard a great distance, penetrating through the layers of vast audiences. Horace White, a reporter who first covered Lincoln at the Lincoln-Douglas Debates and thereafter for the rest of his life, said that the President, even with his "thin, high" voice, could be heard a very long distance, "in spite of the bustle and tumult of the crowd." Such a full-throated voice, like Lincoln's, was a valuable asset when speaking to crowds numbered in the thousands, in an age without electronic amplification.

This day, at Cemetery Hill, the lofty tonation of Lincoln's inspired voice would be wrapped in nobility: a sound that was firm, warm and resonant. Some who heard the President at Gettysburg later said that when he spoke the words, "for which they here gave the last full measure of devotion," that his even-toned delivery voice, uncharacteristically, flinched with emotion, and that he carried that tempered emotion to the end of his speech.

Like his Cooper Union speech, and his Farewell Speech to the people of Springfield, Lincoln had again, as one observer noted, "seemed transfigured" by the strength of his own words. It was true. The words Lincoln spoke at Gettysburg, and the man himself, had become one.

During the delivery of the Gettysburg Address, Lincoln was, as usual, quite conservative in his physical gestures, in obvious contrast to the piston-driven, animated style of Everett. "There was no gesture except with both hands up and down," as Philip Bikle remembered about the President's delivery of his speech. He recalled Lincoln's "grasping the manuscript which he did not seem to need, as he looked at it so seldom." Lincoln needed no grand movements to embellish his words: he had garnished his speech with forceful ideas, rather than forceful gestures.

As Lincoln intuitively paused between the phrased messages of his speech, according to the observations of an *Associated Press* reporter (who later recanted his published version) and other eyewitnesses, there was intermittent applause for the President at least five times during his speech. But the preponderance of credible historical evidence suggests, in reality, that the immense audience was reserved and unresponsive throughout Lincoln's speech, with very little, if any, interrupting applause. It seems the people felt great respect for Abraham Lincoln, and reverence for the occasion. They understood that the President was giving a eulogy. And they were responding, likekind.

The short but gaping interval of silence occurring after the President finished his speech probably caused Lincoln to believe, initially, his speech had failed. For a moment, Lincoln may have flashed back to the cold, brittle silence that followed his ill-chosen words spoken at the Hanover train stop, the day before. His Gettysburg speech had been so brief and concluded so abruptly, many were not sure President Lincoln had even finished. Some people on the outer fringes, shuffling around in restless transition to find a good spot to see and hear the President, missed his speech, altogether.

It was only the body language of the President turning and returning to his seat on the platform at the conclusion of his remarks, his back facing the crowd, that tipped off most of the audience that President Lincoln had finished his speech. Then finally President Lincoln received, according to the *New York Times*, a "long continued applause."

For many, it seemed the President's speech was already over, before it really got cranked up. Lincoln's friend from Illinois, Clark E. Carr, who served on the Gettysburg Cemetery Commission and sat on the speaker's platform that day, acknowledged years later that "so short a time was Mr. Lincoln before them that the people could scarcely believe their eyes when he disappeared from their view. They were almost dazed." Carr even conceded that "Time and time again expressions of disappointment were made to me. Many persons said to me that they would have supposed that on such a great occasion the President would have made a speech." A stunned reporter from the *Philadelphia Press*, John Russell Young, who knew the President quite well and was sitting near Lincoln on the speaker's platform, later told that he leaned over towards Lincoln after he finished his speech, asking the President if that was all of his remarks. As Young explained the moment, "To my surprise . . . it seemed before Mr. Lincoln had begun to speak, he turned and sat down."

Even in those earliest moments after the speech, the President was concerned that his "remarks" at Gettysburg had not come off cleanly, as many years later, Ward Lamon would recall about that day. In reference to the defective plows used out West that allowed dirt to clog-up on the blade and failed to cut cleanly through the ground, Lamon remembered Lincoln telling him as they left the speaker's platform: "Lamon, that speech won't *scour*—it is a flat failure—and the people are disappointed!" Marshall Lamon may have initially shared the President's concern over his speech. Close enough to his old friend Lincoln to speak freely and candidly, Lamon reportedly commented to the President that his speech fell on the audience like a "wet blanket."

Was Lincoln stricken with self-doubt after his speech? Did the President wonder if his most important speech of the war, maybe of his presidency, had missed the mark? On first impression, he probably did. After all, the next day, Lincoln would reply to Everett's compliment of his remarks by writing that he was pleased that his speech "was not entirely a failure." But any hard conclusions on this point are scotched on speculation. If Lincoln felt any doubts or disappointment about his speech, it may have been triggered by the few but terribly awkward seconds of silence that occurred at the end of the President's speech. Or Lincoln may have believed his speech failed to connect with the audience, because of its brevity, especially when matched up against Everett's super-sized speech.

It must be remembered that long speeches were the popular trend and predominant entertainment experience of the day. They were public performances. Like the length of today's feature films, people wanted two hours or more of " good speech-make'in." Perhaps some folks expected a pumped-up, patriotic, hard-line, anti-Confederacy speech like Secretary Seward had given the night before. Perhaps the sudden ending of Lincoln's speech shocked many spectators, leaving them with a visceral reaction of being shortchanged. After all, in those days people would journey all day, and sometimes all night, to hear a famous person make a good speech—much the same way people, today, migrate great distances to rock concerts, or travel to see a Vegas or Broadway show.

Some have argued that the shortness of Lincoln's speech was because he had so little time to prepare it. This is a historical fallacy, akin to the story that Lincoln quickly composed and scribbled the great speech on a scrap of paper, while on the train ride to Gettysburg. Lincoln did struggle to put an ending on his speech, but he had been thinking about the ideas that were the content of his speech for many years. This speech was not slapped together at the last minute; it was a speech of distilled thought and preconceived brevity, painstakingly crafted and revised by Lincoln into the great composition it would be.

Whatever the reasons—perhaps a blending of them all—for that brief, temporary station in time, the President seemed to have reconciled himself to giving a disappointing speech. Or even worse, a failed speech. Lincoln's harsh appraisal of his own performance could have been amplified by his extreme fatigue, or by the variola, a mild form of smallpox that was already invading his body.

Benjamin B. French, a devoted Lincoln fan, whose poem *Consecration Hymn* was very well received at the ceremonies, gave Lincoln's speech only a short, tepid review, writing in his journal that the President, "in a few brief, but most appropriate words, dedicated the cemetery." Even Lincoln's loyal aide John Hay, still a little giddy and smitten by the grandeur of Edward Everett's presentation, was not so generous in his assessment and praise of the President's speech. Hay would blandly describe Lincoln's speech in his diary, by writing that "the President in a fine, free way, with more grace than is his wont, said his half dozen lines of consecration. . . and all the particulars are in the daily papers." Not the most enthusiastic compliment of his boss's speech, to say the least.

Afforded the 20-20 view of historical hindsight, there were other factors having nothing to do with the quality of Lincoln's Gettysburg Address that would explain the blunt silence that followed his speech, and then, the absence of lively applause. First of all, many in the audience that day had loved ones killed at Gettysburg or in the awful War. Daniel Skelly, who was nineteen when he listened to Lincoln at Cemetery Hill, and whose brother, Jack Skelly, Jr., died fighting for the Union, posed the rhetorical question (as to why there was the silence and then only lukewarm applause for Lincoln at the end of his speech), when he asked, "Could there be much applause from such an audience?"

Young Dan Skelly was right. Folks don't often wildly applaud at a funeral. The dedication ceremony at Gettysburg was not much different. Odds are, that everyone in the crowd that day at the soldiers' cemetery had been touched, or knew a family that had been touched, by the tragedy of the War, probably more. Clark Carr, one of the cemetery commissioners on the speaker's platform that day, later remarked that "the occasion was too solemn for any kind of boisterous demonstration." The Civil War would make casualties of between two and five per cent of the Nation's entire population. One of every five soldiers in the War died. The audience at Cemetery Hill had suffered too much death and destruction in their lives, to enthusiastically cheer or applaud anything that day.

Moreover, many in the massive audience were just beginning to mentally settle-in to the President's words, when the speech was suddenly over. Henry Jacobs, who was there that day, explained that "The attention was just beginning to turn from the close study of the speaker . . . to the substance of what he was saying, when he finished." Jacobs went on to say that "The suddenness with which [Lincoln] closed was almost startling." Like the fidgety photographer who missed the photo of a lifetime, lots of folks may have been in the distracted process of mentally nestling into position for a good, long speech. Certainly there were those in the audience that day who believed that the end of the President's speech was only a temporary pause—surely, they thought, there was more speech to come. But there wasn't. The speech was over. This certainly would account for the crowd's delayed applause—and its diminished intensity, when the applause finally did come.

Ultimately, this issue over the few seconds of silence that immediately followed Lincoln's speech would be no more than a tempest in a historical teapot. And eventually, it would have little, if any, lasting impact on Lincoln's self-appraisal of his own remarks.

* * *

But what about media coverage? How would Everett's and Lincoln's speeches fair with the 1863 press corps?

Edward Everett's speech would receive prolific coverage from the country's major newspapers—much more than the Gettysburg Address. Even Reverend Stockton's invocation prayer and Benjamin French's *Consecration Hymn* would receive as much press as Lincoln's speech. Many Republican newspapers ran the complete, unedited version of Everett's speech on the front page, even pushing their other detailed descriptions of the program ceremonies deeper into the newspaper, in order to draw full attention to Everett's voluminous printed oration.

There was, however, a driblet of Northern newspapers (mostly Democratic) that said very little about Everett's speech, or tossed a few scattered barbs at it. John Russell Young, a reporter with the *Philadelphia Press*—a pro-Republican rag (that had become Lincoln's pet publication while in office)—mildly chided the perfection of Everett's oration, describing it "like a bit of Greek sculpture—beautiful, but cold as ice." The *Daily Age* out of Philadelphia would cut even deeper: "Seldom has a man talked so long and said so little. He gave us plenty of words, but no heart. His style was as clear and cold as Croton ice." *Harper's Weekly* joined in with their own sub-zero criticism, assessing Everett's speech as "smooth [but] cold."

Everett expected some of this. But his hide wasn't as tough as Lincoln's.   Especially the "ice" and "cold" adjectives, which really pushed his buttons and the critics knew it. Other critics railed against his speech as being purely partisan; some accused Everett of getting his facts about the battle wrong. These printed criticisms of his Gettysburg speech, even when they were unfounded or politically-motivated, still bothered Everett. With his usual dramatic flair, he described them as "villainous assaults." Such is the way of partisan politics—then and now. However, the overwhelming majority of newspapers were flush with praise about Everett's grand oration at Gettysburg, and gave his speech extensive, front-page coverage.

There is tenaciously-enduring folklore that the Gettysburg Address was either totally ignored or attacked with harsh criticism by every single newspaper and reporter who wrote about it. And, as legend has it, that Lincoln himself was utterly convinced, to his grave, that the Gettysburg Address was a total failure. It is an appealing story that adds another layer to Lincoln mythology. But it is not an accurate historical appraisal of what really happened.

Certainly, Edward Everett's speech would claim the lion's share of media coverage, most of it laudable, along with the generous praise showered on Reverend Stockton's invocation prayer and Benjamin French's poem, the *Consecration Hymn*. But the Gettysburg Address would get its sizeable share of press too, coming in the form of a wildly diverse and schizophrenic bag of reviews. Most newspaper journalism of that era—including reporting on the Gettysburg Address as Lincoln delivered it on November 19th—was deeply rooted in partisan politics.

Although history has spotlighted the ugly press coverage that excoriated the Gettysburg Address, most of the Republican newspapers were actually quite complimentary of Lincoln's speech. After all, there were plenty of reporters in Gettysburg who were friendly to the President's politics. A resourceful Lincoln had helped his own cause in that way. Many had rode with him on the train. For example, *Harper's Weekly*—a Republican-leaning national magazine headquartered in New York City —equated Lincoln's words with those of the great Athenian statesman Pericles, writing that "The few words of the President were from the heart to the heart. They cannot be read without kindling emotion. It was as simple and felicitous and earnest a word that was ever spoken."

Out of Springfield, Massachusetts, the *Daily Republican*, a newspaper that had lionized the President for many years, described the Gettysburg Address in glowing terms that surely dovetail with today's venerated appraisal of Lincoln's speech, calling it "a perfect gem, deep in feeling, compact in thought and expression, and tasteful and elegant in every word and comma." Adding to its editorial tribute, the newspaper wrote: "Surprisingly fine as Mr. Everett's oration was . . . the rhetorical honors of the occasion were won by President Lincoln."

The *Providence Daily Journal* also roundly praised the President's speech, gushing: "We know not where to look for a more admirable speech than the brief one which the President made at the close of Mr. Everett's oration. It is often said that the hardest thing in the world is to make a five minute speech. But could the most elaborate and splendid oration be more beautiful, more touching, more inspiring, than those few words of the President? They had, in [our] humble judgment, the charm and power of the very highest eloquence."

The reporter from the *Cincinnati Daily Gazette* wrote that Lincoln's speech was "the right thing in the right place, and a perfect thing in every respect." And the *Chicago Tribune*—a newspaper that had long backed and bolstered Lincoln—stood out in its lofty praise of the Gettysburg Address, predicting with uncanny accuracy that "The dedicatory remarks of President Lincoln will live among the annals of man." (Interestingly, this same Chicago paper, eighty-five years later, would seem to lose its knack for political prognostication, when it would famously misreport on its front-page headlines—as captured in one of the most memorable photos in American politics—that "Dewey Defeats Truman.")

However, Lincoln received only a lukewarm reception to his speech from a few Republican newspapers, despite Gettysburg being stocked with plenty of reporters who were friendly to Republican politics. This may have chafed Lincoln a bit, although he was never known to comment on it.

There were other newspapers, invariably those of strong Democratic persuasion, that harshly criticized the Gettysburg Address, downplayed it, or completely ignored it. The reason some Democratic newspapers were coldly indifferent to the Gettysburg Address because they considered it no more than a re-election speech for Lincoln. And they rarely said anything good about Lincoln anyway. Other Democratic papers chose not to cover the speech at all, or severely truncated the Gettysburg Address by printing just a small slice of it.

The *Hartford Courant* in Connecticut included in its coverage generous portions of Everett's oration, and even ran two separate renditions of William Seward's evening speech outside the Harper house—but never mentioned one word of the Gettysburg Address. *The Freeport*

Bulletin in Illinois pretended the Gettysburg Address was never spoken, but published a speech that was made that afternoon after the cemetery dedication was over, by the Governor of New York, Horatio Seymour. Both of the local newspapers in Gettysburg, the Compiler (with Democratic, perhaps even Copperhead leanings) and the Adams Sentinel (a pro-Republican newspaper), strangely enough, printed only the raw text of Lincoln's Gettysburg Address, choosing to run no editorial articles commenting on the speech.

And there were many newspapers that inaccurately reported or misprinted the Gettysburg Address. A few misrepresentations of the Gettysburg Address may have been by design. But most misprints were more comical than mean-spirited, resulting from klutzy journalism or mistakes by telegraphers and typesetters—a common journalistic gaffe in an age without tape recorders and amplification equipment for public speakers. For example, the *Rochester Daily Union Advertiser* reported Lincoln as saying **"Our Father"** (seeming to invoke the Lord's Prayer) "brought forth on this continent . . . ," thus substituting the Almighty for the Founding Fathers. Had the *Advertiser's* print been taken literally, Mt. Rushmore would look radically different today. The *Missouri Republican* severely truncated the speech, quoting Lincoln in his immortal conclusion: "that the government for and of the people . . . **might not perish from apathy**." A clerical slip, but perhaps a Freudian one that has meaning even today; good causes are lost far more often to indifference, than war.

The *Philadelphia Inquirer*, along with a number of other newspapers, would report the President as saying, "That from these dead we **imbibe increased devotion**." Perhaps the typesetters at the newspaper or telegraph offices had "imbibed" as well. The *New York Times*, along with many other newspapers, quoted Lincoln as saying that Americans should be "dedicated here to the **refinished work**." "Refinished" work? Like a refinished antique wardrobe? The *Sacramento Daily Union* garbled up the Gettysburg Address by quoting Lincoln as saying: **"The dead will little heed.** Let us long remember what we have." Apparently, some of the reporters who were still alive and well—were paying "little heed" to Lincoln's speech, too.

Then, there were the bare-knuckled criticisms. Most of the journalistic slingstones fired at the Gettysburg Address would come out of a firepot of anti-war or soft-on-slavery press, mostly Democratic newspapers in Northern states, that had a political ax to grind with Lincoln and his policies.

In fact, some newspaper accounts of the speech were downright rabid in their viciousness. The *Chicago Times*, one of the most powerful and broadly circulated newspapers in America (and journalistic friend to Lincoln's old debate opponent, Stephen A. Douglas), posed the rhetorical question: "Is Mr. Lincoln less refined than a savage?" The editorial went on to upbraid Lincoln for introducing "Dawdleism in a funeral sermon" and called the Gettysburg Address "ignorant rudeness" and an "offensive exhibition of boorishness and vulgarity," declaring that the speech "was a perversion of history so flagrant that the most extended charity cannot regard it as otherwise than willful." Continuing with its savage critique, the *Times* spewed, "The cheek of every American must tingle with shame as he reads the silly, flat, and dishwatery utterances of the man who has to be pointed out to intelligent foreigners as the President of the United States."

The *Chicago Times'* fanatical bias against Lincoln would be matched only by its later frothing-at-the-mouth assessment of his peerless Second Inaugural Address, which it called "puerile and slip-shod." Although Lincoln did not specifically mention race in the Gettysburg Address, referring only to the general proposition that "all men are created equal," the *Chicago Times* would unashamedly pull the political lever of race ("playing the race card" is as old as politics, itself), editorializing that Lincoln's speech "libeled the statesmen who founded the government," and that America's Founding Fathers "were men possessing too much self-respect to declare that Negroes were their equals."

The *New York World*, as did other Democratic-slanted print, carved into Lincoln with the serrated edge of the Constitution, lecturing the President that "This United States" did not hatch from the Declaration of Independence, but rather, was "the result of the . . . Constitution"— a document, they emphasized, that never mentions the absurd idea of equality for everyone, especially "Negroes."

Out of Harrisburg, Pennsylvania, political home of Governor Andrew Curtin who had thrown so much personal and governmental support into the Gettysburg event and Soldiers' National Cemetery—came the coverage of the *Patriot and Union*. This newspaper, despite being located in the state capital, a region nestled in the bosom of the Union cause, and located only thirty-six miles from Gettysburg, ran a snarling editorial that read: "We pass over the silly remarks of the President; for the credit of the nation we are willing that the veil of oblivion shall be dropped over them and that they shall no more be repeated or thought of."

Across the great pond, the *London Times* would harshly appraise the content of the Gettysburg Address as follows: "The ceremony was rendered ludicrous by . . . that poor President Lincoln," they dispatched. "Anything more dull and commonplace . . . would not be easy to produce." Perhaps the Blighties had New Orleans and that portrait of Andrew Jackson that Lincoln enjoyed on his office wall, still on their minds.

The Copperhead newspaper, *Crisis*, with its insatiable affection for the invective, charged that Lincoln—the "Despot" as it often called him—trampled on state rights in every move he made. The article mocked the President's words he had used at the end of his Gettysburg Address, that alluded to a government "of the people, by the people, and for the people," growling that state rights was where ultimate government power should rightfully be placed.

One Confederate newspaper, the *Richmond Daily Dispatch*, blisteringly wrote that President Lincoln "acted like a clown." The *Cincinnati Daily Enquirer* gibed that the Gettysburg Address brought "disgrace upon the Nation." Most shocking of all, might be the words of the virulently anti-Lincoln *Ebensburg Democrat* out of Pennsylvania, just a piece up the road from Gettysburg, which venomously printed that when the President gave the Gettysburg Address, he threw-up "vulgar jargon" on "the graves of his countrymen."

And in a sublime stroke of scandalmongering, *MacMillan's Magazine* would invoke the ghost of the Antietam ditty that accused Lincoln and Lamon of singing irreverent songs over the bodies of dead soldiers, by printing: "That Lincoln . . . is a boor, his address at Gettysburg will in itself suffice to prove. Is it easy to believe that the man who had the native good taste to produce this address . . . would call for comic songs to be sung over soldiers' graves?"

And we think politics is dirty and rough, today.

Even Lincoln's most devoted friends and supporters would not see the Gettysburg Address, at the time Lincoln delivered it, as the great speech it would later become. One former Gettysburg seminary student—reminiscing as a clergyman even four decades after being a young witness to Lincoln's historical speech—was still not able to get past his first, uninspired, low opinion of the President, as he blandly remembered him "[w]ith his arms hanging at his side at full length, and holding a slip of paper with both hands on which was written his three minute address, which had been prepared, according to a report then current, on his way from Washington." (Although hindsight is usually 20/20, this minister was as blindly stubborn as a Missouri mule with his first impressions.)

One of the few with the clairvoyance to recognize the Gettysburg Address for the exalted and peerless speech it would someday be, was the great American poet and essayist, Ralph Waldo Emerson, who in the stirring eulogy he gave at Lincoln's funeral about seventeen months later, would forecast that Abraham Lincoln's "brief speech at Gettysburg will not easily be surpassed by words on any recorded occasion."

Ultimately, how the Gettysburg Address was graded in the minds of its listeners depended, almost entirely, on who heard it. Much like the case of modern eyewitnesses who all see the same incident, all at the same time—but later recall and describe the event differently—the thousands gathered at Cemetery Hill that day would leave with a myriad of impressions and recollections about the Gettysburg Address. Some recalled Lincoln reading the speech from his hand; others remember the President folding it away in his coat, and speaking entirely from memory. Some said he gestured with his arms at key points in the speech; others thought the President was restrained and motionless. Some picked up on a Kentucky accent in the President's enunciation (silly as it seems, this offended the sensibilities of some easterners); others heard no such thing. Some reminisced that the subdued crowd released only "sobs of smothered emotion;" others witnessed a "hurricane of applause." Some reported Lincoln as receiving at least five intermittent rounds of applause during the speech; other remembered no applause at all.

But most of the people who heard the President that day, who were not driven by politics or hate. . . loved what he said. George Gitt, still hunkered underneath the speaker's platform, remembered years later that the audience, many in awe of Lincoln's rarified words, "stood motionless and silent." They didn't have to understand the deeper meaning and symbolism of his speech.   One can listen to an Italian opera without understanding the meaning of *mezza voce* or the words themselves, and yet, be enthralled by the beauty, emotion and timbre of the performer's voice. The words their President had spoken that day, and the grace in which he delivered them, in and of themselves, were heartfelt, beautiful—and touched them, deeply. He had reached out to common people, with uncommon assuredness. And, as Lincoln would find out shortly after he delivered the Gettysburg Address, the best speech-maker in the country, Edward Everett—loved what he said. A pretty good endorsement, indeed.

Everett, perhaps deeply moved by the sacred ambiance of the Gettysburg event that day, made handwritten alterations on his personal copy of the program brochure for the ceremonies. In its original printed form, the program was captioned at the top: "The Inauguration of the National Cemetery At Gettysburg." Everett marked through the rather cold and politically-toned word **"Inauguration."**   And in its place, he handsomely wrote a more warm and spiritual title for the brochure—the word, **"Consecration."**   A more worthy substitution of word is hard to imagine. On the same program brochure, Everett also wrote in his name and the names of the program participants beside their listing of assigned parts in the ceremony. Old "EE" may have been a little peeved at the brochure's author, Ward Lamon, who had completely omitted Everett's name (along with the names of all other program participants), although he was the featured speaker. In glaring contrast, Lamon had given his boss, the President, full billing on the program brochure, name and all, for his role in saying a few closing remarks. (Loyalty, not tact, was certainly one of Lamon's attributes.)

In those days, it was a definitive trait of good moral character and decency, especially among hard-working, common folk, for a man to speak to others "forthrightly." At Gettysburg, Lincoln had spoken to the people in a forthright way, without self-conscious platitudes, and without the pretentious use of elevated words. He spoke to them in a language they were raised on. Words they understood and held dear. More than any other words said or written by Abraham Lincoln during his whole life, these in the Gettysburg Address tell us how he felt about the men who fought in the Civil War, and how he felt about his country.

The President had spoken from the heart.

* * *

Eventually the passage of time would prove Lincoln's self-doubt in his own speech to be unjustified, and all of his critics wrong. If nothing else, on November 19, 1863, the words of the Gettysburg Address had reached the masses—although imperfectly so in some newspapers and dispatches— linking up with thousands of people beyond those who stood in the audience at Cemetery Hill. That's because the speech was short enough to print in newspapers all over the country, in its entirety. And the latest communications technology called the "telegraph" would quickly spread the Gettysburg Address across the country, like a flash fire.

Still, it would take time—decades—for the greatness of the Gettysburg Address to be fully absorbed into the Nation's consciousness. Lincoln himself, after Gettysburg, would scarcely mention his speech, ever again. Even after Lincoln's assassination, when grief-driven eulogies, poems, testimonials and exaltations flowed like a mighty river to glorify and venerate a martyred President—the Gettysburg Address was rarely alluded to. It was looking as though Lincoln's harsh initial assessment of his own speech—that it didn't even "scour"—was turning out to be right.

But by the dawn of the twentieth century, Lincoln's words at Gettysburg would not only "scour"—indeed, they would "soar" through the ages. Historians would slowly but surely begin to recognize that Lincoln's speech at Gettysburg had put his hands at the helm of the Nation's rudder at a critical moment in history, allowing him to steer America away from the mouth of the treacherous, dark waters of disunion and human bondage in which she had become dangerously moored.

For Lincoln, the delivery of the Gettysburg Address that day on November 19, 1863 at Cemetery Hill had given birth to the apotheosis of his life. It would just take some time. A long time.

But then again . . .time would change everything.

Lincoln-Douglas Debates were held in seven cities in 1858. The artist's rendering was used for a four cent stamp in 1958 commemorating the event.

Mary, Willie, Robert, Tad and President Lincoln.

Lincoln in front of tent: Photo made when Lincoln visited Antietam battlefield, October, 1862. At left, Allen Pinkerton, Union Intelligence Chief. At right, Gen. John McClernand.

This photograph is from a partial enlargement of the speaker's platform at Gettysburg on November 19, 1863, taken about two and a half hours before Lincoln gave his famous speech. A bare-headed President Lincoln can be seen at left center. Lincoln's presence, in what was originally a distant, wide-angle picture of the massive crowd, would remain unknown until 1952, when it was discovered by the keen eye of Josephine Cobb at the Library of Congress.

Lincoln's Address at Gettysburg, November 19, 1863. A drawing by A. I. Keller which appeared as a two page centerfold in *Harper's Weekly* on February 10, 1900. As many as 20,000 people attended the event.

Lincoln between his two secretaries, John G, Nicolay (l) and John Hay (r). Photo taken eleven days before his speech at Gettysburg. That day Hay would write in his diary "Nico & I immortalized ourselves by having ourselves done in group with the Prest."

Ward Hill Lamon, close friend and bodyguard of Lincoln. Lamon would serve as chief marshal over the dedication ceremonies at Gettysburg. A big, tall barrel-chested man, he was one of very few who could stand eye-to-eye with Lincoln.

Mary Todd Lincoln the first presidential wife known as the "First Lady." The tragedies she suffered during the White House years and afterwards, caused her to weep so much it physically damaged her eyes.

William H. Seward, Lincoln's brilliant Secretary of State and valued friend and advisor. Seward was at Gettysburg with Lincoln. He was viciously attacked the same evening Lincoln was assassinated in what would be known as the "Night of Horrors." Miraculously, Seward would survive his near fatal wounds.

Lincoln and
son Tad reading.

Last Moments of
Lincoln by Max
Rosenthal: Angels
are coming for
Lincoln with George
Washington as a
radiant divinity
looking down.
Apotheosis of
Abraham Lincoln
was in full swing.

CHAPTER FIFTEEN

AFTERWARDS

"I should be glad if I could flatter myself that I came as near to the central idea of the occasion in two hours, as you did in two minutes."
—Edward Everett
Letter to President Lincoln
November 19, 1863

AFTERWARDS . . . FOLLOWING PRESIDENT LINCOLN'S DELIVERY OF HIS Gettysburg Address, a chorale group, made up of volunteers from local Gettysburg churches, accompanied by Birgfield's Band, performed a somber but beautiful dirge. The music had been composed by Alfred Delaney, the words by James G. Percival, just for the day.

Mournfully, yet sweetly, they sang: **"Glory, that never is dim, Shining on with a light never ending . . . Glory, that never shall fade . . . never, O never . . . away."**

Motionless, breathlessly, the people listened. Again, tears flowed among the multitude. Hearts were melted. Souls, uplifted. Hope . . . embraced.

The people rejoiced.

Reverend Doctor Henry L. Baugher, D.D., who was the President of the local Pennsylvania College, would then close with the benediction. Heads uncovered, and bowed, the Rev. Dr. Baugher, in part, prayed:

"O Thou King of Kings and Lord of Lords,
God of the Nations of the earth . . .
Bless this consecrated ground, and these holy graves.
. . . who, by Thy kind providence,

253

hast permitted us to engage in these solemn services,
grant us Thy blessing.

May this great nation be delivered
from treason and rebellion at home,
And from the power of enemies abroad . . .
Amen."

And the people said, "Amen."

The Soldiers' National Cemetery had been consecrated.
"All time," Edward Everett had told the people that day, referring to the fallen soldiers, "is the millennium of their glory." And so it was. Then and forever, holy ground.

U. S. Marshal Lamon, who had opened the ceremonies, would now bring them to a close by announcing to the audience that the Ohio delegation had organized a special patriotic program to be held at the Presbyterian Church at five o'clock that same afternoon.

Suddenly, the military assembly split the crisp November air with an eight-round artillery salute. The Marine Band broke loose with music. The program was over.

Protracted, yet perfect.

Like clumps of a glazier breaking loose in the spring thaw, thousands of people began to move and disband. Most would find a spot at the edges of the road back to town, hoping to get another glimpse of the President.   Some would race towards the Presbyterian Church, to lay early claim for a seat at what would be the last official event of the day. Others, by the thousands, fanned out to the graves and battlegrounds one final time, to pay last respects.

President Lincoln climbed down from the speaker's platform and made a bee-line to the group of about fifty wounded veterans of the Battle of Gettysburg who had stood near the platform during the entire program. They proudly held a banner above their heads, saying, "HONOR TO OUR BRAVE COMRADES." These war-scarred men had traveled from a hospital in nearby York, Pennsylvania, to honor their fallen compatriots. During Lincoln's delivery of the Gettysburg

Address, eyewitness J. Howard Wert specifically recalled that the veterans "appeared to drink in every word," and that many of the soldiers "were weeping" the whole time.

After all of the day's speech-making about the sacrifices of war, Lincoln wanted to speak—face to face—with soldiers who had actually been there on the battlefields, who had wrestled with death and given all they had for their country. And likewise, these veterans carried a deep and abiding admiration for their President. "None seemed to gaze with as much fondness upon the Nation's head," observed Wert, "as did those fifty wounded heroes." Lincoln wanted eagerly to thank them, personally, and shake their hands.

Lincoln would comment that the "very appearance" of these Gettysburg veterans, when compared to the roster of speeches made that day, had "spoke louder than tongues." This band of men with broken bodies, but not broken spirits, had certainly spoken loudly to the President of the United States during the ceremony—with their eyes. And what they said touched him deeply—and in turn, touched the words he spoke that day. In those words of his Gettysburg Address, President Abraham Lincoln had spoken to the broader meaning and significance of the War—to the hope of a resurrected America.

First, there was the Nation's *birth*, in 1776. Then, the *death* suffered by the Nation, through the sacrifices of War. There is no life without death, Lincoln had told the people that day. Only through the awful but necessary sacrifice of death, would life emerge, again, in the future. And finally, by rolling back the stone of slavery, there would be the *rebirth* of the Nation—a new birth of freedom—through rededication of its citizens to the core principles of the Declaration of Independence.

The President had honored the brave sacrifices of the soldiers at Gettysburg, living and dead. And it was only through the supreme sacrifices of those men, Lincoln declared in his speech, that America could be renewed and restored to a new day of freedom and equality for all people. The birth of a Nation. Then death. And then, rebirth of that Nation.

In Lincoln's words were a renewed meaning of human freedom and the American Revolution. And a renewed meaning of America.

Lincoln had spoken of the **resurrection** of America.

After these moments of brief communion with the Gettysburg veterans, it was time for the President to take his position in dignitaries division of the returning procession, still led by Marshall Lamon. Lincoln would mount his horse and return back to town, as John Hay would later write in his diary, "through crowded and cheering streets."

Everett so admired Lincoln's speech that the day after the ceremonies, he wrote the President a letter thanking him for the hospitality shown himself and his daughter Charlotte, saying, "I should be glad if I could flatter myself that I came as near to the central idea of the occasion in two hours, as you did in two minutes." In the same letter, Everett revealed his kind and thoughtful heart when, referring to the telegram Lincoln had received about Tad's improvement, he added, "I hope your anxiety for your child was relieved." It would be one of the most cherished letters Lincoln would ever receive.

Lincoln was both ecstatic and flattered. This was a compliment from the greatest public speaker in the country. He promptly sent back a written reply to Everett, crafted in words of grateful humility that were the essence of the man: "In our respective parts yesterday," the President wrote to Everett, "you could not have been excused to make a short address, nor I a long one. I am pleased to know that, in your judgment, the little I did say was not entirely a failure."

Interestingly, in his reply letter to Everett written from the White House, Lincoln went on to specifically commend the Massachusetts orator for his "tribute to our noble women for their angel-ministering to the suffering soldiers." The President, to his credit, was aware and deeply appreciative of the valuable contributions of these brave, remarkable women, women who volunteered and sacrificed to save the country, at a time when they could not even vote.

Lincoln's U.S. Attorney General, James Speed, later recalled President Lincoln commenting to him that "he had never received a compliment he prized more highly," than the kind words about his Gettysburg speech that came from Edward Everett. Everett's heartfelt praise of Lincoln's speech would be the first wave to touch shore, among the endless ocean tide of praise the Gettysburg Address would gradually receive in the next century, and beyond.

If Edward Everett was the master of style on that autumn day at the soldiers' cemetery, Abraham Lincoln's prayerful words in the Gettysburg Address had been the *magnus opus* of substance. Historian Garry Wills best contrasted the two orators, by explaining that Everett, in his lengthy speech, brought "scholarship"; whereas Lincoln, in the Gettysburg Address, brought "art."

There is a juxtaposition in this story that is both fascinating and true; one that adds historical allure to the Gettysburg Address. Edward Everett's two hour speech, made by the greatest and most acclaimed speaker in America, was put into type by a Boston printer and distributed, in advance, throughout the Northern states; prepared and practiced over a period of two months before the speaking event; and was a speech made of some 13,607 words, inspired by neoclassical literature, and highly praised in its time, and today, no one hardly knows what was in it. In contrast, Abraham Lincoln's two minute speech, made by a good speaker of inconsistent oratory reputation, was written in longhand and got no advanced press; was prepared over a period of two weeks and finished only in the waning hours before it was delivered, with little time to practice it; and was a speech made of less than 300 words, inspired by Biblical scriptures, and harshly criticized in its time— and today, is known by about everyone.

Lincoln and Everett are further juxtaposed by history. Both were mutually indispensable players in a historical moment, which launched the Gettysburg Address into posterity. Had it not been for the presence of Edward Everett at Gettysburg, there may not have been the massive collection of people and press to create the grand and important event that provided Lincoln the historical stage which would anoint his speech with immortality. Likewise, had it not been for the presence of Abraham Lincoln at Gettysburg, whose words forever preserved the event, Everett's speech, which is always mentioned in the context of the Gettysburg Address, would have soon evaporated into total oblivion.

* * *

When the ceremonies at the soldiers' cemetery were over, "a very large company" of dignitaries gathered about 3:00 o'clock that afternoon for a dinner at David and Jennie Will's home. Afterwards, out of the sheer momentum of public enthusiasm, an informal reception for the people was quickly organized. Anyone in the general public willing to come and wait in line to meet the President was welcome. And come, they did.

Thousands of people queued outside the Will's home, now converted to a reception hall. The immense crowd stood in long lines, excited with anticipation, about entering the Wills mansion and shaking the hand of their President. Lincoln stood in the hallway opening on the York Street side of the house, greeting folks as they entered. Governor Curtin, at the other end of the hallway, shook hands with the people as they exited the Wills home, stepping into the public square.

Although weary to the bone, Lincoln, who seemed to always find joy in meeting "ordinary folk," spoke and shook hands, non-stop, for nearly an hour. "Needless to say," recalled Leander Howard Warren, who as a thirteen-year-old Caucasian boy had labored with African-American work crews that transported exhumed bodies to the soldiers' cemetery for re-interment, "the whole town took advantage of the opportunity to shake hands with the Great Emancipator." Young Warren got to shake the President's hand too—and would live a long life, becoming the last survivor of the crew of workers who buried the dead at the Soldier's National Cemetery.

Although he showed an extraordinary vitality for the practice, these long handshaking sessions, no doubt, took a physical toll on the President. Folks in the nineteenth century believed in a good firm handshake. A hand, even as strong and calloused as Lincoln's, could only take so much. Sometimes Lincoln would use his left hand to shake, giving his right one a brief rest. When Lincoln arrived in Washington for his 1861 inauguration, his swollen right hand was gnarled and nearly paralyzed from shaking hands on the twelve-day trip from Springfield. The catenation of handshakes leading up to Lincoln's signing of the final version of the Emancipation Proclamation on January 1, 1863, left his signature hand in trembles. These two days on the Gettysburg trip, most likely, were beginning to do the same.

One of the people waiting patiently in the long, serpentine reception line to meet President Lincoln was a Lutheran pastor from Albany, New York. His name was H. N. Pohlman. This would be the second time Reverend Pohlman would have the opportunity to meet the President of the United States, face-to-face, and exchange some conversation. A rare privilege, for sure.

Reverend Pohlman had first met Lincoln in the previous year, when a delegation of the Lutheran Church visited the White House. During that White House visit, Reverend Pohlman told the President a war story about a Lutheran minister who was brave enough to publicly pray in church for Lincoln, in the Confederate-seized city of Nashville, Tennessee. The way the minister got away with it, as Reverend Pohlman himself explained it with a grin, "prayed in German" and that "the, The Rebels couldn't understand German—but the Lord could!"

Lincoln loved the Reverend's story. It was his brand of anecdote. Even as a young boy, such novel stories always became indelibly imprinted in Lincoln's head, along with the face that launched it. So, a year later, when Reverend Pohlman stepped up next-in-line to meet the President in Gettysburg, just as Governor Seymour was about to give the Reverend an introduction to the President, Lincoln instantly recognized the good pastor, shaking his hand, and with his enchantingly crooked smile, said . . . "The Lord understands German." This encounter at Gettysburg between President Lincoln and Reverend Pohlman, like revered ecclesiastical doctrine, would proudly pass down as oral history through the Lutheran Church for many, many years.

Twelve-year-old Charles Young—barefoot and respectfully holding his cap across his chest—waited his turn in the long reception line at the Wills house to meet the President of the United States, face-to-face. Earlier that day, the towheaded boy had "stood only a few feet" from the President when he gave his speech, remembering his "grave and solemn appearance." He had walked three miles to see the President. Finally, after standing in the reception line at the Wills house a good while, Charles Young found himself standing right next to President Abraham Lincoln. Most folks, as Charles recollected, were "bowing graciously" to the President. Charles had another greeting in mind. "How are you, old Abe?," the spunky farm boy blurted out, as he stared up at the giantly Lincoln like he was looking for a squirrel in the top of a tall hemlock. Charles had five brothers serving in the Potomac Division of the Union Army, who would write letters home to their mother relating stories about how President Lincoln would bravely visit the troops, even in combat zones, shaking their hands and wishing them well. He wanted to shake the hand of this great man, just like his big brothers. A grown-up Charles Young, who would one day become a juvenile court probation officer in Des Moines, Iowa, would write, years later, about his encounter with Abraham Lincoln. He remembered that on that day, November 19, 1863, the President "grasped" him by the arm, then put his other hand gently on the boy's head, and told him, "God bless you, little fellow." It was a sweet memory that never failed to warm Charles Young's heart, all of his days.

Earlier in the day, Gettysburger Mary Elizabeth Montfort had wiggled her way close to the platform steps at the soldiers' cemetery. "As Mr. Lincoln came down the steps," the twelve-year-old recalled, "I looked up into his face." Lincoln reached out his hand to her, and said, "Hello, young lady, who are you?" Nerving herself, she politely replied, "I'm Mary Elizabeth," placing her hand in the President's. The glowing youngster was in awe. She would write in her diary the following day, "It was the greatest moment of my life."

A fidgety little boy, George D. Thorn, only five years of age, and his brother, had been brought to Cemetery Hill by their mother. George's father was superintendent of the Evergreen Cemetery which adjoined the soldiers' cemetery, and the Thorn family had lived in the cemetery house which was located at the epicenter of the Battle of Gettysburg. Like so many others, the Thorne home was converted that summer to an emergency hospital. When Charles' father was called to action for the Union Army, his mother assumed responsibilities for managing the Evergreen Cemetery, even digging graves while she was pregnant. Our mother "wanted us to see the President," Thorn later reminisced about that day on November 19, 1863.

As Lincoln begun his Gettysburg Address, Mrs. Thorn told her boys "to listen carefully, as this was the great man of our country." When the ceremonies came to an end, George was standing with his mother and brother at the edge of a corridor of people that had been separated by parade marshals to allow the President and other dignitaries to pass through the crowd. Suddenly, George's brother impulsively zipped across the passageway of people to stand beside a flashy drum major, who was decked out in a dazzling, gold-trimmed uniform. Caught up in the chase, young George followed suit, and darted right in front of the oncoming President of the United States. Years later he would still remember what happened next. "I felt a hand on top of my head," George recalled, "turning me back to my mother." He had been steered into a U-turn, compliments of the President of the United States. Many years later, George Thorn would nostalgically reminisce that he never "regretted" his boyish horseplay that day, because, as he put it, "it gave me the right to say I was patted on the head by Abraham Lincoln."

A little later in the afternoon, fifteen-year-old Albertus McCreary slipped by a guard and squeezed his way into the Presbyterian Church, along with some other boys, where there was standing room only. They were hoping to make their "strongest wish" come true: to shake the hand of President Abraham Lincoln. Albert had already tried earlier to meet the President at the Wills home, and got within about ten feet of the speaker's platform at Cemetery Hill, but had no luck in getting close enough to shake the President's hand. As Lincoln was working his way through the smothering crowd and exiting the Presbyterian Church near the end of the program, Albert spotted a crack in the crowd, and got a flicker of a chance to get the President's attention. Giving it his full lung capacity, young Albert hollered out for the President: "Mr. Lincoln, will you shake my hand?" It worked. "Certainly," replied the President. Lincoln had a knack (and soft place in his heart) for spotting children in a crowd, little ones otherwise lost like seedlings among the tall, mature trees. As Albert told it, Lincoln gave him "a good, strong grasp." Irrepressibly excited over this once-in-a-lifetime opportunity, Albertus McCreary would later reflect on that November 19, 1863 moment, saying, "I was a proud boy, and to this day feel a thrill of pride to have pressed the hand of one of the greatest men the world has ever known." It was one of the defining memories of his life.

There were hundreds, perhaps thousands, of these personal encounters with President Lincoln in Gettysburg, and at the railroad stops along the journey there. When Abraham Lincoln touched the people—he touched their lives, forever. There was something about the man, something mysteriously wonderful and beyond words, that made it so.

Reminiscent of Michelangelo's famous painting on the ceiling of the Sistine Chapel, depicting God reaching out His finger to the outstretched hand of Adam—where the simple gesture of touch was used to portray the precious gift of life—President Lincoln, that day, through the simple gesture of a handshake, had given those who were reaching out their hands to clasp his, the precious gift of an imperishable memory.

These handshakes would become memories that would last not only for their lifetimes, but for the lifetimes of their descendants—and their descendants, too, who would continue to give the moment eternal life through the legacy of oral history. Sons and daughters, grandsons and granddaughters, great-grandsons and great-granddaughters, the descending consanguinity of ancestral kin who shook Lincoln's hand at Gettysburg, would—until the passing of bloodline extinguished all possibility— tell with great pride, again and again, how they had held the hand of a family member that had once grasped the hand of Abraham Lincoln.

* * *

Shortly before five o'clock that Thursday afternoon, the President decided it was time to retire from the reception line at the Wills house where he and Governor Curtin had met the public for almost an hour. He wanted to walk about a quarter of a mile to the Gettysburg Presbyterian Church, which sat on the corner of Baltimore and High Streets. Lincoln wanted to attend the "Ohio program" to be held at the church, announced by Ward Lamon at the close of the cemetery dedication program. It would be the last formal event of the trip. Seward, as usual, would go with the President. But this time, there was someone else that Lincoln wanted to accompany him. Someone special. He wanted Gettysburg's very own home-grown hero, John L. Burns, by his side.

The seventy-year-old Burns, who already claimed to be a veteran of the War of 1812 (1812-1815), the Florida War (1835-1842) and the Mexican War (1846-1848), along with any political battles he may have fought as a former constable in Adams County, had rejuvenated his local fame by fighting as a civilian soldier with the Yankee First Corps of the Union Army at the Battle of Gettysburg. Four wars. At Gettysburg, Burns had been wounded in combat the first day of battle, although his injuries were not life threatening. A shoemaker with his hands, a patriot with his heart, and wired of gristle and nerve, John Burns, featured on the cover of *Harper's Weekly* in New York (comparable, today, to being on the cover of Time magazine) and described as "the only citizen of Gettysburg who [fought] against the enemies of his country," had become a living folk hero, a legend in his own time. This moniker irritated Gettysburgers, who had at least two hundred of its men from the little town volunteer for Union duty.

Fame sometimes drops on the unexpected. And the unprepared. Here was John Burns, a man who had a past reputation of staying drunk, and was regularly harassed for fun by the local "toughs," now honored and revered by the people of Gettysburg for fighting the Rebels on July 1st , 1863 with all he had, which was the wiliness of old age, a hay wagon's worth of gall, and his old flintlock musket used for squirrel-hunting. Aside from President Lincoln, John Burns was arguably the most famous person in Gettysburg those two days.

In fact, people visiting Gettysburg that week of the cemetery dedication had descended on the cantankerous Burns like a stump of ants on sugar, until, as one reporter observed, he was "overwhelmed with visitors." Like the bearded lady in an old time carnival sideshow, John Burns had become sort of a human novelty item that everyone visiting Gettysburg wanted to see, stiff and stoic sitting under the shade of his porch-steps, his flintlock rifle posed next to his side. Folks gave him money and wanted to hear the legendary stories about John Burns, veteran of four wars and the "hero of Gettysburg." And they wanted to hear those stories from the living legend himself. Burns gladly accommodated them, taking much delight in reliving his colorful (and malleable) experiences in battle.

John Burns—with his habitually sour expression, was eccentric in his ways, cranky, and had no discernable sense of humor. But he was a pretty sly old fox when it came to parlaying his celebrity status into a private business venture. A newspaper correspondent who was in Gettysburg during the President's visit picked up on the old soldier's business acumen, and wrote that Burns did "a thriving business in the sale of photographic views of himself, and his humble abode."

Hearing Lincoln say he was anxious to meet John Burns, David Wills and William Seward arranged for an envoy of three citizens to be dispatched out to his home, to let Burns know the President of the

United States had sent for him. Perhaps Burns' pride had been overinflated a tad by the kingly attention he had received the last couple of days—combined with his crabby disposition—when he initially told the anxious envoy from town, "If anyone wants to see me, let him come here." This was, however, a personal invitation from the President of the United States. So Burns reluctantly reconsidered (no doubt, pausing in silent, sullen-faced reflection for dramatic effect), finally giving in to the appeals of the citizens group. Burns then put on his high hat and joined the assembly back to town.

When "the brave old man" (as the *Adams Sentinel* newspaper called him) was proudly brought to the public square to join the President, Lincoln graciously deflected all of the attention away from himself to John Burns. "It need hardly be told how that patriot of the people, the honest Father Abraham, received this brave and venerable man," wrote the *Adams Sentinel*. "God bless you, old man," Lincoln told Burns, as he warmly took hold of the hand and arm of the venerable warrior. (Lincoln liked a double-handed handshake.) The people who watched all of this were thrilled. Robert Harper would write that at that moment, when their two great men came together and clasp hands in the middle of the street, "perhaps, more than any other, Gettysburg was truly dedicated."

The crowd on Baltimore Street was lively and asphyxiatingly thick. Marshals, now on foot, scraped the way clear as Lincoln and Burns walked side by side, along with Seward, the quarter mile stretch to the Presbyterian Church. The vast crowd that wrapped around this trio of men surged and rolled like a great ocean wave of humanity. It was a rich scene—the alpine, statuesque Lincoln in his lofty stovepipe hat, walking with his usual long-legged strides alongside the diminutive, short-legged, slumping frame of Burns. "They seemed an ill assorted pair . . . and could not keep step," observed J. Howard Wert, "try as they would." For the people in Gettysburg, it was an emotional sight, as well—two men weathered by time and war, physical opposites, yet spiritually bonded by courage and country.

Eventually, Lincoln, Burns and Seward, surrounded by a massive confluence of onlookers, arrived at the Presbyterian Church. As remembered by Thomas (T. C.) Billhiemer, a local college student, the church "was crowded to its utmost capacity . . . for each one within, there was ten without, unable to gain admission." Like modern day rope-line bouncers guarding entrance to the hottest show in town, military guards were stationed at the church doors, allowing in only those who had been invited. Some of the uninvited, like young Billhiemer, were able to sneak around the gatekeepers and get inside the church, cloaked by the chaotic admission process.

Lincoln would enter the sanctuary of the church and sit down in a reserved pew, in a seat next to the aisle. The old warrior John Burns would take a seat beside him. One year later, the famous frontier author Bret Harte wrote a poem about John Burn's exploits (it was, of course, more invented than biographical), making Burns into sort of a living legend. Fifty-one years later, to the day, this pew would be dedicated in a ceremony as the "Lincoln and Burns Pew," where it can be seen today.

Folks were tamped and stuffed into the tiny church, like fill dirt around a posthole. White, dust-filled bars of late afternoon sunlight slanted in the windows, irradiating scattered members of the audience. For many, it was standing room only. A deep breath of air was about as hard to come by, as was a place to sit or stand. Sentries at the church doors would keep out hundreds more that wanted in. The *Adams Sentinel* reported that the church was "filled to repletion, and for everyone inside there were ten on the outside, who wanted to get in."

Although never regularly attending or joining a church during his life, Lincoln was, perhaps, most comfortable in the Presbyterian Church. Thirteen years earlier, when Lincoln's son Eddie died after two months of terrible suffering with a respiratory illness, the pastor of the First Presbyterian Church in Springfield was so devoted to consoling the grief-tormented family, especially Mary Lincoln, that Mrs. Lincoln switched over to that church's particular kind of Presbyterianism. For years, the Lincoln family would reserve pew number 20 at the First Presbyterian Church in Springfield.

This Presbyterian Church in Gettysburg was the same church back in July, just four months earlier, that was filled—not with the joyful voices of choir and congregation—but with the tearful moans and gnashing of teeth of maimed and dying soldiers. North and South. Soldiers who were all Americans . . . excluding none. This convocation at the

Presbyterian Church would be a fitting place to last gather on such a special day. It would be held in the descending, evening shadow that followed the words of Lincoln's Gettysburg Address , words he spoke earlier that day at Cemetery Hill to both the North and South. Words spoken to all Americans . . . excluding none.

Despite some good singing and speech-making going on inside the church walls, people were spellbound by the very presence of the President. No matter where Lincoln had appeared in public during his Gettysburg trip—whether on the train balcony, on the porch of the Wills house, riding a horse to the soldiers' cemetery, sitting on the speaker's platform at Cemetery Hill, or in a pew at the Presbyterian Church—people were intractably drawn to his face. They looked at him, constantly, fixed on every expression, every raised eyebrow, every word. And they were comforted, reassured. Somehow, the alloy of sadness, strength and kindness in Lincoln's face, made it so.

Earlier that day, William Tipton, a scrappy thirteen-year-old boy who was bound and determined to get a good look at the President, rubbernecked for a view from the taller crowd that was congregated in sardine-can fashion on York Street. Eventually, young William was able to lock his eyes on President Lincoln as he was speaking from the steps of the Wills house, and later said, "My eagerness to see and hear the President—whom I regarded as much above all other men, and second only to the Almighty, centered all of my attention on Mr. Lincoln, and no word or movement of him escaped by attention."

In a strange sense, folks could hardly believe they were looking at the President of the United States. They were awe-struck. Entering the Presbyterian Church only about six feet behind the President, and then getting a seat only a few pews behind Lincoln and Burns, T. C. Billhiemer had squeezed himself into the front row of history. "I cannot recollect what the speaker said, nor can I tell what the speaker looked like," Billhiemer later confessed. "My eyes were glued upon the President," he said, adding that "I had never seen a live President, and never one like Lincoln, whose greatness was on every tongue."

If history has failed to adequately underscore anything that occurred in Gettysburg on November 18th and 19th of 1863, it is the sheer magnitude of the awe and adoration that was shown to President Lincoln by the thousands of people who were there. Their view of Lincoln as a man, was stronger than their view of Lincoln as a politician. They saw a man of humble beginnings, like themselves, who had remained humble after attaining the highest office in the land; a man with calloused hands who had lived through poverty and grief, and labored over the soil like they had. They saw a man of practical wisdom who was kind and decent, and who understood their sadness and hardships. And above all else, they saw honesty.

The recently-elected lieutenant governor of Ohio, Robert Anderson, whose brother Charles Anderson was the celebrated Union hero who just about single-handedly defended Fort Sumter until it finally fell to the Confederacy, was the featured speaker for this patriotic program being held at the Presbyterian Church. By all accounts, he did a respectable job on a speech he had already given back in the summer. The local paper, the *Adams Sentinel*, would describe (and perhaps embellish upon) Anderson's speech as "a bold and able exposition" of the causes leading to the Civil War, and "the importance of its termination."

Still, the extended battery of songs and speeches got the best of some, even the venerable warrior John Burns. Burns had often fought the enemy in war, but could not survive the combined forces of a long day, a stemwinder speech, and a stuffy-hot church sanctuary. Alice Powers, who was there in the church, would later explain how Burns became a casualty of the program, writing that "drowsiness claimed" their local hero. (Burns would eventually be buried in the Evergreen Cemetery at Gettysburg, where his gravestone appropriately bears the inscription: "Patriot." His grave is one of only two at Evergreen, where the American flag is flown twenty-four hours a day.)

President Lincoln had to leave the church services a bit early too, but his was a conscious decision; it was almost time for the presidential train to depart. The interrupting train schedule was probably a stroke of mercy for the President, who was becoming very sick.

Finally, it was time for the President to go home.

With a moving barricade of Marshals and Federal soldiers chopping a path through the crowded streets of Gettysburg, President Lincoln departed from the Presbyterian Church and returned to the Wills house, the place where it had all began. The President retrieved his carpetbag, and extended heartfelt words of gratitude to David and Jennie Wills.

Although Lincoln had a strong aversion for leaving the Nation's capital during the War, he had enjoyed the warmth and hospitality the Wills family had extended to him. It had been a fine trip, filled with good food and good fellowship, a pleasurable remission from Washington and the War. He had made some good political contacts along the way. And hopefully, he had delivered a speech to the Nation, which accomplished his two most urgent objectives: honor the sacrifices of the brave men who fought there so they would never be forgotten; and redefine the purpose of the War.

But the President was anxious to return home. Telling his hosts good-bye, Lincoln was chaperoned to the train depot by military guard, where he was bid farewell by music of the Marine Band and the huge concourse of people who had gathered there, hoping for one last look at the President of the United States.

Shortly before seven o'clock that evening, the President's train lumbered out of the Gettysburg train station, its destination, Washington, D. C.

Even after the President pulled up stakes in Gettysburg and returned to Washington, the little community still crackled with activity for a few days. Some people took an extra day or two, to walk about the battlefields; others had to wait that much time just to catch a spot on an outgoing train. Benjamin French, seeming to intuitively sense that he had just been a part of something big and wondrous, stayed over until the next day to soak it all up. He was walking on air. And rightly so. His poem *Consecration Hymn*, beautifully performed, had moved the multitude to tears and received rave reviews.

But most people were scrambling to get out of Gettysburg as quickly as possible. The beleaguered (if not jinxed) Governor's train would depart about an hour after the President's train, only to get stranded at the station in Hanover, Pennsylvania until the following day. Folks on board were angry as wet hornets. Even though the engine was shut down in Hanover for hours, there was still plenty of smoke rising from the Governor's train, from fuming passengers.

Local schoolteacher Sallie Myers, who would later dedicate herself to teaching and bringing equal education to African-American children, wrote in her diary, the day after the ceremonies were over, "The town is all excitement." She then added with her trademark candor (and seemingly, just a smidgen of sarcasm), that "persons from abroad are as anxious to get away, as they were to get here." Within a week, Gettysburg was breathing normal, again.

When the presidential train pulled out of the Gettysburg station in return to Washington, D. C. on November 19th, Lincoln's body was already ransacked by a form of smallpox known as the "variola" sickness. Over the course of those two November days, President Lincoln had shaken hands with hundreds, probably thousands of people during the Gettysburg trip, handshakes that could be vectors of the dangerous illness which was raging in parts of the country. And apparently, it had caught up with him. A throbbing, debilitating headache forced the President, who was ashen-faced and near collapse, to make the journey home stretched out on a side-seat in the "drawing room" of the director's car.

And where was the most unlikely, the most improbable member of the President's guild of men who made the historic trip with him to Gettysburg, the young African-American manservant, William Johnson? As usual, William Johnson was right there by Lincoln's side on the train, draping cool, wet towels on the aching forehead of a feverish and fatigued President. For both Lincoln and Johnson, Gettysburg would mark the commencement of the last chapter of their lives.

Along the way of this return trip, there would be no speeches or public appearances by the President. Many excited people, hoping to hear a few words or get a glimpse of Lincoln at one of the railway stops, would be left congregated on the depot platforms, disappointed. There could be no other way. The President was spent, utterly.

* * *

By the time President Lincoln arrived back in Washington at 1:10 a.m. the next morning, November 20th, he was quite ill. He would remain that way for nearly a month. As a health precaution, Lincoln's physicians placed him under a partial quarantine. They also urged him to get rid of his beard. William Johnson shaved the President. This was the first time that Abraham Lincoln had been without a beard, since eleven-year-old Grace Bedell wrote a letter to the President about three years earlier, during Lincoln's presidential campaign.

In her letter, young Grace expressed her admiration for candidate Abraham Lincoln and kindly suggested that he would "look a great deal better" if he would grow a beard, because, as she put it, "your face is so thin." Four days later, Lincoln wrote the little girl back, saying, among other pleasantries, "As to the whiskers, having never worn any, do you not think people would call it a piece of silly affectation if I were to begin it now?"

A few weeks later, at a campaign stop near Grace Bedell's hometown in Westfield, New York, Lincoln's newly-grown whiskers were conspicuous. He had wisely followed the little girl's advice. Lincoln asked the crowd if Miss Grace Bedell, his "little correspondent," was there, and if so, would she come forward. Suddenly the little girl emerged from the audience, and stood next to Lincoln at the speaker's platform. Lincoln stooped over, and gave her a fatherly kiss on the cheek. It is quite remarkable that. the venerable likeness of President Abraham Lincoln, the bearded Lincoln, that we will see forever, both in marble and in our minds, was sculpted by eleven-year-old Grace Bedell. No doubt, the youngest presidential image consultant in the history of American politics. This would continue to be the most remarkable incident of direct teenage involvement in presidential politics until President Jimmy Carter would reveal, in an October 28, 1980 debate with Ronald Reagan, that his twelve-year-old daughter Amy was a nuclear policy advisor.

The month following the ceremonial consecration of Soldiers' National Cemetery was a languid, roller-coaster recovery for President Lincoln. His body broke out with tiny, sparsely-appointed, blister-like sores that identified his illness as the milder but still dangerous version of smallpox. Infection and blood poisoning is what made the variola deadly. The fact that the President could avoid such complications while using the White House's infectious water supply and living among the putrid, unsanitary conditions of Washington, D.C., was in itself, very fortunate. The Lincoln family washed in the polluted water of the Potomac River, piped directly into the White House wash basins. This was a wonderful luxury installed by President Buchanan, but may have been a carrier of terrible sickness, perhaps even death, as in the case of Willie. Some days Lincoln was strong enough to leave his sickbed and take care of the Nation's most-pressing business, even working on his Annual Address to Congress that was due in early December. At other times, he felt so poorly he did not rise.

His upcoming speech to Congress would be a vitally important one, because it had to address the question that had become the riddle of the Sphinx for Lincoln's administration and the Federal government: under what conditions should the Southern states be reinstated into the Union? President Lincoln would describe this political conundrum as "the greatest question ever presented to practical statesmanship." It was a frightening, gut-wrenching query that hopefully no President of the United States will ever face again.

Even under the strain of sickness, the quality of mercy seemed never strained in Lincoln, who took time to review the steady flow of requests for pardons and stays of execution connected with the War, a responsibility he took very seriously. Lincoln always had a natural, instinctive sensitivity to injustice, and he took it with him all the way to the presidency. He meticulously studied every death penalty case submitted to him (most were for desertion and cowardice), and he always did so through the lens of common sense and compassion.

Lincoln's Secretary of the Interior, the always courteous, genial and snappy-dressed John P. Usher, himself an outstanding trial attorney, recalled with perhaps a smidgen of cynicism that when the President dissected these death sentence cases, "his great effort seemed to be to find some excuse, some palliation for offenses charged." John Hay recalled that earlier in the summer, Lincoln had spent six laborious hours going over the transcripts of one hundred court-martial cases, plowing through pardon applications like a row of potatoes, hoping to find, as Hay, (who was exhausted from the ordeal), noted in droll fashion in his diary, "any fact that would justify him in saving the life of a condemned soldier."

At one signing, Lincoln would commute sixty-two death sentences. On another occasion, Lincoln would write the injured soldier's pardon on his bandages. That December 1863, only a month after his

Gettysburg speech, Lincoln would even offer total amnesty to those in the South who would, by oath, pledge loyalty to the Union and recognize the Emancipation Proclamation. President Lincoln, however, did not always commute death sentences. If "meanness or cruelty" was involved, the death sentence was carried out. In what has become only a historical footnote, Lincoln would not rescue Nathaniel Gordon from the gallows. Gordon was the first American to be convicted and executed for trafficking in the slave trade. This time the quality of mercy in Lincoln apparently was strained and he set a stinging precedent when it came to accountability for the inhuman crime of slave trade.

Throughout his sickness and unrelenting presidential duties, the President still maintained his keen sense of humor, in part by poking fun at the endless cavalcade of people always showing up in dogged pursuit of a job or favor from him. Lincoln would remark about his contagious illness: "For the first time since I have been in office, I have something now to give to everybody that calls."

Tad continued to be quite sick, too. Mary was beginning her annual slide into depression, as February—the month of Willie's death—grew nearer on the calendar. All of this was a difficult postscript to what was, overall, a very good Gettysburg trip. And as usual, his trusted and faithful friend William Johnson was there, tending to the Lincoln family, relaying important presidential messages, watching over the President until he finally recovered.

But there was some good news, too. The Army of the Potomac had just defeated the Confederate troops at Lookout Mountain and Missionary Ridge, near Chattanooga. The Rebels had been chased out of Knoxville too, virtually eliminating the Southern army's presence in the eastern half of Tennessee, and opening the gate for a decisive Union campaign down the throat of Georgia, into the fertile Mesopotamia of the Confederacy. Gettysburg had brought an end to the South's invasion of Northern soil. Grant's key victory on the Mississippi River at Vicksburg that took place back in July, had chopped the Confederacy in half.

The outcome of the War had finally tilted, slightly but indefeasibly, in favor of the Union. Although another violent seventeen months remained before it would all come to an end at the McLean House in

Appomattox Court House, Virginia, and much more blood would be shed—the ax of the Union army was already at the root of the Confederacy tree.

Exactly one week after the dedication of the Soldiers' National Cemetery at Gettysburg, came Thanksgiving Day. The President, at that time, was still quite ill. But he felt a growing surge of hope in the survival of the Union, especially after victories at Gettysburg, Vicksburg and Chattanooga. Sensitive to the public's growing affection for the last Thursday in November, and prodded by the prominent national magazine editor Sarah J. Hale (who, interestingly, composed the venerable children's poem, *Mary Had a Little Lamb*), Lincoln would officially declare Thanksgiving Day as a national holiday.

In conjunction with this new, uniquely American holiday, President Lincoln would issue the Proclamation of Thanksgiving, a wildly popular piece of prose, ironically, that garnered far more print and praise across the country than his Gettysburg Address. Music would even be composed for the poem; it would be called the "Thanksgiving Hymn." Lincoln got the credit for composing the Proclamation of Thanksgiving, although it was actually written by his friend William H. Seward. It reminds us that the Secretary of State was a talented wordsmith, himself, and why Lincoln often ran his speeches by Seward before giving them.

As the years passed, the Nation's collective memory would not only fade about the President's beloved Emancipation Proclamation, but also about Abraham Lincoln's indispensable role in creating one of America's most cherished holidays—*Thanksgiving Day*.

* * *

After Lincoln's speech at Gettysburg and his return to Washington, naturally, all of the focus was on the recovery of a very sick President. But then, unexpectantly, as so often happens, the tireless, loyal caretaker, William Johnson, needed care, himself. Johnson fell ill with smallpox. Privately, Lincoln feared Johnson may have caught it from him. Odds are, he didn't. After all, a lethal epidemic of the disease was rifling through the capital city. While Johnson was bed-ridden with smallpox, the President collected his pay for him, and took care of Johnson's bills.

Lincoln had rallied from his sickbed, but his dear friend would not. Like so many others that year who could not escape the dreadful disease, Johnson died. Death had again reminded Lincoln of its ubiquity in his life.

Taking into consideration the hovering presence of death over Lincoln's family and friends, and how he had to live with the horrifying and painful knowledge that his decisions as President had sent hundreds of thousands of young soldiers to their graves, it is understandable that Abraham Lincoln ruminated about death. Death often co-opted his thoughts. During these times, he frequently sought comfort in poetry. When Lincoln read poetry, to him, it seemed as though cool, soothing breezes flowed from the words. One of his most cherished stanzas was from the poem, *The Last Leaf*, by Oliver Wendell Holmes, which he described as "inexpressibly touching," and often recited aloud, by memory:

> "The mossy marbles rest
> On lips that he has prest
> In their bloom;
> And the names he loved to hear
> Have been carved for many a year
> On the tomb. . ."

Now, another name Lincoln loved to hear, would be carved on the tomb. It was the name of William H. Johnson.

In a personal gesture that put into action the speech that Lincoln had recently given to dedicate the soldiers' cemetery at Gettysburg, in particular the words, "all men are created equal," the President would see to it that the body of William Johnson was honorably laid to rest in Arlington Cemetery. Lincoln would pay for Johnson's burial out of his own pocket. It was a mighty politically-incorrect thing to do, in that day. But to Abraham Lincoln it did not matter. It was really quite simple. Johnson and Lincoln were, at their core, good and decent men. equal men, who took equally good care of each other.

On the headstone of William H. Johnson, servant, another title would be placed underneath his name, another word to better describe the man, it would be the word . . . "CITIZEN." There it is, today, carved in stone. William H. Johnson, citizen. One solitary word placed after Johnson's name, that would be the seedcorn for African-American citizenship in America and the "new birth of freedom" that Lincoln had promised in the Gettysburg Address.

A promise he would keep.

CHAPTER SIXTEEN

ANALEPSIS: JUST TO BE "REMEMBERED"...

". . . that government of the people, by the people, for the people, shall not perish from the earth."
—Spoken at Ground Zero
New York City, NY
September 11, 2002

OVER TIME, THE GETTYSBURG ADDRESS HAS REACHED A MYSTICAL status, as though handed down to us by a Delphic Oracle. Its words distill the wisdom of the Founding Fathers and breathe eternal life into the Declaration of Independence. The words of the Gettysburg Address bring the Declaration of Independence forward to our time, making it real and relevant to the freedom and democracy we now enjoy.

When President Lincoln summoned forth the Declaration of Independence at Gettysburg, like a metallurgical wordsmith, he was forging together moral force with political force. Lincoln was telling those who heard his words that day at Cemetery Hill, and those who would read his words thereafter, the Americans of then, today and tomorrow, that our Nation was founded not only on the promise of freedom for all of its people, but also, on the promise of equality for all of its people. These dual promises of both freedom and equality, Lincoln believed, were self-evident and sacrosanct.

The Gettysburg Address reflects Lincoln's peerless ability and dexterity as a wordsmith. And it reflects his mastery in converting the vaporous substance of thought into the more tangible form of clear and lasting words. In short . . . his power over words.

Lincoln loved to blend together the Elizabethan prose appearing in the *King James Bible* which he always kept on his desk in the Executive Office and knew many verses by heart and the Anglo-Saxon language of the Shakespearean tragedies that he grew up reading. Both strongly influenced him throughout his life. The cadence of Bunyan's prose in *The Pilgrim's Progress*, in rhythmus tandem with the ecclesiastical language of the *King James Bible*, are vibrantly revealed in the Gettysburg Address. And he preferred the short words of the English language to the longer words of Latin origin. Most of all, however, Abraham Lincoln wanted to speak plainly, and be understood when he spoke.

But how does a man with only a smattering of formal education, who did not learn good grammar until he was twenty-two and basic geometry until he was forty, who could give a pretty good stump speech or hold his own in a debate, but just as often was mediocre or fumbling as a impromptu public speaker, a man who delivered all of his speeches with a notoriously scrill and squeaky, Midwestern-twanged, monotone voice, write and give a speech that will take him to Ciceronian heights?

The answer, although lying in a fascinating confluence of factors, is predominately found in Abraham Lincoln's early life— his frontier upbringing, his hunger to read and learn, his love of wordplay and literature, and his wildly-diverse experiences along the path to manhood. Lincoln's writing and speaking abilities were constructed over time—not conceived at birth.

To understand how the Gettysburg Address came to be, one must understand how Abraham Lincoln came to be.

One must go back to the beginning . . .

Abraham Lincoln was born on February 12, 1809. He came into the world dirt poor, in a one-room, windowless log cabin with a floor of packed mud. It was a common home for that time and place, built on a leasehold site called the Sinking Spring Farm. The boy was "born low," as folks put it back then. In the first biography ever composed about Lincoln, Nicolay and Hay would write that the newborn Abraham arrived "in the midst of the most unpromising circumstances that ever witnessed the advent of a hero into this world." This birthplace adjoined the waters on the Big South Fork of Nolin Creek, near the town of Hodgenville, Kentucky. The three hundred acre site had a crystal-clear drinking spring, fed by a cave, just over the hill from their primitive home.

His parents were Thomas and Nancy Hanks Lincoln. They gave him a good, long first name . . . Abraham. It was long and lean and sturdy name, like he would be someday, a name worn by his grandfather. A name straight out of the *Old Testament*. But he came into the world with none of the advantages of blueblood pedigree. He was a boy, some would claim, of uncertain and undignified biological stock.

When Abraham was two years old, the threat of eviction over a shoddy land title and unproductive soil drove the Lincoln family from the Sinking Spring Farm about ten miles, northeastwardly, to a two hundred thirty acre farm in Hardin County, Kentucky, with richer ground. It was called Knob Creek, a beautiful, pastoral site with a creek meandering through it, where Thomas Lincoln rented thirty acres of fertile bottomland in the valley. Corn and beans thrived in the creek-fed soil. The place got its name from the small but distinct hills surrounding the creek, called "knobs," which abruptly emerged from the ground.

"My earliest recollection," Lincoln would later write, "is of the Knob Creek place." Six-year-old Abraham, along with his eight-year-old sister Sarah, walked about two miles from Knob Creek to a little place called Atherton where they first learned the alphabet and numbers by rote memorization at Catholic teacher Zachariah Riney's "A.B.C. School."

Young Abraham would always remember a few strong Knob Creek memories: the infant death of his only brother, little Thomas; his near drowning in the cold, flash-flooded waters of Knob Creek; looking upon his mother's face, as she read the Bible; sticking pumpkin seed in the fertile bottomland of the valley, only to see them washed away the next day by a hard rain; "cooning" it across Knob Creek straddling a log—and although he would not speak or write of it, it was at the Knob Creek place that a youthful Lincoln would likely see people with dark skin, manacled, being marched down the old Cumberland Road towards the states of the Deep South—in what would be his first sickening images of the cruelty of slavery.

The land title system in Kentucky was pernicious and maddening for homesteaders with its overlapping boundary claims, and again, Thomas Lincoln found himself tormented by another "ejectment" lawsuit. This time, over his Knob Creek land title. Even Kentucky's iconic pioneer, Daniel Boone, who was distant kin of the Lincoln family, was a victim of that state's onerous title records. Tom Lincoln was also upset over Kentucky's embrace of slavery (about 40% of Hardin County's male population were slaves), which collided with his anti-slavery Calvinist beliefs and, perhaps even more disturbing to him at the time, knocked him out of job opportunities. Farmers using cheap slave labor had a huge economic advantage over everyone else.

So in 1816, Thomas Lincoln would again pull up stakes after living five years at Knob Creek, taking Nancy and their children west in a grueling winter journey across the Ohio River into Indiana. In his 1860 presidential campaign biography, Lincoln would explain that Thomas Lincoln moved out of Kentucky "partly on account of slavery; but chiefly on account of the difficulty of land titles in Ky."

They would migrate to a remote wilderness community in southwestern Indiana near the town of Gentryville, in Perry (later Spencer) County, known as Little Pigeon Creek. The Lincoln family was now 'Hoosiers." Because there was no roads or even a path, they would hack their way through sixteen miles of what young Lincoln called "the unbroken forest," a place he described as filled with "bears and other wild animals." It was a trek through the dense, swampy undergrowth of briar, matted pea vines and other thick forest vegetation, until finally they would arrive at a place selected by Thomas Lincoln. For Thomas Lincoln the homesite was important, but a clear title even more so. Now, he finally had one.

The boy, Abraham, was seven-years-old. His legendary prowess with an ax would begin in this place.

When the Lincoln's reached their Indiana homestead, as was sometimes said back then, they were "poor as Job's turkey." For the first few weeks, Thomas went ahead of the family to stake out a site and put up a lean-to structure called a "half-face camp" or "pole-shed" which was a shelter having only three sides made of logs, with the fourth side temporarily open to the elements. The open face of the pole-shed looked to the south, away from the blunt force of cold northern winds and snowstorms. For survival from weather and large animals, a blazing fire was maintained near the opening around the clock. Thomas would finish a four-sided cabin before winter to assure the family's comfort and safety, although the first winter would come and go before they could chink the cracks with mud and grass. It would be the family's fourth home with a dirt floor. Lincoln would remember those trying days as "pinching times."

Despite the hardship of moving again, and leaving most of the family's hand-made furniture behind for lack of wagon room (Thomas would make more), the Lincolns had found in newly-formed Indiana, a state where land titles were guaranteed by the government and slavery was illegal. Despite the loneliness of their isolation in the wilderness, it seemed like a better fit for the Lincoln family. Thomas Lincoln would purchase about a hundred acres at $1.25 per acre. There, for a little while, Abraham and Sarah would attend Andrew Crawford's tiny "Blab School," located about a mile from the Lincoln's family's log cabin home, when they could scrape up the dollar or two it cost for a school semester. These schools got their name from a teaching technique where the children, of a wide variety of ages, continuously recited or "blabbed" their lessons, out loud, all at the same time. A quiet child, it was assumed, was a daydreaming child. Lincoln later bluntly remarked that these Blab Schools did "absolutely nothing to excite ambition for education."

By the age of ten, only a few months after his mother's death young Abraham could scribble out his name, and was teaching himself to read and write. Soon, at these "so called schools," as Lincoln sarcastically put it, he was learning " 'readin, writin, and cipherin' to the Rule of Three." Words and numbers mesmerized him. The intellectual fuse had been lit, and it would burn hot the rest of his life.

Lincoln would later recall that during that time he wrote "anywhere and everywhere . . . that lines could be drawn." When paper or slate got scarce, Abraham would even scratch out words on a wooden fire-shovel, a board with a tapered handle carved at one end, used to stoke and move coals around a fire, then shave off the scribblings with a drawing knife and start again. Sometimes he would write on a plank of smooth wood with a piece of charcoal, or with a stick in the dirt or snow. Abe's first pen would be made out of a buzzard's feather, and an "ornery" type of ink would be squeezed from blackberry briar root, mixed with a naturally occurring, crystallized rock called "copperas," which was added for color . Because candles cost too much to make or buy, Abraham would read after dark by burning hickory bark or using a cup of animal grease with a homemade wick in it as a source of light. Most of the time, though, Abraham preferred to read by early-morning daylight.

In just a few years, Abraham would become a precocious and purposeful reader, always scrambling to get his hands on the next book. No one had a better view of Abraham's obsession with books than his second cousin, Dennis Hanks. Hanks, an illegitimate child and first cousin of Nancy Lincoln, was taken in by Lincoln's parents. "Abe" and "Denny," as the cousins called each other, would become tight friends for several years. Hanks, who was ten years older and a bit rowdier than Lincoln, described the boy Abraham as a "Constant and I may Say Stubborn reader." Young Lincoln's pal and neighbor, David Turnham, remembered that "We had but few books at that time and our opportunities were poor." But he added, "what [Lincoln] read he read well and thoroughly—never forgetting what he read." Dennis Hanks further recalled from their childhood days that "Abe was getting hungry for book[s], reading Evry thing he could lay his hands on." Journalist and prolific author Ida M. Tarbell would write that the boy Lincoln's "hunger for books [was] . . . as real as that one feels for food." It was true. Abraham read while walking, plowing, stretched out on the cabin's dirt floor, lying in the woods with his feet propped against a tree, on wood piles he had chopped, and in-between chores.

By the time Lincoln was grown, he would have less than one cumulative year of formal schooling. That's all. Even this one year of abridged formal education, doled out in primitive backwoods schools, was spread out over several of Lincoln's early years. For young Lincoln, it was a meager, piecemeal education, eked out of the few months, here and there, that fell between the steely, overcast days of early winter and the spring planting of crops. Back then, they called it going to school by "littles." An apropos name, since Lincoln learned very "little" in these schools. It was a stunted method of "book learning" that marked the end of the trail for most pioneer boy's formal education. But Abraham was different from most. In reality, Abraham Lincoln was home-schooled, serving as his own teacher and pupil. He was saved from educational poverty by a hungry desire to learn, and a restless curiosity that lifted him out of commonality.

Years later, in his adult years, Lincoln privately harbored regret, perhaps was even ashamed, of his lack of a formal education—particularly a college education. He felt it was a dark stain upon himself and his career. During his time in Congress, Lincoln was asked to complete a question about the extent of his education for the *Biographical Dictionary of Congress*. His blunt, scribbled-in, one word reply: "defective."

In a paradoxical way that is unique to Lincoln's life, the frequent reference to his "lack of formal education" is, in one sense, a self-contradiction. It was Lincoln's sparse classroom learning, perhaps eighteen months in all, along with his insatiable craving for literacy, that over time, educated the man. The unique experiences that Lincoln encountered from his barren, hardscrabble life, the "school of hard knocks" were his learning curve, his real classroom education. His faculty was the harsh realities of life. To Lincoln's credit, later in life, he would never allow his "schooling" to get in the way of his "education." Life had become an education, of its own end. When Lincoln combined these two forms of education, that is, the lessons from both books and life, they would become a powerful force in shaping the greatness of the man.

Still, through it all, young Lincoln's most pleasurable respites from the grating work and setbacks of life were when he read books. Books inspired and rejuvenated him. The challenge for Abraham, was getting his hands on those books.

It is hard to imagine in today's world, but as a boy, Lincoln lived in a world without money. There was very little money to be made or spent. It was a world of barter. Lincoln was deprived of much when it came to material things; but he refused to be deprived of books. "My best friend," the adolescent Abraham once quipped, "is the man who'll git me a book I ain't read." For the teenage Lincoln, a good book was an intellectual tryst; a place of joy away from life's hardships, where the author and the reader would secretly meet.

Young Lincoln would sometimes hire himself out for payment in books, rather than payment in store goods. Abraham would give up the opportunity to buy a pair of desperately needed boots, or highly-prized denim trousers that covered the whole length of his long legs, so he could get a handful of books to read. And he borrowed every book in the neighborhood. His stepmother Sally recalled that "Abe read all the books he could lay his hands on." She said that when young Lincoln "came across a passage that struck him, he would write it down . . . then he would re-write it—look at it—repeat it." This showed remarkable self-discipline and a hunger to learn in young Abraham. It was also a precursor of his revisionist writing style, which would someday be distinctly revealed in his composing the Gettysburg Address.

Lincoln's stepmother sally would bring "luxuries" with her from Elizabethtown, Kentucky, things which must have seemed to the Lincoln children, in their cramped Indiana log cabin, like wondrous proof of a better life waiting on them, someday in their future: feather mattresses in place of cornhusk pallets, spoons and forks, a spinning wheel, and a magnificent walnut bureau for which she had paid the exorbitant price of $45.00 in Kentucky, all to perk up the stark ambiance of their tiny cabin. The walnut bureau was the first piece of furniture the Lincoln children had ever seen.

Sally also brought hugs and encouragement into the home, "luxuries" the Lincoln children had been deprived of since their mother's death. And, more portentously, Sally brought books. Wonderful books. In number they were few; but in value to young Abraham, they were priceless. These were not books for ostentation on the shelf, but for constant, finger-to-thumb use, that left the pages worn and dog-eared. For Abraham's hungry mind, they were books that would become the foundation blocks of his adolescent learning. Books that carried the power of immense impression and are still literary staples today, like *The Pilgrim's Progress, Aesop's Fables, The Arabian Nights, Robinson Crusoe* and the *King James Bible.*

Abraham memorized swaths out of the *King James Bible* (often called the "Saxon Bible" in Lincoln's time), particularly sections from one of his favorites, the *Psalms*. And he soaked up *Aesop's Fables* like a sponge, so much so, he could write out the stories by memory. Once, when young Lincoln was reading *Aesop's Fables*, his cousin Dennis Hanks popped off: "Abe, them yarns is all lies." Abraham paused a moment, glanced up at Hanks with a grin, and replied, "and mighty darn good lies, Denny." Abraham first beefed-up his spelling and grammar with *Dilworth's Spelling Book*. And he got his hands on a popular joke book called *Quin's Jests* sprinkled full of coarse, earthy humor that Abraham read to Dennis Hanks at night, while they both laughed out loud the whole time.

When young Lincoln first took grasp of John Bunyan's *The Pilgrim's Progress*, his family would recall that "his eyes sparkled," and on that evening as he read it, "he could not sleep." Surely, when Abraham read the verse in Part One, Section III of *The Pilgrim's Progress*, his heart was forever touched with those words, which would someday be so befitting of his life:

> "The hill, tho' high, I covet to ascend,
> The difficulty will not me offend,
> For I perceive the way to life lies here.
> Come, pluck up, Heart, let's neither faint nor fear;
> Better, tho' difficult, the right way to go,
> Than wrong, tho' easy, where the end is woe."

Sally couldn't read or write her own name, but she loved books and Believed in the importance of education. And she would come to love and nurture Abraham as if the boy was her own and Lincoln in return would call her his "best friend in this world".

Sally said that Abraham, even at a young age, "read diligently." The modest but eclectic collection of books Sally introduced to the Lincoln household was, in Abraham's isolated and bucolic world, the Library of Alexandria.

During his later teen-age years, Abraham asked a well-off farmer, Josiah Crawford, to borrow his book, *Life of Washington*, the inaccurate but inspirational work of Mason ("Parson") Weems. Lincoln desperately wanted to read the popular and adulatory biography of the first president. He was willing to travel sixteen round trip to Crawford's farm, to lay hands on the book. And he did. Crawford loaned it to him. Excited as a child on Christmas morning, Abraham snugly carried the book back to his log cabin home, where he would read it each morning at sunrise. He would tuck the book away at night in the airy cracks between the unchinked logs, for safekeeping. One night, a fierce thunderstorm belted the log cabin, slinging water between the chinks of the logs. Next morning, Lincoln found the book soggy and warped.

Sick over the damaged book, Lincoln promptly went to see old man Crawford, to confess his responsibility for the accident and offer restitution in the only means of payment he had— manual labor. Crawford, ever the exploitive entrepreneur, figured the book to be worth a value equal to three full days of labor on his farm. Despite Crawford's self-serving appraisal of the book, Lincoln gutted-out the work, pulling fodder for three days, until, as he described it, "there was not a corn blade left on a stalk." Crawford credited him with twenty-five cents per day. To release his bitter frustration over the high-price of sweat-equity Crawford had extracted from him, Lincoln would later compose a variety of comical poems and jingles pasquinading the tightfisted Crawford's colossal nose. One ditty put into rhyme the story of "Josiah blowing his bugle." As he would continue to do all the rest of his life, Lincoln was using humor, along with pen and paper, to modulate his anger. And he had purchased his first book.

But poverty and isolation were not the only roadblocks along Abraham's journey to get an education. There was another obstacle. One made of flesh and blood. It was his father, Thomas Lincoln.

Thomas Lincoln was a muscular, "squarebuilt" man of about five ft.-ten and one-half inches, with black hair, an enormous nose, and hazel eyes. The nose-to-chin part of his face was sectioned off by deep furrows. A rustic man of friendly but awkward disposition, the senior Lincoln could spin a pretty good yarn himself. He was against slavery and very religious (he helped start and build the Little Pigeon Creek Primitive Baptist Church), and had a reputation for unflagging honesty. The Lincoln's family homestead, although they moved several times, was at one time, perched on the dusty, old Cumberland Trail road in Kentucky. The road ran from Louisville down to Nashville. There was a steady stream of diverse folks—vendors and vagabonds, hucksters, frontier families, reverends and rag-and-bone men—navigating their way north and south, who sometimes paused in Knob Creek for a night's rest.

Some evenings, after dark, Tom Lincoln, a natural-born raconteur with an inexhaustible stockpile of tales, would tell funny and spellbinding stories, keeping the travelers and locals laughing and entertained. And sitting right there in the lively crowd, his long, skinny legs folded underneath his arms, was his son Abraham, soaking it all in. Remembering every word. Every mimic. Every clever spin of a phrase. And the art of timing a good punch line. On one occasion, Abraham was harshly chastised by his father for entertaining his buddies with imitations of a local fire-and-brimstone Baptist preacher. This ability to galvanize people through conversation and storytelling would be about the only stock-in-trade young Lincoln and his father would ever share.

Otherwise, Thomas Lincoln lived as a handyman, and a pretty good one at that, having better tools than most settlers, and doing carpentry and cabinet work around the various villages where the Lincoln family lived. He was also a part-time surveyor, subsistence farmer and served a bit in the militia. But he was sorely illiterate. Thomas Lincoln could barely write his name. Maybe this was why he frowned on young Abraham's "hankering" to read books. In his view, books diverted Abraham from work; from Abraham's perspective, work diverted him from learning. It seems that Tom Lincoln saw his son's affection for school and books as a sort of character flaw, once remarking that "If Abe don't fool away all of his time on his books, he may make something yet."

If nothing else, Thomas Lincoln's exasperation at his boy's time spent reading, which he mostly saw as the postponement of chores, when examined through the darker lens of Tom Lincoln's unkind journey through life, is more understandable.

Thomas was one of five children of Abraham Lincoln (President Lincoln's grandfather), who had become somewhat of a land baron, accumulating more than 5500 acres of fertile land in Kentucky. From the horrible moment Thomas Lincoln, just a boy between six and eight years old, watched his father Abraham brutally mauled to death in a field by Shawnee Indians before his tender eyes, he was condemned by fate to live a harsh, survivalist life. Sometimes a child sees something that is unspeakably awful, that changes them, and their life, forever. For Thomas Lincoln, this was such an event. He would not allow himself to forget—nor his son. As Abraham Lincoln would reminisce later in his adult life, "[this] legend, more strongly that all others, [was] imprinted upon my mind and memory."

The sudden violent death of Thomas's father not only was an emotional shock to Thomas, the youngest of three boys, but it would also change his financial fate, forever. Instead of having a promising future which held the possibility of being the adult son of a successful plantation farmer, Thomas Lincoln would be left fatherless and penniless, a genealogical loser with no family legacy in land, destined to make his own way in the world. (At that time, the law of "primogeniture" passed all of a family's inheritance to the oldest son, which was his brother Mordecai.)

Thomas Lincoln, the boy, had become a man at the tender age of eight. He had to. There was no time or place for books. The only learning that mattered to Thomas Lincoln was how to scratch out a living as a subsistence farmer in an unforgiving, unbroken forestland filled with wild animals like bears and panthers, dangerous Indians, fatal diseases and sickness, and brutal winters. After all, you couldn't plant, milk or sleep under a book.

Maybe this is why Lincoln's father, year after year, hired out his teen-age boy, Abe—who was almost freakishly talented with an ax by the age of eleven—to do brutish labor for other farmers at a rate of twenty-five cents a day. And they worked Abraham like a borrowed mule. Contracting out one's children to do hard labor at slave wages, today, would be criminally prosecuted as child abuse; but in the frontier life of the 1820's, it was an accepted parental practice until the child reached the "emancipation" age of twenty-one. The father of the legendary frontiersman David Crockett, hired out his boy at the tender age of twelve, to a cattle driver Davy bitterly described as "a perfect stranger," to drive a herd of cattle, on foot, a distance of more than two hundred miles, from Tennessee to Virginia. A year later, Davy would escape. Young Abraham would dutifully bring back all of his earnings to his father, year after year, but he burned inside with anger about it, referring to it in his adult years as "organized robbery."

This decision of Thomas Lincoln to contract out his slender but strong boy to "grub work", often at the flat rate of twenty-five cents a day, digging stumps, cutting thick undergrowth, plowing rocky ground and chopping down trees and then splitting them up into fence-rails, which was the provenance of his later political moniker, "the rail-splitter," and then keep all of the boy's earnings, must have been a disheartening body-blow to young Lincoln, for it marked the cruel end of any hope for a traditional school education.

As Abraham got older, the daily swinging of an ax left his lanky arms corded with muscle and hard as wire nails. One local who was an eyewitness to his chopping prowess, sized it up by saying it looked like "there was three men at work by the way the trees fell." As powerfully symbolized by Norman Rockwell's painting of a young, lanky and long-legged Lincoln in suspenders, titled *Lincoln the Railsplitter*. This breathtaking painting, once owned by businessman and presidential candidate Ross Perot, can be seen at the Butler Institute of American Art in Youngstown, Ohio, depicting young Lincoln with ax in one hand and book in the other, Abraham would, in fact, have to learn to balance the book and the blade.

Despite the ubiquity of labor levied upon him, often ten or more hours a day, and his hunger to read and learn, Abraham refused to let one foreclose the other. His pluck would save him. He was determined to read and expand his horizons, despite the cultural forces pressing down on his early life. Young Lincoln would use his keen mind like another ax, to break through the frozen river of ambition within himself.

During breaks from the pole-ax and plow horses, Abraham would lean up against a shade tree and read. Lincoln would chuckle today at the people who are walking around everywhere, intensely engrossed in their hand-held technology, completely oblivious to what is right in front of them, because he did the same thing with a book. He was always walking and reading. Even with a long day of grinding work ahead of him, young Lincoln would awaken with the first rays of sunrise, to squeeze-in some reading. This juggling of learning and labor kept Lincoln and his father's relationship festered up, like a boil. For the father, Thomas Lincoln, taming the raw land was ennobling; for the son

Abraham, it was enslaving.   In a speech made before he became President, Lincoln, then a Springfield lawyer, alluded to his exodus from home and escape from a life of subsistence farming after reaching the age of twenty-two, saying with tongue-in-cheek, "I used to be a slave, and now I am so free that they let me practice law."

As a boy, Lincoln never hid the fact that he didn't like the hard physical work of a subsistence farmer's life that was cemented into his father's belief system, a system in young Abraham's view, that put a lid on the rest of your life.   Instead, Abraham eagerly embraced the mental work of reading, mathematics and learning about the world outside of the family farm, that in his belief system, opened the door to a fast-growing, free market economy and a way of life with no limitations on how far an individual could go.

Each day that Thomas Lincoln farmed out Abraham to another man's worksite and kept all of the wages for himself; each conflict they had over books and learning, hammered another small wedge between their lives.

* * *

Another transformative event in young Lincoln's relationship to his father took place shortly after the sudden and tragic death of his mother, Nancy.   Thomas Lincoln had been left alone with three children to raise, Sarah, Abraham and Dennis; two, abandoned by their mother's untimely death; the other, abandoned by "bastardy."   Tom Lincoln decided to travel back down into Kentucky, to the place of Elizabethtown, far from their dirt farm in Indiana. The purpose of the trip was to find himself a replacement wife.   It wasn't the stuff of romance novels, but the brutal reality was this: a man in the frontier wilderness, left alone with small children to take care of, one of them a girl, needed a woman's help. And he had a particular woman in mind for the position. She was a recently-widowed lady with three young children, saddled with the unpaid debts of her late husband, whom Thomas sweetly remembered from his childhood.

Her name was Sarah Bush Johnston. She was lovingly known as "Sally." Thomas would make a "cold call," unannounced, to Sally's door. Sally had three young children of her own. In his own plain, unpolished way, Dennis Hanks explained Thomas and Sally's whirlwind courtship and marriage this way: "Tom had a kind o'way with women," adding that as for Sarah Johnston, "maybe it was somethin' she took comfort in to have a man that didn't drink an' cuss none." Because of her station in life, Sally was likely considered to be a notch or two higher in social class than Thomas's first wife, Nancy. Tom Lincoln paid off Ms. Johnston's debt, they got "hitched" in Elizabethtown, and headed back to the wilderness of Little Pigeon Creek. Thomas Lincoln had "married up."

In what was a real, early nineteenth century version of the movie, *Home Alone*, following spring planting, Thomas Lincoln had left his two children, twelve-year-old Sarah and ten-year-old Abraham, and their twenty-year-old, but rather immature, cousin Dennis Hanks behind in their wilderness homestead to "fetch" himself a wife. He would be gone for several weeks. Sarah, Abraham and Dennis would have to fend for themselves while Thomas was gone. As Abraham Lincoln later wrote in a poem during his adult years, the three of them were left all alone in the deep forest where "the panther's scream filled the night with fear."

For the two young ones left behind, especially Sarah, who fixed meals and kept house, the long, lonesome days of isolation and uncertainty in this "wild region," as Lincoln later described it, without any parental help or protection, were unimaginably harsh and frightening. Abraham and Sarah had first felt abandoned by their mother's death. Here they were, abandoned, yet again. Sometimes, young Sarah, despondent from the loss of her mother, the absence of her father and the isolation, would just sit by the fire and cry. The boys would try to cheer her up, by fetching her a cute baby raccoon or a little turtle. It did little to comfort the overwhelmed girl.

Finally, one day, many weeks later, Tom Lincoln would bring home his new bride. It had been about a year, since Nancy Lincoln's death.

Sally would later describe that unforgettable day of her arrival at the Lincoln homestead by recounting that the hungry, forsaken, "rugged and dirty" children she first laid eyes on were acting "wild" and more animal-like, than human. She "Soaped, rubbed and washed the Children Clean," sharing her own clothes with Abraham and Sarah, so they "looked more human." They "were Sufring greatly for clothes", she remembered. It could have turned out much worse.

Sally brought from Kentucky her two daughters, Elizabeth and Matilda Johnston, and a somewhat shiftless son, John D. Johnston, leaving eight people crowded into Thomas Lincoln's tiny, one-room log cabin. It was a frontier version of the *Brady Bunch*. They lived on top of each other, crammed together in the tiny log cabin like weekend inmates in the holding tank of a county jail. Privacy was as rare as oysters. Despite the unnerving start to their relationship, Abraham would soon come to love Sally. And she came to dearly love young Abraham, later saying he was "the best boy I Ever Saw or Ever Expect to see." Lincoln would always called her "Mama."

Sally would later call attention to how truthful her stepson Abraham was, and also his kindness, saying that "Abe never spoke a cross word to me." Sally was anything but the stereotypical wicked stepmother from the fairy tales of *Hans Christian Andersen*. She would treat her stepchildren with the same love and devotion as she did her own children. Sally pressed upon Thomas to give their log home a face-lift with a proper door, a window (without glass) and wooden floor, and a loft for the boys to sleep in. She exposed the Lincoln children to a better, more comfortable cloth called "denim," in the place of their hot, scruffy buckskins. And, in what would turn out to be a splendid bonus for young Abraham, Sally encouraged reading and supported the idea of the children getting the opportunity to attend school.

Sally Lincoln would become the saving grace and a blessing to the Lincoln family. The tall, kind woman would spruce-up their home and their lives. She had an intuitive mind, that appreciated young Lincoln's hunger to learn. Her presence brought an instant ambience of warmth to the Lincoln home, and provided Abraham with the motherly love and tenderness he had lost since his mother's death, and which he so desperately craved. And Abraham loved Sally. Her soft and patient ways were a counterweight to the harsh and unforgiving ways of Thomas. Sally once said of herself and her stepson Abraham, that "his mind and mine . . . seemed to move together."

But despite Sally's sweet intervention into the family, Thomas Lincoln's temporary abandonment of his children that season to find himself a wife, would cast a long shadow over his only son.

* * *

Today, we have a full personality portrait of a kind and thoughtful Sally Lincoln. But historical assessments of Thomas Lincoln butt heads with one another. Some have portrayed Thomas Lincoln as an industrious, hard-working frontiersman in the idealistic prototype of the Jeffersonian proletariat. Others have painted him as a lowbrow, an unsettled ne'er-do-well with no trace of ambition, who put his boy to work in place of himself, while he shot the bull with neighbors and piddled around with odd jobs. Sally Lincoln would say, shortly after Lincoln's death, that her late husband "took particular Care not to disturb" Abraham, when he was reading. Others have claimed that on occasion he destroyed Abraham's books, and tried to snuff out his boy's love of learning through mind-numbing work. Some in Lincoln's circle of family and friends remembered that Thomas Lincoln was strict but good to Abraham, while others recalled that he mentally and physically mistreated his son.

Dennis Hanks, who once admitted his cousin Abraham could be "lazy" about his chores, also recalled that Thomas, angry with "Abe" over his books, would "Sometimes . . . slash him for neglecting his work by reading," once admitting that he had "Seen his father Nock him Down." The plain fact was, the farmer's son hated the farm. Neighbor John Romine, who occasionally worked young Lincoln on his farm remembered that "Abe . . . didn't love work half as much as his pay," saying Lincoln told him that "his father taught him to work, but . . . never taught him to love it." Romine also observed that Lincoln was reluctant to "pitch in at work like killing snakes." Probably a black mark on one's farming vocation. Of course, in the rigorous context of early nineteenth century pioneer life, Abraham's outspoken preference for a good book rather than a day of plowing north while looking at the south end of a mule, was plenty enough to get the boy labeled as awful "lazy." And it did.

Young Lincoln was not only inquisitive, but he could be intellectually meddlesome as well, which sometimes caused Abe to inject himself, uninvited, into grown-up conversations. Dennis Hanks recalled that just to "tease his father," Lincoln would be sure to ask an approaching stranger "the first question" before his father could speak, for which Thomas would sometimes "knock him a rod." Those moments were a burr in Tom Lincoln's britches. And a bruise underneath Abe's.

Abraham could be a bit of a rascal, too. He loved a good prank. Once, after his stepmother Sally whitewashed the ceiling of their log cabin, and teased the tall, fast-growing Abe to "keep his head clean," so not to leave "tracks on her ceiling," he got the idea for a good joke. The spindly but sturdy Abraham persuaded a local boy to let him be held in the air, feet-first, leaving muddy footprints across the ceiling like Abe had walked across it. When Sally returned to the cabin and saw his handiwork, she told Abraham she should "thrash" him, but then burst into laughter over the innovative stunt. Although Abraham scrubbed the ceiling clean, no doubt wearing a Cheshire cat grin the whole time, it certainly was not Tom Lincoln's brand of humor.

Thomas Lincoln was probably at peace with his son investing a little time in reading and writing, but he got a bit lathered-up when he would regularly hear about Abraham darting under a shade tree to take a break from chores, cornbread under one arm, book under the other. He believed Abe needed to put more shoulder in his work, and less nose in his books. In those days, an able-bodied son had a strict duty to help feed the family and turn a profit on their land so they could barter for the necessities of life.

The intellectual and emotional chasm between father and son had cracked open, and was widening. Books were pulling young Lincoln closer to his future, and pushing him further apart from his father.

Even as a teenager, Abraham turned to humor, and his pen and paper, to calm and steady himself during moments of emotional turmoil. He would take some of the sting out of the ongoing conflict with his father by composing a humorous four-line poem, written privately on sheets of paper sewed together to form his 1826 school workbook. Abe's cathartic little ditty went like this:

> *"Abraham Lincoln*
> *his hand and pen*
> *he will be good but*
> *god knows when."*

Thomas Lincoln saw his life limited to one of using his physical power of labor, where taking risks and tempting fate were to be avoided. A life properly lived, in Thomas Lincoln's Primitive or "Hard Shell" Baptist view, was a morally strict life left to the mercy of the winds of fate, already authored and made unchangeable by God's omnipotent stroke of "predestination." Only those predestined by God would be saved from eternal damnation. In contrast, the son Abraham was tormented by what he saw as a fatalistic doctrine of predestination, and already becoming skeptical of a God, if predestination was true , that scripted and pre-ordained all of the suffering he saw in the world. Young Abraham looked at life radically different from the Calvinist leanings of his father. Lincoln, the son, believed an individual could take control and shape their own future, through the expanded mental power and self-improvement that came with education, and the courage to take chances.

Making things worse, Thomas was chaffed by Abraham's stubborn refusal to become a member of the Little Pigeon Creek Primitive Baptist Church where Thomas was a trustee and the family worshiped. Still, Abraham always obeyed his father by attending services and serving the congregation as a "sexton" (cleaning floors and keeping candles in the sanctuary). Abe "never would sing any religious songs," Dennis Hanks noticed during services. This surely embarrassed Thomas before the congregation, because Hard Shell Baptists placed heavy emphasis on full family participation in church. This father-son church conflict involving Abraham Lincoln the boy, ironically, would be a harbinger of his character, as a man. Even in his youth, he was already showing an intractable, steadfastness in holding on to what he thought was right, no matter the costs. Despite the crushing weight of his father's disapproval bearing down on him for not joining the church, Lincoln would not surrender his deeply-held, core beliefs to a religious dogma he felt was wrong. Nearly four decades later, despite the crushing weight of the Civil War bearing down on him, again, he would not surrender his deeply-held, core beliefs in preserving the Union and abolishing slavery.

Ultimately, Thomas Lincoln should not be venerated or vilified. He simply needs to be understood in the context of his own world. Thomas Lincoln was a respected man in an era when having simple and humble goals was a respected life. He fed his family and put a roof over their head. He developed the skills of a master cabinetmaker. He didn't drink alcohol, gamble or curse, and faithfully attended church. And he stood firm against slavery.

Thomas Lincoln may have talked and moved slower than molasses in January, and there seemed to be a streak of shiftlessness that ran through him, especially later in his life. And there were likely no hugs, no gestures of affection or encouragement, nor any emotional nurturing from Thomas Lincoln for his only son, Abraham. After all, in Thomas Lincoln's sclerotic heart, one hardened by a life of disappointment and deprivation, a boy had to be toughened up to become a man. But it is an unfair and a one-dimensional characterization to label Thomas Lincoln as a brutal father, who indiscriminately inflicted discipline upon his son in a way that was driven by cruelty. His, was a typical paternal approach of many pioneer fathers of the day. A harsh raising prepared a child for a harsh world. The remote wilderness was no place for "time-out" chairs. Thomas Lincoln was teaching his son Abraham how to survive with a discipline that was tough and unsparing— exactly like the world they lived in.

Thomas and Sally would never have children of their own; as Dennis Hanks later explained it, as only he could: ". . . accident and nature stopp[ed] things short." But with the addition of Sally's family, Thomas Lincoln already had a family of eight to support. If "it takes a village," as the modern slogan goes, he already had one. And lessons taught to children had to be learned quickly and learned the first time around, and not forgotten, because the consequences were often cruelly unforgiving.

For the pioneer children who had to carry their share of the load for the survival of the family—often hunting, planting and clearing land in the primeval woods, alone—mistakes could be fatal. And often, they were. Every day in the wilderness was a confrontation with mortality. Frontier life was arbitrary and capricious. Thomas Lincoln was probably doing the best he could to teach his children how to survive, in the only world and way he knew. The problem was, however, that Abraham was a different kind of a boy. His heart was one made of kindness, dreams and solitary sensitivities that made his spirit, paradoxically, both strong and fragile.

The famous educator and psychoanalyst, Eric Erikson, once said that "The most deadly of all possible sins is the mutilation of a child's spirit." Thomas Lincoln, unknowingly, unmaliciously, may have come close to doing just that.

The only bequest Thomas Lincoln had to leave to his son, it seems, was a bleak future of raw-boned work and endless struggles against the land and nature. Tom Lincoln was satisfied and at peace with his way of life. Abraham wasn't. For young Abraham, his father had forced him into Hobson's Choice with his life, and he flat-out rejected it. Certainly, this early life of labor and servitude taught the boy Lincoln the value of work and self-reliance. Hardships were constantly foisted on the youthful Lincoln, but he did not buckle. But bitterness ran through it, too. Through his wounded adolescence, Abraham and his father would steadily grow apart, understanding each other less and less, eventually, leaving nothing between them.

The father had, indeed, cast a long shadow over the son.

* * *

Through the early years in the wilderness forests of Kentucky and Indiana, Abraham Lincoln would grow, in his outer-self, both in strength and rugged tolerance, into a sturdy, ax-wielding backwoods boy of the American colonial tradition; yet his inner-self, his spirit, was always restive in the wilderness. And unhappy. Lincoln wanted out. Ambition kindled hot inside of him, an ambition driven by his need to escape from his father's world.

Young Lincoln realized that the worst prison was a closed mind. He saw that ignorance incarcerated people. A strong mind could outdo a strong back, he believed. So Abraham ferociously devoured any books of knowledge he could get his hands on. It certainly helped that Lincoln was blessed with a naturally keen mind, begat from his mother. Like a moth to a flame, young Lincoln was attracted not only to words, but also to fresh ideas, and fascinated by contraptions and new-fangled machines. He was irrepressibly drawn to all kinds of learning. This love of reading and intellectual curiosity would always remain the driving forces in his life.

The plain fact was, Abraham Lincoln was noticeably different, some may have even said he was a downright peculiar kid, when compared to other frontier boys of his day and place. After all, here was a pioneer boy who could not bear to harm animals, putting baby birds back in their nest and worrying himself sick over his shooting of a wild turkey, when other boys around him eagerly hunted and killed animals for fun and food as an accepted way of life; a pioneer boy who preferred to carry a beechwood stick in the woods with him, when other boys around him preferred to carry a long gun; a pioneer boy who was unusually strong and limber, who could swing an ax with remarkable skill for his age, but didn't hide the fact that he hated the work, when other boys around him quietly accepted the inescapability of a life of hard labor; a pioneer boy who was a prodigy reader, and loved to write words and do math, when most boys around him were wholly illiterate.

Yet, despite all of these obvious differences, "Abe" was never tagged as weird, or ostracized by his backwoods peers. Made fun of at times? No doubt, he was. He was six feet tall at the age of fifteen. There was no way his flagpole legs, shrink-wrapped linen britches and size fourteen feet could escape the "kiddin." But his peculiarities never rendered him an outcast; in fact, young men in his neck of the woods admired and clung to him. How could that be?

First of all, there was something in young Lincoln's persona, that allowed him to be unpretentiously frank about his differences and his feelings. Sometimes he was funny and upbeat; at other times, he was sad and lonely. Still, he seemed to always keep some of himself mysteriously private. And although he had a gift and predisposition for quickly making lifelong friends, and there would be many over Lincoln's lifetime that would carry him into the White House, his really close, intimate friendships could be counted on one hand.

Even as a boy, Abraham seemed to be his own man. Young Lincoln loved literature and poetry, but he was no dandy. Tough as a hogshead of nails and strong as a bull, he was self-reliant, honest, took up for friends in a bind and liked helping people. He didn't chew or smoke tobacco, though most around him did. Although he occasionally got a kick out of barnyard and bathroom humor, he never used vulgar language. And he didn't drink alcohol. He didn't like the "flabby" way it made him feel. Lincoln could be mighty funny at times, and was armed with a razor-sharp wit. And man, could he tell a heckuva good story. Abe could talk the antlers off of a rutting buck. He quickly figured out that a good story or joke was the shortest distance between two folks.

But young Lincoln had, still, another unique gift. It was the gift of empathy. Honest, genuine empathy. When Abraham sized up a situation, he was able to put himself into the shoes of others, to understand how they felt about things. The truth was, Lincoln's feelings and thoughts ran deeper than most others around him. This, somehow, gave him insight and compassion. He could disagree, without being disagreeable. Be moral, without moralizing. Be the smartest one in the room, without being condescending. Make his imposing physical presence felt, without being intimidating. Make judgments, without being judgmental. Because of this peculiar mixture of qualities, simply put, folks liked him. And liked his company. Yes, Abraham Lincoln was different from about everyone else around him. Yet . . . he always fit it. It was these inchoate qualities in young Lincoln that he would carry with him throughout life, and eventually help to carve out his path to the White House.

In the remote, frontier villages where young Lincoln grew up, illiteracy was the prevailing standard, not the exception. In that educationally barren environment, Abraham's early reading skills and acquired knowledge, his physicality and keen mind, probably gave him an aura of almost mystical clout and stature. Even as a teenager, surely young Lincoln began to realize, in his private thoughts, that he was stronger and smarter than any of the other boys around.

David Herbert Donald, eminent historian and author of the masterful biography *Lincoln*, writes of young Abraham's own growing self-awareness that he was gifted, intellectually, something different and special, which was noticed by those who associated with him: "In their eyes," Professor Donald writes of the youthful Lincoln, "he was clearly exceptional, and he carried away from his brief schooling the self-confidence of a man who has never met his intellectual equal." Like iron filings clustered to a magnet, others in his peer group were drawn to Lincoln. His childhood friend, Nathaniel Grigsby, remembered that Abraham's intellect and his ambition to better himself, "soared above us." As Grigsby explained it, Abraham "read and thoroughly read his books, whilst we played. Hence . . . he became our guide and leader."

William H. Herndon, who was privy to many private conversations with Lincoln while they were law partners in Springfield, once famously characterized Lincoln's ambition as the "little engine that knew no rest." Lincoln's cousin, Sophie Hanks, would remember that "Abe always had a natural idea that he was going to be something." Lincoln came to realize, above all else, that if he was really "going to be something," he had to get an education, it was his only way out, even if he had to teach himself. It would be an education, as Lincoln himself later put it, that he "picked up . . . under the pressure of necessity."

But it would be a raw and relentless journey of self-education. To make it, young Lincoln would have to teach himself, above all else, to be patient, in his pursuits and dreams. Patience with one's self, he would figure out, is equally as important and difficult, as patience with others. Not an easy task for a young man with ambition coursing through his veins, who was living a life of harsh drudgery. But eventually, Abraham would learn that although patience is a hard fruit to plant and grow, once it does, the yield is sweet.

* * *

By the spring of 1830, the domicile of the Lincoln family and twenty-one-year-old Abraham, was again in flux. Caught on the tenterhooks of downward economic mobility, Thomas Lincoln again uprooted his family, sold their Indiana homestead, piled their worldly possessions on a wagon lugged by two yoke of oxen, and headed for Illinois. Their cousin John Hanks, already living in Illinois, had encouraged the Lincolns in his letters to join him in a state with wide-open, cheap, fertile land, a place filled with bountiful forests and abundant rivers, and no slavery. Word was also circulating that there might be another outbreak of deadly milk sickness in the southern part of Indiana. The family had already lost too much to the monstrous, mysterious disease. To Thomas Lincoln, the prairie of Illinois sounded like the next Promised Land.

In a miserable passage likened to Napoleon's retreat from Moscow, the Lincoln family, by then thirteen of them, would make the cold and muddy journey of two hundred miles during the spring thaw. They would eventually make an exhausted landing on the banks of the Sangamon River in central Illinois, near the town of Decatur, in Macon County.

It was a brutally difficult and miserable trip. They nearly lost everything in the ice-cold waters of the Kaskaskia River, angry and swollen with snowmelt. Unfortunately, the destination would be worse than the journey. That fall, the Lincoln family got feverishly-sick with a form of malaria, known then as the "ague," and the next winter was even worse. Unimaginably worse. In what came to be infamously known as the "winter of the deep snow," nearly four feet of snow fell, and temperatures never climbed above zero for almost three months. Starvation and cholera killed hundreds. Livestock was wiped out. It was nothing short of a miracle that the Lincoln family survived it all.

After nearly three years at the Sinking Spring Farm, plus five more years in Kentucky at Knob Creek, then nearly fourteen more years toiling on the Little Pigeon Creek farm in Indiana, and then finally settling in Macon County, Illinois, only to be greeted by dreadful sickness and snow, Abraham Lincoln hungered, beyond desperately, for a look and taste of the outside world. He was ready to break out of the garret of deprived, frontier life that had trapped him for so long.

Lincoln wanted to leave the family and start his own life when they first arrived in Illinois, but he didn't. He could have. After all, he was twenty-one. But there was a rectitude in young Abe, that obliged him to honor his father's request for help, yet again, in commandeering a new homestead from the untamed forest. Despite chafing at the constraints of his own life, Lincoln stayed and joined forces with Tom Lincoln, who had become blind in one eye, helping his father to put up another log cabin, clearing about ten acres and planting a garden. Although they worked side by side, they no longer knew each other. Sticking around for another mind-numbing round of breaking prairie ground, hewing logs and planting crops showed remarkable self-control in a grown man emotionally estranged from his father. Just two years earlier at age nineteen, Lincoln had to even ask for his father's approval to work as a "bow hand" on a flatboat hauling meat and grain down the Mississippi River to New Orleans. (He got $8.00 a month for the job, and had to turn the money over to his father.)

As Abraham's ambition grew each day, his father's seemed to wane. There was little conversation between them. No arm laid across the shoulder. No pats on the back. No bond. It was painfully obvious. The tide had run out on their father-son relationship.

In later years, Lincoln would not reminisce fondly about his father, who died in 1851. Dennis Hanks would later say that he "never could tell whether Abe loved his father very well or not; I don't think he did." We will never know how Lincoln truly felt about his father, because he rarely mentioned him at all. In the thousands of writings that Abraham Lincoln produced in his lifetime, remarkably, sadly, not one good word is written about his father. Still yet, during his Springfield years as an attorney, Lincoln constantly sent money to his father and his family back in Coles County, Illinois, and saved Thomas and Sally Lincoln's home from foreclosure.

Thomas Lincoln would not be invited to his son's wedding. Nor would he meet Mary Lincoln, or ever lay eyes on his grandchildren. Abraham Lincoln did not visit his father on his deathbed. He did not go to his father's funeral. And he would never go to Shiloh Cemetery in Coles County, to place a memorial stone at the head of his father's grave (although he would pay for it). Time had not blanched away the hurt. Still, this was not a vengeful or hard-hearted decision by the son. It was, in Lincoln's mind, about looking forward in life, not behind. His father was the gatekeeper to a world of which Abraham was born but never wanted to return, or even take a backwards glance over his shoulder. And he didn't.

Sometimes the most difficult decisions people face in life are trying to figure out which bridges to cross over, and which ones they should burn behind them. Once Lincoln left his family home, he soon faced bridges, and decisions to make about them. Some he crossed . . . others he burned.

Lincoln had been a good son. He had faithfully paid his family dues in obedience and labor in a time when prevailing social mores and the law required an unmarried son to stay home to work and support his family until he reached what was then known as the "age of maturity" (the age of twenty-one). Lincoln had even worked beyond that emancipating day. He was twenty-two, ready to move on, and find a life for himself.

No longer indentured to his father, Lincoln was ready to begin the journey of living his own life. In the life expectancy of his day, he had already spent half of it. When Lincoln gazed out at the horizon of his current life, one built on deprivation and manual labor, he saw a place devoid of intellectual opportunity, and meaning. The need to find meaning in one's life, for some, is as vital as the need for human relationships. It seemed so for Lincoln. There had to be more to life, he meditated, than the harsh and unfulfilling path his name-sake grandfather, and his father, had traveled. And both would die on.

So, the very next Spring (of 1831) following the family's arrival in Illinois, Lincoln, his stepbrother John D. Johnston and his cousin John Hanks, at the request of shady and high-strung businessman Denton Offutt, built a flatboat to haul live hogs, corn and barreled pork down the Mississippi River to New Orleans. Broke, but resourceful and energized, the trio made a sail out of wood planks (folks on the riverbanks laughed when they saw the rig).

It would be Lincoln's second journey down the huge, mysterious river, and another look at both the delight and depravity of an cosmopolitan, international mega-port like New Orleans. Their first trip, as Lincoln later wrote, they were "attacked by seven negroes with intent to kill and rob" them. They hoped for less adventure on this second journey. The Crescent City had become both the business center and slave-trading capital of the world. What he would see, both in human entrepreneurship and human bondage, would change him forever. When young Lincoln took on this three-month job and untethered his flatboat from the crusty-brown shoreline into the dark, moving water, he had taken an irreversible step towards forever renouncing the locust years of his farm life, released himself from his father and his father's land, and stumbled, serendipitously, into his future.

He had finally crossed over the weir.

When there is a river in your youth, you can hear it all of your life. And Lincoln loved rivers. They were the interstate highways of his time. Like many young men, he saw them as a means of liberation. Rivers were movement, beauty, adventure and hope. . . hope fed by books and dreams. The thought of traveling down a river in a flatboat, not knowing what laid around the next bend— the fresh wind blowing in his face, the aroma of the currents filling his nostrils, the planetarium of stars over his head at night thrilled Lincoln the same way riding a convertible down Route 66 thrilled young Tod Stiles and Buzz Murdock in the popular 1960's television show. The river was a turnpike to freedom in one century, like the two-lane highway would be in the next. For young men who were cutting the umbilical cord of familial bonds, both routes, river and road, symbolized emancipation, adventure and pursuit of the American dream.

Returning from New Orleans by steamboat that summer, Johnston and Hanks would return to the farm. They could not escape the gravitational pull of their isolated, familiar, rustic upbringing. But not Lincoln. There was no sylvan spirit left in him. He had passed through the fluvian portal of a new and mysterious life, a Shangri-La of opportunity, that gave him the chance to reshape himself and his life, and there was no going back.

Rivers provided the chance to redesign one's self. Abe, himself, resembled a river, long, thin and sprawling, but impressive. For young Lincoln, hope sprang eternal at the confluence of the Anderson and Ohio waterways. He had no idea what he would do, or what he would become. All that mattered was that he was on his way. To borrow a phrase from Daniel Webster, a man he much admired, Lincoln was about "to push [his] skiff from the shore alone" into the unknown of an rugged sea.

And, somewhere, in the pull of the currents, was the village of New Salem, and the inescapable pull of destiny.

* * *

Eventually, Lincoln would arrive by boat at the little village of New Salem, Illinois. It was July 1831. New Salem had been in existence only two years, when Lincoln first straggled into town. It was a place perched on top of a high bluff overlooking the Sangamon River. When Lincoln got there, he was as broke as the Ten Commandments, had no friends, and had no connections. He arrived, in his own words, "like a piece of floating driftwood." One of the people in town, William Butler, who saw the penniless young Lincoln in his undersized homespun clothes and worn-out stoga shoes, said he was "as ruff a specimen of humanity as could be found." Another observed, "His appearance was very odd."

It was a conspicuously humble start.

Still, New Salem was a nice fit for a raw-boned, uneducated, unsophisticated Abraham Lincoln. It would provide Lincoln, at age twenty-two, with a growth spurt in emotional and financial independence, and give him the freedom to make his own way that he had always longed for. New Salem was a place where a young fellow like Lincoln, unfledged in social skills, could find social acceptance. Lincoln immersed himself in this little community, that held about thirty families. He "batched" in many places, staying with families and in boarding rooms all over the village. He participated in wood-chopping contests, joined a local debating society where Shakespeare, religion and politics were discussed, endeavored to meet women, and fished the riverbanks with his friends.

New Salem was a small, tight-knit community, where most folks knew whose credit was good, and whose husband wasn't. Built around a gristmill and sawmill operations—and not a single church to be found— it wasn't the typical farm village of that era, but a midget-sized commercial town mostly populated by tradesmen, craftsmen and merchants, along with their families, most of them rather poor, all of them struggling to gain a financial foothold in life.

Because its existence tied to the shallow, winding and hard-to-navigate Sangamon River (the river was a terrible route for steamboats), New Salem was on borrowed time. Despite there being a boom–town mentality in New Salem when Lincoln arrived, the little commercial hamlet would eventually die a slow death, especially after trade dried-up and the post office was closed. But before the town's decline, New Salem would give Lincoln his first job—grocery store clerk—that didn't involve back-breaking labor, or surrendering his wages to someone else. It was the break Lincoln so desperately needed. A payday that stayed in his own pocket was true liberation, and energized young Lincoln in a way he had never before experienced.

Hired as an employee at Denton Offutt's general store, where whiskey was typically a "grocery" item in those days and sold in bulk and not by the drink, Lincoln quickly gained acceptance in what was a formidably masculine society, where his attributes of storytelling, stellar honesty and physical strength made him a well known and popular character. Lincoln knew that a good work ethic is something you can always depend on—a loyal, friend-for-life who will never abandon you—and a friend he would count on in New Salem. Offutt was a roguish, hard-drinking and hard-talking businessman (as one local resident curiously noted, Offutt "talked too much with his mouth"), but he liked Abe's honest and industrious work in his store. And Lincoln liked the camaraderie and the conversation of the place, and of course, the pay. Denton Offutt had single-handedly opened up the first door of real economic opportunity for young Lincoln.

Lincoln used his yarns and swapped jokes to entertain Offut's customers. He could be incredibly funny at times. And Lincoln was no Puritan when it came to telling an entertaining story. Sometimes his humor could be as salty, as the salt-of-the-earth customers looking for a drink and entertaining conversation.

For instance, Lincoln liked to tell the story of when Ethan Allen, one of the American heroes in the Revolutionary War, traveled to England after the war was over. Allen discovered that his British hosts, who were providing him with room and board—just to tease and ruffle him, had tacked up a picture of a stoic, distinguished George Washington (as they all seem to be) over the toilet in their English outhouse. As Lincoln told it, Ethan Allen would return from his first visit to the "necessary shed," and turn the tables on his smirking, chuckling British hosts that awaited his reaction, by telling them that he thought the portrait of Washington in the privy was a great idea, because, as Allen put it, "there is nothing that will make an Englishman sh_t so quick as the sight of General Washington."

It was here, in New Salem, because of his conscientious and honest dealings in Offutt's store, including an incident where he walked more than two miles to return a few pennies to a customer he accidentally overcharged, that Lincoln, who seemed congenitally incapable of dishonesty, would earn the moniker, "Honest Abe." It was here, in New Salem, because he out-wrestled the "strongest man" around, the hard-knuckled, lantern-jawed Jack Armstrong of the Clary's Grove boys, that Lincoln would become a local celebrity and earn the title, from vanquished Jack Armstrong himself, as "the best feller that ever broke into this settlement."

It was here, in New Salem, that Lincoln opened his first business with the Lincoln & Berry Store (the store would go bust, or "winked out" as Lincoln put it; Lincoln called the $3,000.00 note he signed and paid-off for the store the "National debt"); and landed a job as postmaster (it only paid a salary of $50.00 per year, but enabled Lincoln to access newspapers).

And it was here, in New Salem, that Lincoln learned the skills of a surveyor. He laid out the boundaries for several towns, and was paid at the rate of $2.50 for each 640 acre section of land surveyed; and joined the state militia for seventy-seven days in the Black Hawk War, where his company of men elected him captain; a "success" Lincoln said after being nominated as President, which "gave me more pleasure than any I have had since."

New Salem was the conjugator between Lincoln's youth and his political career; his first big chance to widen the canvas of life.

Those political ambitions of Lincoln, spawned in New Salem, became evident when he decided to run for the Illinois House of Representatives only after living in New Salem seven months—and a gutsy decision at a time when he was uneducated, untested and flat broke. It also reflected his self-awareness that he was well-liked and respected in the community where he lived. Lincoln was always hobnobbing around the town, visiting one place or the other, batching here or there, all the while making friends and stockpiling social credit.

Lincoln would enter the world of politics as a member of the "Whig" party, whose principal platform argued for "internal improvements" in the community. (In today's political parlance, the Whig platform would be in pushing for "infrastructure," like bridges, roads and dams.) "Abe," as they called him, would lose his first bid for the Illinois legislature. But on his second attempt in 1834, after becoming more politically savvy, Lincoln would be elected to the Illinois House of Representatives at the tender age of twenty-five, eventually serving four rough-and-tumble terms.

Lincoln had a craving to be well-liked, and even more importantly, he wanted to be worthy of being well liked. New Salem gave him his first chance to be that kind of person. Hardly a day passed, in the little town, it seemed, that Abe wasn't extending a helping hand to someone. Folks began to notice, and tell about it. And Lincoln was easy to spot in a crowd. From head to toe, he looked every bit the country bumpkin, a "clodhopper" as they put it in those days, with his linsey-woolsey shirt rolled up to the elbows, his long, string-bean legs hoisted into home-made deer-skin britches that stopped a hand-span short of his ankles, and a thick, rebellious shock of black hair that looked like it had been styled with a wheat thresher.

Lincoln, no doubt, was self-aware of his unorthodox appearance. After all, he had been catechized about it virtually all of his life. Lincoln knew he stuck out in a crowd and somehow, it played into his local popularity. Perhaps it was a natural fit with his self-deprecating humor and personality. Maybe at some point, he chose to look this way. Whatever his reasoning, it seemed to become Lincoln's calling card. In fact, his towering, odd appearance and his skills as an engaging conversationist, not only made him an unforgettable character, but also gave him notoriety in the little log-cabin community, like the folklore of Johnny Appleseed wearing rags and a cooking pot on his head. Lincoln's giantly, protuberant figure and deeply-carved face did not just take up space in a room; once he began to speak, his presence re-shaped the space in the room.

New Salem had provided the young, clever and earthy Lincoln one more rung to climb on, a vantage point to meet people connected to trade and commerce, and look for even bigger and better opportunities, like the town of Springfield, Illinois.

Although it sounds like every great-grandfather's venerable story of "walking five miles to school, up hill, both ways," the unvarnished reality was that Lincoln, as a young man living in the rustic community of New Salem, would sometimes walk or ride nearly twenty miles in a round trip to Springfield, so he could borrow old law books from John Todd Stuart's office and take them back home with him, to study. A local schoolteacher in New Salem, Mentor Graham, insisted that a twenty-two year old Lincoln once walked six miles to borrow a textbook on grammar. Who in the world, today, would do such a thing? Even then, folks in New Salem and Springfield chattered about this towering fellow named Lincoln, who would traipse along in his signature, long-legged canter, mile after mile, just to get a book to read.

Gradually, Lincoln began to think about a new career, a career other than the one he had long dreamed of, steamboat captain, and one that did not involve only manual labor.

It was law.

In fact, Lincoln's unquenchable thirst to read and learn was quite a peculiar habit in the agrestic, roughneck community of New Salem. This cultural chasm was illustrated by an incident involving a farmer from New Salem named Russell Godbey, who often hired Lincoln to work on his place. Godbey once spotted Lincoln sitting barefoot at the "summit" of a woodpile, engaging in the strange and unorthodox practice of reading a book out in plain view. Russell Godbey hollered out, "Abe. . . what are you reading?" Young Lincoln explained, "I'm not reading . . . I'm studying." Godbey snapped back, "Studying what?" **"Law sir,"** Lincoln proudly replied. **"Studying law."** To which Godbey, gawping in sheer astonishment, blurted out in a voice that would have drowned out a saw mill: "GREAT GOD ALMIGHTY!"

Law was a mighty good career for Lincoln. Actually, a perfect fit. He had a rigorous cast of intellect and the common sense to effectively apply it; a knack for marshalling the facts of a case and then recycling them in the form of a good story for a judge or jury; and an intuitive and genuine sensitivity to injustice. All of these qualities made him naturally suited for the practice of law.

In his pursuit of a career in law, Lincoln would move beyond just reading of books, to the study of them. He would first immerse himself in the cornerstone of law, *Blackstone's Commentaries*, reading it over and over, until he mastered every chapter; he bought the legal tome at an auction with money he had grinded out with physical labor. He drilled himself in the legal classic of his day, *Chitty's Pleadings*, backwards and forwards. And he would faithfully study his borrowed volume of the *Revised Statutes of Indiana*, which was loaned to him by a local constable; this book gave him his first exposure to the complete words of the Declaration of Independence and the U. S. Constitution. He would plow through *Story's Equity Jurisprudence*, and *Greenleaf's Evidence*. Lincoln pushed himself so hard in his law studies that some observers said he became "emaciated," and a few of his buddies even worried that he would "craze himself."

He wouldn't, of course. Lincoln may have cracked the books, but he wasn't about to crack-up studying them. What he had done, while in New Salem, was make himself into a lawyer. He would get his law license on March 1, 1837. (In those days, there was no bar exam. The prospective lawyer had to successfully complete a path of learning under the tutelage of an experienced lawyer, called "reading the law," and then get that lawyer's recommendation into the profession. The two key qualifying components were knowledge of the law and good moral character.)

Lincoln's self-taught legal education, without formal schooling, without the advantages of serving in a structured legal apprenticeship, and without training in what was then the important skill of Latin, would eventually reflect an amazing and meteoric rise from a poor, isolated, uneducated farm boy to one of the best lawyers in his part of the country. This is the most overlooked accomplishment of Abraham Lincoln's entire life. Arguably, it was an achievement unparalleled in its time. And the secret to his remarkable academic achievement in law? Lincoln later answered this question, when he bluntly stated in a brief autobiography that he "studied with nobody." Lincoln labored assiduously and alone to learn the law. He wanted none of the distractions of study groups or social chatter in the process. Lincoln believed the grind of quiet, private study worked best. Good advice, perhaps, even for today's law students.

Early in the sixteenth century, the great artist Raphael painted for the library of Pope Julius II his breathtaking concept of what is famously known as *The School of Athens*. This exquisite painting, which finds its home on the walls of the Vatican in Rome, depicts the fanciful collaboration of Plato, Aristotle, Michelangelo, Leonardo de Vinci, Ptolemy, Socrates and other intellectual sages, all of them selected from different fields of knowledge and epochs, gathered together as teachers in an imaginary academy of learning. Had such a school existed, it would have been the supreme place to acquire knowledge of the world and about life.

No one place or person would completely shape Abraham Lincoln.

And many of Lincoln's early acquaintances in New Salem, particularly after his martyrdom, self-inflated their influence upon his life. But during this impressionable time when Lincoln was first breaking all familial bonds, his School of Athens was the place of New Salem. For most part, Lincoln taught himself, but his experiences there were formative, and he carried the weight of them throughout his life. From some he would learn very little; from others, much more. But from them all, he would gain knowledge about the world. From Jack Armstrong, he would learn the physical self-confidence that comes from doing battle, and thereafter, the value of forging a lifetime friendship with your foe. James Rutledge would offer a club to learn and practice debate. From Jack Kelso, the opportunity to discuss the great classics of literature and Shakespeare. John Calhoun would give him the opportunity to survey, his first successful vocation. Bowling Green would show him the internal workings of the local court system. Denton Offutt would let him run a business. Dr. Jason Duncan and William G. Greene, a bit of basic grammar. William F. Berry would introduce him to the pitfalls of taking on a bad business partner. Ann Rutledge would expose him to female love and loss. Mentor Graham would advise in math. John Todd Stuart would open the door to law and politics.

After all, New Salem was the place where Lincoln, who arrived unknown, financially broke and pitifully inexperienced in life, learned the hazards of running a retail business; became seasoned in the military skills of leadership, discipline and improvisation; experienced the joy of keeping and investing the fruits of his own labor; was extended his first sizeable credit; learned the language spoken by the intimate contours of land; had his heart ripped apart by love; developed a love of poetry and classic literature; learned the rhetorical skills of formal debate; encountered the pressures and fears that come with unpaid debt; began the study of law and earned a law license; and was initiated into the fraternity of politics.

The legendary basketball coach, Al McGuire, once philosophized about getting a practical education on the streets of life: "I think everyone should go to college and get a degree," he said, "then, spend six months as a bartender and six months as a cabdriver. Then they would really be educated." In a sense, Lincoln did just that in New Salem, not only studying the treatises of law, but also by selling liquor at Offut's store and taxiing people and goods along the byways of the Sangamon River. New Salem was his real world education.

In New Salem, driven by his insatiable, intellectual curiosity, Lincoln would adapt to the rapidly changing world around him with a Darwinian-like evolution, an exponential growth in life experiences that was dramatically shaping the person, politics and principles of a man who would eventually become President of the United States . . . and compose the greatest speech in American history.

After six years in New Salem, Illinois, likely becoming its most popular and well known citizen, and a short stint thereafter in the Town of Vandalia (it was the state capitol until Lincoln and his political buddies in the Whig party got it moved to Springfield), Lincoln was, again, ready to expand his opportunities. It was 1837. He was twenty-eight. He had studied hard to earn a law license.

And he had shifted his eyes to the city of Springfield, Illinois.

* * *

Much like the modern story of the naïve, talented, small town, Broadway hopeful, who like the old show-biz adage, risks everything on making it in New York City, Lincoln knew that if he could make it in Springfield, he could make it anywhere. Springfield, lying about twenty miles southeast of New Salem, was a place to make something of himself. A place where he could become "somebody." A place where a man could have the chance of doing something with his life that might be remembered.

To make it in Springfield, a bigger and brighter stage to play out his career, Lincoln was cagey enough to realize that he would have to enter through the twin gates that seemed to lead to influence and success in his day, the gates of politics and law.

Despite having no paved roads or railways, Springfield was a progressive, growing town. It was, by no means, a major city. But even with its muddy streets and meandering pigs, the town was pulsating with businesses, trade and professions. Thanks to Lincoln's political maneuvering back in the state legislature, Springfield was about to become the state's capital city. And a place of power and influence. In short,

Springfield was urbanizing, New Salem, wasn't. The curvy, shallow and brush-filled waters of the Sangamon River which made boat navigation extraordinarily difficult, were slowly but surely choking New Salem's economy to death. It was a contrast in culture and opportunities, clearly evident to young Lincoln. Lincoln recognized that a dying New Salem would take a young man's vaulting ambitions down with it. So he replanted himself in Springfield.

As Lincoln established himself as a lawyer and legislator in Springfield, he continued to learn. His intellectual curiosity would remain a driving force to the very end of his life. He loved the realm of ideas. A serious and somber thinker, Lincoln would become intrigued by the origins of language, a discipline called "philology," and became a devotee of the academic discipline of Reason. He found himself immersed in philosophical conversations about metaphysics and free will. Seeming to have the tender soul of a poet, he often ruminated about the mysteries of Creation, of Time, and of life and death. By reading poetry aloud, he could surreptiously express inner feelings to those around him, he could not otherwise openly discuss. John Todd Stuart, Lincoln's law mentor, observed that Lincoln had a "mind of metaphysical and philosophical order . . . of very general and varied knowledge." When Lincoln wrote, he paid close attention to wordplay and the grammatical arrangement of his words, in what today, we call "syntactics."

By plumbing all of these influences, both in life and literature, Lincoln moved himself towards a writing style that was taut and pithy. He recognized that a good thought can be choked to death by too many words. Lincoln wanted every word to count, and by constant revisions of his own work, culled out those that didn't. Lincoln began to gradually realize—in contrast to the lofty, long-worded elocution that was so popular in his day, that language made of simple, direct and heartfelt words becomes eloquent, in and of itself. And persuasive.

For most of his life, Lincoln was painfully insecure about his appearance, women, and social etiquette. His eccentric garb, wildly unkempt hair and prairie twang didn't help much. Lincoln, after all, was a man of rustic, not aristocratic sensibilities. In fact, he found himself quite sad and lonely during his early days in Springfield, feeling socially out of place. But Lincoln was also self-aware that he was blessed with a keen mind. He read constantly to expand his knowledge about the world and gain a mastery over words. If he read it and liked it, he remembered it. Joshua Speed, perhaps Lincoln's best friend ever, once told Lincoln that he thought his mind was a "wonder," in that Lincoln seemed to learn quickly and never forget. "No," Lincoln told Speed, "you are mistaken."   Lincoln revealed to Speed that he was "slow to learn and slow to forget," saying his mind was "like a piece of steel—very hard to stratch any thing on it, and almost impossible after you get it there to rub it out."

Lincoln was always studying the *Bible*, reading thought-provoking books like Thomas Paine's *Age of Reason*, and reciting poetry (especially Robert Burns, Lord Byron and Edgar Allen Poe—he knew *The Raven* by heart). He enjoyed history books, and was an omnivorous but piecemeal reader of newspapers. He carried a lifelong passion for Shakespeare, memorizing soliloquies from *Hamlet*, *King Lear*, and his absolute favorite—the tragic story of depraved, unprincipled power, *MacBeth*. This classic assembly of literature taught Lincoln the power of the properly-placed word. As a result, all of his life he would work, tediously and painstakingly, to put the right word in the right place in everything he wrote.

Although Lincoln had been limited in the books he could borrow or buy in his early years, the ones he did get, for most part, were masterpieces of literature and language. And what he learned from those early books stuck with him throughout his life. During one of Lincoln's famed series of 1854 speeches with Stephen A. Douglas over the heated Kansas-Nebraska Act (legislation designed to open up these new western states to slavery, which was supported by Douglas, opposed by Lincoln)—Lincoln, calling upon his Shakespearean self-education, unleashed a Jovian bolt of oratory from *Hamlet* against the pro-slavery legislation, thundering to the great crowd . . .

"It hath no relish of salvation in it."

Even during his busy years of practicing law in Springfield, Lincoln took to reading Homer's *Iliad and Odyssey*, telling his law partner William H. Herndon that he ought to read them himself, and commenting that Homer "has a grip and knows how to tell a story." Throughout his years of traveling on the judicial circuit, in the same way Alexander the Great carried a copy of Homer with him during his military campaigns, Lincoln kept a copy of *Euclid's Theorems* in his saddlebag, for constant reference. Years later, on his White House desk, President Lincoln would always keep at least four books: the Federal Statutes, a set of Shakespeare's tragedies, the United States Constitution, and the *King James Bible*. Lincoln once confided to a friend, in the last year of his life, that he had yet to read a novel, from beginning to end. Yet, each and every day of his life, Lincoln was always reading something—not usually to finish it cover-to-cover, but to read selected portions that increased his knowledge and word power. Still, no president has ever mastered great poetry and literature, as did Abraham Lincoln.

During the course of his life, books had become Lincoln's professors, and his university. Books had opened up to Lincoln the secret arcanum of language—the power over words.

By increasing his grip and precision over words, over time, Lincoln came to admire the beauty and influence of the spoken word. Lincoln learned early on in life, that if you wanted people to bite the hook of your story, your point of debate, your closing argument in the courtroom, or the gist of your political speech, you'd best bait it with words the listeners were raised on and understood.

And Lincoln began to realize there was often a vast difference in words silently read to one's self, and those same words when spoken aloud. So Lincoln would read his poetry, out loud, and give his speeches a test run on friends, to get feedback on how the words and rhythms really sounded. He told his law partner William Herndon about this technique, explaining that "I catch the idea by two senses, for when I read aloud I hear what is read and I see it." Lincoln wanted his words to not only have meaning, but sound good, as well. It was a technique for composing speeches that would serve him well, as most splendidly displayed in his Gettysburg Address.

By the time Lincoln had settled into Springfield, and dived headfirst into the practice of law and politics, he had self-engineered the ability to pick and parlay words into mesmerizing stories to fit about any occasion. Even as a young man, Lincoln's old schoolmate Nathaniel Grigsby remembered that Abe "argued much from analogy, [and] would almost always point his lesson or idea by some story that was plain and near . . . that we might instantly see the force and bearing of what he said."

Lincoln's skill as a storyteller was so celebrated in Springfield that when former president Martin Van Buren traveled through Illinois in the early 1840's, some of the local big-shots made sure that Van Buren got entertained by the best raconteur in those parts, Abe Lincoln. Lincoln cracked up Van Buren with his limitless stock of homespun yarns and cornpone jokes.

"They say I tell a great many stories," Lincoln once mused. "I reckon I do . . . but I have found in the course of a long experience, that common people take them as they run, [and] are more easily influenced and informed through the medium of a broad illustration than in any other way." For Lincoln, it might be a lesson woven into a knee-slapping tale. Or a story used to blunt "the edge of a rebuke . . . so as to save wounded feelings," as he once described it. Sometimes, it would be a comical analogy to drive home a point. Or a witty one-liner used to disarm an angry heckler. When tension filled a room, President Lincoln could leaven the conversational air with a humorous story, and put everyone there at ease. He had the gift. And it was a gift that served him well all of his life.

"Every one of his stories," moaned Stephen A. Douglas, as he reflected on his and Lincoln's historic senatorial debates, "seems like a "whack" across my back . . . Nothing else, not any of his arguments or any of his replies to my questions, disturbs me. But when he begins to tell a story, I feel that I am to be overmatched."

As Abraham's appetite for words and storytelling grew, so did his fascination with speeches. For a young man who loved to spin a good yarn and tell entertaining stories to a crowd, public speeches seemed to be a natural progression. So, early on, Abe began to practice the art of public speaking by putting to use what he had read and learned. From the time he made imaginary stump speeches as a skinny-legged boy in the boondocks of Indiana, to his "practicing polemics" after a six mile walk to a meeting of the New Salem debating club, from his first political speech in front of Renshaw's Store in Decatur, Illinois, through his emergence as a candidate for state and national offices, Abraham Lincoln gave speeches. Thousands of them.

In his youth, Lincoln had studied the great orations from antiquity like those of Cicero and Romulus in the famous old textbook by William Scott, titled *Lessons in Elocution* (another influential book brought into the family by his stepmother Sally, which first exposed him to Shakespeare). Later as a young man, Lincoln read and imitated the celebrated speeches of his own era like those of "the great triumvirate," John C. Calhoun, Henry Clay and Daniel Webster. Along his path of self-education, Lincoln discovered that words, especially those in great public speeches, have the power to outlive their author, sometimes surviving even centuries beyond the circumstances and events that inspire them. This realization that words, unlike mortal man—could enjoy immortality, intrigued Lincoln. Perhaps this is why Lincoln enjoyed reading and related to *Marco Bozzaris*, a poem by "the American Byron" Fitz-Greene Halleck, where the brave deeds of the Greek war hero would long outlast his tragic death, and assuage the grief of his loss through historical immortality. In the last three lines of the long poem, Lincoln, himself, seems to take the place of the Greek soldier:

"For thou art Freedom's now, and Fame's,
One of the few, the immortal names,
That were not born to die."

Lincoln made stump speeches on hay bales and street corners, under pole sheds and canvas tarps, and in grocery stores and town halls. He made speeches on the circuit before juries, with what presiding Judge David Davis called "sledgehammer logic." He participated in speaking tours. He dueled on the national political stage before thousands in his famous debates with the Little Giant. Giving speeches on the hustings became an inseparable part of Abraham Lincoln's life.

In his days in the State legislature, Lincoln was admired by his peers for his keen intellect and masterful political skills. But he wasn't yet considered to be an outstanding speaker, likely because his speaking style still contained some of the imprints of a backwoods hick spinning entertaining yarns. As one adversarial newspaper put it, Lincoln's speaking style reflected "a sort of assumed clownishness," which, as the Democratic publication put it, "does not become him."

Steadily, however, Lincoln would refine his speaking skills. At a time when illiteracy prevailed among the general public, good oratory skills were often vital to a successful political career. By the time he became President of the United States, Abraham Lincoln was far from being an amateur speaker, in fact, when he applied thought and preparation to a speech, he had become downright good at it.

But to be a good speaker, and to be literate and liked, was not enough for Abraham Lincoln. His ambition, the ambition his law partner William Herndon called "the little engine that knew no rest," was not quenched.

He wanted to be remembered.

* * *

To be "remembered," was deeply important to Lincoln. From his early youth, he was consumed with concern over the shape his life would take. It was a conscious thought coursing through his lifeblood. Abraham Lincoln was plagued by a deep and terrible fear, almost a monomania, that his life would not be remembered for anything worthwhile.

Discover what really matters to a man, and you will find out who he is. Lincoln wanted—as much as a man could want anything—to leave his mark on the world. To not die in futility. He dreamed of leaving "the world a little better for my having lived in it." As a young man, Lincoln once divulged to his best friend Joshua Speed that he did not fear death, except "that he had not done anything to make any human being remember that he had lived."

When Lincoln expressed his longing to be remembered, he wasn't thinking of statues or marble busts. That's because Lincoln, on a personal basis, was not overly impressed with grand historic sites or monuments. He was, instead, deeply intrigued by nature and science, and how things worked. A good example of this was when Lincoln saw Niagara Falls for the first time. He later told his old law partner Billy Herndon, "the thing that struck me most forcibly was, where in the world did all that water come from?" Each day when President Lincoln looked out the upstairs windows of the White House, he had a direct and unavoidable view of the huge and heroic statue of General Andrew

Jackson on horseback that stood just across the street in Lafayette Park (still there, it's the first statue of a person on horseback cast in America), yet he was never known to have commented on it.

Abraham Lincoln wanted to be remembered, as he put it, for one solitary thing: "for helping his fellow man." To borrow a phrase from Thoreau, Lincoln did not simply want to be good; he wanted to be good for *something*. His heart ached to be a man whose life made a notable difference in other human being's lives. A man who lived a life, worth living. "My peculiar ambition" Lincoln once admitted, is to be "truly esteemed of my fellow men, by rendering myself worthy of their esteem." These beliefs, these yearnings, were the fuel cells of his unquenched ambition . . .

. . . and his speech at Gettysburg, Pennsylvania.

CHAPTER SEVENTEEN

LOST IN THE SHADOWS
OF A PROCLAMATION

*"If my name ever goes into history . . . it will be for this act [the
Emancipation Proclamation]."*
—President Abraham Lincoln
Spoken at the White House
1864, Washington, D.C.

ANY DISCUSSION OF THE GETTYSBURG ADDRESS MUST BE DONE IN THE
lighted backdrop of the Emancipation Proclamation. After all, Lincoln
would ratify the rightness of his Emancipation Proclamation with his
speech at Gettysburg. But how ironic history can unfold. President
Lincoln was fully convinced that his best chance at being favorably
remembered by history was surely the Emancipation Proclamation—
not his Gettysburg Address.

Lincoln had composed every word of the Emancipation
Proclamation himself, without counsel or consultation. His pigment
filled every word of the manuscript. Certainly, Lincoln was painstakingly careful in how he worded the proclamation. He did not want to whip-
up the already-frothing emotions of Northerners, especially those in the
Union's fragile border states, or incite interference from the U.S.
Supreme Court. That's why, in part, the Emancipation Proclamation
reads more like a cold and legal military directive, than an inspirational
manifesto of freedom.

Despite his past political moderation in attacking slavery, Lincoln
had courageously composed and signed into law the Emancipation
Proclamation—confronting, head-on, the evil of slavery rather than

shift the responsibility on to later presidents (as his predecessors had done)—and he did so, knowing it would place him in the crosshairs of many who hated him or his politics.

The harder President Lincoln pushed for black emancipation, the harder it became to keep him safe. The emancipation issue was even generating hate and hostility in loyal Union states of the North. Still, the ever present danger did not deter him. To know in your heart what is right, and choose not to do it, is the most wretched form of cowardice. And Lincoln was no coward.

The Emancipation Proclamation had military, political and moral implications. *Militarily*, Lincoln hoped the Emancipation Proclamation would encourage former slaves to join the Union cause, which would strengthen the Federal Army, vest African-Americans in the Union's cause, and begin to choke-off the Confederacy's main economic engine, the agricultural labor force of slavery. *Politically*, it would help to isolate the Confederacy from European assistance and break-ground for the Thirteenth Amendment abolishing slavery. *Morally*, it would serve as America's public, irrevocable pledge of freedom to people of color if the North won the War, so the process could begin of freeing the Nation from its original sin, slavery.

Since its inception on January 1, 1863, the Emancipation Proclamation has provoked swift crosscurrents of both praise and criticism of Abraham Lincoln. Despite its historical significance in the story of America, The Emancipation Proclamation is still viewed with great skepticism by many. When Lincoln placed his bold signature on the Proclamation that day, it was done so, even against the advice of most of his Cabinet. However, the great black abolitionist, Frederick Douglass, proclaimed that the date of January 1, 1863, was even more important to America than the date of July 4, 1776. But critics, then and now, argue that Lincoln crafted the Emancipation Proclamation, not primarily to end slavery or expand citizenship to black Americans, but mostly to accomplish the military goal of crippling the Confederacy. They emphasize that the Emancipation Proclamation was only a legal illusion, a symbolic document that freed no one. That it declared freedom only for those slaves located in the enemy Southern states, places of active rebellion where the Union had no power—and did not even apply to the Northern states, or the slave-owning Southern "border states" which never seceded from the Union, or parts of Southern states under Union control—all places where the Union did have power.

"I never in my life," Lincoln strongly insisted, "felt more certain that I was doing right," as he finished signing Emancipation Proclamation. Still, some historians have attacked Lincoln's motives more than the Proclamation itself, contending that the only reason Lincoln issued the Emancipation order was to throw a political bone to abolitionists in the "radical" wing of his own Republican Party who were pressuring the President to bring an immediate end to slavery. Historian and distinguished author Richard Hofstadter sharply asserted in 1948 that Lincoln's Proclamation "had all the moral grandeur of a bill of lading." (This is still the most parroted, oft-repeated criticism in every article written on the Proclamation.) Even Lincoln's own Secretary of State, William Seward, privately wisecracked that the Emancipation Proclamation was as short-lived and momentary as "a puff of wind."

However, the U.S. Constitution did not allow Lincoln, through executive order of his Emancipation Proclamation, to free slaves in the Union states. It was only because of the War Powers clause in the Constitution, that Lincoln, as commander-in-chief, was able to claim the presidential authority to free slaves in the "rebellion" war zone of the Confederate states. Lincoln was liberating slaves in the only places he could legally reach them; he could not impose the Emancipation Proclamation on the civilian-governed states in the Union.

With all due respect to the late Professor Hofstader, Lincoln did not set out to draft a document of flourishing, inspirational moral niceties. Lincoln, the lawyer President, was attempting to draft a legal instrument of military necessity that would pass constitutional muster. It was more important that the Proclamation work, than inspire. Lincoln accomplished both.

The all-too-pervasive critics who indict the Emancipation as "freeing no one" because it applied only to the ten Confederate states in rebellion, misprize and sell the Emancipation terribly short. When President Lincoln signed the Emancipation Proclamation, on its face a valid, enforceable, War Powers law, he irrevocably pledged to nearly four million slaves located in the Confederacy that when the War was over, or if they could sooner escape and reach the Union states of the North, the federal government would guarantee their freedom. Obviously, most slaves could not walk away from their manacled life to the soil of freedom. But some could. And they did. And for those who could not, it gave them hope.

Certainly, the Emancipation Proclamation was no panacea in the effort to eliminate slavery. It held flaws as well as promise, because it was intended to be a temporary, emergency fix, not a permanent solution. Slavery was too deeply woven into the socioeconomic fabric of America to be eliminated with one, solitary, presidential edict. Lincoln's Proclamation was, paradoxically, both a noble step towards the elimination of human bondage, and an endeavor of unfulfilled expectations. And, perhaps, the primary catalyst of Lincoln's violent doom.

Early in the War, President Lincoln had hinged the success of black emancipation upon the survival of the Union. But with his Emancipation Proclamation, an executive fiat had been issued, that suddenly, with one stroke of Lincoln's pen, expanded the purpose of the Civil War from the single cause of preserving the Nation, instead, to also include the purpose of destroying the very cause that had put the Nation's existence in imminent peril . . . slavery. The Proclamation was the only effective weapon against slavery that Lincoln had at his disposal. The U. S. Supreme Court and a silent Constitution had, otherwise, put slavery in the Southern states beyond the legal reach of Federal power.

No doubt, the President had unleashed a controversial and divisive war-powers order. After the initial euphoria over the signing had waned among abolitionists, a firestorm of angry and impassioned debate followed. And Lincoln's already diminishing chances of reelection seemed to take another hard hit. But by issuing the Proclamation, Lincoln had ratcheted–up the liberty dial another notch. Antislavery proponents were becoming more abolitionist; abolitionists were moving towards black equality. In retrospect, a subtle but steady, ever-increasing wave of public and legislative momentum towards black freedom was building, that would eventually reach shore with the Thirteenth Amendment.

The Emancipation Proclamation also helped to purge the fears and ambiguity that came from the dark cloud of the Dred Scott case. In defiance of that Supreme Court decision, slaves escaping into Union states, under the terms of the Emancipation Proclamation, were guaranteed to be free people, not chattel property. And despite the Emancipation's limited immediate impact when it was ratified, it was still an act of profound moral courage by President Lincoln to sign it. Critics like Richard Hofstader and some contemporary historians have failed to fully recognize what it meant to African-American slaves, at that awful time in history, to have the most powerful man in the country, the President of the United States, give them hope in the form of a written pledge of freedom, when there had been none in the past. After all, survival is often built upon hope.

This symbolic aspect of the Emancipation Proclamation, particularly as an instrument of hope, was arguably more powerful than its technical, legal application. After all, it was America's first, written, no-turning-back promise towards abolishing slavery.

The Emancipation Proclamation marked the primeval dawn of what would become the civil rights movement of the twentieth century.

And how can critics of the Emancipation ignore the significance of the fact that it would make it possible for 180,000 black soldiers to fight for the Union cause? With this instrument written by his own hand, declaring on January 1, 1863 that all African-American slaves in Confederate bondage were *"henceforward . . . . free"* under Federal law, Lincoln had cemented the position of the U.S. Government in direct opposition to slavery, and in turn, quashed any British or French thoughts of granting the Confederacy , now branded as a rogue government intractably committed to the protection and expansion of slavery—any formal diplomatic recognition or war support.

Furthermore, Lincoln had opened the door leading to a future time and place in America where slavery would be abolished and African-American enfranchisement embraced. As men have done since ancient times, Lincoln was struggling to pull good from evil. Still, Lincoln was under no illusions; he realized there was much work left to be done to completely abolish slavery. And he was well aware that the Emancipation Proclamation was on thin legal ice; after all, it was issued strictly under War Powers presidential authority—what would come of the Proclamation when the War came to an end?

In a powerfully-visual metaphor, Lincoln put the enactment of the Emancipation Proclamation and the long, embattled pursuit of black emancipation into realistic perspective: "We are like whalers," the President reflected, "who have at last got the harpoon into the monster, but we must now look how we steer, or with one 'flop' of his tail, he will send us all into eternity."

If, then, the Emancipation Proclamation was so important in its own time, and not as trivial as a "bill of lading," the question must be asked . . . What took President Lincoln so long (almost two years) to do it? It is a fair question, and the answer is this: Had Lincoln signed the Emancipation Proclamation earlier in his presidency, odds are, all of the border slave states still maintaining a frail grip to Union membership would have reflexively abandoned the Union, creating a historical tipping point that, perhaps, permanently split the Nation into two separate countries and indefinitely extended the life and geographical boundaries of slavery. Furthermore, Lincoln desperately needed the political momentum which could come only from military success, that he would finally get in September 1862 with McClellan's victory at Antietam. "It is my conviction," the President would later muse, "that, had the proclamation been issued even six months earlier . . . public sentiment would not have sustained it." Timing was everything.

And despite its dispassionate, lawyerlike language, who can credibly argue that Lincoln's Proclamation was devoid of *all* inspiration, and lacking in *all* rhetorical beauty—that it has no more moral significance than a receipt for shipped goods—when one reads, aloud, its closing provision:

> "And upon this act, sincerely believed to be an act of justice, warranted by the Constitution, upon military necessity, I invoke the considerate judgment of mankind, and the gracious favor of Almighty God."
>
> By the President,
> *Abraham Lincoln*

Francis B. Carpenter, the famed portrait artist who spent about six months living in the White House, quoted President Lincoln as describing his Emancipation Proclamation as the "great event of the nineteenth century." Yet Lincoln, himself, would rarely ever mention his Gettysburg Address. Carpenter, who was deeply moved by the Emancipation Proclamation, compared it to "the immaculate conception of Constitutional Liberty." Yet, neither Carpenter—nor other prominents of his generation—would ever heap such lofty praise upon the Gettysburg Address. In his mammoth-sized, 15-foot-wide oil painting on canvas, titled the First Reading of the Emancipation Proclamation, which now hangs in the U.S. Capitol Building over the west staircase in the Senate wing, Francis Carpenter would exalt the July 22, 1862 moment by portraying President Lincoln, surrounded by his stoic Cabinet, with the Emancipation grasped in his left hand. Yet, there would be no such grand artistic renderings of Lincoln delivering his Gettysburg Address.

In fact, when looking back at the last months of Lincoln's presidency, and the half-century following his death, it is clear that virtually all of the iconic paintings and effigies of Abraham Lincoln focused on one solitary event: the Emancipation Proclamation. Lincoln, himself, believed his Emancipation Proclamation was the "central act of my administration." Paintings and sculptures that celebrated the Emancipation Proclamation depicted the President as the "Great Liberator" and the "Great Emancipator" who freed the slaves, and "broke the chains" of bondage to liberate a people—but there was nothing done on canvas or in stone to embalm the memory of the Gettysburg Address. It seemed as though Lincoln's two minute cemetery speech had been stuffed away like a message in a bottle, floating in a sea of obscurity, until it would wash upon the shoreline of future generations.

Hindsight allows us to eavesdrop on the decisions, conduct and language of our Nation's leaders from bygone eras with a panoramic perspective that none of the players enjoyed. And the awkward reality is this: despite Lincoln's universally recognized greatness as a president—today, we know that these nineteenth and twentieth century images of President Abraham Lincoln that cast him as the unflawed, saintly, paternalistic, later-day Moses of helpless black people, in the context of the realities of what he actually said and did, are robustly overinflated.

The truth is, **the emancipation of African-Americans took the collective effort of countless, courageous advocates and visionaries in the mid-nineteenth century:** fearless, give-no-ground abolitionists; firebrand newspaper editors like William Lloyd Garrison and other journalists who ginned public support for black emancipation and relentlessly attacked the institution of slavery in print; African-American soldiers who bravely fought and died for a country that had not yet freed them, let alone allowed them social and political equality (twenty-four would receive the Congressional Medal of Honor); pastors and preachers who railed from their pulpits against the evils of human bondage; Harriet ("Moses") Tubman, Levi Coffin and other fearless conductors and keepers of the secret depots along the Underground Railroad; the learned, articulate and fierce African-American voice of Frederick Douglass, whose words burned the cause of black emancipation and racial equality into the Nation's consciousness; African-American women like "Sojourner Truth" (Isabella Baumfree), the deep-voiced, spellbinding abolitionist preacher who shattered social and racial boundaries by meeting with the President of the United States at the White House and traveling throughout the North, city to city, homes to hospitals, slums to schools, advancing a Christian, non-violent movement for the civil rights of blacks and women; hundreds of thousands of soldiers, who fought and died profligate, to preserve the United States of America; blacks in Southern bondage who risked torture to attend secret prayer meetings held in the "underground churches" of slave huts, forests and swamps, where they prayed for family and freedom; gutsy and enlightened white politicians like Charles Sumner, Wendell Phillips and Thaddeus Stevens, who went toe-to-toe against angry white supremists, putting their mission to abolish slavery before their own race, their safety, and their own political careers; women advocates like sisters Sarah Grimke' and Angelina Grimke' Weld, and the mothers of children all over the North, both white and black, who circulated petitions, organized meetings and campaigned door-to-door, galvanizing neighborhoods into a social movement for the cause of black freedom; literary warriors for racial justice like Harriet Beecher Stowe; and most importantly, African-American slaves, themselves, who languished in an inhumane world of lashes and bondage during the long, bestial struggle, yet, never lost their own humanity, or their hope.

But there is another immutable truth: **No single human being in nineteenth century America did more to raze the institution of slavery than Abraham Lincoln.** Others in Lincoln's time, no doubt, were more earlier-engaged, outspoken and enlightened than he was, when it came to the cause of black emancipation. Their remarkable courage and contributions were indispensable and immense. But in the social and political climate of that era, none of them could have ever reached the presidency. Ambitiously navigating himself through the American political labyrinth to become President of the United States, Lincoln inherited both the unique powers and historical opportunity to choke off the institution of slavery. As President, Lincoln would choose the road less traveled. He forcibly injected his Emancipation Proclamation into the veins of America, and used the bully-pulpit of the presidency and his uncanny political skills to connive and cajole the passage of the Thirteenth Amendment. He did not have to use those powers or that moment in time to attack slavery. All presidents before him chose not to. But he did. Remove Abraham Lincoln from the story of America—and there might be no America, at least the unified Nation we know today. And the hideous institution of slavery, although inevitably doomed by its intrinsic evil, would have been prolonged, indefinitely.

Although the grandiose monikers of "the Great Emancipator" and "Redeemer President" are over-the-top in their paternalistic beneficence and never used in their literal sense today, for several decades following Lincoln's death, this image of Lincoln was deeply imprinted in the public's mind, enabling the Emancipation Proclamation to take the center stage of history—meanwhile, the words he spoke in Gettysburg on November 19th, 1863 would fade from the public consciousness, lost in the shadows of the Proclamation. It seemed as though the Gettysburg Address had become submerged in the floodwaters of time.

In Lincoln's mind, his signing of the Emancipation Proclamation was that "something" he had always hoped for, the accomplishment of his life for which he would be fondly "remembered," forever. Not the Gettysburg Address. "If my name ever goes into history," Lincoln once said in 1864 as he mused about his Emancipation Proclamation, "it will be for this act."

However, it was not to be so. As antebellum America surrendered to the twentieth century, the Emancipation Proclamation, too, was slowly and steadily fading in its prominence from America's memory, like a distant dream. The image of Lincoln, the "Great Emancipator" who ended slavery, was gradually replaced by Lincoln, the President who "saved the Union." It would be another Lincoln manuscript, as Lincoln scholar William E. Barton put it, whose "worth dawned gradually upon the mind of the American people." It would be a manuscript made of less than three hundred words, and be used as a speech to dedicate a soldiers' cemetery in tiny Gettysburg, Pennsylvania. It would contain words which the President ironically said "the world will little note nor long remember," and eventually dispossess the Emancipation Proclamation from its venerated place, staking-out Lincoln's permanent claim on recorded oratorical history. It would be the Gettysburg Address—not the Emancipation Proclamation, for which Lincoln, as he had deeply yearned all of his life, would be most . . . "remembered."

* * *

Lincoln came up as a boy busting rails and sod on dirt farms in Kentucky and Indiana, wrestling on the bluffs of the Sangamon River, surveying ground with a compass and chain, flatboating down the Ohio and Mississippi, leading a rowdy company of hungry soldiers up the murky, mosquito-infested Rock River, running a mill, working as a postmaster, managing a general store, arguing law before rural juries and judges, campaigning in big and little towns, debating his political opponents and giving speeches on the hottest, most controversial topics of the day—all of it, a life woven inextricably from the conversations, customs and heartbeat of the common, everyday people.

This . . . the poverty, the endless sorrows, the mind-numbing work, the harsh father, the hunger to read and learn, the storytelling, the intellectual prowess, the ambition, the rivers, all of this, was Lincoln's life. This, all of this, was Lincoln's education, the primordium of his word skills and his great speeches. Lincoln, after all, knew little of polite society or universities. And he had only a thimble's worth of formal education. Instead, Abraham Lincoln often labored, laughed and raconteured with the mudsills and tinkers of the uneducated, working class. It was, in its purest form, a plebian language, a people's language, that was eloquent in its own simplicity, rough-hewned out of life. As one Springfield lawyer once put it, Lincoln never spoke "beyond the people."

Through the years, Lincoln would develop a relaxed style of politicking that was frank, easygoing and light-hearted. And when he wrote and spoke, he distilled his thoughts and used language that was simple, precise and pithy—not the showy, elevated words that were so popular among politicians of his day. "My politics is short and sweet," Lincoln liked to say with a smile—"like the old woman's dance." So were his words. When Lincoln wrote or said something important, he wanted to use words in a way that would be remembered. He recognized that the sound, the rhythm, and the origin of the words he chose, meant everything.

Lincoln understood that words are like shiny gemstones; polish and buff them too much, and you're left with dull kernels of rock. He knew there was power in plain, unpretentious, unpolished words—words that threaded the needle of the listener. Words that came from the language they were raised on. It was Lincoln's secret to the power of communication.

Like a master mason with a plumbline in his hand, making sure the next row of brick is laid straight and true—Lincoln, the master wordsmith, stacked and mortared words in the Gettysburg Address that were straight and true. Words forged by the fire, hammer and tongs of his life. And like the strong and sturdy mason's wall that has endured the test of time. . .thus so, has the Gettysburg Address.

CHAPTER EIGHTEEN

PONDERINGS & REFLECTIONS

"Now he belongs to the ages."
—Sec. Of War Edwin M. Stanton
Spoken as Pres. Lincoln died,
Petersen House, Washington, D.C.
April 15, 1865

As THE LIFE PASSED FROM ABRAHAM LINCOLN'S BODY ON THE RAW AND rainy Saturday morning of April 15, 1865 in the Petersen House at 453 Tenth Street in Washington, D.C., taken by an assassin's bullet, Surgeon General Joseph K. Barnes folded the lanky arms of the sixteenth president across his chest, and at 7:22 a.m. said, in a voice trembled with grief, "He is gone."

Lincoln had become the ultimate victim of a war provoked by his own election, his death a bloody coda to the end of a conflict that nearly destroyed America. The President's close friend and Secretary of War, Edwin M. Stanton, a man who had once called Lincoln a "long-armed ape," sobbing convulsively, his knees pressed against the floor after prayer by all in the room, broke the awful silence when he spoke six immortal words:

"Now, he belongs to the ages."

Lincoln had been both loved and hated. Just eight months before his death, the *LaCrosse Daily Democrat* had written, "We trust some bold hand will pierce his heart with dagger point for the public good." The haters had finally got their wish.

Stanton's words at Lincoln's deathbed would prove to be prophetically true. President Lincoln's sudden and unexpected death, shot down as he reached the moment of triumph in the War, inflicted a grand mal seizure upon the country. Abraham Lincoln had become America's first martyr president. The last strand connecting Mary Lincoln to sanity had been destroyed. The gathering momentum towards black enfranchisement was lost. Friends and admirers were overwhelmed by grief. His harshest critics, transmogrified. His bitter enemies rendered mute.

But when Abraham Lincoln was nominated for the presidency only five years earlier, seen by many as an awkward and poorly dressed rube—inexperienced and ill-prepared for the job, the *New York Herald* wrote: "The conduct of the republican party in this nomination is a remarkable indication of small intellect, growing smaller. They pass over . . . statesmen and able men, and they take up a fourth rate lecturer, who cannot speak good grammar."

Just a few months later, another newspaper editorialized about Lincoln's recent election to the highest office in the land with these words: "Who will write this ignorant man's state papers?" Incredibly, this same man, by sunset of his first term as president, would compose and deliver a speech at Gettysburg, Pennsylvania, that would become the most admired and lasting words in American history.

It was a transformative act of almost mythological proportion, like Prometheus stealing fire from the gods—a pinnacle event that revealed the essence of the man. A poor, uneducated boy, who had come from questionable and undistinguished stock, by the time of his Gettysburg speech, had grown into a master wordsmith, and a man of wisdom and courage who carried an unshakeable moral vision for the country.

Lincoln had become a man who not only had the courage to embrace political risks, but also possessed the steely emotional strength to overcome a life-long gauntlet of tragedy, depression and defeats. A man who, somehow, extracted wisdom from the commingling of immense power and pain. As his old law partner Billy Herndon put it, Lincoln had traveled through the "fiery furnace" of life. It was a life both triumphant and tragic, a life, uniquely Lincoln's. No other in American history, seems to compare.

As time marches on, we are learning more and more about Abraham

Lincoln, and his remarkable Gettysburg Address. How ironic, that in 1898, only thirty-five years after the Gettysburg Address was spoken at Cemetery Hill, newspaperman and Lincoln friend Noah Brooks would boldly predict: "There can be no new Lincoln stories. The stories are all told."

Despite Noah Brooks' famously myopic prediction, it is still an exciting time for students of Lincoln, as America has crossed the threshold of two hundred years following his birth, a birth that took place on a humble knob of ground, still watered with the same cool spring that the Lincoln family likely drank from, and that can be visited, today, near Hodgenville, Kentucky.

But will we ever know exactly when and how Lincoln composed his epoch speech delivered on November 19, 1863? Are there more copies of the Gettysburg Address written in Lincoln's own hand, yet to be found? It is unlikely. The great waters of time, like rapids wearing tirelessly against the mighty rock, have eroded much of the historical record. But we should not stop searching. Or wondering. Or even wishing. Sometimes, when it is least expected, like the Bedouin boy who stumbled upon the Dead Sea Scrolls in a shoreline cave, the unabating sands of time reveal a precious historical manuscript in a neighborhood garage sale.

Many of the stories and anecdotes that were related about Lincoln by those of his own era were reduced to writing, for the first time, decades after the occurrence of the recollected event. Then, there were those who became emotionally lashed to a martyred president. They would yearn for a niche in the temple of history, and would fill that need by weaving a Lincoln fantasy into their life. Even the firsthand recollections of the circle of people closest to Abraham Lincoln are not, at times, consistent and congruent. Sifting and sorting out the myth from the man has not been easy. And much separating of the wheat and chaff still remains.

The truth is, there will always be new "Lincoln stories." They are inspiring and mystifying. They are human and flawed. They pull us in and make us want to know the man.

But knowing the real Abraham Lincoln is no easy task. Even Lincoln's loyal friend and law partner for nearly eighteen years, William

Henry Herndon, humbly confessed not long before he died, that he had struggled most of his life to understand Lincoln, but finally concluded that he was a "mysterious, quite an incomprehensible man."

The nineteenth century author and famous writer of *Uncle Tom's Cabin*, Harriet Beecher Stowe, who had met with Lincoln personally (when Lincoln first met her, he reportedly said: "So you're the little lady who started this great war!," metaphorically described President Lincoln, this way:

> "Lincoln is a strong man, but his strength is of a peculiar kind: it is not aggressive so much as passive, and among passive things, it is like the strength not so much of a stone buttress as of a wire cable. It is strength swaying to every influence, yielding on this side and on that to popular needs, yet tenaciously and inflexibly bound to carry its great end and probably by no other kind of strength could our national ship have been drawn so safely thus far during the tossings and tempests which beset her way."

Brilliant, flawed and complex, Lincoln was a man plagued, co-equally, by potent ambition and razor-sharp self-doubts in himself; a man who longed for, yet, was terribly insecure in his relationship with women; a man who was immovably resolute and concreted into his deeply-held beliefs, yet, was steadfast in his search for compromise over conflict when possible; a man who was a prolific storyteller, but who said little about the story of his own life; a man vexed by dark bouts of depression, yet, remained unfailingly stable and clear-headed during time of crisis; a man who had the emotional durability to confront the most harsh and brutal of all realities, and yet, allocated much awakened thought to his dark and profuse dreams.

Politics can be savage and even repulsive, because it often embraces the most basic human cravings for power, prestige and recognition. Noble visions are sometimes there, but under the best of circumstances, politics is a flawed means to an altruistic end. Despite his flaws and gradualist approach, Lincoln used politics to accomplish the ultimate altruistic goal for the country, the dismantling of the institution of slavery.

Today, the lives of most of America's great Presidents have been completely dissected and   evaluated by gifted historians, giving us a mature understanding of those men. But not Lincoln. It seems we can never fully know him. His life is still a puzzle, being assembled. Even two hundred years after his birth, even after more than an estimated 16,000 books being written about his life (only behind, most likely, books about Jesus and Shakespeare), Lincoln remains eternally shrouded in mystery, just beyond our reach. He emerges in today's world more immense, more incomparable—more enigmatic—than ever before.

How beautifully ironic that Lincoln—a man who viewed himself as a failed poet—would be seen by history as one of America's great literati. And it would be the Gettysburg Address, his incomparable "prose poem," that would most contribute to that iconic status.

* * *

Did the Gettysburg Address instantly change America itself, on that day of November 19, 1863?   It is a titillating historical question. The answer, although still debated today, is probably "no," at least in the literal sense. To think there could be a sudden and instantaneous political metamorphosis of a melting-pot nation like America, as a result of one single speech, especially during the era of sluggish mid-nineteenth century communications, is a romantic thought, but very unlikely. After all, the few thousand people who were fortunate enough to actually hear the President's voice at Gettysburg, and those that read his speech in the newspaper the next day, in total number, were like a drop of water going over Niagara Falls, when compared to the millions of people living in America who would not hear or read the speech that week.

Many of the newspapers and telegraph versions of the Gettysburg Address that were sent out all over the country, printed only a small portion of the speech, botched the transcription of it, or intentionally twisted the meaning of its words.   Certainly, most people in the audience who heard Lincoln's voice at Gettysburg that day were touched, emotionally and intuitively, by the beauty and poetry of his words. But, just as surely, most of them did not leave the soldiers' cemetery with the cognitive thought that they had heard the President speak of a new and expanded concept of democratic government.   Nor did they likely fully grasp the future impact of Lincoln's "proposition" of human equality.

On the other hand, did the Gettysburg Address, when it was spoken on November 19, 1863, gradually and over time, change the course of America? The answer, most surely, is a resounding "yes." As historian and Pulitzer Prize author Garry Wills insightfully put it, Lincoln's Gettysburg Address "stealthily . . . remade America."

Certainly, key victories of the Union Army at critical times, the railroad and telegraph, and the economic advantages of the North were all confluent factors that led to the defeat of the Confederacy, permanently shaping our Nation. But when President Lincoln brought *equality for all people* into the working definition of American liberty, as it had never been done before, done with the moral force of his Gettysburg Address, he would, himself, turn the wheel of American law and life in a new direction, forever.

Beginning with a new birth of freedom Lincoln announced on November 19, 1863 at a soldiers' cemetery, the evolutionary lathe of ever-expanding equality for people of color and women began to turn, slowly shapen, and take form: from the 1865 passage of the 13th Amendment only two years after Lincoln's Gettysburg speech (*equal* right of all people to be free from bondage, abolishing slavery); to the 1868 passage of the 14th Amendment (*equal* rights to citizenship and due process); to the 1870 passage of the 15th Amendment (*equal* right to vote); to the 1920 passage of the 19th Amendment (*equal* right of women to vote); to the 1954 U.S. Supreme Court decision in Brown v. Board of Education (*equal* right of black students to attend all public schools, without segregation); to The Civil Rights Act of 1964 (*equal* right to vote, and work, and have access to all public places, without discrimination).

Equality . . . first promised in the Declaration of Independence—and as brought to life in the Gettysburg Address—has become, today, as identic and indispensable as freedom itself, in forming the two key pillars of American liberty.

As brilliant and peerless as the U. S. Constitution was, when it was first conceived by the Founders, it was not whole. It was an imperfect document like those men who drafted it, and the people it was drafted for. Through the years, amendments to the Constitution would be necessary to improve upon and extend the tenets of freedom and equality that define America as a democratic republic.

The Declaration of Independence was no different. In July of 1776, the great document was nulli secundus in concept and words, yet, in its effect, it was empty and unfulfilled. Despite its noble words, all Americans were not equal, not even free. However, in his speech at Gettysburg, Pennsylvania, Abraham Lincoln would issue what would be, in its practical force and effect, a de facto "First Amendment" to the Declaration of Independence. That amendment, which was a document made of only 272 words, would extend the sacred tenet of human equality, as originally promised in the Declaration, to Americans of every race, color and creed. That amendment was the Gettysburg Address. With that speech, the process had begun, finally, to make the Declaration of Independence whole.

President Abraham Lincoln had moved the chess pieces of history.

And how is that? As a speech, the Gettysburg Address is sui generis. Remove the Gettysburg Address from America's story, and who knows what the consequence might have been for the Nation. Lincoln's majestic words spoken at Cemetery Hill, tragically strengthened by his martyr death and the patient passage of time, would serve as a compass to re-orient and guide a lost nineteenth century America out of the moral and political labyrinth that had been created by a country divided by civil war and slavery. They are words that point America in the direction of a richer and more mature democracy, a democracy built upon the eternal covenant of freedom and equality for all people. Two hundred seventy-two words, that over time, would define America's national creed so perfectly, they cannot be improved upon.

So why do Lincoln's words in the Gettysburg Address endure, still today? The answer is actually quite simple. . .

Because the meaning of America is found there.

The Gettysburg Address is now widely recognized as the greatest short speech given since the Sermon On The Mount. Just nine sentences, now securely in the hands of posterity. And posterity is not likely to let go of them, for they are the best known words in American history.

We stand amazed at the poetic beauty of the Gettysburg Address, deeply moved by its substance. By the time Abraham Lincoln delivered his Gettysburg Address, he had learned how to weave the homespun language and experiences of ordinary people into his speeches. Influenced by the *King James Bible* and *Aesop's Fables*, Lincoln loved to use allegories, metaphors and parables. From *Aesop*, Lincoln loved the story of the four bulls, when standing together in a field, were safe from the stalking lion . . . until they separated (influencing his famous 1858 speech at Springfield, "A house divided against itself cannot stand"). Lincoln's language was rich with brushstrokes of imagery, using the idioms of the woods, rivers and barnyard to get across his point. As Civil War historian literati Shelby Foote put it, Lincoln "wrote American."

Lincoln composed and delivered the Gettysburg Address in a style radically different from the great orators of his day. Lincoln's oratorical skills had been forged along the way in his climb from the bottom rung of his social and economic world, up to the highest office in the land, a process of beating down, bending and hammering out the steel in the man which would produce a speaking style that was real and authentic. It was a style that would pull the public to him like a lodestone.

In a sense, November 19, 1863 began a new age and subtle evolutionary trend in political speeches. After Gettysburg, the style and content of political speeches in America would slowly but steadily become less showmanship, and more egalitarian. Less grandiloquent, and more conversational. Lincoln, with his short speech at Cemetery Hill, had become a master of eloquent brevity. It was a prose poem. He had given the American political speech its modern cast. As Professor Garry Wills so aptly stated, "[A]ll modern political prose descends from the Gettysburg Address."

Part of the brilliance of the Gettysburg Address is that President Lincoln had the clarion vision to not lean upon the rhetorical customs of the day, nor chain down his words to his own time and place. By doing so, Lincoln forged a speech that is just as understandable, relevant and meaningful today, as it was on November 19, 1863. In contrast, much of Edward Everett's speech focused on the specific commanders, military strategies and battles that took place at Gettysburg during the first three days of July 1863, and the national crisis then looming over the country, and hardly a single line is remembered today.

Abraham Lincoln saw the Civil War as being fought by the North against a gentry class of slave-owning aristocrats who organized and fueled the Confederacy, not a war against ordinary folk, his fellow Americans, who happened to live in the South. Ultimately, in Lincoln's view, the War was not about North or South, rich or poor, black or white, it was a fight for human liberty and to save the democratic republic that cradled it. So President Lincoln gave the Gettysburg Address universal appeal by avoiding words that so deeply divided the country like "North" and "South," "Yankees" and "Rebels," or the "Union" and "Confederacy." He never even mentioned his proudest executive act, the Emancipation Proclamation. Instead, Lincoln allowed his speech to transcend time and place, by never calling out the names of commanding officers, heroic soldiers, battlegrounds, or even referring to the Battle of Gettysburg by its name; he did not need to, these names were already, forever, written in blood.

Although Lincoln had abiding, moral contempt for slavery, he avoided using that inflammatory, divisive word in his Gettysburg Address. Instead, Lincoln would choose comforting, healing words from the Bible with powerful spiritual connotations that gave the Gettysburg Address eternal life— words like **brought forth . . . conceived . . . consecrate . . . full measure**—words that were warm and real, that conjured up powerful images in the mind's eye, and inspired hope in every listener of faith. By doing these things, he lifted his speech to a higher and broader plane of purpose and meaning.

Lincoln's words at Gettysburg—conceived from the womb of an apocalyptic national conflict—would become the template for a new birth of freedom, and would, forever, define the moral and political tenets of American democracy.

The words of the Gettysburg Address are the only verses of scripture we have left, that are actually a part of our twenty-first century secular government. The Gettysburg Address has become the spiritual voice of democracy in America. By using words at Gettysburg that carried the force and weight of biblical canons, Lincoln was able to speak to the long view, to the greater importance of the War. He had fused together the secular and the sacred. Lincoln was asking all Americans—then and now— to come together for the ideals of freedom and equality.

He was speaking to all humankind.

* * *

It is a remarkable tribute to Abraham Lincoln that people, today, know more words from the Gettysburg Address than they do America's most sacred and revered documents of destiny, like the Declaration of Independence and the U.S. Constitution. The Gettysburg Address is even known around the world. In 1958, when the people of France implemented their last Constitution, they adopted, verbatim, Lincoln's words as a "principle" into their own sacred instrument, which recites in Article II that the French Republic will be a "government of the people, by the people, and for the people."

Whether the words of the Gettysburg Address reinvented the Declaration of Independence by expanding its meaning of equality for all people, or simply resurrected its intrinsic promises, those words spoken by Abraham Lincoln at the Soldiers' National Cemetery reach out from the past to help us, as today's Americans, to better understand the words from the lips of Thomas Jefferson that define and underpin our democracy.

The Gettysburg Address has been chiseled into the memories of generation after generation of schoolchildren, who have learned to stand and recite it. It appears in millions of books. It is etched in bronze, marble, granite and stone throughout our country.

History suggests that the Gettysburg Address was the first speech, ever, for which a monument specifically was built and dedicated. And how precious to America is the manuscript of the Gettysburg Address written in Lincoln's own hand? For a time during World War II, when the very existence of the free world, as we know it today, hung in the balance—the Gettysburg Address was secreted out of Washington, D.C., and given safe, clandestine sanctuary in America's very own safety-deposit box . . . the Bullion Depository at Fort Knox, Kentucky.

Abraham Lincoln believed deeply and fiercely in democracy. In the context of his own time, Lincoln viewed the Confederacy's minie' bullets and cannon-fire just as much as assault on democracy, as an attack on the Union. He also feared for the survival of America, itself.

An 1860's America was reeling from the shock waves of racial, social and political division, war at home, rapid urbanization, a depleted national treasury, international trade concerns, the Gold Rush, the rise of the women's rights and black emancipation movements, and massive immigration. Lincoln wondered whether or not America, as a self-governing, democratic republic, could sustain itself. He worried that the meaning and importance of the principles set forth in the Preambles of the Declaration of Independence—what he saw as the only true blueprint for the American democracy—had taken on the moldy smell of obsolescence.

"Fellow-citizens, we cannot escape history," President Lincoln would tell the Nation in his Annual Message to Congress on December 1, 1862.

Even in his own era, Lincoln recognized that Americans, by their optimistic and adventurous nature, were a forward-looking people; admirable qualities, certainly, that are part of America's collective greatness. But Lincoln worried that America was becoming like a plow horse with blinders fastened to the sides of its eyes, capable of seeing only in one direction, ahead of it. He saw Americans as people increasingly interested only with their present and their future, the things still before them, but disinterested with their own historical past, the things already behind them.

From Lincoln's perspective, this was dangerous thinking. If Americans turned their back on the core principles of democracy that were forged and born of their own historical past,, that is, a form of democracy built upon the bedrock principles of freedom and equality for all people as expressly written in the Declaration of Independence, then America, itself, was at risk.

Lincoln believed that America's values, its most noble and lasting values, are forged from the crucible of remembrance. From its history. By forgetting its historical roots, roots spring-fed by the Declaration of Independence, Lincoln feared that the world's only enduring democratic republic based upon popular sovereignty would slowly and steadily oxidize away. History connects us to all other American lives, past, present and future. The future of America, the kind of nation America was yet to be, would be shaped, in Lincoln's view, to a great extent, by what it chose to remember about itself.

The worries Lincoln had for the survival of democracy, concerns he felt because Americans, in his view, have it in their nature to forget or disregard the lessons and sacrifices of their past, are still the worries of many Americans, today. As in Lincoln's time, our twenty-first century America is feeling the shock waves of racial, social and political division, war abroad, soaring national debt, an international exodus of manufacturing and jobs, the technology rush, the rise of the gay rights and "occupy" movements, and massive immigration.

As millions of immigrants, both legal and illegal, flow into America like a great river each year, the viability of America as a "melting pot" nation, and what the core principles of American democracy should be, continue to be the subject of fierce and passionate debate, even a century and a half after Lincoln spoke at Gettysburg.

And just as Lincoln and Americans of his time struggled with the burning hot issues of a rapidly growing multi-ethnic, multi-lingual, and multi-cultural democracy in the mid-nineteenth century, and as again vigorously debated by Americans after World War I, o do we, today.

On one end of the political spectrum, there are citizens in our country who believe that failed immigration policies have eroded national unity and patriotism in America, undercut jobs and wages for its people, and thus, dangerously weakened the Nation. They see the fracture and diminution of the English language as the primary and most important voice in America. They fear a balkanization of the country, turning America into a heterogeneous populace of ethnic factions, that will inevitably lead to its disintegration. They see an America as a nation with porous borders, doling out government benefits to anyone who can covertly find their way in. In their view, those who cross our southern borders without permission are "illegal." And they are troubled by the "Americanization" of the children of illegal or undocumented immigrants who gain their citizenship only by birth upon American soil, leaving them, they argue, with little historical knowledge or concern for America's 1776 traditions. They view America as a cracked and overflowed melting pot, a case of immigration gone wild, leaving its gate wide-open for anyone and everyone to enter, putting the unity and security of America at terrible risk. After all, they say, a country without secure borders will someday cease to be a country.

Then, on the other end of the spectrum, there are those citizens who believe that diversity of people, language and culture enriches and strengthens America. Thus, they resist all perceived efforts to nationalize the English language. They oppose most immigration barriers, and resist any governmental policies they see as the forced assimilation of those who come to live in America. They fear the strict enforcement of borders and immigration laws, and believe the installation of walls and fences are dangerous movements which could lead the country into a repressive and homogenizing theocracy. In their view, those who cross our southern borders without permission are "undocumented." And they see America as a room-for-all, bottomless melting pot that is brimming with multi-language and multi-cultural influences. After all, they point out, America was conceived in a single, courageous act of immigration from the Old World; an act not unlike the Cuban boat people who sometimes risk all to come to our shores.

And between these two ideological extremes, there are those somewhere in the grayish middle, and of course, those who live in the sublime karma of not-knowing, not-worried or not-caring. This national pageant of divergent and conflicting ideas has created a feeling among many, today, that America is a giddy, unsteady country, on the brink of careening out of control.

But this is nothing new for Americans. In a 1786 letter to John Hay, George Washington would opine: "We [the people of America] are apt to run from one extreme to another."

In a uniquely-American paradox, the fact that such passionate and divisive issues can be openly debated and publicly protested by its citizens (and even by non-citizens living on American soil), free from fear of government reprisals, is a self-affirming validation that democracy, far from perfect, is still alive and well in America. The clanging, head-on collision of these conflicting ideas over the future of America is, in and of itself, the sound of freedom.

To paraphrase F. Scott Fitzgerald's famous definition of "first-rate intelligence," perhaps the test of a first-rate democracy is its ability to hold opposing ideas in tension at the same time, and still effectively function.

Today, the question is often asked—has America become so immeasurably diverse, so multicultural, so diversiform in human and ethnic texture—that it is no longer possible to recognize our Nation's defining principles? Like the divisive issue of slavery in the nineteenth century, could a twenty-first century America that is still deeply divided by political ideology, immigration, borders and language, drift in a direction that undermines its promise of freedom and equality for all people?

What should American democracy look like, in the future? Is the American experiment, itself, at risk? These questions still burn.

So . . . where should we, as today's Americans, look for answers to these questions?

We should look to Lincoln.

Lincoln worried for his country, as we do today. He pondered on these same questions and about the survival of America during the dark hours of his own multiethnic, multicultural, war-torn, politically-fractured time. It was these same fears for the survival and sustainability of democracy that inspired President Lincoln to compose a speech for Gettysburg that would call Americans back to their founding principles, to their history.

At Gettysburg, Lincoln was endeavoring to mend those fractures in the American consciousness by pulling the past into a contemplative connection with the present, so the Nation could gain a sense of direction for the future. If Americans wanted the vision to see what lay ahead for their country, they had to understand history. Their history. And Lincoln knew that to understand . . . is to remember. He found the answers in the American Revolution.

And, if Abraham Lincoln were alive today, what would he tell us?

Lincoln, first, would direct us to 1776—the American Revolution—back to the sacred promises written in the Preamble of the Declaration of Independence. He viewed the Preamble's words as the gold standard for democracy, on equal footing with the Constitution, against which not only America, but all later history would be measured. Then, Lincoln would reorient our Nation's enduring search for the true and perfect model of American democracy, and rekindle our hope for the future, by directing us to the second American Revolution—the Civil War—back to the timeless words of the Gettysburg Address. The Constitution, Lincoln recognized, is indispensable as the blueprint of American government. But the Preamble and the Gettysburg Address, read together, are the American creed; they are the two lens through which the Constitution should br read. Lastly, in this process, Lincoln would remind us, above all else, that freedom and human equality, in tandem, are the soul of true democracy.

After all, America, the 1776 nation, did not invent the freedom and equality that defines it's democratic republic. Alas, it is the opposite. It was the hunger for freedom and equality that invented America.

These two great documents, the Declaration of Independence and the Gettysburg Address, do not pretentiously describe who we are, for America is, in many ways, an imperfect nation, but rather, they humbly describe what we *strive* to be. Americans do not simply live under the words of the Declaration of Independence and the Gettysburg Address, we are characterized by them.

John Dos Passos, the great "Lost Generation" American novelist and artist, in his 1941 book *The Ground We Stand On*, insightfully brought Lincoln's concerns for nineteenth century America forward into the context of our own time, when he wrote in these powerful, lasting passages:

> "In easy times history is more or less of an ornamental art, but in times of danger we are driven to the written record by a pressing need to find answers to the riddles of today. We need to know what kind of firm ground other men, belonging to generations before us, have found to stand on. In spite of changing conditions of life they were not very different from ourselves, their thoughts were the grandfathers of our thoughts, they managed to meet situations as difficult as those we have to face, to meet them sometimes lightheartedly, and in some measure to make their hopes prevail. We need to know how they did it.
>
> In times of change and danger when there is a quicksand of fear under men's reasoning, a sense of continuity with

generations gone before can stretch like a lifeline across the scary present and get us past that idiot delusion of the exceptional Now that blocks good thinking. That is why, in times like ours, when old institutions are caving in and being replaced by new institutions not necessarily in accord with most men's preconceived hopes, political thought has to look backwards as well as forwards.

In spite of the ritual invocation of the names of the Founding Fathers round election time, Americans as a people notably lack a sense of history. We have taken the accomplishments in state building of the seventeenth century colonists and of the thirteen states for granted, as we took the rich forest loam and the coal and the iron and the oil and the buffalo. We have wasted and exploited our political heritage with the same childish lack of foresight that has wrecked our forests and eroded our farmlands and ruined the grazing on the Great Plains.

Now that we are caught up short at the edge of the precipice, face to face with the crowded servitude from which our fathers fled to a new world, the question is how much is left; how much of their past achievement is still part of our lives? It is not a question of what we want; it is a question of what is. Our history, the successes and failures of the men who went before us, is only alive in so far as some seeds and shoots of it are still stirring and growing in us today."

Maybe it is time, again, as Senator Everett Dirksen from Illinois was fond of saying during the years of America's civil rights crisis. . . "We need to get right with Lincoln." And how do we do that?

We should read the Preamble to the Declaration of Independence, and then, the Gettysburg Address. They are, together, our American scriptures. And we should read them aloud, the way they were meant to be. They are words which are most powerful when they are spoken. Their words remain fresh and alive, no matter how many times they are read. All we need to know about what American democracy should be, is found there, among the words of these two ancient manuscripts.

To borrow from the great Senator from Illinois . . . we need to get right with the Declaration of Independence and the Gettysburg Address.

Fortunately, these two uniquely-American manuscripts are still there for us, both as a Nation and as individuals, "stretching like a life-line across the scary present," giving America direction and hope. In fact, the words Lincoln spoke at Gettysburg are so timeless in their call for all Americans to re-connect to their historical past, so we can understand the importance of preserving both freedom and equality as the wellspring of our democracy, that a century and a half later—on September 11, 2002, at the one year memorial service in New York City for the terrorist attack on America . . . it was the Gettysburg Address that was chosen to be read.

The Gettysburg Address was read in New York City precisely at a time, as John Dos Passos wrote, when there was "a quicksand of fear under man's reasoning." It was read without introduction, without stridency or self-promotion of the presenter, and without lavish voice inflections or grand gestures—just as Abraham Lincoln had done on November 19, 1863, allowing the dignity of the words to exalt themselves.

When the words of the Gettysburg Address were read in New York City at Ground Zero, they were spoken to all Americans, to all humanity, just as Abraham Lincoln had done at the soldiers' cemetery in Gettysburg. In the same way that Thomas Jefferson's words in the Declaration of Independence had stretched out from 1776 to the lips of Abraham Lincoln, Lincoln's words were stretching out from 1863 to us. The Gettysburg Address had been summoned forth, once more, to bring the past to the present, and then point to the future.

History, again, triangulated.

And so it was. At Ground-Zero, in the year 2002, the Gettysburg Address was read to the masses, to again honor fallen heroes and to bring solace and hope for America, in a time of great uncertainty. America needed the words of the Gettysburg Address as succor. After all, as Lincoln once said, such memorial services are for "us the living." So that we never forget that freedom and equality are for all people. So that we, as a free people, can go on. So we want to go on.

Truly—the Gettysburg Address—is the hymn of American democracy.

The greatest speech, ever.

EPILOGUE

A Personal Journey

When this book emerges, Abraham Lincoln will be over 200 years old. I have been on a personal journey to know Lincoln for nearly half of a century.

My lifetime relationship with Abraham Lincoln began in the late 1950's, in the first grade. As a young boy attending a rural elementary school in the mountains of eastern Tennessee, near the Kentucky-Tennessee border, our entire education about U.S. Presidents was mortared around the great triumpherate—Washington, Jefferson and Lincoln.

Each February of my early elementary school years, as the day officially designated to honor Abraham Lincoln approached on our calendar, we would go through the obligatory task of cutting out his side-profiled silhouette out of black paper. His kind and rugged face was being put before us, even in our earliest years.

We next pasted the paper bust of Lincoln on a background of brightly-colored construction paper. Finally, we carved our name with a #2 pencil at the bottom of our proud creation. Our handiwork would then be tacked to the classroom wall. Duplicated Lincoln heads covered just about every square inch of wall space. It looked like we were sitting inside of a giant kaleidoscope.

On parent day, moms and dads would proudly saunter around the room like they were at the Smithsonian, their kids swollen with anticipation, waiting for their parents to spot their own "unique" paper edifice of Abraham Lincoln that looked just like every other Lincoln head on the wall. It sounds a bit cynical, but the principal's selection of one "best" Lincoln sculpture, out of that sea of similarities, must have been either random or rigged. The fortunate (or favored) student won a five dollar bill—a doggone fortune in those days—as our teacher pointed out Old Abe's face on the front of the bill.

That same day, our teacher would always read to us about Lincoln. She would teach us that "Mr. Lincoln," as she reverently referred to him, was born on Kentucky soil, in a log cabin with a dirt floor, not too far from where we lived ("near Mammoth Cave," she would tell us, which was a much-anticipated school field trip when we got older). And, of course, she would dutifully teach us that Lincoln "saved the Union," "freed the slaves," and was shot to death by a bad actor. (Actually, Booth was a bad person, but a pretty good actor.)

For most of my elementary school years, this sanitized snippet of Lincoln's life was all we were taught—it was all we knew—about our bearded sixteenth president. All the while, Lincoln remained a dead president.

My first stout memory of the Gettysburg Address was when my third grade elementary teacher, Mrs. Bernice Hatfield, read to us, beautifully, from Mary Raymond Shipman Andrews's tiny book, *The Perfect Tribute*. Of course, I had no earthly idea, then, about the author or title, but I certainly remember being captivated by the beguiling storyline of how President Lincoln, in a moment of spontaneous inspiration and after sharpening his stubby pencil with a silver-colored pocketknife (a lot like mine, I imagined), wrote the Gettysburg Address while riding a train to Gettysburg, scribbling it on a piece of brown wrapping paper left discarded on the railroad car floor.

The Andrews story went on to tell the heartwarming story of President Lincoln's chance encounter with a young boy near the White House. It happened on the day following Lincoln's return to Washington after delivering his famous speech at Gettysburg. As the story went, the boy—tears running down his cheeks—stumbles into a giantly President Abraham Lincoln. The boy is carrying with him the last wish of his older brother, a soldier who fought for the Confederacy, who was dying in a Union prison hospital. President Lincoln personally carries out the dying wish of the young Confederate captain, and in the process, learns that his words spoken at Gettysburg were not a failure, as he first thought, but were lasting words that would inspire people in both the North and the South.

Although Mary Andrews's charming account of how the Gettysburg Address was hurriedly composed on a train (along with the story of President Lincoln's personal encounter with the young boy and his dying Confederate brother) were entirely fiction, for years, I believed the whole thing was true. After all, the story wasn't a tall tale like Paul Bunyan or Johnny Appleseed. Instead, it sounded like a history lesson about a real man, one of our Presidents of the United States. Like so many had since Lincoln's death, I had swallowed a Lincoln fantasy story, hook, line and sinker. Not until I reached high school would I learn in my private reading that this version of how the Gettysburg Address came to be, was nothing more than a fairy tale. I had also discovered than Lincoln's life was encrusted with many layers of mythology, and even counter-mythology, that had to be chipped away to reveal the reality of the man.

It was in my adolescent years that I took a quantum leap in my journey to know Abraham Lincoln. During summers, I spent occasional weekends on a farm with my step-grandfather, who was a country lawyer by trade. We stayed in a rustic, block building known as "the cabin." There was a small library in a corner of the cabin. Of course, it contained some law books (including an old leather-bound version of *Chitty's Blackstone*, interestingly enough, one of the same legal publications that Lincoln studied; I still have it), some of those ubiquitous *Readers Digest "Condensed" Books*, and most notably, Carl Sandburg's Homeric multi-volume work, *Abraham Lincoln: The Prairie Years and The War Years*.

Each trip to the farm was filled with adventures: the daytime adventure of exploring the water's edge of ponds that were throbbing with life, and the Appalachian valleys, hills and bluffs that embraced the old cabin, and the nighttime adventure of exploring Lincoln's life in Sandburg's poetic volumes.

Sometimes, I would read about the life of Abraham Lincoln with a flashlight under the bed covers, long into the night, becoming lost in the words. When Carl Sandburg described young Abraham working all alone in the deep woods, dropping trees and splitting timbers with an ax, companioned only by the primordial sounds of a wilderness place, I wasn't just hearing "the crackling and swaying of branches in the wind," I was the wind. I was hovering above Abraham Lincoln, looking down, watching his life unfold. The lush, melodic prose of the author was surround-sound reading. The words were symphonic. They took me to another place and time. And they ignited in me a yearning to know more about the man, and how he came from nothing, without pedigree or privilege, to become the most beloved and venerated president ever.

I read some of Sandburg's chapters, especially about young Lincoln in *The Prairie Years*, many times. It was, for me, a Eurekian experience in learning. I had discovered that you could read something special, over and over again, and that things new and fresh and interesting would reveal themselves with each reading.

I was smitten.

In Abraham Lincoln, I had found a person who inspired me—a life full of adventure, hardships, sadness and courage. A life worth looking up to. A man of character worthy of emulation. A hero. Lincoln was no longer just a dead president, preserved as a black silhouette pasted on construction paper. In my world, Carl Sandburg had brought Lincoln alive.

My next meaningful encounter with the Gettysburg Address was later, in junior high school. One of the teachers organized a "Gettysburg Address Speech Contest." Alas, It was that wonderful educational era of the late 1950's and early 1960's where it was common for school children to visit factories and firehalls, have art shows, skits and talent contests in the gym, and recite poetry by memory before the rest of the class. It was a time when teachers had sufficient classroom time to occasionally detour from textbooks, so they could teach to the kids, and not to national exam standards.

Why, I don't know. But I entered that speech contest. I practiced and practiced . . . and then I practiced some more. I did not fully comprehend the full purpose and meaning of the Gettysburg Address, but even then, I was inexplicably drawn to the rhythms and cadence of the words. I could feel that the words had mystical power in them, even if I did not understand them all.

When the big day of the contest came, my delivery of the Gettysburg Address was choppy and nervous. I left out a complete line. And mangled up another. When the pressure was on, I had folded like a lawn chair. A student whose mother made him a stovepipe hat out of cardboard and added a mascara beard to his jaw-line, took the winning trophy. The truth is, that he would have won fair and square, even without the wardrobe advantage. But the words—those beautiful, remarkable words of the Gettysburg Address—had been indelibly imprinted in my mind.

Through my high school and college years, I read every Lincoln book I could squeeze-in between school work and activities. Thanks to my parents, many Lincoln books were already on our bookshelves at home. Even as I attended college during the early 1970's, I often sifted through the bargain-bin of the university's student center, searching for Lincoln books I had not read. It was then that I first began to notice a disturbing trend, one that, looking back, found its headwaters in America's turmoil of the 1960's.

Over this landscape of the 1970's blew the winds of social and political change, that seemed to touch the highest levels of academic thought and work. Books about Lincoln, particularly those that had anything good to write about him, seemed increasingly scarce. And the books and articles I found, erudite and thought-provoking as they often were, seemed to focus not only on defrocking Lincoln, but also the Founding Fathers along with him. Looking back at that era, there seems to have been a distain for biographies themselves, what some called "Great Man" biographies and others more sneeringly labeled "Dead White Male" history, perhaps reflecting an academic shift that was already extending more heavily to cultural history and also paying attention to trendy social movements of the time.

Overall, this was a healthy shift, a needed opportunity among a new breed of rising scholars to re-examine the lives of our American icons. But the burgeoning trend of writings (along with lectures at my university) seemed to relish, much too exuberantly, in the human frailties and failures of our great presidents, like Washington, Jefferson and Lincoln. Some on the academic fringes and amateur Freudians were going so far as to recast Lincoln and the Founding Fathers into cunning, manipulative, power-grabbing racists. (A few still try, even today.) A new generation of historians had gained access to the *Lincoln Papers* through the Library of Congress (not made available to the public until after World

War II), and, rightfully so, they began to scrutinize and reappraise the iconographic Lincoln story. Hauling Lincoln and our Founders over the hot coals of historical re-evaluation became nonconformist, free-thinking and avant-garde. The microscopic scrutiny was good. But I suspect that some academians at that time, disillusioned by an unpopular war, the hubris of the Nixon presidency, and the covert dishonesty and blunders of their government, turned their anger and frustration not only towards America, but also against what they saw as America's oversold and overinflated pantheon of Presidential demi-gods.

Perhaps this academic stoning of Lincoln was sort of a cultural acid-reflux to the late 1940's and 1950's, decades at the high tide of the Lincoln myth—the culmination of nearly a century's worth of increasing veneration of Abraham Lincoln in the inescapable form of thousands of biographies and Lincoln-named parks and parkways, odes and edifices, movies and monuments, libraries and lecture halls, roads and rocks (yes—there really is a natural rock in a Washington state park, supposedly bearing a resemblance to Abraham Lincoln), cities and counties, schools and shrines, and of course, Mt. Rushmore —all of it, an epoch that international author and Lincoln biographer Jan Morris referred to as a "sententious mania."   (The first thing named after Abraham Lincoln was probably a town in Logan County, Illinois, in 1853. Lincoln warned the townspeople who proudly told him of their decision, telling them, "Nothing named Lincoln ever amounted to much." The most recent phenomenon, is a book and then movie that portrays Lincoln as a vampire hunter. What would he say about that? No doubt, he would chuckle and somehow use it to poke fun at his political enemies.)

It's true, among the pages of much historical literature and books of that century, Lincoln the man, had sometimes been inflated to superhuman proportions. As the equally brilliant and controversial novelist Gore Vidal, who relished in whacking down American icons to size, including Lincoln, once sarcastically quipped that the worst thing that ever happened to Abraham Lincoln was "to fall into the hands of Carl Sandburg." Despite his trademark invective sarcasm, Vidal had a point about some of the over-the-top, hagiographic treatment of·Abraham Lincoln. During my family's visit to Lincoln's birthplace at the Sinking

Spring Farm near Hodgenville, Kentucky, I had a delightful and informative discussion with a neatly-uniformed and articulate lady who was
working as a ranger for the National Park Service. She was assigned to
keep vigilant watch over the log structure tucked inside a miniaturized
Greek temple apocryphally known as the "Lincoln birthplace." In our
discussion of Lincoln mythology, we both chuckled as she reminded me
of the long running gag-line that satirized the post-World War II
Lincoln "mania," which boasted that "Abraham Lincoln built the log
cabin where he was born with his own hands."

By the time the "mania" subsided and the 1960's and 1970's had
arrived, the idea that Lincoln, Washington or Jefferson were lives worth
celebrating and learning from, had become a position treated in some
academic circles as amateurish, if not downright ridiculed. Some
schools named after these presidents even changed their name.

The Vietnam War, and the culture of American cynicism emerging
from it, had taken its toll. America had lost her innocence. The
Gettysburg Address had lost its relevance. I had lost my nerve to speak
openly and admirably of Lincoln in classroom discussions and academic circles. And my once proud elementary school silhouettes of Lincoln
were becoming an embarrassing memory.

Certainly, there is no redeeming value in biographies of Lincoln or
our Founders that are so romantic and mawkish that they ignore the
infirmities, ambiguities and character flaws of those enormously complex men. There have been plenty of them through the years. Such
writings not only turn these historical figures into inane, marble-cast
caricatures, but they also rob them of their humanity, often, the most
meaningful part of the story of their lives.

To truly understand Abraham Lincoln one must, no doubt, pierce
through the cloak of mythology. I have tried to do so in this book. It is
no easy task. Lincoln's life, from his log cabin birth and ax-wielding
childhood, his public and private tragedies, his leading America from
out of the apocalyptic darkness of a fratricidal war, and then, his shocking assassination on a Good Friday, at the very moment of victory, is a
perfect storm of human events for iconography. Human beings have
always wanted the myth of heroes, to show them the way.

Even Lincoln's dear and loyal friend, and his last law partner before becoming president, William Henry Herndon, had no stomach for sanitized biographies. Soon after Lincoln's death, Herndon, a garrulous, quick-thinking, hard-drinking and sometimes overbearing but popular character, collected hundreds of testimonials from people who really knew Lincoln. He then began to write and lecture about his view of Lincoln, the man, an authentic human being who exhibited greatness and weakness, triumphs and failures, not an iconic saint. Before he got done, Mary and Robert Lincoln probably hated him. In Herndon's time, biographies were more akin to eulogies, intended only to honor the subject. Herndon didn't see it that way. Herndon took pride in his facility to see deep down, as he put it, to "the gizzard of a question." He felt that painting the whole picture of Lincoln's life, warts and all, would not degrade but rather amplify the public's admiration of Lincoln's achievements.

Billy Herndon had it right. Although his reputation would be whip-sawed and his work treated as trifling by historians for many years, time has proved Herndon's contributions to the understanding of Lincoln, the man, as priceless. We are still learning from Herndon's raw observations and assessments about Lincoln. Herndon had little contact with Lincoln after he went to the White House. But without Herndon's personal research, we would know virtually nothing about Lincoln's earliest years. His work reminds us that we are best served by a full, unvarnished and balanced knowledge of our historical figures. For that reason, I have delved into some of Lincoln's flaws and foibles in this book.

But neither should it be an academic sin to praise the extraordinary courage and achievements of flawed men and women. I believe we can admire Lincoln, without lionizing him. As W.E.B. Du Bois poignantly said of Lincoln, "I love him not because he was perfect, but because he was not—and yet triumphed."

Part of the problem was that some contemporary historians in the 1960's and 1970's were reaching back and snatching Lincoln from out of his own era, then, in time machine fashion, fast-forwarding him into the twentieth century, where they harshly appraised Lincoln and his place in history in the strict contextual vacuum of contemporary mores, culture and socioeconomic attitudes. (These time-machine assessments of Lincoln still thrive in the twenty-first century.) From my perspective, this produced a historical snapshot of Abraham Lincoln that was blurred and out of focus from the true and full human profile of the man. Historian James M. McPherson has described it as "looking at history through the wrong end of a telescope." In order to truly understand Abraham Lincoln and grasp his impact on today's America, contemporary historians, looking at Lincoln backward in time, must maintain their sense of fairness and intellectual equilibrium by studying and critiquing Lincoln in his own time and place.

It was in this lingering environment, in 1979, during my final months in law school, that a friend loaned me a brave new book. By now, the demands of law school had cannibalized my time for pleasure reading. Books had become something I studied, not read. But somehow, I had to read this one. From the very first page, it pulled me in. It was unconventional, intelligent . . . and inspiring. And it did what is so incredibly difficult, cast a fresh, new light of understanding on Abraham Lincoln. It was titled *Lincoln and the Economics of the American Dream.*

The author was a remarkable man, Gabor Boritt, a Civil War historian and professor at Gettysburg College. Suddenly, here was a man of esteemed scholarship, ironically, a refugee from Hungary, who dared to celebrate the contributions of Lincoln's life. This must have been heresy to some of the reigning orthodoxy of academia. Professor Boritt's book was taking on the 800 lb. gorilla of mainstream academic thought. He praised Lincoln's vision for America where every person, no matter their skin color or gender, should "have a chance" to keep the fruits of their labor and better their life, what Professor Boritt coined "the economics of the American dream."

Gabor Boritt had, for me, breathed more life and relevancy into Lincoln; he had galvanized my belief that Abraham Lincoln, an incredibly complicated man of flaws and flesh and blood, was also a man of noble ideas and virtues, whose life was still worthy of praise and celebration.

Again, I was smitten.

After graduating from law school, I eagerly returned to my hometown, the small community where I was born and raised. I was going to "hang out my shingle" as was often said in those days, and take up the practice of law. I also hung a copy of the Gettysburg Address on my office wall. I often looked at it, and thought about its words. As I argued cases before judges and juries, I soon realized that my success would be directly tied to the power of communication. And to good "word-smithing"—that is, choosing the right words for the right moment.

As a lawyer, I found myself leaning on Lincoln.

During the early years of my law practice, I continued on my Lincoln journey by reading Albert A. Woldman's *Lawyer Lincoln* (1936) and John P. Frank's *Lincoln as a Lawyer* (1961). Although my Lincoln self-education had focused primarily on his early life and presidency, it was enlightening to study Abraham Lincoln, the practicing lawyer. I could not truly relate to Lincoln the teenage rail-splitter or Lincoln the President of the United States, but I could empathize with Lincoln the lawyer. I began to gain valuable insight from studying how Lincoln, as a lawyer, made a living. And there were also valuable lessons for me in how Lincoln, as a lawyer, made his life.

The most important lesson I learned from Abraham Lincoln about the actual practice of law came from his own words, when he wrote a letter of advice to a young lawyer, J. M. Brockman, and told him, "Work and work, the secret of success in law is work." Lincoln applied a spit-in-the-hand work ethic to practicing law, and it took him to the top of his profession. Lincoln may have launched his legal career as a hayseed lawyer climbing from the bottom rung of his profession; but by the time he ran for president, he had argued more than 300 cases before the Illinois Supreme Court. His example taught me that hard work is the indispensable ingredient of any good or great lawyer, no matter how much natural talent they have.

During his years in Springfield, Lincoln's bethel was his law practice. Riding the circuit in the spring and fall with a group of judges and lawyers in the Eighth Judicial District, Lincoln would cover a grueling eight hundred miles of rough and rutted roads on his horse, Old Buck, or by horsedrawn buggy, crossing at least fourteen counties. It was long days of hard work that took him away from his home and family for months at a time. Lincoln rode the circuit because that is where the cases were, and how a living was made. He loved practicing law, and became extraordinarily good at it, eventually receiving the largest fee ever paid to an Illinois lawyer in his time. Lincoln would argue hundreds of cases before the Illinois Supreme Court, and even a case before the U.S. Supreme Court.

There were other lessons I learned from Lincoln the lawyer. Over a period of a quarter of a century, through his formula of "work and work," Abraham Lincoln strived to build his reputation both as an outstanding lawyer and a prominent citizen by putting food on his family's table, buying their first and only home, developing the skills of how to settle disputes between heated adversaries through negotiation and mediation, bonding with the colorful people and culture of his community, learning how to shape words into powerful and persuasive courtroom arguments, and launching his political career. It was the phenomenal growth of a man from a self-taught, socially-inept, financially-strapped, backwoods lawyer to one of the most-skilled and successful lawyers of his time.

I believe Lincoln's meteoric rise from obscurity to the top of the legal profession, stands as one of his greatest and most understated achievements. Lincoln's growth as a lawyer was pretty good stuff for a novice lawyer like myself to learn from, and be inspired by, a young lawyer, as folks liked to say in these parts, who was "green as a gourd," struggling to make a name and living in a rural judicial circuit.

As I closely observed and soaked-up the courtroom work of some of the best lawyers in eastern Tennessee, I soon recognized one common denominator among them. They all spoke like Lincoln. They had harnessed the power of words. Bespoken words. Their arguments and summations contained no unnecessary garnishments of oral legalese; no flourishes of ornamental doubletalk. Instead, they chose words and spoke with arresting precision, a style that was plain, clear and direct, words that their listeners, whether judges or juries, were raised on.

Our proud native son here in Scott County, Tennessee, Howard H. Baker, Jr., former Senator, Chief of Staff for President Ronald Reagan and Ambassador to Japan began his distinguished career as a young lawyer trying cases in the mountains of what is, like Lincoln's old circuit, our own Eighth Judicial District. Years later, when serving on the Congressional Watergate Committee investigating President Richard Nixon wordsmithed one of the most venerable and widely-borrowed phrases ever spoken in the American political lexicon, when he asked:

"What did the President know, and when did he know it?" Hardly a week goes by in the national news cycle, that someone doesn't paraphrase this iconic question to size up some political figure's proximity to scandal or trouble.

"Billy, don't shoot too high," Lincoln once advised his young law partner, William Herndon, about using fancy, elevated words when trying to communicate with everyday folks. "If you [do]," Lincoln cautioned, "your idea will go over the heads of the masses . . . and only hit those who need no hitting." Lincoln understood that too many words can choke off a good thought. When Senator Baker asked his famous question, he synthesized down the layers of factual complexities regarding President Nixon's culpability and involvement in the Watergate Scandal into one, single, cut-to-the-bone question, that all Americans could understand. When it mattered most to the country, the Tennessee Senator made sure he didn't "shoot too high." It was pure Lincoln-speak.

After a decade of busy law practice in the 1980's, I needed some fresh occupational air, and was blessed with an opportunity to go on the bench. I am still there. As a judge, I keep a copy of the Gettysburg Address on my office wall. And I still regularly look at those words.

Being a judge is a gratifying and humbling job, but it carries its own unique burdens. The heaviest weight a judge shoulders is not so much from the public process of deciding wrenching cases, but from the unavoidable collateral damage to his or her private life, especially a judge who lives in small-town America. The damage reveals itself in the form of strained relationships and personal stress that naturally result from the meting out of criminal sentences, custody rulings, divorce decrees and civil judgments that stretch out and impact the lives of people you live, work and worship among.

When Lincoln lamented to New York journalist Charles G. Halpine about the "public opinion baths" that he often took, I knew just what he meant. While picking up a few groceries, or in the stands watching my children's ballgames, I have been soaked by quite a few of those baths, myself. As my father, with a Lincoln-like quip and a smile, used to remind me when I would occasionally complain a bit: "No one put a gun to your head and made you take the job." Fair enough. It just comes with the territory.

As a judge, again, I found myself leaning on Lincoln.

In Lincoln the President, I saw the example of a man who was compassionate to those in the wake of his decisions, but iron-willed when necessary; a man who kept his ego in check, and never hesitated to share credit among his peers and subordinates; a man who could make tough decisions that adversely affected friends and family, and yet, absorb their angry reactions without forming grudges or responding in kind; a man who kept a firm grip on his emotions, even through times of unbearable pressures and insufferable grief; a man who learned to use humor to soften life's blows; a man who weighed the shortcomings of those around him without putting his thumb on the scales; a man, who in every decision and while at the height of his power, brought into the equation the overarching qualities of honesty, kindness and decency.

Now, as a judge who wields significant power over people's lives, I often reflect on how Abraham Lincoln, during the Civil War, never allowed himself to stray into that callousness of executive power that viewed men as merely pawns in a chess game, to be maneuvered and rearranged here and there, in pursuit of a political checkmate. The crown of fame bestowed upon great men and women should always be measured by the methods they used to gain it. Lincoln's rise to presidential power started with the most humble of origins, and his ascent to the most powerful position in America was based on honesty, masterful political skills and hard work, not by corruption, cruel wielding of power, or climbing up the backs of ordinary folks.

In Lincoln's view, the presidency had not conferred privilege or power—it had imposed awesome responsibility. Lincoln maintained a keen self-awareness of the power intrinsic to his official office, and the need to wield that power with deliberation, restraint and precision to the purpose at hand. Like no president before or since, Abraham Lincoln exercised, unchecked, the full scope of war powers; and yet, through it all, he was never corrupted by it. It was one of Lincoln's greatest attributes. . .he became flush with power, but was never intoxicated by it.

I am still leaning on Lincoln.

As the years have gone by, Lincoln's masterpiece, the words of the Gettysburg Address, have become some of the most important non-biblical passages in my life. Why? Because everything one needs to know about America—and what America should always strive to be—is found in those 272 words of Lincoln's immortal speech.

When I speak to people about the law, or about Abraham Lincoln, I encourage them to not only read the Gettysburg Address, but to read it, out loud. The nobility and elegance of the words, their majestic cadence, when read aloud, make them even more powerful, more moving, more meaningful. Lincoln, surely, meant for them to be read that way, just as Thomas Jefferson composed the Declaration of Independence to be read aloud.

But there is another way the Gettysburg Address should be read. It is a place. A special place. A place like no other, that all Americans should go at least once in their lives, to read the words of the Gettysburg Address. It is the Lincoln Memorial in Washington, D.C. No matter how many times you go there, the power of the experience always gets you.

When I entered the Lincoln Memorial for the first time, many years ago, it was at night. Night is special there. It was quiet, with only a handful of people around. I climbed the steps, and stood in awe as I looked up at the colossus statue of Lincoln. (As a Tennessean, it is a source of pride to know that Lincoln's figure rests on ten feet of Tennessee marble.) Then, I turned to the south wall, which like an ancient petroglyph, holds the deeply-engraved words of the Gettysburg Address. As I read it in the amber glow of light, the haunting power of its words overcame me. For the first time, I truly understood. The Gettysburg Address was not about the past, nor even the present. Lincoln was speaking to me, and to all Americans, about our future, the future of America. In that way, I believe, lies the eternal greatness of the words.

If anyone doubts the immeasurable significance of the Gettysburg Address, they need only reflect back to Ground Zero, New York City, on September 11, 2002, a single year after one of the darkest days in America's history. In the months following the September 11, 2001 attack, Ground Zero had become a somber, hallowed place for Lincoln's words, like Cemetery Hill had been at Gettysburg, in 1863. At a time when America needed hope, the words of the Gettysburg Address would be read. When I heard Lincoln's words spoken over the stark, gray site where so many Americans lost their lives in the twisted steel and ash, cold chills ran my backbone.

It reminded me that we still need Lincoln.

At a time when a frightened, uncertain America needed to be reassured of its future place in the world, and reminded of the eternal truths that would guide the way, the Gettysburg Address was there for us, again. Without fanfare, without introduction of the speaker or speech, without pomp and circumstances, the words of the Gettysburg Address were read at Ground Zero to all America—to all humankind. Why?. . .

Because the meaning of America is found there.

In a sense, when I heard the words of the Gettysburg Address read at Ground Zero in one of America's most desperate times of need, I realized that history had, again, become triangulated: from the 1776 origins of the Declaration of Independence, to the dark days of the Civil War that engulfed our Nation during the mid-nineteenth century, to the "War Against Terrorism" that now threatens America in the twenty-first century. It was a triangulation to reorient our minds to the moral, political and philosophical place where we came from, to take us back to our exact point of origin, so that we understand who and where we are now, and where we are going.

And, thus, it happened: somewhere along the way in my Lincoln journey, a pilgrimage paved with hundreds of books and dozens of places, I was inspired to weave together my own words to tell the remarkable story of the Gettysburg Address, what I believe to be the greatest speech, ever. In that tapestry, I wanted to include threads from many parts of Lincoln's incredible life. I wanted more people to know not only how Lincoln's life shaped his greatest words, but to also know how those words shaped the democracy that baptizes all of us as Americans.

From my boyhood days of making cut-and-paste Lincolns, to a teacher's classroom rendition of *The Perfect Tribute*; from reading the enchanting prose of Sandburg by flashlight under the bedcovers, to nervously reciting the Gettysburg Address aloud, at school; from college days of cautious reluctance to speak openly and admirably of Lincoln's distinguished place in history, to my intellectual rebirth upon discovering Gabor Boritt's *Lincoln and the Economics of the American Dream*; from a twilight epiphany at the Lincoln Memorial, to the tremble of emotions from hearing the words of the Gettysburg Address read from a hallowed place called Ground Zero—I had completed my journey in search of the greatest speech, ever.

Of course, there is more travel and learning ahead, more places to go, and more to understand about Abraham Lincoln. But in my quest, I have already learned from Lincoln's life the most important precept of all. And it is this. . .

Each journey in life starts with a dream. Soon, the dream matures and ripens into a passion, a passion to do something good and worthwhile with your life. The passion, in turn, inspires you to read, and listen, and learn all you can, so you can plan and prepare for the course you will take. Then, at last, you actually begin the journey—a single step, and another, and still another. You keep on moving no matter what comes, shoulder to the wheel, working your way through the hardships, setbacks and disappointments that surely come—until, one day, you arrive . . . at the destination of your dream.

My journey is done. What a marvelous trip it has been.

—James L. Cotton, Jr.
760 Grape Rough Rd.
Oneida, Tennessee

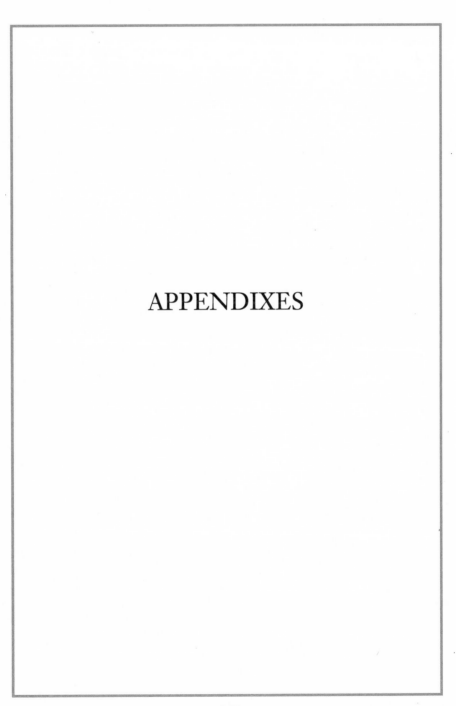

APPENDIXES

THE GETTYSBURG ADDRESS

Four score and seven years ago our fathers brought forth on this continent, a new nation, conceived in Liberty, and dedicated to the proposition that all men are created equal.

Now we are engaged in a great civil war, testing whether that nation, or any nation so conceived and so dedicated, can long endure. We are met on a great battle-field of that war. We have come to dedicate a portion of that field, as a final resting place for those who here gave their lives that that nation might live. It is altogether fitting and proper that we should do this.

But, in a larger sense, we can not dedicate—we can not consecrate—we can not hallow—this ground. The brave men, living and dead, who struggled here, have consecrated it, far above our poor power to add or detract. The world will little note, nor long remember what we say here, but it can never forget what they did here. It is for us the living, rather, to be dedicated here to the unfinished work which they who fought here have thus far so nobly advanced. It is rather for us to be here dedicated to the great task remaining before us—that from these honored dead we take increased devotion to that cause for which they gave the last full measure of devotion—that we here highly resolve that these dead shall not have died in vain—that this nation, under God, shall have a new birth of freedom—and that government of the people, by the people, for the people, shall not perish from the earth.

A. Lincoln

November 19, 1863

GREAT REPLICATIONS

A Brief History and Commentary on the Five Speech Manuscripts

M ANY PEOPLE TODAY ARE SURPRISED TO LEARN THAT THERE IS MORE than one Gettysburg Address. There are, in fact, five of them. All of them were written, beginning to end, by the hand of Abraham Lincoln. And each is a little different from the others. As the great Lincoln scholar James G. Randall wrote, "one can see the turning of the literary lathe," as Lincoln improved upon each of the five drafts, eventually perfecting the last one.

The earliest clues of the future greatness and historical repercussions of the Gettysburg Address would be first revealed by the number of times President Lincoln was asked to write out copies of his Gettysburg speech, after he delivered it. The President had no choice but to copy his speech in longhand; typewriters would not be invented until three years after his death.

Surely, those ongoing requests for handwritten copies of his Gettysburg Address began to calm Lincoln's early concerns that his November 19th speech had failed, and perhaps, even signaled to him that his speech was growing in stature.

When President Lincoln spoke the words of the Gettysburg Address on November 19th, 1863 at Cemetery Hill, he probably did not realize that he would be revising and improving the content of his speech over the next four months. In his own muscular yet beautiful handwriting style, the President would eventually write out at least a total of five clear and handsome copies of the Gettysburg Address. These manuscripts, because they are written entirely in Lincoln's own hand, are sometimes referred to as "autograph" or "holograph" copies.

Lincoln may have penned even more. Some historians speculate that he did. Certainly it is possible. But if so, they have never been found. It is known that Lincoln's host in Gettysburg, attorney David Wills, requested the copy of the speech that Lincoln held in his hand when he delivered it at the soldiers' cemetery, so he could archive it with other official documents from the famous occasion. There's no proof, however, that he ever got his wish. Wills never professed to receiving a draft of the Gettysburg Address. And those close to him, said he never got one. Why Wills never got the autograph copy of the speech he asked for, still remains a mystery. Among "true believers" (i.e., those that believe a sixth copy of the Gettysburg Address still exists, being the one written by Lincoln specifically for David Wills), this is sometimes referred to as the "missing" Gettysburg Address.

If anyone was worthy and deserving of a copy of the Gettysburg Address written in Lincoln's own hand, it was David Wills. Wills was the linchpin of the entire Gettysburg project, from interments to invitations, from cemetery to ceremony. There is an old adage: "Where there's a will, there's a way." When it came to finding a way for the tiny Town of Gettysburg to overcome its overwhelming crisis; when it came to conceiving and organizing the Soldier's National Cemetery at Gettysburg, and planning the magnificent ceremonies that consecrated it, there was certainly the "will" to make it a reality. David Wills.

Of course, Wills did not act alone as he designed and energized a recovery plan for the Town of Gettysburg. Much help and cooperation came his way. In fact, a rival attorney in town, David McConaughy, a dye-in-the-wool Republican and Lincoln supporter, had the earliest vision of establishing a soldiers' cemetery (even before the Battle of Gettysburg), and was the first to begin the process of purchasing seventeen acres north of the Evergreen Cemetery for use as a national cemetery. Eventually, the more comprehensive plan developed by David Wills would supercede, although McConaughy would dedicate the rest of his life to preserving the honor of Union soldiers who fought at Gettysburg. Even so, looking back into the rear-view mirror of history, one can credibly argue that but-for the unique talents and contributions of the young lawyer and public servant, David Wills, there might never have been a Gettysburg Address. Yet, somehow, he never got a handwritten copy for himself. History rudely shortchanged him, in that regard.

Of the five known, surviving handwritten copies of the Gettysburg Address, one (the "Nicolay Copy") was most surely written out by Abraham Lincoln before he delivered his speech on November 19, 1863. Another copy (the "Hay Copy") is the most fiercely debated one, with distinguished Lincoln scholars disagreeing on whether Lincoln penned it before he gave the speech (and then used it as his reading copy when he delivered the speech), or wrote it out afterwards, when he returned to Washington. All of the debate and controversy among authorities and buffs surrounds the provenance of these first two drafts. The other three were indisputably penned by the President after he spoke at Gettysburg. We will likely never know, with unimpeachable accuracy, the exact time and place Lincoln wrote the first two drafts of his famous speech, and whether there really is a "missing" copy out there somewhere, a sixth one, that was penned by Lincoln for David Wills.

Once requests started coming in for handwritten copies of his Gettysburg Address, Lincoln, ever the literary craftsman, became interested in improving—with small but numerous brushstrokes—the rhythm and texture of the speech. These changes were made by Abraham Lincoln to both improve his speech, and perhaps, to closer match the words he actually spoke at the soldiers' cemetery. However, Lincoln was probably more interested in perfecting the text of his Gettysburg Address, than strictly preserving a verbatim account of the words he spoke at the soldiers' cemetery.

The custom of revising and smoothing out a speech after it was given, so it would read better in print, was common in Lincoln's time. Even today, members of the Congress, after making speeches from the speaker's well, often conclude their oratory by expressly reserving the right to later "revise and extend" their remarks, so the words of their speeches can be reshaped into a more clear and coherent form when they appear in print for public consumption. Lincoln was doing the same with his Gettysburg Address.

The three handwritten copies of the Gettysburg Address indisputably made by Lincoln after giving his speech at Gettysburg, were written in Washington, D.C. over a course of about four months, while he was sick from a strain of smallpox. In those last three drafts of his speech, Lincoln would make several word and punctuation changes from what was written in the first two versions of his speech. And all three were donated by Lincoln to charitable causes. Most of the revisions in those last three autograph copies were minor word adjustments and grammatical tweaks to polish up the clarity and cadence of the speech.

However, a few of those changes in his last three drafts were small, but powerful. They would have a major impact on the meaning and message of the speech. For example, by removing a single word from the Third Draft (the "Everett Copy") of his speech, Lincoln would expand his message to reach beyond America and include the audience of the entire world. This revision had a major impact on the meaning of the speech and was done when Lincoln deleted (from how it had last appeared in his Second Draft) the word "this" from the phrase, "that [this] government of the people, by the people, for the people. . ." (words that spoke only to the United States government). By omission of that single word, Lincoln was left with a more universal phrase in the Third Draft of his speech: "that government of the people, by the people, for the people. . ." (words of boundless reference, that spoke to all humanity). And, of course, Lincoln would insert the iconic words "under God" into his Third Draft, words he had extemporaneously added to his speech from the rostrum at Gettysburg.

Admittedly, it is a bit presumptuous (and perhaps unscholarly) to identify Lincoln's five handwritten copies of the Gettysburg Address simply as the "First Draft," the "Second Draft," and so on, after all, the sequential place of some of those great writings are still, and will likely always be, the subject of scholarly debate. However, those labels seem to help those who are first encountering the five drafts to wrap their mind around their literary evolution.

Each of the five extant copies of the Gettysburg Address, all of them written entirely by Lincoln's hand, have their own unique story and historical journey. They cast a fascinating light on Lincoln's mental process of speech revision, and his techniques used for rhythm, cadence, sound and wordplay. They also reveal the human sensitivities of the man. These great replications reveal the work of a master craftsman as he composes, and seeks to perfect, what Carl Sandburg would later call "the great American poem."

The Implausible Conception: The First Draft

At the conception of this famous family of five manuscripts, lies the First Draft of Lincoln's Gettysburg Address. It is commonly known as the "Nicolay Copy," because of its close connection to John G. Nicolay, the President's top private secretary. Nicolay may have ended up owning this manuscript, as a private gift from the President.

The historical evidence is very strong, that President Lincoln wrote about half of the Nicolay Copy with a pen before pulling out of Washington on his way to Gettysburg, and then finished the manuscript in pencil at the Wills home in Gettysburg the evening of November 18th, 1863. It is the earliest-written version of the five surviving copies of the Gettysburg Address.

The Nicolay Copy consists of two pages. The first page (in ink) was written by Lincoln on letter-sized stationery, engraved at the top with the letterhead of the "Executive Mansion." The second page of the Nicolay Copy (in pencil) was written on a lined, longer "foolscap" sheet of paper.

"Foolscap" paper was the term commonly used in Lincoln's time to describe what would be roughly comparable in size to today's larger, legal-sized paper. It was also called "diplomatic" size paper. Lincoln and lawyers of his era routinely took these extra-large sheets of foolscap paper and creased them in the middle, and then, they would cut or rip them along the crease to create two separate "half-sheets" of paper. The second page of the Nicolay Copy is written on a "half-sheet" of foolscap paper, that has a coarse edge from being separated from the other half. Also, the two pages of the Nicolay Copy shows faint creases of being folded into thirds. These folds on the two sheets match, suggesting they were, at some point, folded up together.

The predominant view (that Lincoln wrote out the first part of the Nicolay Copy in Washington, D.C., and finished it at the Wills house in Gettysburg) is powerfully corroborated by James Speed, Lincoln's second-appointed Attorney General. Several months after the Gettysburg ceremonies were over, President Lincoln would tell Speed that just before he left Washington for Gettysburg, he had written "about half of the speech." Speed quoted President Lincoln as joking that "he [Lincoln] took what he had written with him to Gettysburg, and then was put in the upper room of a house," where the President said he asked "to be alone" for a while. Lincoln also told Speed that he "then prepared the speech," but that the commencement of the Gettysburg ceremonies arrived so quickly after completing his address, that Lincoln "had not time to memorize it."

John Nicolay, a man in the presence of President Lincoln as much as anyone, confirmed Attorney General Speed's version. While his eyes were absorbed in the mystic qualities of the First Draft of Lincoln's speech, and seeming to feel a personal sense of awe in the moment, Nicolay would write twenty years after Lincoln's death:

"It is true that Mr. Lincoln wrote the Gettysburg address (but in part only) in his [David Wills'] house. The original ms. [manuscript] is now lying before my eyes. Half of it is written with ink on a half sheet of letter paper; this the President wrote in Washington and brought in his pocket. The other half in pencil, on a half sheet of foolscap (diplomatic size); this he wrote in Mr. Will's house, and I was with him at the time."

John G. Nicolay was a man devoted to restrained emotion and accuracy when he transcribed accounts occurring within the Executive Office, and he also remembered being present with President Lincoln at the Wills house on the morning of November 19th. Nicolay specifically recalled seeing President Lincoln in his second floor room after the breakfast hour, working on his speech, writing it with a "lead pencil." In Nicolay's words, he "remained with the President while he finished writing the Gettysburg Address."

The President's own recollected version of the process of composing his speech (that is, writing the first part of it in Washington, and the last part in Gettysburg), as told by Lincoln to Attorney General Speed only about a year after the Gettysburg event, rings with trustworthiness. Time has disclosed nothing, whether in Speed's own words, or the words of his contemporaries, to suggest that he was psychologically captured by a Lincoln fantasy or was trying to reconstruct history. Speed had no motive to prove that he had some intimate connection to the Gettysburg Address. In fact, Speed was never involved in the Gettysburg trip or its planning, because he did not become U.S. Attorney General until a year after the Gettysburg cemetery dedication. When quoting Lincoln on this historical point, James Speed would appear to be rock-solid credible.

Although we will never know with absoluteness, strong odds are, based on reliable eyewitness accounts and the predictability of Lincoln's writing habits, that Lincoln wrote about half of the First Draft of his Gettysburg Address in Washington, and the other half in Gettysburg at the Wills house.

* * *

Another intriguing question yanks on the Nicolay Copy. Was it the very same two sheets of paper that Lincoln clasped in his hand, his "reading copy." when he spoke the words of the Gettysburg Address from the podium at the soldier's cemetery? Again, historians are splintered on this issue. And delving into the debate can become a bit tedious.

There are a series of arguments that are traditionally offered in support of the theory that the Nicolay Copy, Lincoln's First Draft of his speech , was, in fact, his reading copy. The crux of those arguments are as follows: First, one journalist with the *New York Tribune* reportedly saw the "Executive Mansion" heading on the paper Lincoln held while delivering his speech at the soldiers' cemetery. (The Nicolay Copy is the only version of the five autograph copies of the Gettysburg Address that is written on Executive Mansion letterhead.) Secondly, it was John Nicolay's belief, a man with historical clout when he wrote and spoke about Lincoln, that Lincoln used his First Draft as a reading copy. Nicolay, along with security guard Sergeant Rebert, saw Lincoln in the Wills home that morning of November 19th, working on his speech with a pencil (which probably led Nicolay to believe the First Draft was the reading copy, because it was finished with a pencil). Thirdly, according to archival scholars, the Nicolay Copy shows faint but certain signs of being folded; many spectators at the soldiers' cemetery said that Lincoln, before giving the speech, removed a folded text from his vest pocket. Moreover, these folds (in thirds) in the two pages of the Nicolay Copy seem to match, suggesting they were folded together. (To bring contextual weight to these arguments supporting the Nicolay Copy as the reading version, it must be noted that the Second Draft of Lincoln's speech, the "Hay Copy," which other historians contend was the actual reading copy, is not written on "Executive Mansion" stationery, is not written in pencil and shows no visible signs of folding.)

The problem with these historical postulates—according to dissenting Lincoln authorities who contend that the Nicolay Copy was not the reading copy—is that they seem to place far too little weight or importance on what they believe is the most compelling fact of all: there are just too many significant differences between the words of the Nicolay Copy, and the words Lincoln spoke publicly at the soldiers' cemetery, for the Nicolay Copy to be the reading copy.

Lincoln surely extemporized a bit when he delivered his speech at Gettysburg. But there is an entire phrase that Lincoln spoke at Gettysburg which is omitted from the Nicolay Copy (i.e., ". . . here to the unfinished work which they have, thus far, so nobly carried on . . . "). To accept the Nicolay Copy as being the reading copy held in Lincoln's hand at Cemetery Hill, one must also accept the remarkable assumption, historians argue, that Lincoln would dare to dramatically deviate no less than three times from his prepared text and ad-lib before a huge crowd on one of the most important speeches of his life—and that Lincoln, who often struggled with impromptu public speeches—could, in a pressure-packed, two minute speech, improvise with such precision and perfect compactness of thought.

Lincoln was exhaustive and painstakingly thorough in his preparation of important speeches. The President was well aware that he was a hit-or-miss extemporaneous speaker. Sometimes he could deliver splendid off-the-cuff remarks, as when he addressed Union soldiers in the field. And at other times, he flat-out missed, as he did at the Hanover railway station in route to Gettysburg. Lincoln historians who argue against the Nicolay Copy as the reading copy, underscore that it is extremely unlikely that the words spoken by President Lincoln at the soldiers' cemetery, as most accurately reported by Joseph Gilbert with the *Associated Press* and Massachusetts journalist Charles Hale with the *Boston Advertiser*, which varied strikingly from the words written in the Nicolay Copy, were improvised on the podium that day. (However, scholars point out that the Hay Copy, the other manuscript that some believe is the reading copy, also deviates from what Lincoln likely spoke that day from the podium.)

Those who discount the Nicolay Copy as the reading copy emphasize it has a troubling composition gap between its first page (written in ink) and its second page (written in pencil). Put another way, there is a glaring disconnect of grammar and content between the transition sentences of the Nicolay Copy's two pages, making it almost inconceivable, they would contend, that Lincoln could have extemporized the connections as smoothly and perfectly as he delivered the words of his speech from the rostrum at Gettysburg. When one steps back and surveys the Nicolay Copy as a whole, it does create a strong first impression as being a composition draft, not a final draft from which a live speech would preferably be made.

Further, those who place heavy weight on the one *New York Tribune* reporter's observations (that he saw "Executive Mansion" stationery in Lincoln's hand) to underpin their belief that the Nicolay Copy is the reading copy, must deal with the knotty problem that when boiled down, that reporter's version is at best, a single, even shaky, eyewitness account. After all, a 6 ft. 4 inch tall Lincoln was standing on a three-foot high platform, built on a hill, holding the paper in his moving hand. And most likely, the edge of the paper with the words "Executive Mansion" printed at the top, was curved toward Lincoln's face, as a result of being inwardly folded, making it very difficult, especially in the sun's glare, to read by a person standing below or even on the platform. And with hundreds of people surrounding the speaker's platform, all of their eyes laser-locked on Lincoln, why would only one man see the "Executive Mansion" stationery that so indelibly identifies the Nicolay Copy?

But what about John Nicolay's belief that the Nicolay Copy was Lincoln's reading copy? Nicolay may have simply got this one wrong.

Lincoln's top aide may have mistakenly presumed that when he saw the President writing with a pencil on the morning of November 19th, that the President was working exclusively on the First Draft of his Gettysburg Address (which was, in fact, finished with a pencil). However, we know from the observations of the security guard who was in Lincoln's room that morning, that the President was likely sorting through other pencil-written pages of work, aside from his speech.

When Nicolay saw Lincoln writing in his room at the Wills house with a pencil, and later discovered that the last half of Lincoln's First Draft of his speech was also written in pencil , he then, understandably, may have assumed that Lincoln's pencil-written version of the Gettysburg Address was the only one the President had worked on that morning, and thus, must have been the same one used by Lincoln later in the day as his reading copy. However, Nicolay was not with the President every minute of the entire morning. Far from it. Young Liberty Hollinger would see Lincoln through the window of the Wills house, shortly before the procession to the cemetery assembled, where the President appeared to be alone and practicing his speech. Lincoln certainly had a whirlwind schedule that morning, but he still had enough time to dash out, entirely in ink, a cleaner, more refined copy of his short speech to read from at the soldiers' cemetery , that is, arguably, his Second Draft (the Hay Copy).

And what about the crowd's observation at the soldiers' cemetery, that Lincoln's reading copy was removed from his pocket, folded? After all, the Nicolay Copy clearly shows forensic signs of being folded. (A possible answer to this mulish historical question is deferred until Lincoln's Second Draft, the "Hay Copy," is hereinafter examined.)

The orthodox view among historians, today, seems to be leaning in favor of the First Draft (Nicolay Copy) as the reading copy. However, even if Lincoln did not use his First Draft as the reading version at the soldier's cemetery, it cannot be automatically assumed that he used the Second Draft (Hay Copy) for that purpose. Other possibilities exist to fertilize the historical debate. Lincoln experts will be divided on this issue for many years to come.

* * *

What journey would the First Draft of the Gettysburg Address—the Nicolay Copy, take after Lincoln's death?

Lincoln's presidential aides, John G. Nicolay and John M. Hay, who lived in a corner room on the second floor of the White House, had performed their duties for the President extraordinarily well. The serious, health-fragile Nicolay was hired first by Lincoln. In turn, Nicolay recommended Lincoln employ the young, exuberant and mildly-cocky Hay. They were a great team for the President, and the two presidential aides would be lifelong friends. Loyalty, sharp minds and sheer occupational stamina were hallmarks of their service to President Lincoln. There were in twenty-four hour contact and proximity of the President. It was not unusual for Nicolay and Hay to put in twelve-to-fifteen hours a day, for six or seven days each week. It was organized chaos, as they scheduled the President's appointments, handled Lincoln's massive amounts of correspondence, answered most of his letters, lobbied, served as ombudsmen and emissaries for Lincoln's important political missions, and vigilantly but tactfully guarded access to the President of the United States. In the early years, these two acolytes of the President ran the whole machinery of the Executive Office.

Even more importantly, Nicolay and Hay were like family to Lincoln. They were enthralled by Lincoln's stories, and shared his affection for humor, Shakespeare and poetry. They enjoyed the world of politics as he did, deeply respected the President's wisdom and integrity, and provided him the companionship and conversation of two devoted sons. Thus, Nicolay and Hay, who were closer to Abraham Lincoln on a daily basis, than anyone, were the natural choice of the president's oldest son, Robert Todd Lincoln (following Lincoln's death in April 1865), to be named as custodians to collect and organize the assassinated President's papers. After Nicolay and Hay completed their daunting archival task, this collection of what would become known as the "Lincoln Papers" were then vaulted away for almost a decade, under the aegis of a U.S. Supreme Court justice.

Later, in 1874, with Robert Lincoln's blessing, this same assemblage of *Lincoln Papers*, no doubt containing the First Draft of the Gettysburg Address (the Nicolay Copy), and probably the Second Draft (the Hay Copy), were entrusted to the man who had served dutifully as Lincoln's senior secretary and aide, John G. Nicolay, who was still living in Washington. Although these papers were in the primary fiduciary care of the serious and introspective Nicolay, he unselfishly allowed Hay to have unfettered access to them, as Nicolay and Hay begun writing about the sixteenth president.

The Nicolay-Hay biography of Lincoln first appeared as serials in *The Century Illustrated Monthly Magazine* from 1886 until 1890, and was later published in ten-volume book form. It was the first official biography of Abraham Lincoln. And it was a massive, monumental task. It would take Nicolay and Hay nearly a quarter century to complete it. There is no question that the First Draft of Lincoln's Gettysburg Address was stacked among the collection of Lincoln papers handled by Nicolay and Hay. At one point during their years of literary collaboration after Lincoln's death (1885), Nicolay wrote a letter to Richard Watson Gilder, editor of the widely-circulated and popular *Century* magazine, in which he described his examination of the First Draft of the great speech, and that it was spread out, as he exulted, "now . . . before my eyes."

Although records do not explicitly tell us, there is the possibility that Lincoln gave the First Draft of his speech to Nicolay. Certainly, Lincoln was deeply appreciative of his loyal and hard-working first secretary, and would have liked Nicolay to have a souvenir from the Gettysburg event. If so, after Lincoln's death, when Nicolay examined and held in his hand the irreplaceable First Draft of the Gettysburg Address, he may have been more than a custodian of the manuscript, he may have been its proud owner. But this, too, is uncertain. After all, why would John Nicolay fail to ever mention, to anyone, his receipt of such a momentous gift from the President of the United States?

After Nicolay's death in 1901, the Nicolay Copy seemed to vanish into thin air. It was, in all probability, unknowingly turned over with the other Lincoln Papers to the possession of John Hay, who was then Secretary of State, by John Nicolay's daughter, Helen Nicolay. Helen Nicolay, who had previously served as her father's secretary, apparently did not realize that she had included her father's manuscript nonpareil in the packaged assortment of *Lincoln Papers* delivered to the stewardship of John Hay in December 1901. This transfer of *Lincoln Papers* to

John Hay, allowed Hay to garner into his personal control, perhaps, under questionable authority, the First Draft of the Gettysburg Address, most likely the Second Draft of the great speech, Lincoln's private 1864 letter when he predicted his own defeat in the upcoming presidential election, and also Lincoln's immortal Second Inaugural Address. It was a collection for the ages. Even after Hay's death in 1905, the Nicolay Copy, a public domain manuscript deriving from the Lincoln Papers, was secreted in the Hay family and treated as a part of their private collection for more than a decade.

For those many years that the First Draft of the Gettysburg Address found safe coverture in the Hay family, Robert Todd Lincoln and Helen Nicolay frantically combed through boxes of documents and chased dead-end leads in a persistent but futile search to find it. For most of those years, they knew only of the existence of the First Draft (what they called the "original manuscript"), but towards the end of their quest, and to their surprise, they learned that a Second Draft of the great speech also existed. Adding to the urgency of their search, autograph copies of the Gettysburg Address, at a time which was the peak of pre-World War I mania for all things Lincoln, were rapidly escalating in both monetary and historical value. They apparently had no idea that the Hay family, who remained mum throughout the desperate search, still possessed the First Draft (and unbeknownst to them, the Second Draft) they so earnestly sought.

Some would assert that the failure of John Hay and his family to disclose the whereabouts of these irreplaceable presidential manuscripts for so many years, while the Lincoln family searched in earnest, was, when held under a most favorable light, bewildering, and at worst, ethically disturbing.

And it raises even a more disturbing question. Did John Hay allow himself, in a shocking breach of trust, to purloin the Second Draft from the public collection of Lincoln Papers? Otherwise, why would John Hay keep the existence of a second autograph copy of the great speech a secret from his closest friend and biographical collaborator, John Nicolay? Nicolay died, it seems, never knowing the Second Draft ever existed. And was Hay's family, following his death, culpable as accessories-after-the-fact? These are uncomfortable, but fair historical questions.

Finally, in 1916, the Hay family went public, in an orchestrated "discovery" of the Nicolay Copy, perhaps feeling the weight of Robert Todd Lincoln's intercession and fearing they were on the cusp of being portrayed in an embarrassing scandal. To their lasting credit, on April 11, 1916 the Hay family, in generous collaboration with Helen Nicolay (who would later become a distinguished author in her own right), jointly donated both the First Draft (Nicolay Copy) and the Second Draft (Hay Copy) to the American public, by releasing them to the permanent guardianship of the Library of Congress, where they belonged in the first place. They also included in this historic gift Lincoln's 1864 secret memorandum forecasting his own defeat in the upcoming presidential election, and his incomparable Second Inaugural Address. This donation of four priceless Lincoln manuscripts was an honorable act by the Nicolay and Hay families, that guaranteed their preservation, hopefully forever. They remain at the Library of Congress, today, in strict archival isolation.

The Most Mysterious of all: The Second Draft

The Second Draft of the Gettysburg Address (commonly known as the "Hay Copy") could, according to some historians, be the mysterious "reading copy." Lincoln wrote out the Hay Copy entirely in ink on the same type of lined stationery that he used for the second page of the Nicolay Copy. If so, it is President Lincoln's first re-write of the Gettysburg Address.

However, this too, like the contradictions that emerge at every step of Lincoln's biographical journey, is a matter of continuing debate and controversy. The Hay Copy has been called "the most inexplicable" of all of the five known facsimiles of the Gettysburg Address. It is a perfect moniker. That's because the Hay Copy has kept historians in clover, arguing over when and where it was drafted, and whether or not Lincoln used it as his delivery text at Cemetery Hill.

Like the Nicolay Copy, the Hay Copy is also wrapped in a chrysalis of questions. Was the Hay Copy the one President Lincoln held in his hand at Cemetery Hill, when he gave the speech? Or was it the first of several revised copies Lincoln would pen, after he returned to

Washington? Or did the President write the Hay Copy out before he went to Washington, only to forget to take it with him to Gettysburg, and thus, was forced to mentally reconstruct his speech in what would become the rough draft known as the Nicolay Copy?

Scholarly consensus, which has teetered back and forth through the years, currently seems to be that the Hay Copy was not Lincoln's delivery text, but most likely, was written out by Lincoln after he returned to Washington from Gettysburg. This school of thought believes that the Hay Copy was the first of several revisions Lincoln would make as he experimented with and improved upon the words of the speech he gave at the soldiers' cemetery. Other Lincoln authorities surmise that the Hay Copy is a version of the speech that Lincoln hurriedly wrote out as a souvenir for John Hay, again, after the President returned to Washington. Other historians contend that the Hay Copy was written by Lincoln while at David Wills' home in Gettysburg and used as his reading copy when he delivered the speech. Some say the Hay Copy may even be the one Lincoln made and meant for David Wills, that mysteriously never reached the Gettysburg attorney. It is also conjectured that Lincoln's reading copy is none of the five known to us, and may have been lost, forever. All of these are possibilities.

In his brilliant book, *Lincoln's Sword: The Presidency and the Power of Words*, Douglas L. Wilson makes a powerful case that the Hay Copy was not Lincoln's reading copy. Wilson, who like most Lincoln scholars has wrestled with the "inexplicable" nature of the Hay Copy, proposes that the Hay Copy was written by Lincoln after he returned from Gettysburg to Washington, in the predictable process of Lincoln reappraising, revising and rewriting his Gettysburg speech for public consumption. Wilson points to an 1885 well known letter written by John Nicolay, which in recent years has been cast in a fresh light by historians, led by insightful Lincoln scholar Martin P. Johnson. In that letter, Nicolay is focusing his attention on Lincoln's First Draft (the Nicolay Copy). However, Nicolay digresses a bit and calls sidebar attention to a separate manuscript which he intriguingly refers to as a "revision," a manuscript, which Nicolay goes on to say, was penned by Lincoln after the President "returned [from Gettysburg] to Washington." It raises a fascinating question: could that "revision" manuscript mentioned by

Nicolay have been the Hay Copy? Wilson concurs with Johnson that, most likely, it is.

Wilson also heavily emphasizes the absence of creases in the Hay Copy, to evict it from consideration as Lincoln's reading copy, and eloquently opines that Lincoln's omission of the words "under God" from the Hay Copy was Lincoln's revisionist experimentation with the absence of those powerful words. In Douglas Wilson's ultimate view, the Hay Copy makes more sense when analyzing its provenance and chronology, if it is seen simply as a medial step in Lincoln's continuing process of improving his Gettysburg Address after he returned from Gettysburg. Certainly, Lincoln was a compulsive revisionist of his prepared speeches.

And it is true. The Hay Copy shows no traces of ever being creased or folded like the Nicolay Copy, which would, at first impression, seem to forensically eliminate the Hay Copy as the one Lincoln tucked away in his coat pocket during his ride to the soldiers' cemetery and used as his reading copy when he delivered the speech. After all, many people indisputably saw Lincoln unfold his speech before he delivered it. But as journeyman public speakers know, pages of a speech can be softly bent and placed in the vest or side pocket of a suit coat, without putting a hard crease in the paper. The technique of a "soft" fold, without making creases in the paper, is important because a hard crease, especially a document apparently folded into thirds like the Nicolay Copy, can obscure the words that appear in the fold lines and tends to curl up, which prevents the paper from laying flat on the speaker's lectern, thus making it difficult to read from.

Historians who argue that the Hay Copy (and not the Nicolay Copy) is the reading copy, call attention to the fact that the Hay Copy is written on the same type of lined, foolscap paper Lincoln obtained at the Wills house and used for the second page of his First Draft (the Nicolay Copy); a sturdy and forcible argument, it would seem, that the Hay Copy was written at the Wills house in Gettysburg where Lincoln got the paper and not when the President later returned to Washington. (On the other hand, Lincoln could have easily brought a few sheets of that paper he received at the Wills house, back to Washington with him, later writing out the Hay Copy.)

Furthermore, as Gabor Boritt has persuasively demonstrated in his extraordinary work, *The Gettysburg Gospel: The Lincoln Speech That Nobody Knows*, the Hay Copy seems closer in content (than the Nicolay Copy) to the words Lincoln may have actually spoken at the soldiers' cemetery in Gettysburg. There are key words and phrases in the Hay Copy that are included in transcribed versions of Lincoln's live speech—taken down in real time by reporters at the scene , but which are conspicuously absent from the Nicolay Copy.

And when a close, scrutinizing look at Lincoln's penmanship is taken, the Hay Copy leaves the palpable (but subjective) impression that it was being quickly reproduced from another text. Experienced public speakers who are in the throes of revising and improving their speech, and the process of imprinting it into their memory, often hurriedly write out one last "clean" of "fair" copy, shortly before their speaking engagement. It becomes their delivery copy. The Hay Copy seems to fit this profile. Even to the amateur eye, content seems more settled, and neatness seems to slightly but steadily wane in the Hay Copy as you read through it, suggesting that Lincoln may have quickly wrote it out, as if approaching a looming deadline. Mistakes made and fixed by Lincoln in the Hay Copy seem to be errors commonly produced by rushing, not the process of composition. Words omitted in the seemingly hurried process are stuck back in with a caret. And, arguably, it would seem a composition draft would be more likely to be written in pencil so changes could be easily made (like the second page of the Nicolay Copy), whereas a final reading copy, where content is settled, would be more likely to be written in ink (Hay Copy). Again, admittedly, these are distinctive, but subjective impressions.

The morning of his speech, Lincoln was extremely busy before leaving for the soldiers' cemetery, and no doubt, would have been rushed as he prepared a final, clean copy from which to deliver his speech. Furthermore, if Lincoln had waited until he returned to Washington to write out the Hay Copy, as some historians argue he did, then he had no reason to be rushed (and a bit sloppy) in preparing it. The President could have cherry-picked some quiet, unhurried moments in his Executive Office or the Soldier's Home to write out a clean, neat, error-free version of his address. In the three copies of Lincoln's Gettysburg

Address that he unquestionably prepared after he gave the speech and returned to Washington, none of them show signs of a rush job, like the Hay Copy. He later commented that the Gettysburg ceremonies seemed to arrive so quickly, he didn't have adequate time to memorize the speech.

Proponents of the Hay Copy as the reading copy also hammer home what may be their most compelling argument of all: if the President really had used the Nicolay Copy (his First Draft) as his reading copy, and thus, wrote out the Hay Copy (his Second Draft) after he delivered the speech, there is no way in the world Lincoln would have omitted from the Hay Copy the words "under God," inspired and unforgettable words, that he had extemporaneously spoken from the platform at Cemetery Hill.

These two words, "under God," were heard not only by three reporters who telegraphed out the text of Lincoln's speech, but also by thousands of people at the soldiers' cemetery, and would be printed in newspapers all over the country. If for no other reasons, it can be powerfully argued, that Lincoln's growing spiritual sentiments and his political adroitness would not have allowed him to omit those words invoking the Divinity from versions of the speech he would write out after returning back from Gettysburg. America was, at the time, a homogeneously Christian nation. Evangelicals, many of them united in religion through the abolitionist movement, were still a vibrant political and social force in America. And Protestantism was thriving. Both religious sects paid close attention to the words of their President. Lincoln thought these two words so essential to the perfecting of his speech, that he included them in the next three drafts he would write, including his fifth and final, most-perfect draft of the Gettysburg Address. So, if the Hay Copy was written after Lincoln gave the speech and returned to Washington, why in the world would he leave out the words "under God" from that one post-speech draft, but keep them in the last three? Arguably, some historians insist . . . he wouldn't.

Through the looking glass of time, it would seem that the words "under God" in Lincoln's Gettysburg speech, were both spiritually and politically indispensable. They were unscripted, spontaneous words spoken by the President, from the heart. Although possible, it is difficult to imagine that Lincoln, for any reason, even with his natural tendency to experiment and play with words, would leave out these two sacred words from any copy of the Gettysburg Address that he wrote out, after giving the speech. This gives weight to the argument that the Hay Copy was written out by Lincoln in Gettysburg, and thus, used as his reading copy.

There is another, more subjective argument that further shores up the belief, among others, that the Hay Copy is also the reading copy. Most veteran public speakers, when giving a speech in an outdoor venue, prefer their handwritten speaking notes to be in ink, rather than pencil. Words in ink are typically sharper, and easier for the eyes to clutch, upon quick glances. Lead pencil markings of the time could be a dull charcoal in tone, and easier lost in the glare of the sun. Lincoln, especially since he needed the assistance of reading glasses, would have surely preferred his reading copy written in the bolder strokes of ink. Half of the Nicolay Copy, including the powerful crescendo finish of the speech, is in pencil. *The Hay Copy is written entirely in ink.*

Then, there is still another possibility, albeit remote. Maybe there is a reason both the Nicolay Copy and Hay Copy, as square pegs, don't fit nicely into the round hole of a reading copy: because neither of them were the reading copy. Perhaps Lincoln, for his reading copy, used the first page of the Nicolay Copy (thus explaining the one reporter's story that he saw "Executive Mansion" stationery) and a second page we have never seen, lost forever to posterity. Or, perhaps, Lincoln wrote out another private copy of his Gettysburg Address to read from on the speaker's platform, which was somehow lost, discarded or secretly tucked away, and never seen again. If so, there you have it. The mysterious, missing sixth copy of the Gettysburg Address. Our own American version of the Dead Sea Scrolls, waiting on a serendipitous discovery in the cave of someone's garage.

Before his death, John Hay, himself, was asked whether the Second Draft, the very one he may have owned, was the manuscript Lincoln held in his hand when he spoke at Gettysburg. Hay's candid and concise reply? "Don't know." If Hay did not know, in all likelihood, neither will posterity.

So . . . is the Nicolay Copy or the Hay Copy the reading copy? This is part of the Lincoln story where we find ourselves, out of necessity, substituting speculation for the scarcity of hard facts. Objectively, as an neophyte historian—and intuitively, as a frequent public speaker—I believe that the Hay Copy was probably Lincoln's reading copy. If it wasn't, the reading copy is likely lost forever. The Nicolay Copy's striking content differences from the words Lincoln likely spoke at the cemetery and its overall rough-draft condition, create reasonable doubt for the author as it being the reading copy. But Lincoln savants still respectfully part company on this question. The better weight of current scholarly opinion, it appears, would reject the Hay Copy as the one Lincoln held in his hand at the cemetery. Perhaps the better odds are that the reading copy is unknown to us, and lost forever. No doubt, this intriguing historical debate will continue for many years.

As Joseph Joubert, the French philosopher best put it: "It is better to debate a question without settling it, than to settle a question without debating it."

* * *

Not until 1906, its existence first revealed in a lecture by an eminent Lincoln manuscript collector, William H. Lambert, would the world learn of the Hay Copy. And not until February 1909, nearly a half century after Lincoln may have held this copy in his hand at the soldiers' cemetery at Gettysburg, and on the centennial of his birth, would the Hay Copy be first mass printed for the general public, in *Putnam's Magazine*.

Although it is not certain, the Hay Copy was likely inadvertently included in the original collection of *Lincoln Papers* Helen Nicolay turned over to John Hay in 1901, along with the Nicolay Copy. Whether it was written before or after Lincoln delivered the Gettysburg Address, it is remotely possible that Lincoln gave this Second Draft of his speech to John Hay, privately, as a personal memento of the Gettysburg event. This was the Hay family's version of events. It is easy to envision that Lincoln would have thought that the marked-up, hurriedly-written pages of this Second Draft of his speech, a copy that did not even include the words "under God" that everyone heard him say at the soldiers' cemetery, would have been of little historical or monetary value. And it would have been a nice token of the occasion—similar to modern presidents handing out to their colleagues the signature pens used to sign new bills into law—to give to the dedicated and loyal Hay. We can conjecture that Lincoln secretly gave the Second Draft to Hay, to balance out his secret gift of the First Draft to Nicolay. And if so, was this the draft of the speech intended for David Wills, who had requested a copy?

If Lincoln extended such a gratuity to Hay, the historical record does not vouch for it. Surprisingly, and even suspiciously, Hay himself never mentioned owning this Second Draft of the Gettysburg Address, although he extensively and frequently spoke and wrote about Lincoln, his relationship to Lincoln, and Lincoln manuscripts. In fact, during the last century, there has been a dark cloud of mystery hanging over John Hay's acquisition of the First and Second Drafts of the Gettysburg Address, and his family's sequestration of those precious manuscripts long after his death.

In the same way the Nicolay family asserted a personal claim to the First Draft (as a gift from Lincoln to John Nicolay), the Hay family, likewise, seemed to drive claim stakes into the Second Draft. But both claims, it seems, were on thin ice. In legal-speak, the assertions by family members that these two irreplaceable speech manuscripts were personal gifts from Lincoln to Nicolay and Hay are supported only by historical speculation (as to whether Lincoln would have given the manuscripts away to them as gifts) and the inconsistent hearsay statements offered by Nicolay's and Hay's heirs—all of them arguably motivated by self-interest and having something to gain by "owning" the priceless manuscripts.

If Lincoln truly made a gift of the first two drafts of his Gettysburg Address to Nicolay and Hay, which he may have done, thereby converting his private secretaries from stewards of the manuscripts to lawful owners, there is no hard, documented proof of it. Notably, even Nicolay's and Hay's own written words, and there are thousands and thousands of them, do not mention or corroborate such gifts. Whatever the circumstances, like the First Draft, Lincoln's Second Draft of the Gettysburg Address was given stealthy sanctuary by the Hay family for many years, until 1916, when it was presented by them to the Library of Congress.

In J.R.R. Tolkien's famous *Lord Of The Rings* series, the longer Frodo possessed the precious ring in his trusted stewardship, the more it clouded his thinking. On his mission to properly dispose of the ring, Frodo began to convince himself that the ring was his, and his alone, although he had no rightful claim to it. Frodo had developed an addictive-like, psychological bond with the ring. Although drawing a comparison with a fictional fantasy novel is a bit unorthodox if not precarious, especially for historical analysis , one cannot help but wonder, when contemplating the analogy, whether Hay's peculiar and prolonged possession of the increasingly valuable Lincoln speech manuscripts, over the passage of time, began to cloud his thinking. After all, the Lincoln mythology was reaching the proportion of a Tolkien tale. Is it possible that Hay, somehow convinced himself that the precious assortment of Lincoln manuscripts in his possession and control had become his, and his alone. Is it possible that Hay, in his lifelong mission to write and speak about his revered boss, had psychologically bonded with the Lincoln manuscripts? After all, no one was closer to Abraham Lincoln in the White House than John Hay, who was like a son to the President. We will never know. No matter, since the Hay family ultimately left these priceless manuscripts with the American people, right where they belong.

Great efforts have been taken to preserve and protect both the Nicolay Copy and Hay Copy. Several decades ago, the internationally-recognized archivist, Dr. Nathan Stolow, designed and built special environmental containers for these two treasured manuscripts. Built of heavy gauge stainless steel, fastened together with neoprene gaskets and bolts, covered with quarter inch plexiglas allowing viewing from both sides, and filled with low-temperature argon gas to purge the containers of oxygen, these state-of-the-art, hermetically sealed containers were constructed to shield the Nicolay Copy and Hay Copy from ultraviolet light and eliminate moisture. This would, hopefully, extend the life of these two manuscripts for hundreds of years. Even a special non-adhesive, gauze-like product, called Tetex™, was developed to safely suspend the documents in place inside their containers. During recent years, even further technological advancements have contributed to the long-term preservation of these two Lincoln speeches.

Abraham Lincoln would surely be amused, if not stunned, to learn that no money, science or technology of the twenty-first century has been spared to safeguard these first two rough drafts of his short speech. The cost of designing, building and maintaining this technology to house four sheets of paper: millions. The value of preserving these manuscripts . . . *priceless*.

The Gift (To Everett) That Keeps On Giving: The Third Draft

Another handwritten copy of the Gettysburg Address, the Third Draft prepared by Lincoln, unquestionably written out after he delivered his speech at the soldiers' cemetery , went to Edward Everett (this draft is also known as the "Everett Copy" and the "Everett-Keyes Copy").

Unlike Lincoln's first two drafts of his speech, there is little historical controversy about the last three. The last three drafts of the Gettysburg Address were written by Lincoln at the direct request of others. Everett would ask first, personally requesting this Third Draft from the President the day after Lincoln delivered the speech. On February 4, 1864, as a companion to the handsomely reproduced speech, Lincoln would write to Everett the following succinct and humble note:

"My dear Sir: Herewith is the copy of the manuscript which you did me the honor to request. Yours truly, A. Lincoln"

When, a few weeks later, Everett received his copy of the Gettysburg Address from Lincoln, he assembled it, along with a personal manuscript of his own speech, a copy of Saunder's plan for the Soldiers' National Cemetery, pictures of military commanders and soldiers, maps of Gettysburg, and other public remarks made at the ceremony, and sent them to a bindery. Everett numbered the pages of this remarkable compilation preserving the Gettysburg event. The faint numbers 57 and 58 can still be seen where he wrote them at the top right corners of this Third Draft of the Gettysburg Address.

Along with polishing up his speech with a few stylistic refinements,

President Lincoln would also make two momentous revisions between the Hay Copy and the Everett Copy, in an effort to closer reproduce the words he had actually spoken at the soldiers' cemetery. As previously noted, Lincoln would add the words, "under God," and then expand the audience of his speech from America only (". . . that this government of the people. . ."), to a boundless, world-wide audience (". . . that government of the people. . .").

The Everett Copy, as Lincoln's Third Draft, is an unhurried, neat and methodically-written facsimile of the Gettysburg Address. It was originally meant to be sold along with the other manuscripts Everett had assembled in his book, at the New York Metropolitan Fair in 1864, to raise money for a soldier's charity fund. For this reason, this version of the Gettysburg Address is sometimes referred to as the "New York Metropolitan Fair Copy."

Everett provided his leather-bound book of manuscripts, which contained Lincoln's Third Draft of the Gettysburg Address, to Mrs. Hamilton Fish (wife of the New York Governor), who chaired the committee which would auction off the book. However, for reasons that still remain a mystery, it was never sold at the fair, despite the auction of the book being publicly advertised.

Eventually, the Everett Copy would find passage into the open marketplace, where it was privately bought and sold numerous times, and passed by inheritance, the precious collection of Gettysburg manuscripts still bound together. Even during the Great Depression era of the 1930's when the wealthy went bust and money was brutally scarce, the Everett Copy and its surrounding bindery of Gettysburg manuscripts sold at private sale, twice: once for the lofty amount of $100,000—and again, a few years later, for what was then an eye-popping price of $150,000.

Thomas F. Madigan, an avid collector and dealer of rare manuscripts during the early part of the 20th Century, at one juncture in time, not only proudly owned the Everett Copy of the Gettysburg Address, but also Lincoln's Fourth Draft known as the "Bancroft Copy." Madigan also possessed in his personal collection the only known autographed copy of Edgar Allen Poe's poem *The Raven*, and a rare letter signed by Galileo.

In his fascinating book, *Word Shadows of the Great: The Lure of Autograph Collecting*, Thomas Madigan, in 1930, seemed as awestruck over looking at the Gettysburg Address as John Nicolay was in 1885 ("[it] is now lying before my eyes," Nicolay said), when Madigan laid his own eyes on the Everett Copy he had recently purchased. Caught up in sublime moment, Madigan would passionately write: "Before me as I write lies the most precious American transcript, literary or historical—and this is both—which has not yet found its way into a public institution." (The author understands the exuberance expressed by both Nicolay and Madigan, when with shameless adoration, I first laid eyes on the actual Everett Copy.) Only six years after writing these words, Madigan would die. Before he passed, he was sadly forced into a distress sale of these two precious Lincoln manuscripts he so dearly admired. For Madigan, it was surely a painful separation.

After years of private ownership, the Everett Copy would eventually find its way to the Illinois State Historical Library where it was kept in the Old State Capitol Building in Springfield, Illinois, thanks to money donated by the philanthropic family of Marshall Fields III the department store entrepreneur and funds raised by Illinois schoolchildren in the 1940's.

Now, the Everett Copy is safely housed at the Abraham Lincoln Presidential Library and Museum (which is repository for the entire Illinois State Historical Library), also in Springfield, where it is occasionally brought out for public viewing. The Everett Copy has been separated from the original bindery of manuscripts, so it can be observed alone—a majestic and fitting isolation.

Written By a "President Without Brains": The Fourth Draft

Lincoln, by his own hand, wrote out a Fourth Draft of the Gettysburg Address (also known as the "Bancroft Copy"). The preeminent historian of Lincoln's time, George Bancroft, interestingly, also a hardcore Democrat, took advantage of a White House reception in February 1864 and asked President Lincoln to write out a copy of the Gettysburg Address for him.

Bancroft, a former secretary of the Navy, was famous in his own right, authoring a commercially-successful ten volume work titled *History of the United States*, which would eventually earn him the esteemed moniker of "the father of American History." When Bancroft buttonholed President Lincoln for a handwritten copy of the Gettysburg Address, he was carrying water for his stepson, Colonel Alexander Bliss, who was on a committee soliciting popular manuscripts for a new book. The book would be reproduced by the predominant method of mass-printing at that time, called "lithographing."

With the most famous historian in the country dogging him for an autograph copy to put in a nationally-published book, any thoughts inside Lincoln's head that his speech at Gettysburg had failed, were surely evaporating away, if not already gone.

Despite the fact he was still recovering from his tough bout with variola and extremely busy with the War, Lincoln generously wrote out and sent Bancroft a handwritten facsimile of the Gettysburg Address from Washington on February 29, 1864. This was only four weeks after Lincoln had mailed Edward Everett the Third Draft of his speech. Bancroft loaned the newly-copied manuscript to Colonel Bliss, so he could arrange that this Fourth Draft of the Gettysburg Address be printed and included in a marvelous anthology of handwritten essays and manuscripts Bliss was publishing, titled *Autograph Leaves of Our Country's Authors*. This book would contain the work of a wide variety of famous literary figures. The plan was that this book be sold at the Baltimore Sanitary Fair to raise money for sick and wounded soldiers and sailors. Accordingly, this copy has also been labeled after its namesake event, as the "Baltimore Sanitary Fair Copy, No. 1."

Lincoln mailed this Bancroft Copy (Fourth Draft), along with the Everett Copy (Third Draft) to their respective destinations on the same day. There would be only one word change from the Everett Copy (Lincoln would use the word "on" in the first sentence, instead of "upon"), and make a handful of other minor punctuation adjustments.

Unfortunately, when the President wrote out this copy of the Gettysburg Address, he left virtually no margins with his penmanship, gave the manuscript no title, and wrote on the first and third pages on a larger creased sheet of paper, rendering it useless for reproduction by the lithograph method. Also, the editor wanted the President's signature on it, which Lincoln had left off. The publisher must have cringed (and perhaps, cried) over the lost opportunity. So George Bancroft, who once wrote during Lincoln's early tenure in office, "We have a President without brains," kept this "obsolete" Fourth Draft within the confines of his own family. Apparently, his early appraisal of President Lincoln had changed.

After spending decades in the Bancroft family, the Bancroft Copy would, in 1929, find itself finally passing into the hands of a private collector.

One uniquely distinguishing aspect of the Bancroft Copy is that it is the only copy of the Gettysburg Address that is companioned by both a transmittal letter from Lincoln and the original transmitting envelope that is addressed and franked by President Lincoln.

The Bancroft Copy of the Gettysburg Address, unlike its counterparts, would be the only handwritten copy of the Gettysburg Address, out of the five, to find its final resting place in private ownership. and it still is. In 1949, it was generously donated to Cornell University in Ithaca, New York by Nicolas and Marguerite Lily Noyes of Indianapolis, Indiana, who were its last private owners. Cornell remains its proud archival home. It is held there in the Division of Rare and Manuscript Collections, located in the Carl A. Kroch Library.

A Long, Strange Trip: The Fifth Draft

Lincoln wrote a Fifth Draft of the Gettysburg Address (also referred to as the "Bliss Copy"), again, to be "lithographed" for sale of reproductions at a Baltimore Sanitary Fair. This was the second of two copies Lincoln vouchsafed to Colonel Bliss for charitable purposes. Thus, this facsimile of the Gettysburg Address is sometimes called the "Baltimore Sanitary Fair Copy, No. 2."

This version of the speech, written in longhand by Lincoln like the others, was intended to replace the Bancroft Copy that was unsuitable to be lithographed. Accordingly, the editor of *Autograph Leaves of Our Country's Authors*, John P. Kennedy, asked the White House for another handwritten Gettysburg Address. Colonel Bliss would send a letter of apology to Lincoln on March 7, 1864 for the difficulty in the process, and enclosed ruled stationery for the President to write on, a type of paper that worked best for lithographing. Kindly accommodating Kennedy's request, the President wrote out still another draft of the Gettysburg Address.

This would be the fifth one—and the last.

Although all five versions of the Gettysburg Address have minor distinctions in punctuation and text, this one is extraordinarily unique from the others. Lincoln gave this copy a caption at the top of the manuscript ("Address delivered at the dedication of the ceremony at Gettysburg"), and dated it for the day he made the speech—November 19, 1863. And then, in a rare act, he placed his full signature on it, first name and last. Today, in the manuscript world, this Bliss Copy would be known as an ACS, or "autograph copy signed."

This Bliss Copy is viewed as the "official" version of the Gettysburg Address. Much of the public is under the impression that there was only one Gettysburg Address, and this, the Bliss Copy, is the one. It has generally been accepted as the standard version of the great speech, the text so often duplicated and displayed in commercial print today, as *the* Gettysburg Address.

After this Fifth Draft was lithographed for public consumption, it remained the precious property of the Alexander Bliss family for years. The Bancroft and Bliss families, through the commingling of influence, gall and luck, at one remarkable place in time, had stockpiled two copies of the Gettysburg Address (the Fourth and Fifth Drafts), both of them written in Lincoln's own hand. In fact, they had retained ownership of the entire cornucopia of original manuscripts that were anthologized in *Autograph Leaves of Our Country's Authors*. It was, truly, a collection of rare manuscripts that must have brought them "bliss."

Eventually, on April 27, 1949, the entire collection from Autograph Leaves was auctioned-off in New York City by the Bliss heirs. The fifth and last surviving copy of the Gettysburg Address would be sold for what was then the lofty price of $54,000, to Oscar B. Cintas, a wealthy Cuban entrepreneur and collector of rare manuscripts and art, who was living in Havana. At that time, it was the highest price ever paid for a manuscript at a public auction (although private sales had previously brought more).

Cintas would eventually become the Cuban Ambassador to the United States. When Cuba fell to the control of Fidel Castro's communist government, Cintas escaped to America. Grateful to the country that offered him the freedom and equality that was beautifully defined by Lincoln on the pages of the Gettysburg Address that he owned, Cintas bequeathed the rare manuscript, at his death, back to its home in America, where it belonged, conditioned upon it resting permanently in the White House. It is still there, today, on display in the "Lincoln Bedroom" (which is, actually, Lincoln's former office) on the second floor of the White House. The White House Historical Association now supervises the care of this manuscript.

This manuscript bequest took place at Cintas' death in 1957, which was, fortuitously, two years before the Castro Government seized all of Cintas' assets in the Cuban Revolution. The Bliss Copy of the Gettysburg Address had traveled a long and strange adventure. Amazingly, because of the farsighted bequest in a Cuban refugee's last will and testament, it is now in safe repose in the Lincoln Bedroom of the White House, exactly where the testator wanted it to be.

Without Cintas' bequest, the Bliss Copy of the Gettysburg Address would likely still be in Cuba, considering Cuba's strong and strange affection for America's sixteenth president. Ironically, there are probably more schools named after Lincoln in Cuba than in his birth state of Kentucky. And a statue of Lincoln awaits those who drive up the Avenida de los Presidentes into the city of Havana. Perhaps Cubans hold great affection for Lincoln because the hero of the Cuban Independence Movement and beloved poet, Jose' Marti (1853-1895), himself, carried great admiration for Abraham Lincoln. Perhaps it is because the master class of Southerners, during the Civil War, coveted Cuba as a site to expand their slave-driven agricultural businesses, a motive no doubt repulsive to the Cuban people.

Historian Garry Wills has written that the Bliss Copy is "stylistically preferable" to Lincoln's other facsimiles, in one distinctive way, because the President apparently spotted his own redundant use of the word "here," and thus deleted it from the phrase ". . . that cause for which they [here] gave the last full measure of devotion. . .". In all four of the previous drafts of his speech, Wills points out, Lincoln inserted this seventh "here." Lincoln's redaction of this word may have been by design, or simply a scrivener's error.

One must wonder if our contemporary presidents—late at night, sleepless with the burdens of the Nation pressing down upon their chest—ever go up to the Lincoln Room of the White House, alone—a room once wall-papered with Civil War maps and where the Emancipation Proclamation was signed—and look, deeply and meditatively, at the words of the Gettysburg Address, which is placed there on a desk in quiet repose, written in the hand of the sixteenth president a century and a half ago. Surely, they must. Surely, they find hope and inspiration there.

And what a moment that must be.

UFO Sightings

During the last few hectic days of mid-November 1863, before President Lincoln would travel to Gettysburg to deliver his speech, did anyone know what would be in it? Or see it? Possibly.

There were a number of individuals who would later claim UFO ("Unidentified Formal Oration") sightings of the great speech while in its infancy. But like modern day UFO's, those close encounters with the Gettysburg Address are lean on hard evidence, clouded by questions of credibility, and wrapped in controversy. They are, however, fodder for interesting historical debate.

Out of the numerous UFO encounters claimed with the great speech, most would be completely discredited. However, three of these sightings, in the past, have garnered a good deal of historical attention. The three men involved, who were all men devoted to Lincoln, would eventually say they had a private rendezvous—a close encounter, so to speak—with the Gettysburg Address, before Lincoln left Washington to go to Gettysburg. They were Noah Brooks, John Defrees and Ward Lamon.

The first significant bleep on the radar screen of historical record, indicating that Lincoln was beginning to assemble the word-pieces of his Gettysburg Address, reportedly occurred just a few days before the Gettysburg ceremonies. It was the incident told on many occasions by journalist (and later Lincoln biographer), Noah Brooks. Brooks enjoyed liberal access to the White House and close friendship with both President and Mrs. Lincoln (which was unusual).

Brooks never laid claim to seeing the Gettysburg Address with his own eyes. But he came pretty doggone close . . . at least according to his version. Brooks asserted that in early November—just days before Lincoln delivered his Gettysburg Address at the soldiers' cemetery— he accompanied the President in Washington, when Lincoln went to have pictures made at Alexander Gardner's photographic studio. While they were on their way from the White House to the photo shop, as Brooks recalled, the President told him that the "long envelope" in his hand contained an advance copy of "Edward Everett's address," and that Brooks got a good slant at the printed speech when Lincoln removed it from the envelope. Brooks emphasized as corroboration for his account, that the envelope containing Everett's speech can be clearly seen, laying by Lincoln's right hand on a table in one of Gardner's sitting portraits of the President taken that day. Brooks also remembered the President gently wisecracking about the length of Everett's speech ("Solid men of Boston, make no long orations."), and going on to tell Brooks that his own "written, but unfinished" Gettysburg speech would be "short, short, short." Sometimes, when Brooks told this captivating story— which he did quite often—Lincoln would be confessing to Brooks that he had revised his Gettysburg speech several times, and that it still needed, in Lincoln's own words, "another lick" before the President would be "satisfied" with it. This is the Brooks UFO encounter.

It was just one week or so before the Gettysburg ceremonies were to take place that the outside world, for the first time, may have got its first actual glimpse of an unmilled, unfinished version of the Gettysburg Address. Or at least, that was the story of John D. Defrees.

Defrees was a newspaperman who had positioned himself to have tremendous control over Republican politics in Indiana. In one of Lincoln's legion of political appointments, the President had named him first superintendent over the Government Print Office, a department oozing with patronage. Historical records do confirm that exactly one week before the Gettysburg event, Defrees was asked by President Lincoln, in a November 12th note, to make inquiries with a young woman in his office and then come by the White House to discuss the matter, which involved the welfare of a young man in prison.

This all happened, because a few weeks earlier, on October 24th, Lincoln had dropped in at the Government Print Office to make a brief talk to government employees (perhaps to keep things calm in a federal department where employees, about two years earlier when the War escalated the Union's need for printed materials, had initially refused to work a ten hour day, under the demands of their "Trade Union"). One of Defrees's female employees there, somehow, asked (or possibly wrote) the President for help in checking on her incarcerated brother. Incredibly—but predictably—Lincoln was again taking time, despite the weight of the War and a Gettysburg speech bearing down on him, to follow up and help someone he didn't even know.

John Defrees, of course, went by to see the President, presumably during the next few days. While he was there meeting with the President, as the episode was originally described for the public in a later newspaper article, Lincoln suddenly bolted the door for privacy. Lincoln then laid a "paper" before Defrees, and invited Defrees to " read this carefully and make any changes your judgment dictates." Defrees then reads the manuscript, and reaching it back to the President, supposedly says, "Don't change a word of it—it is perfect." According to the gist of this story, President Lincoln was requesting Defree's advice on his composition, which would later turn out to be, as proudly described by Defrees in the newspaper account, "the famous Gettysburg speech." There is no historical mention of Lincoln discussing with Defrees the subject which was the primary purpose of their meeting (i.e., the fate of the young man in prison), although such a discussion likely occurred. This is the Defrees UFO encounter.

The third sighting of the Gettysburg Address would come from the man who seemed to be everywhere (and then some), Ward Hill Lamon. Lamon would assert in his memoir (published after his death, by his daughter, Dorothy Lamon Teillard), that he crossed the path of the great speech just "a day or two" before Lincoln went to Gettysburg. Lamon would describe his private brush with history like this:

> "Just before the dedication of the national cemetery at Gettysburg, Mr. Lincoln told me he would be expected to

make a speech on the occasion—that he was extremely busy and had no time to prepare himself for it, and feared he would be unable to do himself and the subject justice. He took out of his hat (the general receptacle of his notes and memoranda) a page of fools cap, closely written, and read me what he called a memoranda of what he intended to say, which proved to be in substance . . . what was printed as his Gettysburg Address. He remarked that if he got time he would try to write something worthy of the occasion."

This is the Lamon—and last known—UFO encounter.

The credibility of these close encounters with the Gettysburg Address that allegedly took place before Lincoln left Washington for Gettysburg, as related by Brooks, Defrees and Lamon, have been extensively dissected through the years by top Lincoln scholars, and are still debated today. The fact that some of the most respected and preeminent Lincoln scholars differ about the veracity of these encounters adds to the historical intrigue. Conclusions are difficult, because these stories contain just enough historical plausibility, to make them tantalizingly possible. However, when a closer look at these UFO sightings is made, all three events seem to rest upon evidence which raises serious questions about their authenticity. Let's revisit them.

First, there is Noah Brooks. Brooks claimed he had personally been in the company of President Lincoln on specific dates at Gardner's photo studio when —based on a cross-check with other reliable, contemporaneously-made documents of Brooks's time —it was, most likely, impossible. President Lincoln did, in fact, go to Gardner's Gallery on November 8th. We know this because his assistant John Hay preserved the event in his diary, and listed everyone who accompanied the President. Hay and Nicolay even got "immortalized" that day by making their picture with "the Pres^t," as Hay proudly described in his diary. And Noah Brooks was not mentioned or photographed . . . because he wasn't there.

Brooks further gnawed away at his own leg of credibility with many historians when he said he heard Lincoln comment, as they strolled together towards the photo session, on the length of Edward Everett's printed speech—comments supposedly made by President Lincoln on a date before the President could have even received his advanced copy of Everett's oration from the Boston printer and possibly known what was in it.

Lincoln did drop by Gardner's studio the very next Sunday, on November 15th. But no independent historical record or reminiscence remains, verifying that Brooks was with the President on that date, either. Even if Brooks was with Lincoln at the photo shop on the 15th, his lifetime insistence that Lincoln had a copy of Everett's speech with him, again . . . seems impossible. Everett, himself (as entered in his diary), did not receive his own printed galley of his Gettysburg speech until the late afternoon of November 14th. The idea that Everett, in Boston, could (or needed to) get a copy of his speech to Lincoln, in Washington, by the next day, is pretty incredible. David C. Mearns, the esteemed Librarian for the Library of Congress for a half century, harshly concluded that Brooks's chronologically dysfunctional story, which he told over and over through the years, put the "Kibosh" on the Brooks's encounter, or what Mearns called the "Brooks' fantasy."

In Brooks's defense, in what is, perhaps, the most common of all human errors, it can be argued, that he simply got his dates confused. And that he really was with Lincoln at Gardner's Gallery just before the Gettysburg trip (even though there is no historical corroboration of it), and that the President really did let him have an early look at Everett's keynote address, and talked about his own "short" speech. The problem is, however, that Brooks was also wrong about other specific details when he described Lincoln's copy of Everett's speech. And would President Lincoln, who so deeply admired Edward Everett, the greatest living orator, pop off to a journalist with a snarky one-liner about the length of Everett's keynote speech, a speech expected to be lengthy and being given at such an important and somber event? Facts are mighty stubborn things, and in this case, they do not seem to surrender to the story of Noah Brooks.

Next, is the close encounter of John Defrees. The intriguing tale of John Defrees receiving a private showing of the Gettysburg Address by Lincoln, with the President locking down the room as though it was a secret military conclave, and then laying his draft of the Gettysburg

Address before Defrees, giving him carte blanche authority, on the
spot, to edit and improve the speech, also carries the suspicious scent of
a fantasy.

It was a story hatched into life through a newspaper article that was
colorfully narrated by Defrees' son-in-law, a fellow named J. O. Smith.
The historical record is clear and convincing, perhaps unimpeachable,
that Lincoln did not even complete the last half of the Gettysburg
Address, until he arrived in Gettysburg, Pennsylvania. It seems very
unlikely that Lincoln would show Defrees his speech, let alone invite
him to "make any changes" he wanted, on a speech still under construction, a speech only half completed. And since Lincoln's speech was
unfinished, which we know to be historically true, why would Defrees,
in his own words, tell the President: "Don't change a word of it,—it is
perfect."? Defrees was either the world's worst speech critic (and greatest brown-noser), or it is just another tall tale. We cannot be absolutely sure. But, most likely, it was the later. Although John Defrees was,
in fact, summoned to see the President at his Executive Office by way of
Lincoln's November 12, 1863 note, the astonishing details of this
encounter suggest it is, sadly, another example of a Lincoln taradiddle.
A sure way to ruin the truth is to stretch it; and it seems Defrees, in an
effort to convince the world of his intimate proximity to the great
speech and a martyred presidential saint, may have done just that.

Lastly, there is Lamon's encounter. The saga of Ward Lamon's early
sighting of the Gettysburg Address also lacks plausibility, in the view of
many historians. Lamon said he was in Washington, D.C. when he
crossed the path of the newborn Gettysburg Address. Most vexing about
Lamon's early encounter with the speech is that he mentions it for the
first time in 1887, almost twenty-five years after the incident. A troubling factor, in and of itself. Also, Lamon claimed that he first discovered that President Lincoln would be giving a speech at Gettysburg only
at the last moment before Lincoln left Washington, as he put it, "Just
before the dedication of the national cemetery." Critics of Lamon's
close encounter point out that his story stretches credulity mighty
thin—especially since Lamon had been designated by David Wills as
chief marshal over the dedication ceremonies.

If anyone knew that Lincoln would be speaking at Gettysburg, then surely one of the first to know would have been Ward Hill Lamon, who was a Lincoln confidant and the architect of the program under which the President would speak. In short—he was in charge. U.S. Marshall Lamon was there at the planning table in Gettysburg with David Wills and Benjamin French from Friday November 13th until Monday November 16th; then, he quickly returned to Washington on the 16th to organize a crew of parade marshals; and finally, he scrambled back to Gettysburg on the 17th to set up security and accommodations for the President's arrival, staying there until Lincoln arrived at dusk on the 18th.   Lamon, superbly capable at it, was caught in a whirlwind schedule of logistical planning for the Gettysburg ceremonies.

It is difficult for many historians to swallow the story that Lamon—so close to the President and as chief marshal over the event—would first learn that Lincoln would give a speech at Gettysburg "just before" the event occurred. And exactly when did Lamon have both time and opportunity to meet with a very busy President Lincoln in the "day or two" before the Gettysburg trip (possibly on the morning of the 17th, but otherwise, Lamon was mostly in Gettysburg). And why would Lamon, an incurable raconteur, wait a quarter-century to relate his epic tryst with history? Historian Garry Wills has referred to Lamon's encounter with the Gettysburg Address as "notoriously imaginative."

Looking back, history insinuates that the loyal and fun-loving Lamon enjoyed drawing attention to himself, by telling stories about Lincoln that no one else was privy to. Some of Lamon's memories may have come more from what he felt in his heart for his treasured friend Abraham Lincoln, rather than what he had actually seen or heard. This, probably, is one of them. Reminiscences, especially sentimental ones—are precious memories, that always claim close kinship to the truth. But they are not identical twins.

Does Brooks' story hold water? Did Defrees and Lamon actually see, with their own eyes, an early version of the Gettysburg Address, before Lincoln went to Gettysburg? Historians are still divided.

A thick fog of implausibility seems to shroud all three of these stories. Even if one examines the accounts of Brooks, Defrees and Lamon individually, and initially gives them the benefit of the doubt as being remotely possible—still, when overlayed and taken together as a whole, these three stories suffer a glaring shortage of factual congruity. However, like most UFO sightings, we will likely never know, with absolute certainty, the truth about these close encounters.

Most poignantly, and perhaps, just as painfully , it reminds us of the seductive, almost intractable psychological pull felt by these three men, in their longing to be historically close to their good and gallant president, martyred by an assassin's bullet.

Ultimately, the preponderance of historical evidence seems to indicate that during the two weeks in Washington that preceded the President's trip to Gettysburg, that Lincoln kept his thoughts and notes about his speech very close to the vest. Odds are, when the President left Washington, D.C. on the morning of November 18, 1863, in route for a small Pennsylvania town to make a speech over the graves of fallen soldiers, no one—not even his closest friends and advisors—had laid eyes on the Gettysburg Address.

The time to reveal the great speech had not yet come.

Other Missing Drafts?

Movies like the *Indiana Jones* and *National Treasure* series waken fantasies of archaeological adventures that still secretly linger in all of us, as faint residuals from our childhood books and dreams. We cannot help but wonder: are there missing drafts of the Gettysburg Address, in Lincoln's own hand, left to be found?

Some scholars believe the Nicolay Copy, although it is Lincoln's First Draft, is too neat and orderly to be the composition draft, even with obvious revisions. If so, what happened to the composition drafts of the Gettysburg Address, the ones where Lincoln rough-hewed out the words of his speech? Could those close encounters with the great speech in Washington, D.C. claimed by Brooks, Defrees and Lamon the week before the Gettysburg event—actually be true? After all, Ward Lamon reminisced that just before the Gettysburg trip, that President Lincoln read his speech to him from a single page of the odd-sized foolscap paper—not the letter-sized stationery on which Lincoln's First Draft is written. It is conceivable that Lincoln, the inveterate revisionist, drafted an early, work-in-progress version of his speech on a half-sheet of foolscap, before he bettered it with the Nicolay Copy.

It raises the tantalizing question: if Lincoln did write other drafts of the Gettysburg Address— could they still be out there, somewhere? It is possible. . . but not probable.

Every few decades, rumors circulate among purveyors of rare manuscripts, spreading the tantalizing tale that another "Gettysburg Address," or at least a part of one, has suddenly emerged from the anonymity of an old attic trunk or been discovered between the crispy, tea-brown pages of an ancient book. But, without fail, they are eventually dismissed by experts as forgeries. And how? Because they often imitate, with foolish, too-perfect exactness, one of Lincoln's true originals (which are easily accessible for viewing in the public domain), a handwriting feat of reproduction Lincoln himself could not have pulled off.

This is exactly what happened in 1990, when distinguished Lincoln collector, historian and international artist Dr. Lloyd Ostendorf and several other Lincoln experts were fooled by a forgery that was tantalizingly proffered to be a page from the famous "missing copy" of the Gettysburg Address—the manuscript intended for David Wills. After a sophisticated battery of expert analysis and forensic tests failed to expose the counterfeit document (remarkably, expert forgers can obtain nineteenth century paper, writing instruments and ink, complicating the authentication process), it took the brilliantly simple procedure of a Lincoln authority named Richard Sloan—who simply laid a transparency of Lincoln's Second Draft of his Gettysburg Address (the "Hay Copy") on top of the forgery—which revealed the two writings to be a near perfect match. It was, pure and simple, a forgery by tracing.

Joseph Cosey made a career out of crafting Lincoln forgeries and other historical figures like Mark Twain and George Washington, until he died in the early 1950's. Cosey, an ex-con who discovered and developed his amazing talent during the Great Depression (he forged freehand, and not by tracing), using paper, writing instruments and ink of the era he was forging, fooled several experts through the years with his Lincoln imitations. In fact, Cosey took pride in that he never sold his work to amateurs. Some of Cosey's Lincoln forgeries are probably still lurking around in the shadows of the manuscript collection world waiting on another victim. Ironically, Cosey's forgeries have developed their own unique collector's value.

The serendipitous discovery in recent years of original versions of famous historical manuscripts like the Declaration of Independence tease our hope that another Gettysburg Address—the Holy Grail of American historical manuscripts—may, someday, turn up in a garage sale or flea market, somewhere. But chances of that are pretty slim—and as the old saying goes . . . "Slim has left town."

One can only imagine what an autograph copy of the Gettysburg Address — arguably, the most famous speech in American history—would bring in today's market. Twenty. . .thirty. . .even fifty million dollars? The auction price of much more modest Lincoln manuscripts suggest it is possible.

On February 12, 2009, the 200th anniversary of Lincoln's birthday, Christie's auction house in New York City sold an autograph copy of Lincoln's 1864 victory speech (delivered by Lincoln on November 10, 1864, two days after his reelection), for 3.44 million dollars—the highest amount ever paid for any American historical document.

And on June 26, 2012, David M. Rubenstein, co-founder of the Carlyle Group, paid over 2 million dollars for a copy of the Emancipation Proclamation signed by Lincoln. His remarkable collection already included a copy of the Declaration of Independence, a signed copy of the 13th Amendment abolishing slavery and the Magna Carta.

Great, one-of-kind paintings have super million dollar price tags. Why wouldn't comparable historical manuscripts like the Gettysburg Address command the same? In November 2006, Jackson Pollock's painting known as "No. 5, 1948" reportedly sold, privately, for 140 million dollars. Could the Nicolay Copy, that is, "No. 1, 1863"– or Lincoln's most-famous Fifth Draft of the Gettysburg Address, that is, "No. 5, 1864"—bring such a Pollock-like price?

In 1930, Thomas F. Madigan, the famous manuscript collector, writing in insuppressible admiration of his own personal copy of the Gettysburg Address , handsomely penned in Lincoln's own hand, wrote: "No American manuscript of equal interest or importance has thus far come into the market-place."

And, nearly a century later . . . nothing has changed.

NOTES

ABBREVIATIONS

CWAL The Collected Works of Abraham Lincoln, chiefly edited by Roy P. Basler (9 vols.; New Brunswick, NJ: Rutgers University Press, 1953—1955) and *Supplement*, 1832—1865 (2 vols.; Westport, CT: Greenwood Press, 1974). These documents are generously available online at http://quod.lib.umich.edu/l/lincoln/.

ACHS Adams County Historical Society in Gettysburg, Pennsylvania.

GNMP Gettysburg National Military Park, Library Division, in Gettysburg, Pennsylvania.

Chapter One
PROLOGUE: A HOUSE DIVIDED

23. Soldiers . . . 160,000 of them: John W. Busey and David G. Martin, *Regimental Strengths and Losses at Gettysburg*, 4th ed. (Hightstown, NJ: Longstreet House, 2005), pp. 3, 159. A precise calculation of combat soldiers is about impossible. Sometimes military battle records are flawed estimates or even inflated for dramatic effect on history, but there is compelling data that suggests this 160,000 figure is an undercounted, conservative number. There were also thousands of non-combat military personnel, and perhaps thousands of African-American soldiers who fought for both the Union and Confederate armies, not listed in these casualty statistics.

24. The Confederacy would suffer: These casualty numbers for the North and South, which temporary studies indicate may be understated, were compiled in the U.S. Govt. publication entitled *The War of the Rebellion: A Compilation of the Official Records of the Union and Confederate Armies; prepared under the direction of the Secretary of War*, by BVT. Lieut. Col. Robert N. Scott, Third U.S. Artillery and published pursuant to Act of Congress (1880), hereafter referenced as the Official War Records, are available both in print and online under their title.

24. a bullet hit a human being: The author readily acknowledges this statistic is a reasoned estimation, using available historical data. To derive this com-putation, reference was first made to information on the *Battle of Gettysburg Timeline*, available online under its title. Again, this is a raw estimation because fighting on July 2, 1863 was taking place before dawn, and continued into the night. To calculate battlefield entries on July 2nd that referred to a "dawn" start rather than a specific time, the author arranged for a reference to the Starry Night Pro desktop planetarium (software), setting the date of July 2, 1863. Because time zones did not exist in those days, and the program uses only Eastern Time, a small estimated adjustment of 15 minutes "earlier" was made to arrive at a more accurate (but not precise) local Gettysburg time (based upon that town's GPS location to the Eastern Time Baseline) for the dawn start of the second day of battle. Those 51 hours of total battle time were converted to seconds (183,600 battle seconds), and then divided by total battle casualties which were 51,112 (North: 23,049 and South: 28,063). These casualty num-bers were acquired from the *Official War Records* (1880). These computations suggest one "casualty" every 3.59 seconds, which the author rounded-up to 4 seconds. Considering the tremendous number of armed forced engaged in this battle (North: 82,289 and South: 75,000), these averaged numbers regarding the frequency of human bullet strikes may be significantly understated. Although these numbers, by their inherent nature of being imperfect raw data placed into an averaging process, cannot be scientifically precise and are not represented as such, they do create a true and accurate historical picture of the panoramic intensity of the ballistic combat at the Battle of Gettysburg. A real-istic visual of this combat might be the opening 27 minutes of the Steven Spielberg film, *Saving Private Ryan* (1998), depicting the June 6, 1944 attack on Omaha Beach, during the Normandy Invasion of World War II.

24. **A war . . . claim more than 750,000 lives:** The Battle of Gettysburg is still one of the bloodiest battles ever fought by American soldiers, certainly the bloodiest on American soil. Only the World War I Battle of Meuse-Argonne, and the World War II Battle of the Bulge and invasion of Okinawa, Japan—bat-tles which were fought on foreign soil with modern weapons and lasted much longer—may have claimed more lives. Recent studies seriously undermine the 620,000 American Civil War casualties number that has been relied upon by his-torians for generations. *The Civil War Desk Reference* (p. 373) at the Library of Congress, states the total of combat dead to be 620,000. See "Scholars look at Civil War anew during anniversary," *Wall Street Journal*, May 29, 2012. Also, for those interested in this subject, there is an interesting television broadcast that broached this subject (transcript available), which is "Civil War more deadly than thought," *NBC Nightly News with Brian Williams*, first broadcast on April 4, 2012. J. David Hacker, Ph.D., History Professor at Binghamton University in New York, has led the way in bringing new light to the question of the final Civil War death toll, undermining the accuracy of the original and largely uncriticized

1870 census data which may have understated Civil War casualties as much as 20%. Professor Hacker persuasively makes the case that the Civil War death toll exceeded 750,000, and possibly reached as high as 850,000. His article "Recounting the Dead," Disunion Opinionator Blog, *New York Times*, September 20, 2011, available online under its title, provides an interesting theory of how these casualty numbers may have been so grossly understated.

25. the Nation's first "situation room": Tom Wheeler, *Mr. Lincoln's T-Mails: The Untold Story of How Abraham Lincoln Used the Telegraph to Win the Civil War* (New York: HarperCollins Publishers, 2006), p. 3.

25. "I suppose it is good": Don E. Fehrenbacher and Virginia Fehrenbacher, eds., Statement of Noah Brooks, *Recollected Words of Abraham Lincoln* (Stanford, CA: Stanford University Press, 1996), pp. 42-44.

25. sometimes just "keeled over": Allan Nevins, *The War for the Union*, Vol. 1, *The Improvised War, 1861-1862* (New York: Charles Scribner's Sons, 1959), p. 58.

25. "the last President of the United States": Horace Greeley, *The Autobiography of Horace Greeley: or, Recollections of a Busy Life* (New York: E.B. Treat, 1868), p. 359.

25. "Well, boys, your troubles": Philip B. Kunhardt, Jr., Philip B. Kunhardt, III, and Peter W. Kunhardt, *Lincoln: An Illustrated Biography* (New York: Alfred A. Knopf, 1992), p. 130.

27. Most Southerners: This information is available from the *United States Census of 1860*, found online under its title. Despite the complications of the nation being mired in the Civil War, remarkably, that governmental bureau was still able to produce an abbreviated set of public data (without cartographic charts, however), which are informative of the general scope and location of slave populations during the early war era. See also *Time Magazine Special Issue*, "Uncovering The Real Abe Lincoln," July 4, 2005, pp. 60, 61.

27. mopped up with . . . "handkerchief": This statement is infamously attributed to LeRoy Pope Walker, who was briefly Secretary of War for the newly-formed Confederate government when it was in Montgomery, Alabama. Pope was a mouthy, out-of-sync, loose cannon in Jefferson Davis's administration, making not only this embarrassing-bad prediction, but also guarantying in a speech he made after Fort Sumter, that the Confederacy flag would soon be flying over the White House. The source of this information is the *Encyclopedia of Alabama*, available online under its title. Research from the *North Carolina History Project*, also available online (reference the "secession" topic), reveals a similar prediction from A.W. Venable in Granville County, NC. Recoiling to the notion that secession would lead to war, Venable proclaimed that he would be able to "wipe up every drop of blood shed in the War with this handkerchief of mine." The eminent Civil War historian and author, Shelby Foote, sometimes commented, with tongue-in-cheek to chide the men who made these absurd predictions, that this subject would make an excellent dissertation study to calculate how many handkerchiefs it would have really taken for the blood shed in the Civil War.

28. And they wanted them, forever. In a famous speech (the "Cornerstone Address") made in Savannah, Georgia on March 21, 1861, the Vice President of the Confederacy, Alexander Stephens, proclaimed that slavery was the "cornerstone" of the Confederate government. "Our new Government," Stephens stated, "is founded upon exactly opposite ideas; its foundations are laid, its cornerstone rests, upon the great truth that the negro is not equal to the white man; that slavery, subordination to the superior race, is his natural and normal condition." Lincoln had been in office less than a month, when this speech was made. Two excellent books examining this speech, and its historical repercussions, are Thomas E. Schott, *Alexander H. Stephens of Georgia: A Biography* (Baton Rouge, LA: Louisiana State University Press, 1988), and Harry V. Jaffa, *A New Birth of Freedom: Abraham Lincoln and the Coming of the Civil War* (Lanham; Rowman & Littlefield Publishers, Inc., 2000).

29. "to play with Seward": Russell McClintock, *Lincoln and the Decision for War* (Chapel Hill: North Carolina Press, 2008), p. 216.

29. "acknowledges that slavery": Letter from Abraham Lincoln to John D. Defrees, December 18, 1860, *The Collected Works of Abraham Lincoln*, chief ed., Roy P. Basler (9 vols.; New Brunswick, NJ: Rutgers University Press, 1953-1955) and *Supplement, 1832-1865* (2 vols.; Westport, CT: Greenwood Press, 1974), hereafter referred to as *CWAL*, 4:155.

29. "he [Lincoln] lacks will": Howard K. Beale (Howard Kennedy) and Mary Parker Ragatz, eds., *The Diary of Edward Bates*, 1859-1866 (Washington, D.C.: Government Printing Office), p. 220.

30. "Nobody believes in him": George Templeton Strong, diary entry of September 13, 1862, Allan Nevins and Milton Halsey Thomas, eds., *The Diary of George Templeton Strong, 1835-1875*, reference vol. 3, *The Civil War 1860-65* (4 vols.; New York: The Macmillan Company, 1952), p. 3:256.

30. "Lincoln is gone": John C. Waugh, *Reelecting Lincoln: The Battle for the 1864 Presidency* (Cambridge, MA: Da Capo Press, 2001), p. 262.

31. Secession would break loose: An excellent discourse on the impact of secession on Lincoln's administration and the nation is by the eminent historian David M Potter, *Lincoln and His Party in the Secession Crisis* (New Haven, CT; Yale University Press, 1942).

32. "Tippet: Crazy-Man": Harold Holzer, comp. and ed., *Dear Mr. Lincoln: Letters to The President* (Reading, MA: Addison—Wesley, 1993), pp. 191-93.

32. "aeronautic machinery": Kunhardt, *Lincoln: An Illustrated Biography*, p. 326. A good photograph taken on June 1, 1862 of T.S.C. Lowe inflating one of his hot-air balloons for use as an aerial observation post is shown in this superlative Lincoln book at pp. 182-183.

32. **checking out . . . Halleck's Elements of Military Art:** Dr. Louis A. Warren, *Lincoln Lore*, No. 129, "Borrowed Books In The White House," September 28, 1931. Lincoln checked out this book, which was then listed as *Halleck's Science of War*, from January 8, 1862 until March 24, 1864 (surely they waived late fees for the President). This fascinating compilation by Dr. Warren (he credits Judge Henry Horner), identifies every book ever checked-out during Lincoln's administration, and how long it was borrowed. The last book checked-out before Lincoln's assassination? *Tableau de Paris* on March 25, 1865; surely borrowed by Mary Lincoln who was fluent in French and fascinated by Paris.

33. **"the Tycoon":** Letter from John Hay to John G. Nicolay, August 7, 1863, Tyler Dennett, *Lincoln and the Civil War in the Diaries and Letters of John Hay* (New York: Dodd, Mead & Company, 1939), hereafter *Hay Diaries*, p. 76. On this day Hay would write: "The Tycoon is in fine whack. I have rarely seen him so serene and busy. There is no man in the country, so wise, so gentle and so firm. I believe the hand of God placed him where he is."

33. **"The old man sits here":** Letter from John Hay to John G. Nicolay, September 11, 1863, Ibid., p. 91.

34. **"Now, my man, go away!":** Philip B. Kunhardt, Jr., *A New Birth of Freedom: "Lincoln at Gettysburg"* (Boston: Little, Brown and Company, 1983), pp.49-51 (p. 50 is photograph).

34. **The country's "fiery trial":** Abraham Lincoln in his Annual Message to Congress, December 1, 1862, *CWAL*, 5:537.

34. **The teenage soldier, Private August Blittersdorf:** Letter from Abraham Lincoln to George G. Meade, October 8, 1863, *CWAL*, 6:506.

35. **"I am unwilling for any boy":** Ibid.

35. **"Abraham Africanus I":** The Library of the University of Illinois at Urbana-Champaign, in its Digitized Book of the Week, titled *Abraham Africanus I: His Secret Life* (posted September 3, 2007).

36. **"And its one, two, three":** *I Feel Like I'm Fixin' To Die Rag*, ("And, it's one, two, three, what are we fighting for?"), Words and Music by Joe McDonald and performed by Country Joe and the Fish, appearing on Vanguard Records. Published by Alcatraz Corner Music Co. Thanks to Alcatraz Corner Music, and especially to Bill Belmont, administrator of this song, for his generous time and interesting input about it's fascinating history.

37. **"I do not like this arrangement":** Letter from Abraham Lincoln to Edwin M. Stanton, November 17, 1863. *CWAL*, 7:16.

37. **"I do not wish to so go":** Ibid.

38. **"of abundant margin":** Louis A. Warren, *Lincoln's Gettysburg Declaration: "A New Birth of Freedom"* (Fort Wayne, IN: Lincoln National Life Foundation, 1964), p. 57. This was in a reply from John W. Garrett, president of the Baltimore & Ohio Railroad to Secretary of War Edwin M. Stanton, who was

assuring Stanton that the train scheduling had been changed to assuage the President's concerns.

39. "They will eat you up!": Carl Sandburg, *Abraham Lincoln: The Prairie Years and The War Years*, (1 vol. edition; New York: Galahad Books, 1993), hereafter *Abraham Lincoln: TPY & TWY*, p. 216.

39. His "compound Cabinet": Frederick W. Seward, *Seward at Washington as Senator and Secretary of State, 1846-1861* (New York: Derby & Miller, 1891), p. 518. William H. Seward, accepting the post of Secretary of State, would write to his wife that "The President is determined he will have a compound Cabinet."

39. "the president is the best of us": Ibid., p. 590.

40. "There's a d _ _ n good scripture": James G. Smart, ed., *A Radical View: The "Agate" Dispatches of Whitelaw Reid, 1861-1865* (2 vols.; Memphis, TN: Memphis State University Press, 1976), 2:152.

Chapter Two
A DUBIOUS START

42. "Abraham—if you go": James C. Humes, *The Wit & Wisdom of Abraham Lincoln: A Treasury of Quotations, Anecdotes, and Observations* (New York: Gramercy Books, 1996), p. 123.

42. "His melancholy dripped": William H. Herndon and Jesse W. Weik, *Herndon's Life of Lincoln*, with introduction and notes by Paul M. Angle (New York: Albert & Charles Boni, 1930), p. 473.

42. "settled form of melancholy": Ida M. Tarbell, *Abraham Lincoln and His Ancestors* (Lincoln: University of Nebraska Press, 1977), pp. 226-227. The definitive book on Lincoln's struggles with melancholy, and how he transformed that suffering into strength, wisdom and compassion, is Joshua Wolf Shenk's extraordinary work, *Lincoln's Melancholy: How Depression Challenged a President and Fueled His Greatness* (Boston: Houghton Mifflin, 2005).

43. "He who learns must suffer": *Agamemnon*, by the Greek dramatist, Aeschylus (525 B.C.—456 B.C.), as it appears translated in *Quotations For Public Speakers: A Historical, Literary, and Political Anthology*, Robert G. Torricelli, ed. (New Brunswick, NJ: Rutgers University Press, 2001), p. 134.

44. the inspirational slogan, "Victory or Death": Charles H. Coleman, *Abraham Lincoln and Coles County, Illinois* (New Brunswick, NJ: Scarecrow Press, 1955), pp. 198-199.

45. "whistle off sadness": Douglas L. Wilson and Rodney O. Davis, eds., quoting David Davis in an interview with William H. Herndon, September 20, 1866, *Herndon's Informants: Letters, Interviews, and Statements About Abraham Lincoln* (Urbana: University of Illinois Press, 1998), p. 350. Professors Wilson and Davis, as a result of this scholarly and yeoman work, have assembled a permanent and iconic research tool in Lincolniana.

45. "Ashley—I have great confidence":   James M. Ashley quoted in *Recollected Words of Abraham Lincoln*, p. 19.

46. "I leave it to my audience": Harold Holzer, " 'If I Had Another Face, Do You Think I'd Wear This One?'" *American Heritage*, No. 34 (February/March 1983), pp. 56-63. This article was adopted from a speech Holzer gave to the Abraham Lincoln Association in Springfield, Illinois. The focus is on Lincoln's penchant for getting his picture made, portrait painted and submitting to the uncomfortable ordeal of life masks. Holzer references this quote in his opening paragraph with qualifiers ("Lincoln is said to have replied . . . "), but he does not fully dismiss the account. There is no hard proof Lincoln said this during the epic Lincoln-Douglas debates, but it certainly sounds like something Lincoln would say.

46. One of the elderly ladies: Clifton Fadiman, ed., *The Little, Brown Book of Anecdotes* (Boston: Little, Brown, 1985), p. 358, Item No. 19.

46. "I have endured": Letter from Abraham Lincoln to James H. Hackett, November 2, 1863, *CWAL*, 6:559.

46-47. life expectancy . . . when Lincoln elected: For excellent research and demonstrative graphics on American life expectancies for 1850-2000, see *The Mapping History Project*, online under its title, developed by the University of Oregon, Dept. of History, James Mohr and John Nicols, editors for the American History compilation.

47. his "angel mother": Joshua F. Speed, *Reminiscences of Abraham Lincoln and Notes of a Visit to California: Two Lectures* (Louisville, KY: John P. Morton and Co., 1884), p. 19. When Lincoln, in his adult years, spoke of his biological mother Nancy Lincoln that he lost at age nine, he called her his "angel mother." This sweet moniker not only reflected the memories of maternal love and affection he had for her, but also was a way to differentiate Nancy Lincoln from his living stepmother, Sarah (Sally) Johnston Lincoln, whom he lovingly called "Mama."

47. "milk sickness": Called the "trembles" by farmers when they observed it in animals, or "tremetol vomiting" in humans, the sickness is very rare today because of modern animal husbandry practices. It is caused by the toxin "tremetol" that is in the plant known as "white snakeroot." In the nineteenth century, the horrible sickness claimed thousands of lives, particularly in geographical belt of Tennessee, Ohio, Indiana, Kentucky and Illinois. The tall, white-blooming plant was typically not found in open pastures but thrived in the woods and on riverbanks. Pioneers often let their cattle, horses and sheep (which are the most vulnerable animals) roam and graze freely, unknowingly exposing them. Not until 1928, when advances in biochemistry unlocked the mystery and identified tremetol, was the sickness significantly curtailed. Legend has it a Shawnee Indian woman, who was wise about plants and herbs, was the first to make the direct and proximate connection between the snakeroot plant and the illness. Interestingly, pasteurization of milk does not neutralize the tremetol toxin. However, the modern production method of pooling milk from multiple and diverse cattle sources does dilute and lower the tremetol risk. A good article on this subject is Walter J. Daly, " 'The Slows,' The Torment of Milk Sickness on the Midwest Frontier," *Indiana Magazine of History*, Vol. 102, No. 1, March 2006.

47. "the joy and care of her life": Caroline Hanks Hitchcock, *Nancy Hanks: The Story of Abraham Lincoln's Mother* (New York: Doubleday & McClure Co., 1900), p. 87.

47. "to be good and kind": Dennis F. Hanks in an interview with William H. Herndon, June 13, 1865, *Herndon's Informants*, p. 40.

48. cut out of green pine: John G. Nicolay and John Hay, *Abraham Lincoln: A History* (10 vols.; New York: The Century Company 1890), 1:31. This publication is available online through Project Guttenberg.

48. "All that I am": Michael Burlingame, *The Inner World of Abraham Lincoln* (Urbana and Chicago: University of Illinois Press, 1994), p. 42. Lincoln reportedly made this statement to his old law partner and friend, William H. Herndon.

48. raining on her grave: William G. Greene interview with William H. Herndon, *Herndon's Informants*, p. 21. See also William E. Barton, The *Women Lincoln Loved* (Indianapolis, IN: The Bobbs-Merrill Company, 1927), pp. 167-186.

48-49. "Eddie" . . . died: For an account of Edward Lincoln's passing, see Ruth Painter Randall, *Lincoln's Sons* (Boston: Little, Brown & Company, 1955), pp. 22-24.

49. "in such a man, in such a place": Ruth Painter Randall, *Colonel Elmer Ellsworth: A Biography of Lincoln's Friend and First Hero of the Civil War* (Boston: Little, Brown & Company, 1960), p. 262.

49. "May God give you": Letter from Abraham Lincoln to Ephraim D. and Phoebe Ellsworth, May 25, 1861, *CWAL*, 4:386.

50. "even the Heavens are hung in black": Abraham Lincoln giving a speech at the Great Central Sanitary Fair at Philadelphia, Pennsylvania, June 16, 1864, *CWAL*, 7:394.

53. "he was anxious to go [to Gettysburg]": Lloyd A. Dunlap, David C. Mearns, John R. Sellers and Douglas L. Wilson, commentators, *Long Remembered: Lincoln and his five versions of the Gettysburg Address* (Delray Beach, FL and Washington, D.C.: Levenger Press in association with the Library of Congress, 2011), p. 36, referencing as historical derivation an interview with James Speed, reprinted from *The Daily Louisville Commercial* in the *Illinois Daily State Journal* (Springfield), November 17, 1879.

Chapter Three
BOARDING PASSES INTO HISTORY

55. "Boys, you needn't be in such a hurry": Quoting James B. Fry, Allen Thordike Rice, ed., *Reminiscences of Abraham Lincoln by Distinguished Men of His Time* (New York: North American Review, 1888), p. 403.

57. "I wanted to wring their little necks": Statement of William Henry Herndon to Jesse William Weik, November 19, 1865, Herndon-Weik Collection of Lincolniana, Manuscript Division, Library of Congress.

57. "had they sh__t in Lincoln's hat": Statement of William Henry Herndon to Jesse William Weik, February 18, 1887, Herndon-Weik Collection of Lincolniana, Manuscript Division, Library of Congress.

57. the law office in Springfield: For a vivid description of the disheveled state of the Lincoln-Herndon Law Office, see the previously-referenced *Herndon's Life of Lincoln*, pp. 254-55. Being a country lawyer myself for many years before taking the bench, and hanging around rural law offices as a boy, the author can assure readers that Lincoln's and Herndon's "horizontal filing" system (that is, "sideways" filing that covers everything flat in the room), was the rule for most country lawyers, not the exception. In their defense, Lincoln and Herndon had no file cabinets. Lincoln thought the young, bright, energetic Billy Herndon would bring some organizational skills to their new law partnership. He didn't.

57. It was a plush . . . "director's car": Gabor Boritt, *The Gettysburg Gospel: The Lincoln Speech That Nobody Knows* (New York: Simon and Schuster, 2006), pp. 50-51. Professor Boritt provides a picturesque description of the luxurious coach in which the President and his entourage rode. As security and convenience for the President, the train was discharged from its regularly scheduled station stops, and given first and unconditional right of passage in its ingress-egress to and from Gettysburg.

58. "flub dubs": Benjamin Brown French, *Witness to the Young Republic, A Yankee's Journal, 1828-1870*, eds., Donald B. Cole and John J. McDonough (Hanover, NH: University Press of New England, 1989), p. 382. French would record in his diary on December 16, 1861, that President Lincoln said it would "stink in the land" if Mary overspent a $20,000 White House refurbishment appropriation while "poor freezing soldiers could not have blankets," declaring that he would never approve bills for "*flub dubs* for that damned old house!"

59. "a brainless egotistical fool": Norma B. Cuthbert, ed., *Lincoln and the Baltimore Plot, 1861: From Pinkerton Records and Related Papers* (San Marino, CA: Henry E. Huntington Library, 1949), p. xx.

59. "I regret that you do not appreciate": Edward Steers, Jr., *Blood on the Moon: The Assassination of Abraham Lincoln* (Lexington: University of Kentucky Press, 2001), p. 16.

60. "I cannot discharge my duties": Ward Hill Lamon, *Recollections of Abraham Lincoln, 1847-1865*, ed., Dorothy Lamon Teillard (Washington, D.C.: 1911), p. 266.

60. "Hereafter, when you . . . strike": Kunhardt, *A New Birth of Freedom*, pp. 45-46.

60. "He [Lincoln] has got stacks": Steers, *Blood on the Moon*, p. 16.

61. Although the details of the "Baltimore Plot": There is an excellent account of the "Baltimore Plot" written by historian Edward Steers, Jr. in his superlative book, *Blood on the Moon*, pp. 16-22. See also the previously referenced Cuthbert, *Lincoln and the Baltimore Plot*.

62. "Abe, you can't play": Cuthbert, *Lincoln and the Baltimore Plot*, p. 82.

62. "this surreptitious nocturnal dodging": Diary entry of George Templeton Strong, February 23, 1861, *The Diary of George Templeton Strong*, 3:102.

63. "Plug Uglies": The Plug Uglies were a rough and rowdy street gang, operating generally between 1854-1860, in Baltimore. The Herbert Asbury novel, *Gangs of New York* (1927) and the Martin Scorsese film of the same name (2002), have created the misconception that the Plug Uglies were located in New York City. Actually, Baltimore was their origin and home base. See the *New York (Daily) Herald*, July 6, 7, 1857, for a narrative about this gang.

64. "many an assassin's knife": Maurice Bucke, Thomas B. Harned and Horace L. Traubel, eds., *The Complete Writings of Walt Whitman* (New York: G.P. Putnam's Sons, 1902), 15: 243-244.

66. "William goes with me": Abraham Lincoln to S. Yorke, November 18, 1863, *CWAL: Supplement*, pp. 210-11. In his masterful work, *The Gettysburg Gospel*, at pp. 54, 170, Professor Boritt, in just a few succinct paragraphs, provides the most insightful picture of William H. Johnson and his special relationship with Lincoln, than we have ever had before. It is a beautiful, poignant story that has brought William Johnson out of historical obscurity. At times, writers and historians have confused William Johnson with another black servant during that same era at the White House, William Slade. Both African-American men worked for Lincoln on the White House staff, and references in diaries and memos by those around Lincoln to only "William," using the first name only, no doubt, caused the confusion. For further information about William Johnson, see "William Johnson, Lincoln's First Body Guard," in John E. Washington, *They Knew Lincoln* (New York: Dutton, 1942), pp. 127-134.

Chapter Four
THE RIDE TO GETTYSBURG

68. For most part, the Republican press: John Russell Young, *Men and Memories: Personal Reminiscences*, May Russell Young, ed. (2 vols.; New York:

Tennyson Neely, 1901; reprint by BiblioLife, LLC), 1:64. Young tells how one Democratic reporter who did not like Lincoln, making himself obnoxiously conspicuous with hat and cigar, stood near the speakers platform, "jeering now and then at the ceremonies." But apparently, not for long. The other reporters who were of Republican slant and in the clear majority at the event—to avoid any disturbance of the President's reception—took matters into their own hands and, as they tactfully put it, "adjusted that incident."

68. "Shields is a fool": "The 'Rebecca' Letter" from the "Lost Townships," *Sangamo Journal*, September 2, 1842, in *CWAL*, 1:295. The definitive analysis of these events which lead to Lincoln's "scrape" with James Shields and their near-duel with swords on the Missouri side of the Mississippi River, is found in Douglas L. Wilson's brilliant book, *Honor's Voice: The Transformation of Abraham Lincoln* (New York: Alfred A. Knopf, 1998), pp. 265-272.

69. "code duello": Ibid. See also the lively account of the Lincoln-Shields imbroglio described by James E. Myers, in *The Astonishing Saber Duel of Abraham Lincoln* (Springfield, IL: Lincoln-Herndon Building Publishers, 1968). The contest rules for the duel appear in William Henry Herndon and Jesse William Weik, *Abraham Lincoln: The True Story of a Great Life*, with Horace White introduction (2 vols.; New York: D. Appleton and Company, 1892; reprint by Nabu Public Domain), 1:239.

70. It offended him if: Justin G. Turner and Linda Levitt Turner, *Mary Todd Lincoln, Her Life and Letters* (New York: Alfred A. Knopf, 1972), p. 296-299. On one occasion during Lincoln's presidential years, when an imprudent military man mentioned the Lincoln-Shields incident, the President, mildly angry and a bit shamefaced, sternly told the officer, "I do not deny it—but if you desire my friendship, you will never mention it again." Lincoln and the First Lady had a lifetime pact between them, "never to speak, of it." This account also appears in F. B. Carpenter, *Six Months at the White House With Abraham Lincoln* (New York: Hurd and Houghton, 1869), pp. 304-305.

71. "Public opinion in this country is everything": Abraham Lincoln in a speech given in Columbus, Ohio, September 16, 1859, *CWAL*, 3:424.

72. "Father Abraham, come out": Boritt, *The Gettysburg Gospel*, p. 67. Professor Boritt brings together the scattered historical fragments of eyewitness accounts, newspaper articles and even residual oral history of the city to eloquently piece together a full tapestry of what Lincoln said, and what the atmosphere was like, during the eight minutes the President's train stopped at the Hanover, Pennsylvania station. I leaned heavily on Dr. Boritt's impeccable research, in composing my section that tells about Lincoln's Hanover stop. This account is also briefly alluded to in Kunhardt, *A New Birth of Freedom*, p. 100, where Rev. Alleman is similarly quoted, "Father Abraham, your children want to see you."

72. "Well, you have seen me": Ibid.

72. "You had the Rebels here": Ibid.

73. "Well . . . did you fight them any": Ibid.

74. group of ladies . . . to present flowers: Ibid.

74. little fella brought . . . an apple: *Philadelphia Inquirer*, November 21, 1863.

74. "Flowerth for the Prethident": Warren, *Lincoln's Gettysburg Declaration*, p. 59. See also E.W. Andrews quoted in Rice, *Reminiscences of Abraham Lincoln*, p. 511, where the child is quoted in a slight variation, "Flowrth for the President!"

74. "Papa-day": Donald, *Lincoln*, p. 428.

75. "You're a sweet little rose-bud": E.W. Andrews quoted in Rice, *Reminiscences of Abraham Lincoln*, p. 511.

75. "We are coming, Father Abraham": Words by James Sloan Gibbons, Music by Luther Orlando Emerson. The complete words of this Civil War song can be found online under its title, *We are coming Father Abraham—Poetry and Music of the War*. Another fine rendition of this song, both lyrics and music, is beautifully performed by the *97th New York Regimental String Band* on YouTube.

76. "Lorena": Marc McCutcheon, *Everyday Life in the 1800's: A Guide for Writers, Students & Historians* (Cincinnati: Writer's Digest Books, 1993), pp. 300-301.

77. Why it was when Andrew Carnegie: George S. Hellman, *Lanes of Memory* (New York: Alfred A. Knopf, Inc., 1927), pp. 125-126.

77. "The Rubber Room Phenomenon": This subject it comprehensively covered by Harold Holzer and Frank J. Williams in their fascinating book, *Lincoln's Deathbed in Art and Memory: The "Rubber Room" Phenomenon* (Gettysburg, PA: Thomas Publications, 1998).

78. "William, now how does that sound?": Kunhardt, *A New Birth of Freedom*, pp. 117-118. Philip B. Kunhardt, Jr. (1928-2006), who was a distinguished author, journalist, producer of historical docudramas and member of the family who originated the renowned Meserve Collection (now the Meserve-Kunhardt Collection) of Civil War photographic plates—as was common in the decade of his well-done book—mistakenly has William Slade in Gettysburg, not William Johnson. Johnson was likely the only African-American who made the trip with Lincoln. This is confusion understandably perpetuated, as the author has previously addressed, because both Slade and Johnson were African-American "manservants" on the White House staff, who were often referred to in historical documents only by their first name. Slade's claim of being in Gettysburg was impossible.

80. "The Perfect Tribute": Mary Raymond Shipman Andrews, *The Perfect Tribute* (New York: Scribner, 1906). The preeminent Lincoln scholar and museum curator, Dr. Louis A. Warren, was chaffed raw by the broad school readership, the image of historical accuracy, movie adaptation, and the prominent literary status enjoyed by *The Perfect Tribute.* "It is to be regretted that American Youth for over half a century," Warren wrote, "have received the impression that the finest oration in our language, was belatedly, hurriedly, and even slovenly, written on a railroad train." Hitting the beautifully-written little Andrews book even harder, Warren bluntly concluded, "The story [as told in *The Perfect Tribute*] is a travesty on how masterpieces are created." These comments appear in Warren, Lincoln's *Gettysburg Declaration,* p. 63. No Lincoln book has ever been assaulted by critics with the ferocity directed at *The Perfect Tribute.* However, it is a fond and lasting memory the author has of my third grade teacher reading this sweet, mesmerizing story about Abraham Lincoln; we just needed someone to tell us it was fiction . . . not history.

80. Robert, still believed the story: William E. Barton, *Lincoln at Gettysburg: What He Intended to Say; What He Said; What He Was Reported To Have Said; What He Wished He Had Said* (Indianapolis: Bobbs, Merrill, 1930), p. 107.

80. "in a few moments, while on the way": Harriet Beecher Stowe, *Men Of Our Times* (Hartford, CT: Hartford Publishing Company, 1868), p. 80.

81. "his high hat . . . as a makeshift desk": Quoting the observations of George D. Gitt, Rufus Rockwell Wilson, ed., *Intimate Memories of Lincoln* (Elmirg, N.Y.: Primavera Press, 1945), p. 476.

81. "no recollection seeing him [Lincoln] writing": James Barnett Fry quoted in *Reminiscences of Abraham Lincoln,* p. 403.

81. The President's trusted assistant, John G. Nicolay: John G. Nicholay, "Lincoln's Gettysburg Address," *The Century Illustrated Monthly Magazine,* XLVII, February 1894, p. 601. See also Lincoln Lore, No. 1497 (November 1957).

82. "Apparently . . . every time the President": Warren, *Lincoln's Gettysburg Declaration,* p. 71.

Chapter Five
MISGIVINGS

86. "the skinning of Thomas": Herndon, *Abraham Lincoln; The True Story,* 1:188-189. See also the previously-referenced Wilson, *Honor's Voice,* pp. 206-209.

87. "I shall do nothing in malice": Letter from Abraham Lincoln to Cuthbert Bullitt, July 28, 1862, *CWAL,* 5:346.

88. "Copperheads": A excellent examination of the scope and power, the emergence and collapse, of this virulent political faction is Jennifer L. Weber's *Copperheads: The Rise and Fall of Lincoln's Opponents in the North* (New York: Oxford University Press, 2006). James M. McPherson's epic work, *Battle Cry of Freedom: The Civil War Era* (New York: Oxford University Press, 1998), also provides valuable insight into the political activities of the Copperheads.

88. "the fire in the rear": Edward L. Pierce, *Memoir and Letters of Charles Sumner, 1860-1874* (Boston: Roberts Brothers, 1893), 4:114.

89. "the bottom is out": Frank Abial Flower, *Edwin McMasters Stanton: The Autocrat of Rebellion, Emancipation, and Reconstruction* (New York: Saalfield Publishing Company, 1905; reprint by ULAN Press), p. 179.

90. First Lady spent thousands of dollars: Regarding Mary Lincoln's purchase of four hundred pairs of gloves, see Frank Freidel and William Pencak, eds., *The White House: The First Two Hundred Years* (Boston: Northeastern University Press, 1994), p. 71. Regarding Mary Lincoln's overspending of her White House refurbishment budget, see Jean H. Baker, *Mary Todd Lincoln: A Biography* (New York: W. W. Norton, 1987), pp. 187, 191. Regarding her demand to pay for a White House dinner from the manure fund, see Martin Crawford, ed., *William Howard Russell's Civil War: Private Diary and Letters, 1861-1862* (Athens, GA: University of Georgia Press, 1992), p. 162. An outstanding contemporary work which insightfully delves into all psychological and financial aspects of Mary Lincoln's spending and budgetary woes, and brings historical balance to contemporary assessments of Mary Lincoln, is Catherine Clinton, *Mrs. Lincoln: A Life* (New York: HarperCollins Publishers, 2009). Another informative narrative of these matters can be found in Michael Burlingame, "Mary Todd Lincoln's Unethical Conduct as First Lady," found in Appendix 2, pp. 185-203. of the previously referenced *At Lincoln's Side: John Hay's Civil War Correspondence and Selected Writings.*

91. "already conquered and ruined us": Abraham Lincoln's response to a serenade, November 10, 1864, *CWAL*, 8:101. In Basler's footnotes [*CWAL*, 8:101n-102n], he quotes John Hay's *Diary*, which reveals Lincoln's growing disdain for making off-the-cuff, impromptu speeches. Lincoln had just made a speech out of a window, saying, "Not very graceful," and then added, "I am growing old enough not to care much for the manner of doing things."

91. "Mr. Lincoln is already beaten": Letter from Horace Greeley to George Opdyke, David Herbert Donald, ed., *Inside Lincoln's Cabinet: The Civil War Diaries of Salmon P. Chase* (New York: Longmans, Green, 1954), p. 238.

91. "You think I don't know": Jessie Ames Marshal, ed., *Private and Official Correspondence of Gen. Benjamin F. Butler* (Norwood, M.A.: Plimpton Press, 1917), 5:35.

91. "It will be an interesting ceremony": Letter from Abraham Lincoln to Stephen T. Logan, November 9, 1863, *CWAL*, 7:7.

92. "The proposition to ask": Clark E. Carr, *Lincoln At Gettysburg* (Chicago: R.R. Donelley & Sons Company, 1906), p. 21. One of the author's treasured books is a Fourth Edition of this book (1909), beautifully clothbound, which was presented as a souvenir for a banquet held on November 19, 1913, at the Hamilton Club of Chicago, in honor of the 50th Anniversary of Lincoln's Gettysburg Address. This 4-1/2 x 7-1/2 inch book contains a fold-out facsimile of the Nicolay Copy (First Draft) of the Gettysburg Address, deeply-textured lithograph photos of Everett, Meade and Seward, and a fold-out facsimile of the Gettysburg Cemetery map prepared by William Saunders. Carr was present at this event, and signed the book "Clark E. Carr, the author." Carr's signature and handwriting is beautiful and muscular, reminiscent of Lincoln's.

93. "it did not seem to occur": Ibid., pp. 21-22.

93. "there was immediate and vigorous objection": Warren, *Lincoln's Gettysburg Declaration*, p. 43.

94. "Howdy": Emanuel Hertz, ed., *The Hidden Lincoln: From the Letters and Papers of William H. Herndon* (New York: Viking Press, Inc., 1938), p. 414.

94. "Mr. Cheerman": Charles Bracelen Flood, 1864: *Lincoln at the Gates of History* (New York: Simon & Schuster, 2009), p. 2.

95. As the slanderous story went: There is an excellent and comprehensive account in Warren, *Lincoln Lore*, No. 230, "The Antietam Song-Singing," September 4, 1933. The article states that the ugly story ran in the *New York World*, on a daily basis, for three months, and was widely circulated by General McClellan's friends, reaching its peak when Lincoln was nominated for re-election.

95. "Abe may crack his jolly jokes": Kunhardt, *A New Birth of Freedom*, p. 37.

96. The truth was: Lincoln Lore, No. 230.

96. "finally yielded to my demands": Warren, *Lincoln's Gettysburg Declaration*, p. 43.

97. "set apart these grounds": For the full text of Wills invitation, see Warren, *Lincoln's Gettysburg Declaration*, pp. 45-46. For a full-color facsimile of the original Wills manuscript, printed in its actual size, see the previously referenced *Long Remembered*, pp. 11-14, which is a unique, beautifully-done publication, rich in scholarship and commentary by distinguished Lincoln historians.

97. "a few appropriate remarks": Ibid., p. 45.

97. "a confidence that they who sleep": Ibid.

Chapter Six
THE BIRTH OF A SPEECH; A DECLARATION, REBORN

99. he had half of his first draft: *New York Times*, April 20, 1887.

99. "ancient faith": Abraham Lincoln giving a speech in Peoria, Illinois, October 16, 1854, *CWAL*, 2:276.

100. "Would rather be assassinated": Abraham Lincoln giving a speech in Independence Hall at Philadelphia, Pennsylvania, February 22, 1861, *CWAL*, 4:240.

100. "It was that which gave promise": Ibid.

100. "This is the sentiment": Ibid.

100. "I do most sincerely": Abraham Lincoln giving a response to a serenade,

July 7, 1863, *CWAL*, 6:319.

101. "How long ago is it": Ibid.

101. "an effort to overthrow": Ibid., 6:320.

102. immigrants . . . "cannot carry themselves back": Abraham Lincoln giving a speech at Chicago, Illinois, July 10, 1858, *CWAL*, 2:499-500.

103. "a self-evident lie": *CWAL*, 2:275.

103. "Near eighty years ago": Ibid.

103. "Let us re-adopt": Ibid., p. 276.

103. "I have never had a feeling": *CWAL*, 4:240.

104 " monstrous injustice": *CWAL*, 2:255.

104. "As I would not be a slave": Abraham Lincoln in a writing, speculated to be dated August 1, 1858, *CWAL*, 2:532.

104. "naturally anti-slavery": Letter from Abraham Lincoln to Albert G. Hodges, April 4, 1864, *CWAL*, 7:281.

105. "I . . . am in favor of the race": *CWAL*, 3:16. This is part of Lincoln's reply to Stephen A. Douglas, in their First Debate of the Lincoln-Douglas Debates held on August 21, 1858, in Ottawa, Illinois.

106. "I have no purpose": Ibid.

106. "Negro [should be] entitled to all of the natural rights": Ibid.

107. "nothing but a goddern": Kunhardt, *Lincoln: An Illustrated Biography*, p. 19.

108. between the seventy-two years: See the interview with James Oliver Horton on the *PBS Newshour* originally broadcast on January 25, 2007, appearing online under the caption of "Exhibit Reveals History of Slavery in New York City," at www.pbs.org/newshour.

109. not "interfere with the institution slavery": Abraham Lincoln's "First Inaugural Address—Final Text," March 4, 1861, *CWAL*, 4: 263.

109. "I would save the Union": Letter from Abraham Lincoln to Horace Greeley, August 22, 1862, *CWAL*, 5:388.

110. "By giving away six points": Quoting Leonard Swett in a statement to William H. Herndon, appearing in William H. Herndon and Jesse William Weik, A.M.: *An Illustrated Herndon's Lincoln: The True Story of a Great Life* (2 vols.; Chicago: Bedford, Clarke & Company, 1889), 2:334.

111. not Don Quixote: No matter what position Lincoln took, he always had plenty of critics. Often, those criticisms were in the form of cartoons savagely lampooning the President. One political cartoonist who felt Lincoln was over-ly idealistic, actually portrayed Lincoln as Don Quixote on his horse, with General Benjamin Butler caricatured in the role of his sidekick, Sancho Panza. This editorial cartoon can be seen in Keith W. Jennison, *The Humorous Mr. Lincoln* (New York: Bonanza Books, 1965), p. 89.

113. "a reverence for the Constitution": Abraham Lincoln in an Address given before the Young Men's Lyceum at Springfield, Illinois, January 27, 1838, *CWAL* 1:15.

114. "I WILL BE HEARD": William Lloyd Garrison, an article "To the Public," printed in the first edition of *The Liberator* (No. 1), January 1, 1831.

115. "a covenant with death": William Lloyd Garrison is quoted in James Brewer Stewart, "William Lloyd Garrison and the Challenge of Emancipation," as it appears in the *American Biographical History Series* (Arlington Heights, IL: Harlan Davidson, 1992), p. 164. Garrison remains an enigmatic historical figure. He has been portrayed both as a front-line, selfless, take-no-prisoners warrior in the fight to abolish slavery, and also as self-promoting, power-hungry journalist who was more interested in fame and agitating the planter class than the cause of black emancipation. Over time, shifts in the assessment of Garrison have become increasingly more hostile. An excellent first-foray into the historiography of abolitionism is Harry L. Watson, *Liberty and Power: The Politics of Jacksonian America* (1990).

115. "I think to lose Kentucky": Letter from Abraham Lincoln to Orville H. Browning, September 22, 1861, *CWAL*, 4:532.

116. black people at hotels: *New York Times*, November 20, 1863.

116. For every black soldier: See the American Experience pbs.org website, appearing online under the general article heading of "The Civil War By the Numbers."

117. "There may be times": See the Nobel Lecture of Elie Wiesel titled *Hope, Despair and Memory*, given on December 11, 1986 at the Nobel Peace Prize Award Ceremony, as it appears online @ http://www.nobelprize.org/nobel-prizes/peace/laureates/1986/wiesel-lecture.html.

117. "the Gorilla": Stephen W. Sears, ed., *The Civil War Papers of George B. McClellan: Selected Correspondence, 1860-1865* (New York: Ticknor and Fields, 1989), p. 515.

119. "there is a moral fitness": Abraham Lincoln giving an eulogy for Henry Clay, July 6, 1852, *CWAL*, 2:132.69. "I strongly favor colonization,": Abraham Lincoln would proclaim in his annual Message to Congress, December 1, 1862, *CWAL*, 5:534.

120. Frederick Douglass . . . invited to White House: When Douglass first arrived at the White House, he was initially blocked by two officers, who told him they could not admit anyone "of color." Eventually, Douglass made it to the East Room, where President Lincoln called out in a loud voice, "Here comes my friend Douglass." They warmly shook hands, with Lincoln telling Douglass "I am glad to see you." Lincoln then asked Douglass, "How did you like [my inaugural address]?," going on to say, "there is no man in the country whose opinion I value more than yours." Douglass replied, "Mr. Lincoln, that was a sacred effort." For a full picture of Douglass's White House visit, reference Frederick Douglass, *The Life and Times of Frederick Douglass, Written By Himself* (Hartford: Park Publishing Co., 1882), pp. 402, 784-786; see also Philip S. Foner, *Frederick Douglass* (New York: Citadel Press, 1950; reprinted

1964), p. 216; and further, the previously-referenced Rice, *Reminiscences of Abraham Lincoln*, in Section 15, "Lincoln and the Colored Troops."

120. Africans were brought to Jamestown . . . 1619: An insightful work on this subject is Carl Schneider and Dorothy Schneider, *Slavery in America* (New York: Infobase Publishing, 2007).

120. "I am glad the President": John Jay, diary entry of July 1, 1864, Dennet, *Hay Diaries*, p. 203.

121. It was "compensated emancipation": See Steers, *Blood on the Moon*, pp. 39-41, providing excellent insight into this subject.

121. "think anew, and act anew": *CWAL*, 5:537.

121. I shall try to correct errors: Letter from Abraham Lincoln to Horace Greeley, August 22, 1862, *CWAL*, 5:389.

123. "the father of moral all principle": Abraham Lincoln in a speech given at Chicago, Illinois, July 10, 1858, *CWAL*, 2:499.

123. Dred Scott v. Sandford, 60 U.S. 393 (How.), a decision rendered by the U.S. Supreme Court in the December term of 1856, can be found online in its entirety at http://laws.findlaw.com/us/60/393.html. The Dred Scott case was not only a highly-charged, divisive experience for the nation, but also involved a complicated set of facts and entanglement of state and federal laws, stretching the litigation out for more than a decade before it was finally decided by the U.S. Supreme Court on March 6, 1857. Dred Scott was a slave living in the slave state of Missouri. His master, an army physician named John Emerson, took Scott with him for extended stays into the free state of Illinois and the free Wisconsin Territory (future Minnesota), where slavery was prohibited. Those free territories recognized the doctrine "once free, always free," meaning once a slave stayed for extended time in a free territory, they could be declared permanently free. While in these free territories, Dred Scott and his wife could have, but never ran away to freedom, instead choosing to stay loyal to their owners. Eventually, the Dred Scott family, still living under slave conditions, was moved back to the slave state of Missouri, and the brother-in-law of Dr. John Emerson (Dred Scott's original slaveowner, who had died), a man named John Sanford, took over the family's legal affairs, which is why his name is on the case style. Sanford coldly refused to let Dred Scott's family have or buy their freedom, claiming they had to remain slaves because they were now living back in a slave state. Thus, the case was filed on behalf of Dred Scott for his freedom. In a 7-2 decision, that was destructively panoramic in its scope and hard to fathom today, the U.S. Supreme Court determined that black people were never intended to be citizens of America under the U.S. Constitution, and thus, Dred Scott had no right to even bring his case to court (that is, he had "no standing" to sue his slaveowners). Chief Justice Roger Taney extended his cruel ruling even further, declaring that the Declaration of Independence and Constitution did not apply to the black race, and that Congress did not have the authority to pass laws that prohibited slavery in any of the states, because African-Americans were only property rights, that could be moved around the country with their owners, without interference from state or federal law. The highest court in the nation, in one breathtaking decision, had turned America into a lawful slavocracy. This was, undoubtedly, the worst decision in the history of the U.S. Supreme Court. The definitive work on this subject is Don E. Fehrenbacher, *The Dred Scott Case: Its Significance in American Law and Politics* (New York: Oxford University Press, 1978).

124. "Negroes had no rights": Ibid.

125. "If slavery is not wrong": Letter from Abraham Lincoln to Albert G. Hodges, April 4, 1864, *CWAL*, 7:281. Oxford University historian Richard Carwardine in his Lincoln Prize book, *Lincoln: A Life of Purpose and Power* (New York: Alfred A. Knopf, 2006), pp. 32, 329 (Note No. 46), insightfully writes that this Lincoln statement may have been influenced by Rev. Leonard Bacon, a Congregationalist pastor, whose uncle was a teacher in Springfield, Illinois and who once wrote: "If those laws of the southern states, by virtue of which slavery exists there, and is what it is, are not wrong—nothing is wrong."

126. "That is the last speech": John Wilkes Booth quoted in William Hanchett, *The Lincoln Murder Conspiracies* (Urbana, IL: The University of Illinois Press, 1983), p. 37. This was the statement of Booth to a Confederate soldier Lewis Powell (a/k/a Lewis Paine), as they listened to President Lincoln make a speech on April 11, 1865 from his second floor window of the White House, announcing the end of the War, to an exuberant crowd of thousands that had gathered there. Lincoln had just publicly expressed his hope for black suffrage, which triggered Booth's murderous comment. Booth was so angry ("that means ni _ _ er citizenship," he growled), he demanded Powell shoot Lincoln right there and then, in full public view. Three days later, Booth would do it himself, at Ford's Theatre.

Chapter Seven
WHY, GETTYSBURG

127. shortfall of gravediggers: It is a sort of quirky and remote causal connection, that has undoubtedly passed through the mind of every Lincoln historian. However, credit should be given to James C. Humes, a prominent speechwriter for several presidents, for being perhaps the first to plainly state that the overwhelming crisis at Gettysburg in dealing with thousands of unburied soldier corpses—that is, the "lack of gravediggers"—was the catalyst which put into motion the chain-of-events that eventually led to Lincoln's Gettysburg Address. Obviously the historical fortuity of Lincoln's speech at Gettysburg is the complex concursion of many human forces, but it all started on July 4, 1863 when there were too many bodies for the little town to bury.

See Humes's brief narrative captioned "Grave Diggers" in the previously referenced *The Wit & Wisdom of Abraham Lincoln*, p. 119.

128. "To all Citizens, Men, Horses and Wagons": (Gettysburg) *Star and Banner*, July 9, 1863.

129. "Every name . . . is a lightening stroke": (Gettysburg) *Compiler*, July 7, 1863.

129. Union Sergeant Charles Blanchard: Charles H. Blanchard, from his recollections of service in the 111th Pennsylvania Volunteers, as archived with the Erie County Historical Society in Erie, Pennsylvania.

129. "you could feel the body": The Journal of John Blair Linn, from his "Journal of My trip to the Battlefield at Gettysburg, July 6 & 7, 1863" [unpublished account] copy, GNMP.

130. "lying on their backs": Daniel A. Skelly, *A Boy's Experience During the Battles of Gettysburg* (Gettysburg, PA: privately printed, 1932), p. 22.

130. "vast bone yard": Boritt, *The Gettysburg Gospel*, p. 46.

130. "I fear we shall be visited by pestilence ": Ibid., p. 7, referencing as historical derivation Sarah M. Broadhead, *The Diary of Lady of Gettysburg, Pennsylvania from June 15 to July 15, 1863* (n.p., [1864], July 11, 1863), p. 22.

130. William T. Livermore: Letter from William T. Livermore of the 20th Maine Infantry to his brother, Charles Livermore, July 6, 1863, captioned" "camp in the field near Gettysburg Penna," archived with the GNMP Library.

131. "The terrible smell": Diary entry of Mary Elizabeth Montforth, July 4, 1863, in Lester Trauch, "How a Twelve-Year-Old Girl Saw Gettysburg," *Doylestown* (PA) *Daily Intelligencer* (May 30, 1959), copy, ACHS.

131. "festering corpses at every step": J. Howard Wert, *A Complete Hand-Book of the Monuments and Indications and Guide to the Positions on the Gettysburg Battlefield* (Harrisburg, PA: R.M. Sturgeon & Co., 1886, 2010), hereafter the *Wert Monument Book*, p. 109; this book is available online at Google Books. See also J. Howard Wert, "Twas Fifty Years Ago," *Harrisburg Telegraph* No. 13 (published June-December 1913), hereafter the *Wert Telegraph Article*.

131. Heavy rains: *Wert Monument Book*, p. 109.

80. no song birds could be heard: Jennie Smyth Croll, ed., "Days of Dread," Philadelphia *Weekly Press*, November 16, 1887.

133. "God pity us!": Letter from Nurse Harris to her husband, July 9, 1863, *Fifth Semi-Annual Report of the Ladies' Aid Society of Philadelphia with Letters and Extracts From Letters from the Secretary of the Society, written from Various Places While attending to the Sick and Wounded of the Union Army* (Philadelphia: Sherman, 1863; reprint Cornell University Library), hereafter the *LAS Letters*, p. 13.

133. "The site of the greatest": Boritt, *The Gettysburg Gospel*, p. 3 [Preface].

133. And how was the ominous lit? J. David Petruzzi, "The Battle of Gettysburg: Who Really Fired the First Shot?," *American Civil War Magazine* (July 2006).

135. "When This Cruel War Is Over": This seductively sad song (it was also known as "Weeping Sad and Lonely") was one of the most popular of the Civil War. Music was by Henry Tucker, Words by Charles Carroll Sawyer. By the end of the war, an estimated million copies of the sheet music had been sold. The lyrics are available, along with the music, online under its title.

135. "white trash": In September 1861, Senator Benjamin F. Wade, angry over Lincoln's position on the Fre'mont proclamation, told Zachariah Chandler that it was the President's "poor white trash" upbringing that was to blame for Lincoln's decision. It was, and still is, most often used as a disparaging slang term for poor, white Southerners, that has dug itself into the American lexicon like a Tennessee tick.

135-36. "Those above in the barn": (Gettysburg) *Compiler*, March 15, 1887.

136. "by any thing short of arch-angels": William Quentin Maxwell, *Lincoln's Fifth Wheel: The Political History of the United States Sanitary Commission* (New York: Longmans, Green & Co. 1956), p. 211.

137. "The thick foliage caused dark shadows": Charles H. Weygant, *History of the One Hundred and Twenty-Fourth Regiment, N.Y.S.V.* (Newburgh, NY: Journal Printing House, 1877; reprint by Manu Public Domain), pp. 182-185.

138. "for seven days, it literally ran blood": Kunhardt, *A New Birth of Freedom*, p. 9.

138. "The amputation-table is plainly in view": Boritt, *The Gettysburg Gospel*, p. 16, referencing as historical derivation various letters from Emily Souder to family and friends, containing her observations about the gruesome amputation process.

138. a father and his son lying side by side: Ibid., p. 13.

138. "Too horrible to describe": Fannie J. Buehler; *Recollections of the Rebel Invasion and One Women's Experience During the battle of Gettysburg* (Gettysburg, PA: Star and Sentinel Printing, 1896; reprint by Gary T. Hawbaker), p. 26.

138. "the Regimental Bands": Ibid.

138. the town "was filled up every day": Skelly, *A Boy's Experience*, p. 23.

139. "A word of well meant advice": *Philadelphia Public Ledger*, July 15, 1863.

139. "one vast hospital": Ibid.

139. "great fluttering pairs": Boritt, *The Gettysburg Gospel*, p. 180 (+), quoting from the second page (following p. 180) of the glossy photograph section of the book, captioned under a photograph titled as THE HOSPITAL.

140. "The dead lay all about": John W. (John Whiting) Storrs, *The Twentieth Connecticut, A Regimental History* (Naugatuck, CT: Press of the "Naugatuck Valley Sentinel," 1886; reprint, HardPress Publishing), p. 102.

140. "The sights and smells": Robert Stiles, Major, Army of Northern Virginia, *Four Years Under Marse Robert* (New York: The Neal Publishing Company, 1903; reprint, R. Bemis Publishing, Ltd., 1995), pp. 219-220.

141. "The ground was still marked": Alfred B. McCalmont, *Extracts From*

Letters Written By Alfred B. McCalmont, 1862-1865: From the Front During the War of Rebellion (Franklin, PA: private printing by Robert McCalmont, 1908; reprint, Metalmark Books), p. 47.

142. the "Plum Run" stream: *Wert Monument Book*, p. 109, and *Wert Telegraph Article*. This stream, after the Battle of Gettysburg, got the name of the "Bloody Run" stream; see also N.A. Meligakes, *The Spirit of Gettysburg* (Gettysburg, PA: Times and News Publishing, 1950), p. 68. Interestingly, this author granted standing permission for excerpts from his book to be freely used "if the purpose or objective is to further Democracy and Freedom, and credit is acknowledged." Thus, it is.

142. "magnified the surrounding horrors": John L. Smith, compiler, *History of the Corn Exchange Regiment, 118th Pennsylvania Volunteers, From their First Engagement at Antietam to Appomattox* (Philadelphia, PA: J.L. Smith, 1888), p. 257.

142. One Union soldier . . . x-rated horror: Leander H. Warren, *My Recollections of What I Saw Before, During and After the Battle of Gettysburg, July 1st, 2nd and 3rd, 1863* (unpublished account, 1926), p. 12, copy, ACHS. See also the *Wert Monument Book*, p. 163.

144. "In many instances arms and legs": Letter from David Wills to Governor Andrew G. Curtin, July 24, 1863, *Pennsylvania State Archives*, Harrisburg, PA.

145. "Felt the need for artful words": Garry Wills, *Lincoln at Gettysburg: The Words That Remade America* (New York: Simon and Schuster, 1992), p. 23.

146. Out of the thirty-four bids: See the "Report of David Wills", March 21, 1864, from the *Revised Report of the Select Committee Relative to the Soldiers' National Cemetery, Together with the Accompanying Documents, as Reported to the House of Representatives of the Commonwealth of Pennsylvania, March 31, 1864* (Harrisburg: PA: Singerly & Myers, State Printers, 1865; reprint from the collection of the University of Michigan Library), hereafter the *SNC Report*, p. 8.

146. Wills . . . employed Samuel Weaver: Ibid.

146. "I saw every body taken out: See the "Report of Samuel Weaver," March 19, 1864, *SNC Report*, p. 151.

147. "It may be asked how": Ibid., p. 151.

149. Weaver firmly believed: Ibid., Weaver confidently reported "I firmly believe that there has not been a single mistake made in the removal of the soldiers to the Cemetery by taking the body of a rebel for a Union soldier." Despite Weaver's and his worker's yeoman efforts in this gruesome process, undoubtedly, bodies of Union and Confederate soldiers were inadvertently commingled in the cemetery. Over time, this seems more comforting, than disturbing; first and foremost, they were all Americans.

149. "It is the grounds": See the "Correspondence of David Wills," August 17, 1863, *SNC Report*, p. 166.

150. "the idea of death": Lydia Marie Child, *The Mother's Book* (Boston:

Carter, Hendee and Babcock, 1831; reprinted Pierides Press, 2006), pp 80, 81.
151. "The prevailing expression": See the "Remarks of William Saunders," [undated manuscript], *SNC Report*, p. 148.
153. 3,512 Union soldiers: See the "Report of Samuel Weaver," March 19, 1864, *SNC Report*, p. 149.

Chapter Eight
LINCOLN ARRIVES IN GETTYSBURG

156. "a very imposing and solemnly impressive": Letter from David Wills to Abraham Lincoln, November 2, 1863, from the Robert Todd Lincoln collection of the Abraham Lincoln Papers, Library of Congress, Vol. 130, f.27783. A color, full-sized facsimile of this historic letter can be seen in the previously referenced Dunlap, *Long Remembered*, pp. 11-14.
158. "a continual torment to me:" Letter from Abraham Lincoln to Joshua F. Speed, August 24, 1855, *CWAL*, 2:320.
158. Wills, Everett and General Darius Couch: *The Philadelphia Inquirer*, November 21, 1863.
159. "fill the measure of public expectation": Lamon, *Recollections of Abraham Lincoln*, pp. 172-179.
159. Moonlight was beginning to shimmer: *The Philadelphia Inquirer*, November 21, 1863.

Chapter Nine
THE PRESIDENT BECOMES A HOUSE GUEST

162. Lincoln "became invisible": John Russell Young, *Men and Memories: Personal Reminiscences*, ed., May D. Russell Young (2 vols.; New York: F. Tennyson Neely, 1901 reprint by BibiloLife, LLC), 1:59.
162. "could not be enticed": Ibid.
162. "in gentlemanly appearance . . . peer of any man": (Springfield) *Illinois Daily State Journal*, November 30, 1864. See also Edward Everett, *Orations and Speeches on Various Occasions* (4 vols.; Boston: Charles C. Little & James Brown, 1850), 4:744.
162. Lincoln "would listen to everybody": Letter from Leonard Swett to William H. Herndon, January 17, 1866, *Herndon's Informants*, p. 167.
163. Hurrah for "Old Abe": J. Howard Wert, "Lincoln at Gettysburg," The (Harrisburg) Patriot, February 12, 13, 1909, copy, ACHS. See also *New York Times*, November 21, 1863.
163. "Nothing would do": Rev. Dr. Henry C. Holloway, "Lincoln at Gettysburg," *The* (Gettysburg) *Compiler*, November 21, 1914, copy, ACHS.
163. "Never did a mortal": Wert, "Lincoln at Gettysburg."

163. **"Thank you for this compliment"**: Abraham Lincoln in remarks he made to the citizens of Gettysburg, Pennsylvania, November 18, 1863, in *CWAL*, 7:16-17. See also Boritt, *The Gettysburg Gospel*, p. 74, in which Professor Boritt provides an interesting alternate version of these serenaded remarks Lincoln made on November 18th, in front of the Wills House. In his informative End Notes (p. 317), Boritt explains the confluence of various newspaper sources that he used to reconstruct the account in his book, which concludes with the President saying, "I must beg you from saying . . . one word." It is impossible to know exactly what Lincoln said that night, although both accounts are consistent in describing the atmosphere and repartee of the event.

164. **"for several substantial reasons"**: *CWAL*, Ibid.

164. **"In my position"**: Ibid.

164. **"Believing that is my present condition"**: Ibid.

164. **catawamptiously chawed up**: McCutcheon, *Everyday Life in the 1800's*, p. 9.

164. **physical description of W.H. Seward:** Frederic Bancroft, *The Life of William H. Seward* (2 vols.; New York: Harper & Brothers, 1900), 1.184.

165. **"treason that is without justification"**: *SNC Report*, p. 174.

165. **"the purest, the best, the wisest"**: Ibid.

165. **"the richest, the broadest, the most beautiful"**: Ibid.

165. **"Seldom, if ever, met with a man"**: Diary entry of Benjamin B. French, November 22, 1863, Benjamin Brown French, *Witness to a Young Republic*, p. 434.

166. **Seward's "conversation, no matter . . . what subject"**: Ibid.

166. **"Bewildering the night"**: Young, *Men and Memories*, 1:59.

167. **"The fear of having"**: *Edward Everett Diary*, entry in his diary, November 18, 1863. Most of the Edward Everett papers are archived at the Massachusetts Historical Society in Boston, where they are available by microfilm (microfilm call no. P-349, 54 reels). The Edward Everett papers include a treasure trove of other incredible American manuscripts beyond his own compilations, including correspondence and letters of Daniel Webster, George Washington, John Adams and John Quincy Adams. Reel no. 18 contains documents connected with Everett's time in Gettysburg.

167. **The entire cast of twelve singers:** Reference the "Reminiscences" of Kate McCreary, November 19, 1914, in the "Lincoln-Burns Event," *The Gettysburg Times Commemorative Edition* issued November 19, 1963, Lincoln's Farewell Address, copy, ACHS.

168. **"There was so many people"**: Letter from Susan Holabaugh White to her husband, Alonzo V. White, November 20, 1863, copy, ACHS.

168. **"The President appeared at the door"**: Dennett, *Hay Diaries*, p.120.

Chapter Ten
THE NIGHT BEFORE

170. "People from all parts of the country": *New York Times*, November 19, 1863.

173. "The tranquility of the little town": Emily B. Souder to her cousin, November 20, 1863, Mrs. Edmund A. Souder, *Leaves from the Battle-field of Gettysburg. A Series of Letters from a Field Hospital and National Poems* (Philadelphia, PA: Caxton Press of C. Sherman, Son & Co., 1864), p. 137.

106. Sergeant Bigham would maintain: For a detailed account of Sergeant Hugh Paxton Bigham's observations and experiences during Lincoln's stay in Gettysburg, see "Great-Uncle of Attorney Bigham Was Lincoln Guard When President Was a Guest at Home of Judge David Wills," *The Gettysburg Times Commemorative Edition*, November 19, 1963, Lincoln's Farewell Address, Section 15. See also the Kunhardt, *A New Birth of Freedom*, pp. 117-121 (which refers to Sergeant "Bingham").

173. "with paper, prepared to write": Orton H. Carmichael, *Lincoln's Gettysburg Address* (New York: The Abingdon Press, 1917); the photograph located between pp. 86 and 87. This is a photograph of the actual David Wills typed and autographed statement describing some of the events in his home involving President Lincoln, occurring on November 18th and 19th, 1863.

173. "just seated himself to put upon paper": Ibid.

173. "What was expected of him": Ibid.

173. a "full talk" with President Lincoln: Ibid.

174. "Very large yellow envelope": This is an account based upon a May 1885 conversation between Andrew G. Curtin and Horatio King in Gettysburg, as published in *The Washington Critic* on February 18, 1888. This historical reference is provided in the End Notes (p. 116, n. 55) of Dunlap, *Long Remembered*.

174. Lincoln and Seward spent: Diary entry of Benjamin B. French, November 22, 1863, *Witness to a Young Republic*, p. 434.

174. "As they sat together by the fireside": Seward, *Seward at Washington . . . 1861-1872*, p. 197.

176. "No one but Abraham Lincoln": John M. Taylor, *William Henry Seward, Lincoln's Right Hand* (New York: HarperCollins, 1991), p. 224.

177. "like Egyptian locusts": Letter from John Nicolay to Therena Bates, March 5, 1865, John G. Nicolay, *With Lincoln in the White House: Letters, Memoranda and Other Writings of John G. Nicolay, 1860-1865*, Michael Burlingame, ed. (Carbondale: Southern Illinois University Press, 2000), p. 175.

178. "hanging himself": See the notes following Lincoln's meditation on the Divine Will, September 2, 1862 [?], *CWAL*, 5:404n.

178. "There are too many pigs": Kunhardt, *A New Birth of Freedom*, p. 63.

178. "public-opinion baths": Statement of Charles G. Halpine, Fehrenbacher, *Recollected Words*, p. 194.

179. "I can't speak tonight, gentlemen": Kunhardt, *A New Birth of Freedom*, p. 120-121.

179. "The way was very dark": Letter of Hugh Paxton Bigham to Charles M. McCurdy, January 14, 1922, Charles M. McCurdy, *Gettysburg: A Memoir* (Pittsburgh, PA: Reed and Witting Company, 1929; reprint by Retro Books, 2013). This book was first presented at an event held in 1929 at the Soldier's National Cemetery. Charles M. McCurdy, then 76 years old, attended. First edition prints of his recollection manuscript are extraordinarily rare, because none have been printed since 1929.

179. "You clear the way": Ibid.

179. "the paper on which he had written his speech": Carmichael, *Lincoln's Gettysburg Address*, photo between pp. 86-87. Because of the small size of this book (5-1/2 in. x 7 in.), magnification is very helpful, if not essential, in reading the facsimile of the Wills manuscript. See also *Lincoln Lore* No. 1437 (November 1957).

113. "the doll Jack is hereby pardoned": Randall, *Lincoln's Sons*, p. 88.

Chapter Eleven
A GLORIOUS MORNING USHERS IN THE SPEECH

182. "It was one of those": Henry Eyster Jacobs, "Gettysburg Fifty Years Ago," *The Lutheran*, August 7, 1913, copy, ACHS.

183. Afterwards, President Lincoln: The President and Seward's carriage ride into the battlefields is described in the *Washington Daily Chronicle*, November 21, 1863. These men enjoyed each others company because they could, as peers, talk freely about many things, other than the War. Mary Lincoln resented Seward for this, partly because of lingering hard feelings over Seward opposing Lincoln for the 1860 Republican nomination, and perhaps because she saw their closeness encroaching upon her self-perceived role as Lincoln's chief confidant.

184. President Lincoln "took much interest in it": In *William Saunders Journal (1898-1999)*, which is available via microfilm copy examination at the Library of Congress Manuscript Division, and photocopy at the U.S. Department of Agriculture National Library in Washington, D.C., Saunders gives this account of his interactions with President Lincoln about the Soldiers' National Cemetery.

184. the President was "much pleased": Ibid.

186. there were the morbid remnants: For a vivid description of the battlefields as littered with the remains of human warfare, see the previously referenced Warren, *Lincoln's Gettysburg Declaration*, p. 133, derived from an article in the *Adams Sentinel* (Gettysburg). In February 1864, only seven months after the Battle of Gettysburg, the *Adams Sentinel* would report that 2800 musket rifles had been retrieved from the battlefields since combat ceased on July 4, 1863.

188. "like a drop of quicksilver": Diary entry of John Hay, November 20, 1863, Dennet, *Hay Diaries*, p. 119.

188. "in his pocket": Dunlap, *Long Remembered*, p. 41. See also *Lincoln Lore*, No. 1437 (November 1957).

188. "in Mr. Wills house": Ibid.

188. "I was with him [Lincoln] at the time": Ibid.

188. "he took what he had written": Ibid.

188. "to wait a few minutes [outside the door]": Carmichael, *Lincoln's Gettysburg Address*, pp. 87-88.

189. "had several sheets of note paper": Ibid.

189. "he folded them all together": Ibid.

191. "was a clear autumn day": Emily B. Souder to her cousin, September 20, 1863, *Leaves from the Battle-field*, p. 23.

Chapter Twelve
CORTEGE TO THE SOLDIERS' CEMETERY

192. "The hum of life was everywhere": Wert, *"Lincoln of Gettysburg."*

193. "pacing back and forth": Mrs. Jacob A. Clutz [as a child, known as "Liberty Augusta Hollinger"], *Some Personal Recollections of the Battle of Gettysburg* (Gettysburg, PA: 1925), p. 19, copy, ACHS, p. 19.

193. "A hush stole over the girls": Ibid.

193. "apparently engaged in deep thought": Ibid.

193. "inexpressible sadness of his face": Ibid.

193. "was to stand by the officers of the army": *Pittsburgh Daily Commercial*, November 23, 1863.

194. They cheered, applauded and hurrahed: *Washington Daily Morning Chronicle*, November 21, 1863.

194. "as he was about to start down": W.C. Storrick, "When I Saw and Heard Mr. Lincoln," (unpublished, August 11, 1939), copy, GNMP.

194. "he was the tallest man": Ibid.

194. "I had the honor": Ibid.

195. "Such homage I never saw": *Josephine Roedel Diary*, November 19, 1863, Library of Congress.

195. "Every available spot": (Gettysburg) *Adams Sentinel*, November 24, 1863.

195 chestnut horse: Sandburg, *Abraham Lincoln: TPY & TWY*, p. 443.

196. "If there had been an accident": Jacobs, "Gettysburg Fifty Years Ago."

197. During this organized mayhem, a telegram: Kunhardt, *A New Birth of Freedom*, p. 159.

197. "pranced about in time to the music": Clutz, *Some Personal Reflections*, p. 22.

198. "the President's face looked "lined and sad": Daniel Alexander Skelly, *A Boy's Experiences During the Battles of Gettysburg* (Gettysburg, PA: privately published, 1932; reprint by Gary T. Hawbaker), p. 27.

198. "He seemed like the "chief mourner": Warren, *Lincoln's Gettysburg Declaration*, p. 83.

198. "waves of warm, loud cheers": Wert, "Lincoln at Gettysburg."

198. "illuminated with smiles": Ibid.

198. "his heart was touched": Ibid.

198. "He looked rather odd": Annie M. Skelly (unpublished account, December 8, 1941), copy, ACHS.

199. "I must do the President justice": *Boston Journal*, November 20, 1863.

199. Seward . . . unaware that his pants: Marine lieutenant Henry Clay Cochrane quoted in Doris Kearns Goodwin's monumental Lincoln book, *Team of Rivals: The Political Genius of Abraham Lincoln* (New York: Simon & Schuster, 2005), p. 585.

199. "the mass of people who passed through": Josephine Forney Roedel, "Diary Related Dedication of Cemetery Here," *The Gettysburg Times*, November 14, 1946, copy, ACHS.

199. "long before the hour": Michael Colver, "Reminiscences of the Battle of Gettysburg," *The Spectrum* (Pennsylvania College Yearbook, 1902), p. 181.

200. "Saw the President": Diary entry of Salome (Sallie) Myers, November 19, 1863, Sarah Sites Rodgers, *The Ties of the Past: The Gettysburg Diaries of Salome Myers Stewart 1854-1922* (Gettysburg, PA: Thomas Publications, 1996), hereafter *Salome Myers Diary*, p. 167.

200. "because of the great crowd": Clutz, *Some Personal Reflections*, p. 23.

200. "Everything passed off very pleasantly": *Josephine Roedel Diary*, November 19, 1863, Library of Congress.

Chapter Thirteen
THE DEDICATION CEREMONY BEGINS

202. "an orphanly sort of way": Diary entry of John Hay, November 20, 1863, Dennett, *Hay Diaries*, p. 121.

203. "There was "perfect silence": *Washington Morning Chronicle*, November 20, 1863.

203. "was one of respect": Wert, "Lincoln at Gettysburg."

203. Thirty chairs, in three rows of ten: Frank L. Clement, *The Gettysburg Soldiers' Cemetery and Lincoln's Address: Aspects and Angles* (Shippensburg, PA:

White Mane Publishing Company, Inc., 1993), pp. 45, 90.

203. "an old, dingy, uncushioned settee": *Cincinnati Daily Gazette*, November, 1863.

203. Military units would peel off the procession: Kunhardt, *A New Birth of Freedom*, p. 181.

204. "immense crowd": *New York Times*, November 20, 1863.

204. "Oh, what a jam it was": Rev. Dr. Philip M. Bikle, "Mr. Lincoln's Gettysburg speech," February 12, 1926, notarized account, ACHS.

204. "I have never been so wedged": Ibid.

205. "on account of infirmities": Telegram from Winfield Scott to David Wills, November 19, 1863, *SNC Report*, p. 172.

205. "This army has duties": Letter from George G. Meade to David Wills, November 13, 1863, Ibid., pp. 171-172.

206. "golden opportunity": Letter from Abraham Lincoln to George G. Meade, July 14, 1863, telling Gen. Meade, "Your golden opportunity is gone," [never sent or signed by Lincoln], *CWAL*, 6:328, 328[n].

206. "It disappoints me greatly": S.P. Chase to David Wills, November 16, 1863, *SNC Report*, p. 173.

206. "hornswoggle": McCutcheon, *Everyday Life in the 1800's*, p. 22.

207. "President Chase": Sandburg, *Abraham Lincoln: TPY & TWY*, p. 217. In an interesting turn of the phrase, Sandberg writes that this story "was easily half-true."

207. "just risen from the tomb": *Chicago Times*, November 21, 1863.

207. "O God our Father": See the "Prayer of Rev. Dr. Stockton," *SNC Report*, pp. 179, 180.

208. "Our Father, who are in Heaven": Ibid., p. 181.

208. "Mr. Stockton made a prayer": Diary entry of John Hay, November 20, 1863, Dennett, *Hay Diaries*, p. 121.

208. "Old Hundred": Also known as "Old Hundredth," it is, perhaps, one of the best known hymn tunes in the history of Christian music. It is believed the melody was composed in the 16th Century by Frenchman Loys Bourgeois. It derives its name from the 100th Psalm, but is often sung in churches across the world with varying lyrics. The words sung by the audience at Gettysburg is commonly known as the "Doxology," written in 1674 by Bishop Thomas Ken who was both poet and pastor in the Church of England. Ken is considered, historically, as one of the fathers of modern English hymnology. For more history on this iconic hymn tune, see Rev. W.H. Havergal, MA, *A History of the Old Hundredth Psalm Tune: With Specimens* (New York: Mason Brothers, 1854), which is available both in print and online under its title.

209. In the previous decade, Everett had raised: There is no universally recognized formula by which to convert the worth of money, between eras, with empirical precision; even the best methodologies are educated estimates and vulnerable to scholarly criticism. However, an excellent site for obtaining a credible conversion calculator is found at Samuel H. Williamson, "Six Ways To Compute the Relative Value of a U.S. Dollar Amount, 1774 to Present." Reference the working website online under this title. More extensive information about Everett's remarkable speech tour to rescue a disgracefully run-down Mount Vernon, is found at the previously referenced Everett, *Orations and Speeches*, 4:3-17. Another good source about Everett's Mt. Vernon speech tour is Paul Revere Frothingham, *Edward Everett, Orator and Statesman* (Boston: Houghton Mifflin Co., 1925).

210. "It is . . . wholly out of my power": Letter from Edward Everett to David Wills, September 26, 1863, *SNC Report*, p. 168.

212. "mutilated by . . . reporters": Warren, *Lincoln's Gettysburg Declaration*, p. 102.

212. "Standing beneath this serene sky": *SNC Report*, pp. 182-209. Also, the full text of Everett's remarkable speech can be found in two of the most important and inimitable books ever written on the Gettysburg Address, which are the previously referenced Boritt, *The Gettysburg Gospel*, pp. 207-233, and Wills, *Lincoln at Gettysburg*, pp. 213-247.

213. "sweet, clear voice": Jacobs, "Gettysburg Fifty Years Ago."

213. "no lapse of time, no distance of space": *SNC Report*, p. 209.

213. Everett, with his piercing black eyes: Henry Eyster Jacobs, *Notes on a Life of a Churchman: Memoirs of Henry Eyster Jacobs*, ed., Henry E. Horn (Huntington, PA: Church Management Services, Inc., 1974), 1:63.

213. "next to a defeat": *SNC Report*, p. 197.

213. "apostolic fame": Young, *Men and Memories*, 1:62.

214. Lincoln listened pensively to Everett: *Chicago Tribune*, November 21, 1863.

214. At one point, Everett inadvertently: *Ohio Statesman*, November 22, 1863 (wire news story).

214. "The President became nervous": Jacobs, *Notes on a Life of a Churchman*, 1:64.

215. "as we bid farewell": *SNC Report*, p. 209.

215. "I am more than gratified": *Diary of Edward Everett*, November 19, 1863.

215. "Magnificent oration": *Washington Daily Chronicle*, November 20, 1863.

216. "Mr. Everett spoke as he always does": Diary entry of John Hay, November 20, 1863, Dennet, *Hay Diaries*, p. 121.

216. Everett left "his audience in tears": Benjamin B. French, entry in his diary, November 22, 1863, *Witness to the Young Republic*, p. 435.

216. A blanket was placed: Kunhardt, *A New Birth of Freedom*, p. 203.

216. A two hour speech . . . bareheaded: Young, *Men and Memories*, 1:66.

217. "one of the most imposing and interesting": *Philadelphia Inquirer*,

October 13, 1863.
218. "Tis holy ground": See the "Hymn" composed by B.B. French, Esq., *SNC Report*, p. 210.
218. "Mr. Idiot": Boritt, *The Gettysburg Gospel*, p. 112.

Chapter Fourteen
A TWO-MINUTE SPEECH; THE BIRTH OF APOTHEOSIS

220. "The stillness was very noticeable": Bikle, "Mr. Lincoln's Gettysburg Speech," p. 3.
221. "Lincoln was moved": Richard Hofstader, *The American Political Tradition and the Men Who Made It* (New York: Vintage, 1948), p. 172.
221. "For him [Lincoln], it was impossible": Ibid.
221. "I remember distinctly": Quoting Charles Young, "'How Are You, Old Abe?' He asked Lincoln," *The Gettysburg Times* (February 17, 1937), copy, GNMP Library.
222. "like a telescope": *Young, Men and Memories*, 1:68.
222. platform boards creaked and popped: Wilson, *Intimate Memories of Lincoln*, p. 478.
222. "flutter and motion": Ibid.
222. Near the front . . . stood about fifty veterans: See the "The National Cemetery," *SNC Report*, p. 161.
223. Verse Ten of the 90th Psalm: "The days of our years are threescore years and ten; and if by reason of strength they be fourscore years, yet is their labour and sorrow; for it is soon cut off, and we fly away." *King James Version.*
223. "Four score and seven years ago": See *CWAL*. 7:17-23 for the entire text of the version of the Gettysburg Address appearing in this book. Basler has included all five versions of the Gettysburg Address, including an additional "Newspaper Version" derived from the *New York Tribune* and *New York Herald*, November 20, 1863 editions. The Gettysburg Address appearing in this book is the version Basler refers to as the "Final Text" at pp. 22-23; it is the last and fifth version of the Gettysburg Address that Lincoln would pen with his own hand (often referred to as the "Bliss Copy"), and the one currently archived in the Lincoln Room of the White House.
227. Then, with perhaps the only prominent gesture: See the "Reminiscences" of William H. Tipton, November 19, 1914, found in "The Lincoln-Burns Event," *The Gettysburg Times Commemorative Edition* (November 19, 1963), Lincoln's Farewell Address section, copy, ACHS.
228. Verse One of the 121st Psalm: "I will lift up mine eyes unto the hills, from which whence cometh my help." *King James Version.*
228. "monstrous injustice" of slavery: *CWAL*, 2:255.
229. Verse Eighteen of Proverbs, the 29th Chapter: "Where there is no

vision, the people perish: but he that keepeth the law, happy is he." *King James Version.*

229. photographer assigned to capture the event: Rice, *Reminiscences of Abraham Lincoln,* pp. 510-511. See also Kunhardt, *A New Birth of Freedom,* p. 208. This account has been questioned by some scholars through the years. However, it would seem to lend authenticity to the story that John Russell Young—a reporter with the Philadelphia Press who stayed close to the Gettysburg event, and was later a nationally-recognized journalist and Minister to China—apparently observed this incident. In his personal reminiscences he would write that "when Lincoln was speaking . . . [there was] sympathy for the forlorn photographer who failed to take his picture;" see the previously-referenced *Men and Memories,* 1:70.

230. It would be almost a century: This fascinating "Lincoln on the speaker's platform" photograph taken by an unknown photographer and made historically significant through its discovery by Ms. Josephine Cobb can be seen not only in this book, but also online at the *American Treasures of the Library of Congress* web-site, under "The Dedication Ceremony, November 19, 1863." In 2007, two other photographs of Lincoln at Gettysburg, made by Alexander Gardner, were discovered. Both photographs of Lincoln, thanks to the efforts of Civil War enthusiast John Richter and modern digital technology, were pulled out of the murky, obscure background of other primary images. They show what is most likely Lincoln arriving at horseback at the soldiers' cemetery through corridors of soldiers. These photographs can also be seen online at the web-site of *The Center For Civil War Photographs,* under "Lincoln Discovered in Gettysburg Photos." In the Philip B. Kunhardt, Jr. book, *A New Birth of Freedom,* he enlarged this "platform" photograph into a two-page spread (pp. 192-193), and provides interesting commentary about the plethora of people located on the speakers platform around Lincoln. Some dignitaries are clearly identifiable; others invite enjoyable debate and historical sleuthing. This is only one of many treasures of Lincoln information, both factual and myth, in this very nicely done, richly pictorial book produced in 1983.

230. "The will of God prevails": Abraham Lincoln in his meditation on the Divine Will, [September 2, 1862?], *CWAL.* 5:403. This is Lincoln's bold, opening line in his "Meditation."

230. "He, from Whom all blessings flow": Abraham Lincoln giving his last public address, April 11, 1865, *CWAL,* 8:399.

231. "felt religious More than Ever": Mary Todd Lincoln in an interview with William H. Herndon, September [?], 1866, *Herndon's Informants,* p. 360.

231. "There was no gesture except": Bikle, "Mr. President's Lincoln's Gettysburg Speech", p. 4.

232. "grasping the manuscript": Ibid. There is many conflicting eyewitness accounts of how much, and if, President Lincoln relied upon his reading copy when delivering the speech. Historian Gary Wills in *Lincoln at Gettysburg* (previously referenced) has concluded that Lincoln essentially read his entire speech to the audience; this would fit with Lincoln's own version of his speech preparation, which he later related to his Attorney General James Speed, telling Speed that he "concluded it [his speech] so shortly before it was to be delivered, he had not time to memorize it." Historian Frank L. Klement, in his excellent work *The Gettysburg Soldiers' Cemetery and Lincoln's Address* (previously referenced), suggests Lincoln held his reading copy in his left hand, speaking to the crowd from memory. Colonel Clark E. Carr said Lincoln held the papers of his speech in his left hand, and "read them in part and in part spoke without them." (see Carr quoted in Barton, *The Life of Lincoln*, p. 218). In the author's assessment, the answer lies somewhere in the middle. Lincoln clearly did not have time to cold memorize his speech, barely getting an imperfect fair copy written (to read from) before the ceremonies began. But many of the phrases in his speech had formulated in Lincoln's mind during the previous decade, and he had used similar phraseology in his past speeches. By Gettysburg, Lincoln had become a very good journeyman speaker from a prepared, written speech, and was skilled at stealing glimpses from his delivery notes without losing connection to his audience. Such a skill works, in principle, like modern "teleprompters," where the speaker appears to keep eye-contact with the audience, but is visually assisted by the words crawling across the teleprompter screen. Most likely, Lincoln kept good eye-contact by looking out and over the immense audience (which appeared to be memorization), but skillfully and intermittently flashed his eyes down to his reading copy for stealthy assistance. This is essentially what Philip M. Bikle observed, with Lincoln "seldom" looking at his speech, which he "did not seem to need."

232. But the preponderance of credible: Other than the question of how, when and if Lincoln wrote his famous speech on the train ride to Gettysburg, the most maddening contradictory and divergent firsthand accounts in Lincoln lore could be over how much, applause Lincoln got during and after his remarks at the soldiers' cemetery. William E. Barton, in his excellent but elongated title, *Lincoln at Gettysburg: What He Intended to Say: What He Said; What He Was Reported to Have Said: What He Wished He Had Said*, skillfully documents—through the statements of "those who heard" the speech (29 eyewitnesses)—at least two dozen inconsistent versions of the applause story (see pp. 161-210). Most likely, Lincoln got the bulk of his applause at the end of his speech, in restrained, reverential form (he had just given a eulogy), after a few seconds of uncomfortable silence; silence due, mostly, to his quick ending to a short speech which caught the audience by surprise. From historical standpoint, the question of how much applause (if any) Lincoln got—although fodder for interesting debate—in its significance, is a tempest in a teapot.

232. a "long continued applause": *New York Times*, November 20, 1863.

232. "so short a time was Mr. Lincoln":   Carr, *Lincoln at Gettysburg*, pp. 58-59.

233. "Time and time again": Ibid., p. 59.

233. "To my surprise . . . it seemed": Young, *Man and Memories*, 1:69.

233. Lamon, "that speech won't scour": Lamon, *Recollections of Abraham Lincoln*, pp. 173.

233. "wet blanket": Ibid.

233. "was not entirely a failure":   Letter from Abraham Lincoln to Edward Everett, November 20,1863, *CWAL*, 7:24.

234. "in a few brief, but most appropriate words":   Benjamin B. French, entry in his diary, November 22, 1863, *Witness To The Young Republic*, p. 435.

234. "the President in a fine, free way": Dennett, *Hay Diaries*, p. 121.

235. "Could there be much applause?": Skelly, *A Boy's Experiences*, p. 27.

235. "the occasion was too solemn": Barton, *The Life of Abraham Lincoln*, 2:218.

235. "The attention was just beginning": Jacobs, "Gettysburg Fifty Years Ago."

235. "The suddenness with which [Lincoln"] closed: Ibid.

236. "like a bit of Greek sculpture": *Philadelphia Press*, November 24, 1863.

236. "Seldom has a man": *The Daily Age*, November 26, 1863.

236. "Smooth [but] cold": *Harper's Weekly*, December 5, 1863.

236. "villainous assaults": *Edward Everett Diary*, entries of November 25, 27, 1863.

237. "The few words of the President": *Harper's Weekly*, December 5, 12, 1863.

237. "a perfect gem": *Springfield Daily Republican*, November 20, 1863.

238. "Surprisingly fine": Ibid.

238. "We know not where to look": *Providence Daily Journal*, November 20, 1863.

238. "the right thing": *Cincinnati Daily Gazette*, November 26, 1863.

238. "The dedicatory remarks": *Chicago Tribune*, November 20, 1863.

239. "Our Father": *Rochester Daily Union Advertiser*, November 21, 1863.

239. "government . . . not perish from apathy": *Missouri Republican*, November 20, 1863.

239. "That from these dead . . . we imbibe": *Philadelphia Inquirer*, November 20, 1863.

239. "dedicated here to the refinished work": *The New York Times*, November 20, 1863.

239. "The dead will little heed": *Sacramento Daily Union*, November-December 1863.

240. "Is Mr. Lincoln less refined": *Chicago Times*, November 20, 1863.

240. "The cheek of every American": Ibid.

240. "libeled the statesmen": Ibid.

240. "This United States" did not hatch: *New York World*, November 27, 1863.

241. "We pass over the silly remarks": *Harrisburg Patriot and Union*, November 21, 1863.

241. "The ceremony was rendered ludicrous": *London Times*, quoted in *Lincoln and the Press*, Robert S. Harper (New York: McGraw-Hill Book Company, Inc., 1951), p. 288. See also Warren, *Lincoln's Gettysburg Declaration*, p. 148.

241. the "Despot": *Crisis* (in Ohio), November 25, 1863.

241. Lincoln "acted like a clown": *Richmond Daily Dispatch*, November 25, 1863.

241. brought "disgrace upon the Nation": *Cincinnati Daily Inquirer*, November 29, 1863.

241. "vulgar jargon": *Ebensburg Democrat* (in Pennsylvania), December 2, 1863.

241. "That Lincoln . . . is a boor": *MacMillan's Magazine* quoted in Barton, *The Life of Abraham Lincoln*, 2:223.

242. "with his arms hanging": Rev. M. Colver, "Reminiscences of the Battle of Gettysburg," 1902 *Spectrum* [Gettysburg College Yearbook, Special Collections], pp. 179-180.

242. Lincoln's "brief speech at Gettysburg": Ralph Waldo Emerson, "Abraham Lincoln Remarks at the Funeral Services Held in Concord, April 19, 1865" in *Abraham Lincoln* (Cleveland: Chautangua Press, 1899), p.80.

243. "stood motionless and silent": George Gitt quoted in Wilson, *Intimate Memories of Lincoln*, p. 478.

Chapter Fifteen
AFTERWARDS

253. Dirge dedicated to Gov. Andrew Curtin: This hauntingly beautiful composition, played immediately after Lincoln gave his Gettysburg Address, can be heard online at the site of *American Civil War Music (1861-1865)*. Delaney, a composer of numerous Civil War songs, dedicated this dirge to Governor Andrew G. Curtin.

253. "O Thou King of Kings": *SNC Report*, p. 212.

254. "All time . . . is the millennium": Ibid., p. 209.

254. President Lincoln climbed down: *Washington Chronicle*, November 21, 1863.

254. group of . . . fifty wounded veterans: *SNC Report*, p. 165.

255. "appeared to drink in every word": Wert, "Lincoln of Gettysburg."

255. "None seemed to gaze": Ibid.

255. "very appearance . . . spoke louder": *Washington Chronicle*, November 21, 1863.

256. "through crowded and cheering streets": John Hay, entry in his diary, November 20, 1863, Dennet, *Hay Diaries*, p. 121.

256. "I should be glad": Letter from Edward Everett To Abraham Lincoln, November 20, 1863, Nicolay, *Abraham Lincoln: A History*, See also *CWAL*, 7: 24n-25n. Everett wrote Lincoln in this letter that he was particularly grateful "for my daughter's accommodation on the Platform," so she could sit close to her father, whose health was worse than anyone knew at the time. Everett also inquired about the health of little Tad, back in Washington. Everett's kindness and eloquence are both on display in this letter.

256. "In our respective parts": Letter from Abraham Lincoln to Edward Everett, November 20, 1863, *CWAL*, 7:24.

256. "tribute to our noble women": Ibid.

256. "he had never received": *New York Times*, April 20, 1887. See also Warren, *The Gettysburg Declaration*, p. 138.

257. "a very large company": Warren, *Lincoln's Gettysburg Declaration*, p. 134.

258. Lincoln stood in the hallway: Ibid.

258. "Needless to say": Warren, *My Recollections*.

259. "The Rebels couldn't understand German": See Frederick Gebhart Gotwald, *Gettysburg; Lincoln's Address and Our Educational Institutions* (Published by the Board of Education of the General Synagogue of the Evangelical Lutheran Church in the United States, Frederick G. Gotwald, General Secretary, York Pennsylvania, 1907), digitized in 2010 and appearing online under the title, p.2.

259. "How are you, old Abe?": Quoting Charles Young, " 'How Are You, Old Abe?' He Asked Lincoln."

260. God bless you, little fellow": Ibid.

260. "As Mr. Lincoln came down": Diary entry of Mary Elizabeth Montfort, November 20, 1863, "How a Twelve-Year-Old Girl Saw Gettysburg," *Doylestown* (Pennsylvania) *Daily Intelligencer*, May 30, 1959, copy, ACHS.

260. "It was the greatest moment": Ibid.

260 "wanted us to see the President": "Memories Unlocked at Gettysburg Anniversary Fete for Geo. D. Thorn," *The* (Gettysburg) *Compiler*, July 9, 1932.

260. "to listen carefully": Ibid.

261. "I felt a hand on top": Ibid.

261. "it gave me the right to say": Ibid.

261. "strongest wish": Albertus McCreary, "Gettysburg: A Boy's Experience of the Battle," *McClure's Magazine* 33 (July 1909), copy, ACHS.

261. "Mr. Lincoln, will you shake": Ibid.

261. "I was a proud boy": Ibid.

262. Shortly before five o'clock: Barton, *Lincoln at Gettysburg*, p. 93.

263. "overwhelmed with visitors": Timothy H. Smith, *John Burns: "The Hero of Gettysburg"* (Gettysburg, PA: Thomas Publications, 2000), p. 95. Smith's well written and richly researched book is the only comprehensive biography of John Burns, and provides a valuable and interesting look into the

life of this accidental hero of Gettysburg, where myth and the man have inter-
twined.

263. "a thriving business in the sale": Ibid.

264. "If anyone wants to see me": Ibid., p. 96.

264. "the brave old man": Ibid, See also the *Adams Sentinel*, November 24,
1863.

264. "God bless you, old man": Ibid, *John Burns*, and *Adams Sentinel*.

264. "perhaps, more than any other": Ibid.

264. "They seemed an ill assorted pair": Wert, "Lincoln at Gettysburg."

265. "was crowded to its utmost capacity": McCreary, "Gettysburg: A Boy's
Experience."

265. Like modern day rope-line bouncers: Ibid.

265. "Bret Harte wrote a poem": Bret Harte, *Poems* (Boston: James R.
Osgood and Company, 1871) pp. 48-51.

266. "My eagerness to see and hear": See the "Reminiscences" of William
H. Tipton, November 19, 1914, "The Lincoln-Burns Event; Unique
Ceremony; Citizens Relate Recollections; Memorial Tablets Unveiled in
Gettysburg Presbyterian Church, Nov. 19, 1914," *The Gettysburg Times
Commemorative Edition*, November 19, 1963, Lincoln's Farewell Address.

266. "I cannot recollect": See the "Reminiscences" of T.C. Billheimer,
November 19, 1914, "The Lincoln-Burns Event; Unique Ceremony; Citizens
Relate Recollections; Memorial Tablets Unveiled in Gettysburg Presbyterian
Church Nov. 19, 1914," *The Gettysburg Times Commemorative Edition*,
November 19, 1963, Lincoln's Farewell Address.

267. "a bold and able exposition": Warren, *Lincoln's Gettysburg Declaration*,
p. 137.

267. "drowsiness claimed": Smith, *John Burns*, p. 98. See also the
(Gettysburg) *Compiler*, February 18, 1903.

269. "The town is all in excitement": Diary entry of Salome (Sallie) Myers,
November 20, 1863, *The Ties to the Past*, p. 167.

270. "look a great deal better": Letter from Grace Bedell to Abraham
Lincoln, *CWAL*, 4:130n.

270. "As to the whiskers": Letter from Abraham Lincoln to Grace Bedell,
October 19, 1860, *CWAL*, 4:129.

271. "the greatest question": John Hay, entry in his diary quoting President
Lincoln, July 31, 1863, Dennett, *Hay Diaries*, p. 73.

271. "any fact that would justify": John Hay, entry in his diary, July 18, 1863,
Dennett, *Hay Diaries*, p. 68.

272. "meanness or cruelty": Ibid.

272. "For the first time": *New York Times*, December 18, 1863.

273. Proclamation of Thanksgiving: *CWAL*, 6:496-497. Sarah Josepha
Hale, the seventy-four year old editor of the nationally-popular magazine

Godey's *Lady's Book*, advocated for fifteen years for our much beloved Thanksgiving Day holiday, eventually persevering on President Lincoln who, unlike previous presidents, responded promptly to her request. Lincoln signed the beautifully written "Proclamation of Thanksgiving" into law on October 3, 1863, declaring the fourth Thursday of November to be "a day of Thanksgiving and Praise."

274. One of his most cherished: Herndon, *Herndon's Life of Lincoln*, p. 258.

274. "The mossy marbles rest": Cambridge Edition of the *Complete Poetical Works of Oliver Wendell Holmes* (New York: Houghton Mifflin & Company, 1895).

274. In a personal gesure: For a different and interesting perspective on Lincoln's involvement with the burial and headstone of William H. Johnson, see the article by Phillip W. Magness and Sebastian Page in the *New York Times Opinionator* entitled "Mr. Lincoln and Mr. Johnson," February 1, 2012, appearing online under these captions. The authors question the motive and extent of Lincoln's participation in Johnson's interment in Arlington, and the significance of the "citizen" inscription on Johnson's headstone, which they insist was originally made of wood.

Chapter Sixteen
ANALEPSIS: JUST TO BE "REMEMBERED" . . .

277. "in the midst": Nicolay, *Abraham Lincoln: A History*, 1:25.

278. "My earliest recollection": Louis A. Warren, *Lincoln's Parentage and Childhood: A History of the Kentucky Lincoln's Supported by Documentary Evidence* (New York: The Century Company, 1926), p. 143.

278. Six-year-old Abraham: Roger H. Futrell, "Zachariah Riney: Lincoln's First Schoolmaster," *Lincoln Herald* 74 (Harrogate, TN: Lincoln Memorial University, Fall 1972), pp. 136-142.

278. "cooning" it across Knob Creek: Nicolay, *Abraham Lincoln: A History*, 1:27.

279. So in 1816: Albert J. Beveridge, *Abraham Lincoln 1809-1858* (2 vols.; Boston: Houghton Mifflin Company, 1928), 1:37.

279. "partly on account of slavery": Abraham Lincoln in an autobiography written for John L. Scripps, June 1860, *CWAL*, 4:61-62.

279. "bears and other wild animals": Letter (enclosing autobiography) from Abraham Lincoln to Jesse W. Fell, December 20, 1859, *CWAL*, 3:511.

279. poor as Job's turkey: McCutcheon, *Everyday Life in the 1800's*, p. 33.

279. "half-face camp": This shelter was described by Dennis Hanks in a statement to William H. Herndon, December 1865 [?], *Herndon's Informants*, p. 149. See the myth-busting article by Charles H. Coleman, The Half-Faced Camp in Indiana- Fact or Myth?," *Abraham Lincoln Quarterly* 7 (Springfield, IL:

Abraham Lincoln Association, September 1952), pp. 138-146, which makes a strong case that Thomas Lincoln did not allow his family to suffer through a bitter Indiana winter in a shed with only three walls.

280. "absolutely nothing to excite": Letter (enclosing autobiography) from Abraham Lincoln to Jesse W. Fell, December 20, 1859, *CWAL*, 3:511.

280. "so called schools": Ibid.

280. "readin, writin, and cipherin": Ibid.

280. When paper or slate got scarce: Sarah Bush Lincoln in an interview with William H. Herndon, September 8, 1865, *Herndon's Informants*, p. 107.

281. Abe's first pen . . . buzzard's feather: Ibid., p. 37.

281. copperas: The chemical compound of iron (II) sulfate or ferrous (copper) sulfate, with the formula $FeSO(4)$. Used by the Romans, it has gone by many names through the centuries, such as "blue vitriol," "blue copperas," "bluestone," and "Roman vitriol." It is a naturally-occurring crystalline substance that is cobalt blue in color and extremely toxic. Many years ago, it was used by rural people to color ink and was mixed with lime to create a pesticide. Today, it is used industrially as a reducing agent in creating cement. In addition to its industrial use, it is also used to treat iron-deficiencies that cause anemia in humans, and to fortify food products.

281. "Constant and I may Say": Dennis F. Hanks in an interview with William H. Herndon, June 13, 1865, *Herndon's Informants*, p. 41.

281. "We had but few books": David Turnham in an interview with William H. Herndon, September 15, 1865, *Herndon's Informants*, p. 121.

281. "Abe was getting hungry": *Herndon's Informants*, p. 41.

281. "hunger for books": Ida M. Tarbell, *Boy Scouts' Life of Lincoln* (New York: The Macmillan Company, 1922), p. 33.

281. school by "littles": Barton, *The Life of Abraham Lincoln*, 1:192.

282. "defective": Abraham Lincoln in a brief autobiography, June [15?], 1858, *CWAL*, 2:459.

282. "My best friend": Sandburg, *Abraham Lincoln*, p. 13.

283. "Abe read all the books": Sarah Bush Lincoln in an interview with William H. Herndon, September 8, 1865, *Herndon's Informants*, p. 107.

283. "came across a passage": Ibid.

283. Lincoln's stepmother Sally would bring: Written statement of A..H. Chapman, September 8, 1865, *Herndon's Informants*, p. 99.

283. bureau . . . exorbitant price of $45.00: Sarah Bush Lincoln in an interview with William H. Herndon, September 8, 1865, *Herndon's Informants*, p. 106.

283. Abraham memorized swaths: There is a very informative article about the books Lincoln had access to in Douglas L. Wilson, "What Jefferson and Lincoln Read," *Atlantic Monthly* 267 (January 1991), pp. 51-62. See also Beveridge, *Abraham Lincoln*, 1:70, 73-77.

284. Abraham first beefed-up his spelling: Nathaniel Grigsby told William

H. Herndon on September 12, 1865, that Lincoln "started" with *Dilworth's Spelling Book*; see reference to this in *Herndon's Informants*, p. 112.

284. When young Lincoln first took grasp: Beveridge, *Abraham Lincoln*, pp. 70, 72.

284. "The hill, tho' high": *The Pilgrim's Progress* is available free online, in several formats, at the website of the Christian Classics Ethereal Library.

284. "best friend in this world": Charles H. Coleman, *Abraham Lincoln and Coles County, Illinois* (New Brunswick, NJ: Scarecrow Press, 1955), p. 199.

284. "read diligently": Sarah Bush Lincoln in an interview with William H. Herndon, September 8, 1865, *Herndon's Informants*, p. 107.

284. During his later teen-age years: This legendary "pulling fodder for a book" story, or the "Josiah Crawford story," involving Lincoln and neighbor Josiah Crawford, has appeared in a plethora of Lincoln books through the years. Both Dennis Hanks and John Hanks, cousins of Lincoln (on his mother's side) who grew up around "Abe" as they called him, related the Josiah Crawford story in interviews with William H. Herndon. See also the written statement of A. H. Chapman given to William H. Herndon, September 8, 1865, *Herndon's Informants*, p. 101, and also the " 'Pulling Fodder' For A Book," in *Lincoln's Yarns and Stories* (Project Gutenberg: released: February 2001), online under its title.

285. description of Thomas Lincoln: Dennis F. Hanks in an interview with William H. Herndon, June 13, 1865, *Herndon's Informants*, p. 37.

287. "[this] legend, more strongly": Letter from Abraham Lincoln to Jesse Lincoln, April 1, 1854, *CWAL*, 2:217.

287. The father of . . . David Crockett: Bob Thompson, *Born on a Mountaintop: On the Road with Davy Crockett and Ghosts of the Wild Frontier* (New York: Crown Trade Group, 2013), p. 29.

288. Lincoln would chuckle: Robert B. Rutledge, in an interview with William H. Herndon, November 30, 1866, describing young Lincoln always having a book with him as he walked, *Herndon's Informants*, p. 426.

289. "I used to be a slave": Statement of John E. Roll, quoting Abraham Lincoln in a speech, *Recollected Words of Abraham Lincoln*, p. 383; deriving from Roll's statement in the *Chicago-Times Herald*, August 25, 1895.

289. She was a recently-widowed lady: Beveridge, *Abraham Lincoln*, pp. 57-58.

290. "Tom had a kind o'way": Sandberg, *Abraham Lincoln*, p. 12.

290. "the panther's scream": Letter from Abraham Lincoln to Andrew Johnston, with enclosed poem "The Bear Hunt," September 6, 1846 [?], *CWAL*, 1:386.

290. "wild region": Letter from Abraham Lincoln to Jesse W. Fell with enclosed autobiography, December 20, 1859, *CWAL*, 3:511.

290. Sometimes, young Sarah: Louis A. Warren, *Lincoln's Youth: Indiana Years, Seven to Twenty-One, 1816-1830* (New York: Appleton-Century-Crofts,

1959), p. 58. This remains one of the definitive works on Lincoln's youth.

290. She "Soaped—rubbed": Dennis F. Hanks in an interview with William H. Herndon, June 13, 1865, *Herndon's Informants*, p. 41.

290. "looked more human": Ibid., p. 106.

291. "the best boy": Sarah Bush Lincoln in an interview with William H. Herndon, September 8, 1865, *Herndon's Informants*, p. 108.

291. "Abe never spoke": Ibid, p. 107.

291. "his mind and mine": Ibid., 108.

292. "Sometimes . . . slash him": Dennis F. Hanks in an interview with William H. Herndon, *Herndon's Informants*, p. 118.

292. "Abe . . . didn't love work": Statement of John Romine to William H. Herndon, September 14, 1865, *Herndon's Informants*, p. 118.

292. to "tease his father": Quoting Dennis F. Hanks, Ibid., p. 39.

293. "knock him a rod": Ibid.

293. "Keep your head clean": Ingri and Edgar Parin d' Aulaire, *Abraham Lincoln* (New York: Doubleday, Doran & Company, Inc. 1939), p.19.

293. "Abraham Lincoln, his hand and pen": *CWAL*, 1:1.

294. "Hard Shell" Baptist view: Primitive or Hard Shell Baptists also go by the names of "Old School Baptists", "Predestinationists" and "Anti-Mission Baptists." Characterized by intense religious conservatism, such as their belief in predestination, their strict adherence to the traditions of foot washing, *a capella* music in church and unpaid ministers, and their opposition to the idea of Sunday School—their origin comes from the church's split from other mainstream Baptist denominations that supported mission boards and Bible tract organizations. Although they are sometimes referred to as "Calvinist," they generally avoid the label, and reject certain Calvinist theology. Their churches are concentrated in the Blue Ridge and Appalachia Mountain regions. See also the comments of William A. Barton regarding the Lincoln family's Primitive Baptist worship, in *The Life of Abraham Lincoln*, 1:127-129. John G. Rowley, who has much expertise on this subject, provides interesting insight into this religious sect in his essay, "The Primitive or Old School Baptists," found in *The Baptist River: Essays on Many Tributaries of a Diverse Tradition*, W. Glenn Jonas, Jr., ed. (2006).

295. "accident and nature": *Herndon's Informants*, p. 41.

296. "The most deadly": Eric H. Erikson, *Young Man Luther: A Study of Psychoanalysis and History* (New York: The Norton Library, 1958), p. 70. Dr. Erikson coined the term "identity crisis," now a universally accepted part of the psychoanalytical lexicon.

296. The father had, indeed: One of the definitive and most intriguing works on the relationship between Abraham Lincoln and his father Thomas, is John Y. Simon, *House Divided: Lincoln and his Father* (Fort Wayne, IN: Louis A. Warren Library and Museum, 1987).

298. "In their eyes": Donald, *Lincoln*, p. 32.

298. "soared above us": Nathaniel Grigsby in an interview with William H. Herndon, September 12, 1865, *Herndon's Informants*, p. 114.

299. "little engine that knew": Herndon, *Herndon's Lincoln*, 2:375.

299. "picked up. . . under the pressure": Letter from Abraham Lincoln (enclosing autobiography) to Jesse W. Fell, December 20, 1859, *CWAL*, 3:511.

299. By the Spring of 1830: For an account of the Lincoln family's move from Indiana to Illinois, see Barton, *The Life of Abraham Lincoln*, 1:138-143.

300. They nearly lost everything: Nathaniel Grigsby in an interview with William H. Herndon, September 4, 1865, *Herndon's Informants*, p. 103.

300. He got $8.00 a month: Ibid., p. 114.

301. "never could tell whether Abe loved his father": Dennis F. Hanks in a letter to William H. Herndon, January 26, 1866, *Herndon's Informants*, p. 176.

302. "attacked by seven negroes": Abraham Lincoln in an autobiography written for John L. Scripps, June [?], 1860, *CWAL*, 4:62. John Romine, Lincoln's neighbor in Spencer County, Indiana, remembered Lincoln telling him about this attack, telling William H. Herndon that he "saw the scar" on Lincoln from the incident; see this account in *Herndon's Informants*, p. 118.

303. "like a piece of floating driftwood": Herndon, *Abraham Lincoln; The True Story*, p. 70.

303. "as ruff a specimen": David C. Mearns, ed., *The Lincoln Papers* (2 vols., Garden City, NJ: Doubleday and Co., 1948), 1:51.

305. For instance, Lincoln liked to tell: Abner Y. Ellis in an interview with William H. Herndon, January 23, 1866, *Herndon's Informants*, p. 174.

305. "Honest Abe": In his book *Honor's Voice*, distinguished Lincoln historian Douglas L. Wilson explains that Lincoln likely acquired this moniker in the early 1830's for his honest judging of horse races in New Salem, Illinois.

305. out-wrestled the "strongest man": For a comprehensive, superbly researched and written account of the famous Lincoln versus Jack Armstrong wrestling match, see Wilson, *Honor's Voice*, pp. 19-43. Dr. Wilson is the Saunders Director of the International Center for Jefferson Studies at Monticello in Charlottesville, Virginia, and is one of the preeminent Lincoln scholars on Lincoln's writing methodologies and his pre-presidential years. He was kind enough to communicate with the author (by fax) many years ago, on recondite Lincoln questions I had during the conceptional stages of this book, for which I am most grateful and indebted.

306. "winked out": Abraham Lincoln in an autobiography written for John L. Scripps, June [?], 1860, *CWAL*, 4:65.

306. "National debt": Mearns, *The Lincoln Papers*, 1:153.

306. "success . . . gave me more pleasure": Abraham Lincoln in a letter (enclosing autobiography) to J.W. Fell, December 20, 1859, *CWAL*, 3:512.

307. A local schoolteacher: Mentor Graham in an interview with William H.

Herndon, May 29, 1865, *Herndon's Informants*, p. 10.

308. This cultural chasm . . . Russell Godbey: Herndon, *Abraham Lincoln: The True Story*, p. 102.

308. first immerse himself . . . Blackstone's Commentaries: Letter from Lynn McNulty Greene to William H. Herndon, July 30, 1865, *Herndon's Informants*, p. 81. See also Barton, *The Life of Abraham Lincoln*, 1:194.

308. He drilled himself . . . Chitty's Pleadings: William H. Herndon quoting Abraham Lincoln, advising a young man how to gain knowledge of the law, *Herndon's Life of Lincoln*, p. 261.

308. He would plow through . . . Story's Equity . . . Greenleaf's Evidence: Ibid.

309. he became "emaciated": Henry McHenry in an interview with William H. Herndon, May 29, 1865, *Herndon's Informants*, p. 14.

309. "craze himself": Ibid.

309. "studied with nobody": Abraham Lincoln in an autobiography written for John L. Scripps, June [?], 1860, *CWAL* 4:65.

309. No one place or person: Historian William E. Barton felt New Salem had such a profound influence on Lincoln, he referred to it as "Lincoln's Alma Mater," in Barton, *The Life of Lincoln*, 1:201. The weight of New Salem influence on Lincoln, however, is debated by scholars. When reading about Abraham Lincoln during his years in the New Salem community, there is one "must read." It is the excellent and incomparable work of Douglas L. Wilson, in his previously-referenced *Honor's Voice*.

310. "I think everyone": Roger Jaynes, *Al McGuire: The Colorful Warrior* (Champaign, IL: Sports Publishing, L.L.C., 2004), p. 17.

312. "mind of metaphysical": *Herndon's Informants*, p. 519.

313. "you are mistaken": Joshua Speed in a letter to William H. Herndon, December 6, 1866, *Herndon's Informants*, p. 499.

313. his absolute favorite . . . MacBeth: Letter from Abraham Lincoln to James H. Hacket, August 17, 1863, in which Lincoln writes, "I think nothing equals MacBeth." *CWAL*, 6:392.

313. "It hath no relish": Abraham Lincoln in a speech given at Peoria, Illinois, October 16, 1854, CWAL, 2:270. This three hour speech (which was one of a series of three against Stephen A. Douglas in 1854), was a comprehensive and revealing insight into Lincoln's moral, economic and legal arguments against slavery. It was a key speech in building his political future and his most important, until his Cooper Union speech made in New York City on February 27, 1860. For an in-depth understanding of the significance of the Peoria speech on Lincoln's political career, see the brilliantly-done book by Lewis E. Lehrman, *Lincoln at Peoria: The Turning Point* (Mechanicsburg, PA: Stackpole Books, 2008).

314. Euclid's Theorems: Abraham Lincoln in an autobiography for John L. Scripps, June [?], 1860, *CWAL*, 4:62, in which Lincoln relates that he "studied and nearly mastered the Six-books of Euclid, since he was a member of Congress."

314. "I catch the idea": Quoting Abraham Lincoln, Herndon, *Herndon's Lincoln*, 2:332.

314. "argued much from analogy": Nathaniel Grigsby in an interview with William H. Herndon, *Herndon's Informants*, p. 114-115.

315. "They say I tell": Statement of Chauncey M. Depew, quoting Abraham Lincoln, Fehrenbacher, *Recollected Words*, p. 137.

315. "the edge of a rebuke": John Wesley Hill, *Abraham Lincoln—Man of God* (New York: G.P. Putnam's Sons, 1920), p. 323.

315. "Every one of his stories": P.M. Zall, ed., *Abe Lincoln Laughing* (Berkley, CA: University of California Press, 1982), p. 5.

316. For thou art Freedom's now": "Marco Bozzaris," by Fitz-Greene Halleck, *Historic Poems and Ballads*, ed., Rupert S. Holland (Philadelphia: George W. Jacobs & Co., 1912). See also Roy P. Basler, *A Touchstone for Greatness: Essays, Addresses, and Occasional Pieces about Abraham Lincoln* (Westport, CN: Greenwood Press, Inc., 1973), p. 223.

317. "the thing that struck": Herndon, *Abraham Lincoln; The True Story*, p. 297.

318. "My peculiar ambition": Springfield's *Sangamo Journal*, March 15, 1832.

Chapter Seventeen
LOST IN THE SHADOWS OF A PROCLAMATION

319. The Emancipation Proclamation: *CWAL*, 6:28-30. There is a cornucopia of scholarly writing on this subject. A good place to start is the Lincoln prize winning book of Allen Guelzo, *Lincoln's Emancipation Proclamation: The End of Slavery in America* (New York: Simon & Schuster, 2004).

321. "I never in my life": Seward, *Seward at Washington . . . 1861-1872*, 2:151.

321 "had all the moral grandeur": Hofstader, *The American Political Tradition*, p. 169.

322. But some could: Significant numbers of slaves escaped to thick wooded areas and marshy backroads until Northern troops passed through. Slaves who were in bondage in the areas of Confederate front lines, often successfully slipped over to the sanctuary of the Union army. Slaves also became indispensable sources of intelligence for Federal troops penetrating into Southern territories, particularly towards the end of the War when slaves often had much less supervision and were able to more fully assist the Union cause. For a magisterial work delving into slave rebellion and escapes, see the Lincoln Prize winning book by John Hope Franklin and Loren Schweninger, *Runaway Slaves: Rebels on the Plantation* (Oxford: Oxford University Press, 1999).

323. 180,000 black soldiers: Eric Foner, *Reconstruction: America's Unfinished Revolution, 1863-1877* (New York: Harper & Row, 1988, 1989), p. 8. See also Kunhardt, *Lincoln: An Illustrated Biography*, pp. 226-227. On these same pages in Kunhardt, a color facsimile of an 1863 recruiting poster is shown. An excellent discourse on the experience of African-American soldiers in the Civil War is Dudley T. Cornish, *The Sable Arm: Black Troops in the Union Army, 1861-1865* (Lawrence, KS: University Press of Kansas, 1956, 1987).

323. "henceforward . . . free":   Abraham Lincoln's Emancipation Proclamation, January 1, 1863, *CWAL*, 6:29-30.

324. "We are like whalers":   Abraham Lincoln quoted in Nicolay, *Abraham Lincoln: A History*, 10:74.

324. It is my conviction":   Carpenter, *Six Months at the White House*, p. 77.

324. "And upon this act":   *CWAL*, 6:30.

325. "the immaculate conception":   Carpenter, *Six Months at the White House*, p.12.

325. First Reading of the Emancipation Proclamation: After the Civil War ended (on April 9, 1865), Francis B. Carpenter's painting, when engraved for mass production, would become the top-selling lithograph print in the nation for several years.   Carpenter lived in the White House about six months while he completed the enormous oil-on-canvas painting, which he worked on in the State Dining Room.   His unique observations are in the above-referenced Carpenter, *Six Months at the White House*.

327. Although the grandiose monikers: In the six decades following Lincoln's death, perhaps reaching high tide with the dedication of the Lincoln Memorial in 1922, virtually all of the art, sculpture and literature focused on his "Great Emancipator" image.   Even book titles during that era, reflected the ever-growing, self-inflating "liberator" status of Lincoln, as his image evolved from "nation" to even "world," to-wit: *Abraham Lincoln, The Liberator* (Charles Wallace French, 1891); *Lincoln, Emancipator of the Nation* (Frederick Trevor Hill, 1928); *Lincoln. The World Emancipator* (John Drinkwater, 1920).

327. "If my name":   Carpenter, *Six Months at the White House*, p. 269.

328. "worth dawned gradually":   Barton, *The Life of Abraham Lincoln*, 2:23.

329. "my politics is short":   Herndon, *Herndon's Lincoln*, 1:104.

Chapter Eighteen
PONDERINGS AND REFLECTIONS

330. "He is gone":   Emerson Reck, A. *Lincoln: His Last 24 Hours* (Columbia: University of South Carolina Press, 1994), p. 157.

330. "Now he belongs":   Barton, *The Life of Abraham Lincoln*, 2: 348.

330. "We trust":   *The La Crosse* (Wisconsin) *Democrat*, quoted in William A. Tidwell, James O. Hall and David Winfred Gaddy, *Come Retribution: The Confederate Secret Service and the Assassination of Lincoln* (Jackson, MS: University Press of Mississippi, 1988), p. 234.

331. "The conduct of":   *New York Herald*, May 19, 1860.

331. "Who will write": Warren, *Lincoln's Gettysburg Declaration*, p. 48.

332. "There can be no": *New York Times*, February 22, 1898.

333. "Lincoln is a strong man": Harriet Beecher Stowe, "Abraham Lincoln," *Living Age*, January 2, 1864, p. 284.

336. Just nine sentences: Some historians allude to the Gettysburg Address as having ten sentences; both counts are correct. The final count depends on how punctuation and hyphenation are analyzed, and which of the five extant versions are being examined. Most counts are referring to the last and fifth draft, known as the "Bliss Copy."

337. Lincoln "wrote American": "Shelby Foote on Lincoln's Literary Genius/Facebook," based upon interview done in Memphis, TN on March 28 and April 7, 1987, found online under its title.

337. "[A]ll modern political prose": Wills, *Lincoln at Gettysburg*, p. 148.

339. In 1958 . . . France implemented: *The Constitution of France* (5th Republic, Established October 4, 1958), as it appears in English online at http:/www.assemblee-nationale.fr/English/8ab.asp.

339. For a time during World War II: Mearns, *The Lincoln Papers*, 1:135.

340. "Fellow-citizens, we cannot escape": Abraham Lincoln in his Annual Message to Congress, December 1, 1962, *CWAL*, 5:37.

342. To paraphrase: F. Scott Fitzgerald said, "The test of a first-rate intelligence is the ability to hold two opposed ideas in mind at the same time, and still retain the ability to function."

344. "In easy times history": John Dos Passos, *The Ground We Stand On* (New York: Harcourt, Brace & Company, 1941), pp. 3, 4.

346. "stretching like a lifeline": Ibid., p. 3.

346. "a quicksand of fear": Ibid.

BIBLIOGRAPHY

Books

Guy Allison, *Man's Most Valuable Words* (Gettysburg: L.E. Smith, 1956).
Mary Raymond Shipman Andrews, *The Perfect Tribute* (New York: Charles Scribner's Sons, 1906).
George E. Baker, ed., *The Works of William H. Seward* (Boston: Houghton, Mifflin & Co., 1884).
Jean H. Baker, *Mary Todd Lincoln: A Biography* (New York: W.W. Norton, 1987).
Frederic Bancroft, *The Life of William H. Seward* (2 vols.; New York: Harper & Brothers, 1900).
Roy P. Basler, *A Touchstone for Greatness: Essays, Addresses, and Occasional Pieces about Abraham Lincoln* (Westport, CN: Greenwood Press, Inc., 1973).
_____, chief ed., Marion Delores Pratt and Lloyd A. Dunlap, asst. eds., *The Collected Works of Abraham Lincoln*, 8 vols.; (New Brunswick, NJ: Rutgers University Press, 1953-55) and Supplements 1832-1865 (Westport, CT: Greenwood Press, 1974, 1990).
_____, *Abraham Lincoln: His Speeches and Writings* (New York: Da Capo Press, 1990).
William E. Barton, *The Life of Abraham Lincoln*, (2 vols.; Arrowsmith, London, Indianapolis: The Bobbs-Merrill Company, 1925).
_____, *Lincoln At Gettysburg: What He Intended to Say; What He Said; What He Was Reported to Have Said; What He Wished He Had Said* (Indianapolis, IN: The Bobbs-Merrill Company, 1930; republished New York: Peter Smith, 1950).
_____, *The Soul of Lincoln* (New York: George H. Doran, 1920; republished Chicago: University of Illinois Press, 2005).
_____, *The Women Lincoln Loved* (Indianapolis, IN: The Bobbs-Merrill Company, 1927).
Howard K. Beale (Howard Kennedy) and Mary Parker Ragatz, eds., *The Diary of Edward Bates, 1859—1866* (Washington, D.C.: Government Printing Office).
Lerone Bennett, Jr., *Forced into Glory: Abraham Lincoln's White Dream* (Chicago: Johnson Publishing, 2000).
Albert J. Beveridge, *Abraham Lincoln* (Boston: Houghton Mifflin Co., 1928).
Linda Giberson Black, *Gettysburg Remembers President Lincoln: Eyewitness Accounts of November 1863* (Gettysburg, PA: Thomas Publications, 2005).
Gabor S. Boritt, *Lincoln and the Economics of the American Dream* (Memphis, TN: Memphis State University, 1978; republished Urbana: University of Illinois Press, 1994).

_____, *The Gettysburg Gospel: The Lincoln Speech That Nobody Knows* (New York: Simon & Schuster, 2006).

Noah Brooks, *Abraham Lincoln, Centennial Edition 1809-1909* (New York, London: G.P. Putnam's Sons, 1888).

Maurice Bucke, Thomas B. Harned, and Horace L. Traubel, eds., *The Complete Writings of Walt Whitman* (New York: G.P. Putnam's Sons, 1902).

Fannie J. Buehler; *Recollections of the Rebel Invasion and One Women's Experience During the battle of Gettysburg* (Gettysburg, PA: Star and Sentinel Printing, 1896; reprint by Gary T. Hawbaker, 2002).

F. Lauriston Bullard, *"A Few Appropriate Remarks": Lincoln's Gettysburg Address* (Harrogate, TN: Lincoln Memorial University, 1944).

Michael Burlingame, ed., *An Oral History of Abraham Lincoln: John G. Nicolay's Interviews and Essays* (Carbondale, IL: Southern Illinois University Press, 1996).

_____ and John R. Turner Ettlinger, eds., *Inside Lincoln's White House: The Complete Civil War Diary of John Hay* (Carbondale, IL: Southern Illinois Press, 1999).

_____, *The Inner World of Abraham Lincoln* (Urbana and Chicago: University of Illinois Press, 1994).

_____, ed., *Lincoln Observed: The Civil War Dispatches of Noah Brooks* (Baltimore: John Hopkins University Press, 1998).

John W. Busey and David G. Martin, *Regimental Strengths and Losses at Gettysburg*, 4th ed. (Hightstown, NJ: Longstreet House, 2005).

Orton H. Carmichael, *Lincoln's Gettysburg Address* (New York: Abingdon, 1917).

F.B. Carpenter, *Six Months at the White House with Abraham Lincoln: The Story of a Picture* (New York: Hurd & Houghton, 1866).

Clark E. Carr, Lincoln at Gettysburg: An Address (Chicago: A.C. McClurg & Co., 1906).

Robert G. Carter, *Four Brothers in Blue* (Austin, TX: University of Texas, 1978).

Richard Carwardine, *Lincoln: A Life of Purpose and Power* (New York: Alfred A. Knopf, 2006).

Bruce Catton, editor, *The Battle of Gettysburg* (Boston, MA: Houghton Mifflin Company, 1969).

Lydia Marie Child, *The Mother's Book* (Boston: Carter, Hendee and Babcock, 1831; republished Pierides Press, 2006).

L. Pierce Clark, Lincoln; *A Psycho-Biography* (New York, London: Charles Scribner's Sons, 1933).

Frank L. Clement, *The Gettysburg Soldiers' Cemetery and Lincoln's Address: Aspects and Angles* (Shippensburg, PA: White Mane Publishing Company, Inc., 1993).

Catherine Clinton, *Mrs. Lincoln: A Life* (New York: HarperCollins Publishers, 2009).

Mrs. Jacob A. Clutz [as a child, known as "Liberty Augusta Hollinger"], *Some Personal Recollections of the Battle of Gettysburg* (Gettysburg, PA: 1925).

Gregory A. Coco, *A Strange and Blighted Land, Gettysburg: The Aftermath of a Battle* (Gettysburg, PA: Thomas Publications, 1995).

Charles H. Coleman, *Abraham Lincoln and Coles County, Illinois* (New Brunswick, NJ: Scarecrow Press, 1955).

Eileen F. Conklin, *Women of Gettysburg* (Gettysburg, PA: Thomas Publications, 1993).

Dudley T. Cornish, *The Sable Arm: Black Troops in the Union Army, 1861-1865* (Lawrence, KS: University Press of Kansas, 1956, 1987).

Martin Crawford, ed., *William Howard Russell's Civil War: Private Diary and Letters, 1861-1862* (Athens, GA: University of Georgia Press, 1992).

Norma B. Cuthbert, ed., *Lincoln and the Baltimore Plot, 1861: From Pinkerton Records and Related Papers* (San Marino, CA: Henry E. Huntington Library, 1949).

Tyler Dennett, *Lincoln and the Civil War in the Diaries and Letters of John Hay* (New York: Dodd, Mead & Company, 1939).

David Herbert Donald, *Lincoln* (New York: Simon & Schuster, 1995).

_____ and Harold Holzer, eds., *Lincoln In The Times; The Life Of Abraham Lincoln As Originally Reported In The New York Times* (New York: St. Martin's Press, 2005).

Frederick Douglass, *The Life and Times of Frederick Douglass, Written By Himself* (Hartford: Park Publishing Co., 1882).

Samuel Adams Drake, *The Battle of Gettysburg* (Boston: Lee and Shepard Publishers, 1892).

Lloyd A. Dunlap, David C. Mearns, John R. Sellers and Douglas L. Wilson, commentators, *Long Remembered: Lincoln and his five versions of the Gettysburg Address* (Delray Beach, FL and Washington, D.C.: Levenger Press in association with the Library of Congress, 2011).

Donald Charles Durman, *He Belongs to the Ages: The Statues of Abraham Lincoln* (Ann Arbor, MI: Edwards, 1951).

Eric H. Erikson, *Young Man Luther: A Study of Psychoanalysis and History* (New York: The Norton Library, 1958).

Edward Everett, *Orations and Speeches on Various Occasions* (4 vols.; Boston: Charles C. Little & James Brown, 1850).

Clifton Fadiman, ed., *The Little, Brown Book of Anecdotes* (Boston: Little, Brown, 1985).

Drew Gilpin Faust, *"Republic of Suffering": Death and the American Civil War* (New York: Alfred A. Knopf, 2008).

Don E. Fehrenbacher, *The Dred Scott Case: Its Significance in American Law and Politics* (New York: Oxford University Press, 1978).

Don E. Fehrenbacher and Virginia Fehrenbacher, eds., *Recollected Words of*

Abraham Lincoln (Stanford, CA: Stanford University Press, 1996).

Frank Abial Flower, *Edwin McMasters Stanton: The Autocrat of Rebellion, Emancipation, and Reconstruction* (New York: Saalfield Publishing Company, 1905; reprint, ULAN Press).

Eric Foner, *Reconstruction: America's Unfinished Revolution, 1863-1877* (New York: Harper & Row, 1988, 1989).

James P. Frank, *Lincoln as a Lawyer* (Urbana: University of Illinois Press, 1961).

John Hope Franklin and Loren Schweninger, *Runaway Slaves: Rebels on the Plantation* (Oxford: Oxford University Press, 1999).

Benjamin Brown French, *Witness to the Young Republic: A Yankee's Journal, 1828-1870*, Donald B. Cole and John J. McDonough, eds., (Hanover, N.H.: University Press of New England, 1989).

Frank Freidel and William Pencak, eds., *The White House: The First Two Hundred Years* (Boston: Northeastern University Press, 1994).

Paul Revere Frothingham, *Edward Everett, Orator and Statesman* (Boston: Houghton Mifflin Co., 1925).

George D. Gitt, *Intimate Memories of Lincoln* (Elmira, NY: Primavera, 1945).

Joseph Glatthaar, *General Lee's Army: From Victory to Collapse* (New York: Free Press, 2009).

Barbara Goldsmith, *Other Powers: The Age of Suffrage, Spiritualism, and the Scandalous Victoria Woodhull* (New York: Alfred A. Knopf, 1998).

Doris Kearns Goodwin, *Team of Rivals: The Political Genius of Abraham Lincoln* (New York: Simon & Schuster, 2005).

Horace Greeley, *The Autobiography of Horace Greeley: or, Recollections of a Busy Life* (New York: E.B.Treat, 1868).

Allen C. Guelzo, *Lincoln's Emancipation Proclamation: The End of Slavery in America* (New York: Simon & Schuster, 2004).

Fitz-Greene Halleck, *Historic Poems and Ballads*, ed., Rupert S. Holland (Philadelphia: George W. Jacobs & Co., 1912).

Charles Hamilton, *Great Forgers and Famous Fakes: The Manuscript Forgers of America and How They Duped the Experts* (Lakewood, Colorado: Glenbridge Publishing Ltd., 1980).

_____ and Lloyd Ostendorf, *Lincoln In Photographs: An Album of Every Known Pose* (Norman: University of Oklahoma Press, 1963; republished Dayton, Ohio: Morningside Books, 1985).

William Hanchett, *The Lincoln Murder Conspiracies* (Urbana, IL: The University of Illinois Press, 1983).

Rev. W.H. Havergal, MA, *A History of the Old Hundredth Psalm Tune: With Specimens* (New York: Mason Brothers, 1854).

William H. Herndon and Jesse W. Weik, *Herndon's Life of Lincoln*, with introduction and notes by Paul M. Angle (New York: Albert & Charles Boni, 1930).

_____, and Jesse William Weik, A.M, *An Illustrated Herndon's*

Lincoln: The True Story of a Great Life (2 vols.; Chicago: Bedford, Clarke & Company, 1889).

Emanuel Hertz, ed., *The Hidden Lincoln: From the Letters and Papers of William H. Herndon* (New York: Viking Press, 1938).

_____, *Lincoln Talks; An Oral Biography* (New York: Viking Press, Inc., 1939; republished New York: Bramhall House, 1986).

Caroline Hanks Hitchcock, *Nancy Hanks: The Story of Abraham Lincoln's Mother* (New York: Doubleday & McClure Co., 1900).

John Wesley Hill, *Abraham Lincoln—Man of God* (New York: G.P. Putnam's Sons, 1920)

Richard Hofstadter, *The American Political Tradition and the Men Who Made It* (New York: A.A. Knoph, 1948).

Oliver Wendell Holmes, *Cambridge Edition of the Complete Poetical Works of Oliver Wendell Holmes* (New York: Houghton Mifflin & Company, 1895).

Harold Holzer, author and compiler, *Dear Mr. Lincoln: Letters to the President* (Reading, Mass: Addison-Wesley Publishing Company, 1993).

_____ and Frank J. Williams, *Lincoln's Deathbed in Art and Memory: The "Rubber Room" Phenomenon* (Gettysburg, PA: Thomas Publications, 1998).

John B. Horner, *Sgt. Hugh Paxton Brigham: Lincoln's Guard at Gettysburg* (Gettysburg, PA: Gettysburg Personalities of the Civil War Series, Horner, 1994).

James C. Humes, *The Wit & Wisdom of Abraham Lincoln: A Treasury of Quotations, Anecdotes, and Observations* (New York: Gramercy Books, 1996).

Harry V. Jaffa, *A New Birth of Freedom: Abraham Lincoln and the Coming of the Civil War* (Lanham; Rowman & Littlefield Publishers, Inc., 2000).

Roger Jaynes, *Al McGuire: The Colorful Warrior* (Champaign, IL: Sports Publishing, L.L.C., 2004).

Keith W. Jennison, *The Humorous Mr. Lincoln* (New York: Bonanza Books, 1965).

Edward J. Kempf, *Abraham Lincoln's Philosophy Of Common Sense* (New York: Special Publications of The New York Academy Of Sciences, 1965).

Philip B. Kunhardt, Jr., *A New Birth of Freedom: Lincoln at Gettysburg* (Boston: Little, Brown and Company, 1983).

_____, Philip B. Kunhardt, III and Peter W. Kunhardt, *Lincoln: An Illustrated Biography* (New York: Knopf, 1992).

Ward Hill Lamon, *Recollections Of Abraham Lincoln 1847-1865*, Dorothy Lamon, ed. (Chicago: A.C. McClurg, 1895; republished by Dorothy Lamon Teillard, ed.: Washington, D.C., 1911).

Thomas F. Madigan, *Word Shadows of the Great: The Lure of Autograph Collecting* (New York: Stokes, 1930; republished Lancaur Press, 2007).

Jessie Ames Marshal, ed., *Private and Official Correspondence of Gen. Benjamin F. Butler* (Norwood, M.A.: Plimpton Press, 1917).

William Quentin Maxwell, *Lincoln's Fifth Wheel: The Political History of the United States Sanitary Commission* (New York: Longmans, Green & Co. 1956).

Russell McClintock, *Lincoln and the Decision for War* (Chapel Hill: North Carolina Press, 2008).

Alfred B. McCalmont, *Extracts From Letters Written By Alfred B. McCalmont, 1862-1865: From the Front During the War of Rebellion* (Franklin, PA: private printing by Robert McCalmont, 1908; reprint, Metalmark Books).

Charles M. McCurdy, *Gettysburg: A Memoir* (Pittsburgh, PA: Reed and Witting Company, 1929; reprint by Retro Books, 2013).

Marc McCutcheon, *Everyday Life in the 1800's: A Guide for Writers, Students & Historians* (Cincinnati, Ohio: Writers Digest Books, 1993).

James M. McPherson, *Battle Cry of Freedom: The Civil War Era* (New York: Oxford University Press, 1988).

David C. Mearns, *Lincoln and the Gettysburg Address: Commemorative Papers*, Allan Nevins, ed. (Urbana: University of Illinois Press, 1964).

_____, ed., *The Lincoln Papers* (2 vol,; Garden City, NY: Doubleday & Co., 1948).

Earl Schenck Miers and others, eds., *Lincoln Day by Day: A Chronology, 1809-1865*, (3 vols.; Washington, D.C.: Lincoln Sesquicentennial Commission, 1960).

Misc. Letters, *Fifth Semi-Annual Report of the Ladies' Aid Society of Philadelphia with Letters and Extracts From Letters from the Secretary of the Society, written from Various Places While attending to the Sick and Wounded of the Union Army* (Philadelphia: Sherman, 1863; reprint Cornell University Library).

Misc. Reminiscences, *The Gettysburg Times Commemorative Edition* issued November 19, 1963, Lincoln's Farewell Address, copy, ACHS.

Herbert Mitgang, *Abraham Lincoln: A Press Portrait: His Life and Times from the Original Newspaper Documents of the Union, the Confederacy, and Europe, 3rd edition* (Athens: University of Georgia Press, 1989).

James E. Myers, in *The Astonishing Saber Duel of Abraham Lincoln* (Springfield, IL: Lincoln-Herndon Building Publishers, 1968).

Salome (Sallie) Myers, *The Ties of the Past: The Gettysburg Diaries of Salome Myers Stewart 1854-1922* (Gettysburg, PA: Thomas Publications, 1996).

Mark E. Neely, Jr., ed., *The Abraham Lincoln Encyclopedia* (New York: McGraw-Hill, 1982).

John G. Nicolay and John Hay, *Abraham Lincoln: A History* (10 vols;. New York: The Century Company, 1890).

_____, *With Lincoln in the White House: Letters, Memoranda and Other Writings of John G. Nicolay, 1860-1865*, Michael Burlingame, ed. (Carbondale: Southern Illinois University Press, 2000).

Allan Nevins and Milton Halsey Thomas, eds., *The Diary of George Templeton Strong, 1835-1875* (4 vols.; New York: The Macmillan Company, 1952).

_____, *The War for the Union, Vol. 1, The Improvised War, 1861—1962* (New York: Charles Scribner's Sons, 1959).

John Dos Passos, *The Ground We Stand On* (New York: Harcourt, Brace and Company, 1941).

Merrill D. Peterson, *Lincoln in American Memory* (New York: Oxford University Press, 1994).

_____, *"This Grand Pertinacity": Abraham Lincoln and the Declaration of Independence* (Fort Wayne, IN: The Lincoln Museum, 1991).

J. G. Randall, *Lincoln The President: Springfield To Gettysburg* (2 vols.; New York: Dodd, Mead & Co., 1945).

David M. Potter, *Lincoln and His Party in the Secession Crisis.* (New Haven, CT: Yale University Press, 1942).

Ruth Painter Randall, *Colonel Elmer Ellsworth: A Biography of Lincoln's Friend and First Hero of the Civil War* (Boston: Little, Brown & Company, 1960).

_____, *Lincoln's Sons* (Boston: Little, Brown & Company, 1955).

Emerson Reck, A. *Lincoln: His Last 24 Hours* (Columbia: University of South Carolina Press, 1994).

Allen Thorndike Rice, ed., *Reminiscences of Abraham Lincoln by Distinguished Men of His Time* (New York: North American Publishing Company, 1888).

Salome (Sallie) Myers, *The Ties of the Past: The Gettysburg Diaries of Salome Myers Stewart 1854-1922* (Gettysburg, PA: Thomas Publications, 1996).

Josephine Roedel, *The Josephine Roedel Diary*, Library of Congress. Some of the Roedel diary entries used herein also specifically appear for November 18, 19, 1863 in "Diary Related Dedication of Cemetery Here," *The Gettysburg Times*, November 14, 1946, copy, ACHS.

Carl Sandburg, *Abraham Lincoln: The Prairie Years and The War Years* (1 vol. edition New York: Galahad Books, 1993).

Frederick W. Seward, *Seward at Washington as Senator and Secretary of State, 1846-1861* (New York: Derby & Miller, 1891).

Thomas E. Schott, *Alexander H. Stephens of Georgia: A Biography* (Baton Rouge, LA: Louisiana State University Press, 1988).

Carl Schneider and Dorothy Schneider, *Slavery in America* (New York: Infobase Publishing, 2007).

Stephen W. Sears, ed., *The Civil War Papers of George B. McClellan: Selected Correspondence, 1860-1865* (New York: Ticknor and Fields, 1989).

Joshua Wolf Shenk, *Lincoln's Melancholy: How Depression Challenged a President and Fueled His Greatness* (New York: Houghton Mifflin Company, 2005).

John Y. Simon, *House Divided: Lincoln and his Father* (Fort Wayne, IN: Louis A. Warren Library and Museum, 1987).

Daniel Alexander Skelly, *A Boy's Experiences During the Battles of Gettysburg* (Gettysburg, PA: privately published, 1932; reprint by Gary T. Hawbaker). This entire account (as transcribed in 1998 by John Heiser, GNMP historian) appears on the Voices of Battle Gettysburg National Military Park Virtual Tour, at www.nps.gov/archive/getttour/sidebar/skelly.htm.

James G. Smart, ed., *A Radical View: The "Agate" Dispatches of Whitelaw Reid, 1861-1865* (2 vols.; Memphis State University Press, 1976).

John L. Smith, compiler, *History of the Corn Exchange Regiment, 118th Pennsylvania Volunteers, From their First Engagement at Antietam to Appomattox* (Philadelphia, PA: J.L. Smith, 1888).

Timothy H. Smith, *John Burns "The Hero of Gettysburg"* (Gettysburg, PA: Thomas Publications, 2000).

Emily Bliss Thacher Souder (originally published as "Mrs. Edmund A. Souder"), *Leaves from the Battle-field of Gettysburg. A Series of Letters from a Field Hospital and National Poems* (Philadelphia: Caxton Press, 1864; currently available in reprint).

Joshua F. Speed, *Reminiscences of Abraham Lincoln and Notes of a Visit to California: Two Lectures* (Louisville, KY: John P. Morton and Co., 1884).

David E. Stannard, ed., *Death in America* (Philadelphia: University of Pennsylvania Press, 1975).

Edward Steers, Jr., *Blood On The Moon; The Assassination Of Abraham Lincoln* (Lexington, KY: The University Press of Kentucky, 2001).

Robert Stiles, *Four Years Under Marse Robert* (New York, NY: The Neale Publishing Company, 1903).

John W. Storrs, *The Twentieth Connecticut, A Regimental History* (Naugatuck, CT: Press of the Naugatuck Valley Sentinel, 1886).

Harriet Beecher Stowe, *Men of Our Times* (Hartford, CT: Hartford Publishing Co., 1868).

Ida M. Tarbell, *Abraham Lincoln and His Ancestors* (Lincoln: University of Nebraska Press, 1977).

John M. Taylor, *William Henry Seward, Lincoln's Right Hand* (New York: HarperCollins, 1991).

Benjamin P. Thomas, *Lincoln's New Salem* (New York: Alfred A. Knopf, 1954).

Bob Thompson, *Born on a Mountaintop: On the Road with Davy Crockett and Ghosts of the Wild Frontier* (New York: Crown Trade Group, 2013).

Morris K. Udall, Too Funny To Be President (University of Arizona: 2001).

Robert G. Torricelli, ed., *Quotations For Public Speakers: A Historical, Literary, And Political Anthology*, (New Brunswick, NJ: Rutgers University Press, 2001).

Justin G. Turner and Linda Levitt Turner, *Mary Todd Lincoln, Her Life and Letters* (New York: Alfred A. Knopf, 1972).

Leander H. Warren, *My Recollections of What I Saw Before, During and After the Battle of Gettysburg, July 1st, 2nd and 3rd, 1863* (unpublished account, 1926; reprint by Gary W. Hawbaker.).

Louis A. Warren, *Lincoln's Gettysburg Declaration: "A New Birth of Freedom"* (Fort Wayne, IN: Lincoln National Life Foundation, 1964).

_____, *Lincoln's Parentage and Childhood: A History of the Kentucky Lincoln's Supported by Documentary Evidence* (New York: The Century Company, 1926).

_____, *Lincoln's Youth: Indiana Years, Seven to Twenty-One, 1816-1830* (New York: Appleton-Century-Crofts, 1959).

John E. Washington, *They Knew Lincoln* (New York: E.P. Dutton, 1942).

Jennifer L. Weber's, *Copperheads: The Rise and Fall of Lincoln's Opponents in the North* (New York: Oxford University Press, 2006).

J. Howard Wert, *A Complete Hand-Book of the Monuments and Indications and Guide to the Positions on the Gettysburg Battlefield* (Harrisburg, PA: R.M. Sturgeon & Co., 1886; also online under Google Books.)

Charles H. Weygant, *History of the One Hundred and Twenty-Fourth Regiment, N.Y.S.V.* (Newburgh, NY: Journal Printing House, 1877).

Tom Wheeler, *Mr. Lincoln's T-Mails: The Untold Story of How Abraham Lincoln Used the Telegraph to Win the Civil War* (New York: HarperCollins Publishers, 2006).

John C. Waugh, *Reelecting Lincoln: The Battle for the 1864 Presidency* (Cambridge, MA: Da Capo Press, 2001), p. 262.

Harry L. Watson, *Liberty and Power: The Politics of Jacksonian America* (1990).

David Wills and other reports, speeches, etc., *Revised Report of the Select Committee Relative to the Soldiers' National Cemetery, Together with the Accompanying Documents, as Reported to the House of Representatives of the Commonwealth of Pennsylvania, March 31, 1864* (Harrisburg: PA: Singerly & Myers, State Printers, 1865; reprint from the collection of the University of Michigan Library).

Garry Wills, *Lincoln at Gettysburg: The Words That Remade America* (New York: Simon & Schuster, 1992).

Douglas L. Wilson, *Honor's Voice: The Transformation of Abraham Lincoln* (New York: Alfred A. Knopf, 1998).

_____ and Rodney O. Davis, eds., *Herndon's Informants: Letters, Interviews and Statements About Abraham Lincoln* (Urbana: University of Illinois Press, 1998).

_____, *Lincoln's Sword: The Presidency and the Power of Words* (New York: Alfred A. Knopf, 2006).

Rufus Rockwell Wilson, *Intimate Memories of Lincoln* (Elmira, New York: Primavera Press, 1945).

Albert A. Woldman, *Lawyer Lincoln* (Boston: Houghton Mifflin Co., 1936).

John Russell Young, *Men and Memories: Personal Reminiscences* (2 vols.; New York: Tennyson Neely, 1901).

P.M. Zall, ed., *Abe Lincoln Laughing* (Berkley, CA: University of California Press, 1982).

Internet

The **Abraham Lincoln Papers at the Library of Congress** in Washington, D.C., in their electronic editions as they appear online at http://memory.loc.gov/ammen/alhtml/malhome.html. This site includes the *American Memories Archives*, where images of many of Abraham Lincoln's letters, speeches and other manuscripts can be found.

William Alden, "Rubenstein Buys a Copy of the Emancipation Proclamation for $2 Million," DealBook.com (June 27, 2012).

American Experience on PBS, "The Civil War By the Numbers," appearing online @ pbs.org/w3gbh/americanexperience/features/general-article/death.

The **Center For Civil War Photography**, as it appears online at http://www.civilwarphotography.org/. This site is a wonderful clearinghouse and resource for information about civil war and battlefield photography, including standard and stereoscopic images.

The **Constitution of France (5th Republic, Established October 4, 1958)**, as it appears in English online at http://www.assemblee-nationale.fr/english/8ab.asp.

The **Ford's Theater Center for Education and Leadership**, @fords.org/home/explore-lincoln/Lincoln-book-tower. See also the derivative website article, "Just how many books about Abe Lincoln have there been written? Three stories worth." *The Inquisitr*, @ www.inquisitr.com.

The **George Washington Papers at the Library of Congress (1741-1799)**, in their electronic editions as they appear online at memory.loc.gov/ammen/gw tml/gwhome.html.

James Oliver Horton, Interview on the PBS Newshour originally broadcast on January 25, 2007, appearing online under the caption of *Exhibit Reveals History of Slavery in New York City*, at www.pbs.org/newshour.

Sergey Kadinsky and Christina Boyle, "On Abraham Lincoln's 200th birthday, handwritten speech breaks auction record at Christie's," New YorkDailyNews.com (February 12, 2009).

The **Library of Congress: Information Bulletin**, dated February 6, 1995 (regarding the work of Dr. Nathan Stolow in designing environmental containers for Lincoln's first two drafts of the Gettysburg Address). This publication can be found online under its title.

The **Library of the University of Illinois at Urbana-Champaign**, Digitized Book of the Week, posted September 3, 2007, titled "Abraham Africanus I: His Secret Life . . .". Reference online at http://www.library.edu/blog/digitized-botw/2007/09.

The **Mapping Project: Life Expectancy 1850-2000**, prepared through the University of Oregon Dept. of History, James Mohr and John Nicols, eds. Reference online at www.uoregon.edu/~maphist/english/US/US32-01.html.

Elie Wiesel, His Nobel Lecture titled *Hope, Despair and Memory*, given on December 11, 1986 at the Nobel Peace Prize Award Ceremony, as it appears online at http://www.nobleprize.org/nobel-prizes/peace/laureates/1986/wiesel-lecture.html.

The U.S. Supreme Court case of *Dred Scott v. Sandford*, 60 U.S. 393 (How.), rendered in the December term 1856, can be found online in its entirety at http.//laws.findlaw.com/us/60/393.html.

Samuel H. Williamson, "Six Ways To Compute the Relative Value of a U.S. Dollar Amount, 1774 to Present," Measuring Worth, 2009. Reference the working website online at www.measuringworth.com/uscompare/.

Authors Note: *The Collected Works of Abraham Lincoln* is generously made available at no charge by The Abraham Lincoln Association, in electronic version online at www.alincolnassoc.com, along with *The Lincoln Log: A Daily Chronology of the Life of Abraham Lincoln* (which includes the Lincoln Sesquicentennial Commission publication, *Lincoln Day–by–Day: A Chronology, 1809-1865*). Valuable information about Lincoln's boyhood home at the Knob Creek Farm near Hodgenville, Kentucky, can be found online at http:/www.nps.gov/abli/. Also, a cornucopia of information about the Lincoln Memorial National Monument in Washington, D.C. can be found at http:/www.nps.gov/line/. Many of the books referenced above, including nineteenth century publications, are in the public domain and available in their original content through digital scanning at Google Books.

Music

Dirge Sung At The Consecration Of The Soldiers' Cemetery, Gettysburg, PA, Nov. 19, 1863, Words by James G. Percival, Music by Alfred Delaney (In C Major, Arranged for Four Voices; Philadelphia: Lee & Walker). An instrumental of this dirge can be heard online at the site of American Civil War Music (1861-1865), which is the excellent work of Benjamin Robert Tubb, at pdmusic.org/civilwar2.html.

I Feel Like I'm Fixin' To Die Rag, ("And, it's one, two, three, what are we fighting for?"), Words and Music by Joe McDonald and performed by Country Joe and the Fish, appearing on Vanguard Records. Published by Alcatraz Corner Music Co. Thanks to Bill Belmont, administrator of this song, for his time and interesting input about it's fascinating history.

Lorena, Words by Rev. Henry D. L. Webster, Music by Joseph Phibrick Webster (1857). An instrumental of this song can be heard online at the site of American Civil War Music (1861-1865) at pdmusic.org/civilwar2.html.

We Are Coming, Father Abraham, Words by James Sloan Gibbons, Music by Luther Orlando Emerson. An instrumental of this song can be heard online at the site of American Civil War Music (1861-1865) at pdmusic.org/civil-war2.html. Another fine rendition of this song, both lyrics and music, is performed by the 97th New York Regimental String Band on YouTube.

Recorded Recollections

Reference the "Reminiscences" of Philip M. Bikle, 19 November 1914, in "The Lincoln-Burns Event; Unique Ceremony: Citizens Relate Recollections; Memorial Tables Unveiled in Gettysburg Presbyterian Church Nov. 19, 1914," *The Gettysburg Times Commemorative Edition* (November 19, 1963, Lincoln's Gettysburg Address, section 13). [This article hereafter referred to, in abridged form, as "The Lincoln-Burns Event"], copy, ACHS.

Reference the "Reminiscences" of T.C. Billheimer, 19 November 1914, in "The Lincoln-Burns Event," *The Gettysburg Times Commemorative Edition* (November 19, 1963, Lincoln's Farewell Address, section 6"), copy, ACHS.

Reference the "Reminiscences" of Kate McCreary, 19 November 1914, in "The Lincoln-Burns Event," *The Gettysburg Times Commemorative Edition* (November 19, 1963, Lincoln's Farewell Address, section 8"), copy, ACHS.

Reference the "Reminiscences" of William H. Tipton, 19 November 1914, in "The Lincoln-Burns Event," *The Gettysburg Times Commemorative Edition* (November 19, 1963, Lincoln's Farewell Address, section 7"), copy, ACHS.

Reference the "Reminiscences" of Judge David Wills, known as the Judge Wills "Statement" which he wrote and gave to a friend (Charles M. McCurdy) on or about 1890, which was later published in a 1929 book, copy, ACHS.

Diaries & Journals

Reference the Diary Entries of Sarah Broadhead, published as "The Diary of a Lady of Gettysburg, Pennsylvania, from June 15 to July 15, 1863," available online at the Cornell University Library Digital Collections at www.librarycornell.edu.

Reference the Journal of John B. Linn, July 6 & 7, 1863, "Journal of My Trip to the Battlefield at Gettysburg" [this account was not published]. GNMP.

Reference the Diary Entries of Mary Elizabeth Montfort, 4 July 1863 & 20 November 1863, in Lester Trauch, "How a Twelve-Year-Old Girl Saw Gettysburg," *Doylestown* (Pennsylvania) *Daily Intelligencer* (May 30, 1959). ACHS.

Reference the Diary Entries of Josephine Forney Roedel, 18 & 19 November 1863, at the Library of Congress; also in "Diary Related Dedication of Cemetery Here," *The Gettysburg Times* (November 14, 1946), copy, ACHS.

Articles

Lee Bowman, "Civil War was even bloodier than previously thought," writing about a new analysis of 1870 census data conducted by David Hacker, Professor at Binghamton University, *The* (Knoxville) *News Sentinel* (November 13, 2011).

Jennie Smyth Croll, ed., "Days of Dread," *Philadelphia Weekly Press* (November 16, 1887).

Elizabeth Daniels, "The Children of Gettysburg," *American Heritage Magazine* (May/June 1989, Vol. 40, Issue 4).

Joseph George, Jr., "The World Will Little Note? The Philadelphia Press and the Gettysburg Address," *The Pennsylvania Magazine of History and Biography* (July 1990).

Rev. Dr. Henry C. Holloway, "Lincoln at Gettysburg," The (Gettysburg) Compiler, (November 21, 1914), copy, ACHS.

Henry Eyster Jacobs, "Gettysburg Fifty Years Ago," *The Lutheran* (August 7, 1913), copy, ACHS.

Martin P. Johnson, "Lincoln Greets the Turning Point of the Civil War, July 7, 1863," *Lincoln Herald* (Fall 2004).

Thomas W. Knox, "The Battle Field at Gettysburg. Scenes after the Battle. Visit to the Battle-Field," *New York Herald* (July 9, 1863).

_____, "Who Stole the Gettysburg Address," *Journal of the Abraham Lincoln Association* (Summer 2003).

Robert McClean, "A Boy at Gettysburg—1863," *The* (Gettysburg) *Compiler* (June 30, 1909), copy, ACHS.

Albertus McCreary, "Gettysburg: A Boy's Experience of the Battle," *McClure's Magazine* (July 1909), copy, ACHS.

Annie M. Skelly, (December 8, 1941) [this account not published], copy, ACHS.

W.C. Storrick, "Here and There: News Collected at Random," *The Gettysburg Times*, (February 19, 1943), copy, GNMP.

W.C. Storrick, "When I Saw and Heard Mr. Lincoln," (August 11, 1939) [this account not published], copy, GNMP.

George D. Thorn, "Memories Unlocked at Gettysburg Anniversary Fete for Geo. D. Thorn," *The* (Gettysburg) *Compiler*, (July 9, 1932), copy, GNMP.

Carol Vogel, "A Pollock is Sold, Possibly for a Record Price," *The New York Times* (November 2, 2006).

J. Howard Wert, "Lincoln at Gettysburg," *The* (Harrisburg) *Patriot*, (February 12-13, 1909), copy, ACHS.

Charles Young, " 'How Are You, Old Abe?' He asked Lincoln," *The Gettysburg Times*, (February 17, 1937), copy, GNMP.

ACKNOWLEDGMENTS

The poet and author Kent Gramm wrote, "If we Americans can't find Lincoln, we are lost." Without the work of innumerable, devoted Lincoln scholars who came before me—far too many to personally mention—from whose bountiful fruits of labor I have partaken to write this book, I too, would have been lost.

First and foremost, to my publisher Don Bracken and History Publishing Company, LLC, I extend my deepest gratitude and appreciation, for giving me the opportunity to tell this story. Don, you are a gentleman and historian in every sense of the word, and it has been an honor and privilege to write for your company.

As a writer, it is a distinguished accomplishment to cast new light on Abraham Lincoln's life and his Gettysburg Address. By no means, do I claim to have done so; only a rarified group of past and contemporary historians have joined that class through the years. No book like this is a solitary endeavor. As often said, I hoisted myself up upon the shoulders of giants—countless historians and authors who have, for many decades, impeccably researched and exquisitely written about Lincoln, *a priora* my literary effort. This book was not possible without them. Because of the contributions of those gifted predecessors, I suspect Lincoln has become the most alive of all the dead presidents.

Speaking of great scholars, I tender special appreciation to Gabor Boritt, Ph.D., Robert Fluhrer Professor of Civil War Studies and former Director of the Civil War Institute at Gettysburg College, for his incomparable body of work on Lincoln and the Civil War. I have cloistered myself in his learned books for many years, and been inspired by them all. I have never met this remarkable man (I certainly would like to), but his most recent major book, *The Gettysburg Gospel: The Lincoln Speech That Nobody Knows* (2006)—is exhaustively researched, richly detailed and splendidly written. I was nearly halfway through my own book project, when *The Gettysburg Gospel* was released; it brought closure for me (and challenged my conclusions) on some of the vexing questions about the Gettysburg Address that I had chased, researched

467

and struggled with during my life. In that book, Dr. Boritt's beautiful-
ly-told story of Lincoln's personal servant, William Johnson—and the
moving photo of his grave at Arlington Cemetery—are tiny nuggets
of historical gold, among many others, that gild the masterful work.

Then there is the electrifying Pulitzer Prize winner, *Lincoln at
Gettysburg: The Words That Remade America* (1992), by Garry Wills.
Remarkably, more than two decades after its ground-breaking appearance, even with the quantum advances in Lincoln research that have
occurred since, it still stands out and illuminates. Professor Wills lit the
fuse of contemporary intellectual thought about Lincoln's immortal
speech. Most books on the Gettysburg Address that follow these two
seminal works by Dr. Boritt and Dr. Wills are destined to remain, forever, in their long and distinguished shadow.

Also, I extend a word of appreciation to the late Civil War author,
Gregory A. Coco (1946-2009). And kudos to his publisher, Thomas
Publications. Mr. Coco's books are not typically of broad appeal that
make best-seller lists, but they are important, scholarly and rich with
valuable information about the Civil War. He honored his country and
his family as a distinguished Vietnam Veteran and park historian at
Gettysburg. I often leaned on Mr. Coco's unique and extensive body of
work as a windvane to primary sources and to gain a deeper understanding of the horrible aftermath of the Battle of Gettysburg.

Librarians, our faithful stewards of books and historical records, do
noble and indispensable work, with little credit or recognition. Much
appreciation to Dawn Claiborne, Head Librarian in my small hometown
of Oneida, Tennessee, and her ever-helpful assistants, Christy Simmons
and Crystal Jolly. The Oneida Library, although small and operating on
a shoestring budget, is a special place loved and used by many—a place
always filled with warm greetings, good books and cheerful help. Thanks
for going the extra mile to find what I needed, somewhere, in the river of
books that flow through the State of Tennessee's partnership library system. I commend my beloved home state for this service.

I am fortunate to live only ninety minutes from Lincoln Memorial
University in Harrogate, Tennessee, a fine repository of Lincolniana,
rare photographs and nineteenth century books on Lincoln. Much
appreciation to the library staff at that university, who offered pleasant

clerical support early in this project. Wonderful, expedited assistance also came from Michelle Ganz, University Archivist-Librarian.

To Dr. Charles M. Hubbard—author, Lincoln scholar, recipient of the prestigious Order of Lincoln Award and distinguished Professor of History at Lincoln Memorial University in Harrogate, Tennessee— thanks for the precious office chat on Lincoln, and for your intellectual generosity. You are, truly, a gentleman and scholar.

I am hugely indebted to The Adams County Historical Society (ACHS) in Gettysburg, Pennsylvania, who produced copies for me of rare journals and newspaper articles, particularly of eyewitness accounts of Lincoln at Gettysburg. Many thanks to the ACHS Executive Director, Wayne E. Motts, and especially to Administrative Assistant, Jan Beebe, for her extraordinarily pleasant and unstinting assistance; your knowledgeable, patient and polite assistance never wavered.

Also, I extend my gratitude to Librarian Scott Hartwig and Park Ranger/Historian John Heiser with the Gettysburg National Military Park library, who provided me with copies of nineteenth and twentieth century publications that give us contemporary accounts of President Lincoln's historic trip to Gettysburg.

Impeccable and friendly help was always available from James Cornelius, Curator of the Abraham Lincoln Presidential Library and Museum.

Many thanks to my friend, M. Fred Marcum, for his valuable assistance on administrative matters for this project.

Over my many years on the Adjunct Faculty at Roane State Community College, and working for its former but exceptional Dean of Social Science, Business and Education, Dr. Christopher L. Whaley, J.D.—who is now the President of that outstanding institution of higher learning— hundreds of students have passed through my law classes, where we regularly discussed Abraham Lincoln's remarkable abilities as a wordsmith and lawyer, and his enduring impact on America. In the words of the French essayist, Joseph Joubert: "To teach is to learn twice." Thanks, Chris for the opportunity. Many thanks to Tammy Guge while you were in Dr. Whaley's office; your years of cheerful assistance were indispensable. And thanks, most of all, to my students. I have learned much from you!

I will always be grateful to the former Chair of the Political Science Department at Tennessee Technological University in Cookeville, Tennessee, Professor Paul G. Stevenson. In 1975, Dr. Stevenson helped me to select a diverse and thought-provoking batch of books to read and discuss with him, as one of my last courses at the university. They were books, as he wryly put it, "no self-respecting political scientist should fail to read" before getting a college diploma. In this process, he put me on to the extraordinary author and artist John Dos Passos, in particular, his 1941 work, *The Ground We Stand On.* This largely forgotten book contains passages, I believe, that further illuminate the timeless wisdom of the Gettysburg Address, and are full of karma on the future of America. Some of those passages—which had a lasting impact on me—are contained in this book, thanks to the generosity of his daughter, Lucy Dos Passos Coggin, for which I am most grateful. My first edition of this publication is a cherished title in my personal library.

Lincoln scholars are an amazingly generous and helpful genus of folks, no matter who and where they are. Through the early years of my Lincoln journey, I occasionally corresponded with two remarkable Lincoln experts, Rodney O. Davis, Ph.D. and Douglas L. Wilson, Ph.D., who are co-directors at the Knox College Lincoln Studies Center in Galesburg, Illinois. Professor Wilson's chapter on the Gettysburg Address in his award-winning book, *Lincoln's Sword,* is about as perfect as a single chapter on a historical subject can be researched and written. Although Professors Davis and Wilson did not "know me from Adam," as the old expression goes around here, they always found time to reply by fax or note with valuable guidance and input. These two men, of course, are not the only great contemporary Lincoln scholars—but the class they're in, it certainly doesn't take long to call the roll.

Further, I want to thank other contemporary Lincoln scholars whose writings have inspired and profoundly impacted my Lincoln studies through the years (although there are too many to individually thank), such as Michael Burlingame, David Herbert Donald, Harold Holzer, Doris Kearns Goodwin, Edward Steers, Jr., Ronald C. White, Jr., Allen C. Guelzo, James M. McPherson, and the body of work and contributions of the Meserve and Kunhardt families. And, of course, the incomparable Civil War commentator and literati, the late Shelby

Foote. There are many other Lincoln historians who have strongly influenced me through the years, both past and present, but who are not directly drawn upon for this book; however, the subliminal echoes of their voices are likely woven herein.

I will always be indebted to Senator Howard H. Baker, Jr.—once the Chief of Staff to President Ronald Reagan, Ambassador to Japan, and perhaps, this nation's last, truly great statesman—for your exquisite Foreword in this book and the priceless talks in your office about Lincoln, and his affection for East Tennesseans.

Words are sorely inadequate to express the love and gratefulness to my parents, James L. Cotton, Sr. and Carolyn Cotton, for a wonderful childhood and the steadfast encouragement they gave all of their four children to read. Like Sarah Bush Lincoln, our mother brought stimulating and eclectic books into our home, and our father guided us with Lincoln-like wit and wisdom, that shaped all of our lives. When he was a traveling salesman, my father brought home from Philadelphia in February of 1965 (he dated and signed all of his books) a paperback published by Pyramid Books, titled *Lincoln For The Ages*. It was an amazing smorgasbord of Lincoln articles from seventy-six distinguished authors, from Carl Sandburg to Adlai Stevenson, covering the entire scope of Lincoln's life. I read it then—and still read it now. That tattered little paperback remains a personal treasure. Thanks, Dad; I miss you.

To Lou Ann Smith, my loyal, smart and irreplaceable legal assistant who has been with me for more than three decades of practicing and then making rulings on the law, I extend my profound gratitude for all you do. This book was not possible without you. Your superhuman patience and endurance in the long and tedious slog of converting my pitiful handwriting to the typewritten word ("working on Abe" as you call it), will be forever appreciated.

And lastly, but most importantly, I thank my wonderful wife, Lisa Bishop Cotton—mother, Sunday School teacher, community volunteer and engineer extraordinaire—for your love, support and companionship on my Lincoln journey. I could not have made it without you. Our Lincoln sojourn to Springfield, with our great kids Caroline and Luke aboard, was an unforgettable family trip (especially when I left the rear-door of our van open on our pre-dawn departure, silently dumping our luggage just outside Lincoln and Herndon's old law office). The mother's milk of any Lincoln library is *The Collected Works of Abraham Lincoln*, chiefly edited by Roy P. Basler. Years ago, Lisa gave this collection to me as a gift; it is one I will always cherish.

There are, undoubtedly, mistakes and misinterpretations lurking among the words of this book, notwithstanding my abiding commitment to historical accuracy. And, surely, there are historical conclusions I have drawn, extracted from the anecdotes, papers and memoirs of Lincoln's life, that will find disagreement among respected scholars. Accordingly, I take full responsibility for them.

INDEX